CliffsNotes®

Praxis II® Mathematics Content Knowledge Test (0061)

SECOND EDITION

by
Ennis Donice McCune, Ph.D.,
and Sandra Luna McCune, Ph.D.

WILEY

John Wiley & Sons, Inc.

About the Author

Prior to his death, Ennis Donice McCune was Regents Professor in the Department of Mathematics and Statistics at Stephen F. Austin State University in Nacogdoches, Texas. Sandra Luna McCune is a former Regents Professor and math specialist in the Department of Elementary Education also at Stephen F. Austin State University, where she received the Distinguished Professor Award. She now is a full-time author and consultant and resides in Austin, Texas.

Author's Acknowledgments

Sandra Luna McCune wishes to thank her late husband Donice for his brilliant understanding of mathematics that made this book possible.

Editorial

Acquisition Editor: Greg Tubach

Project Editor: Kelly Dobbs Henthorne

Copy Editor: Christy Scannell

Technical Editors: Mary Jane Sterling and David Herzog

Composition

Proofreader: Tricia Liebig

John Wiley & Sons, Inc., Composition Services

CliffsNotes® Praxis II® Mathematics Content Knowledge Test (0061), Second Edition

Published by:
John Wiley & Sons, Inc.
111 River Street
Hoboken, NJ 07030-5774
www.wiley.com

Copyright © 2012 John Wiley & Sons, Inc., Hoboken, NJ

Published by John Wiley & Sons, Inc., Hoboken, NJ
Published simultaneously in Canada

Library of Congress Control Number: 2011945012
ISBN: 978-1-118-08555-4 (pbk)
ISBN: 978-1-118-20485-6; 978-1-118-20483-2; 978-1-118-20484-9 (ebk)

Printed in the United States of America

10 9 8 7 6 5 4 3 2

Table of Contents

PART II: FULL-LENGTH PRACTICE TESTS

Introduction

General Description

The PRAXIS Mathematics: Content Knowledge test (test code 0061, Mathematics CK) is designed to assess the mathematical knowledge and skills that an entry-level teacher of secondary school mathematics needs to possess. As listed in the *Mathematics: Content Knowledge (0061) Test at a Glance* (www.ets.org/Media/Tests/PRAXIS/pdf/0061.pdf), the test addresses five broad areas:

I.   Algebra and Number Theory

II. Measurement, Geometry, and Trigonometry

III. Functions and Calculus

IV. Data Analysis, Statistics, and Probability

V.   Matrix Algebra and Discrete Mathematics

The test consists of 50 multiple-choice questions. Each multiple-choice question contains four response options. You record your answer choice in the separate answer booklet by filling in the space corresponding to **A**, **B**, **C**, or **D**. No penalty is imposed for wrong answers (you merely score a 0 for that test question). The test booklet provides a mathematics reference sheet containing information organized under three labels: NOTATION, DEFINITIONS, and FORMULAS. You are given two hours to complete the test.

Calculator Requirements

You are required to bring a graphing calculator to use while taking the Mathematics CK. The calculator that you bring must have the following built-in capabilities:

- graph a function within an arbitrary viewing window
- find the zeros of a function
- compute a numeric derivative of a function
- compute a numeric integral of a function

You will have to clear the memory of your calculator before and after you take the test. Be sure you know how to clear the memory on the calculator you plan to use during the test.

You are NOT allowed to bring computers, including powerbooks and portable/handheld computers, calculators with QWERTY keyboards (for example: TI-92 PLUS, Voyage 200), cell-phone calculators, or electronic writing pads or other pen-input/stylus-driven devices.

Allocation of the Test Content

According to the *Mathematics: Content Knowledge (0061) Test at a Glance* (see "General Description," earlier in this chapter for the Internet address), the content categories for the test and approximate number of questions and percentage of the test for each content category are as follows:

Allocation of the Test Content		
Content Category	Approximate Number of Questions	Approximate Percent of Test
Algebra and Number Theory	8	16%
Measurement	3	6%
Geometry	5	10%
Trigonometry	4	8%
Functions	8	16%
Calculus	6	12%
Data Analysis and Statistics	5–6	10–12%
Probability	2–3	4–6%
Matrix Algebra	4–5	8–10%
Discrete Mathematics	3–4	6–8%

In addition to mathematical knowledge and skills, the PRAXIS Mathematics CK assesses five process categories: Problem Solving, Reasoning and Proof, Connections, Representation, and Use of Technology. These process categories refer to the ways through which mathematical knowledge is acquired and used. The first four process categories are adopted from the National Council of Teachers of Mathematics Process Standards (available at www.nctm.org/standards/content.aspx?id=322) and are as described here:

Problem Solving

- Build new mathematical knowledge through problem solving.
- Solve problems that arise in mathematics and in other contexts.
- Apply and adapt a variety of appropriate strategies to solve problems.

Reasoning and Proof

- Make and investigate mathematical conjectures.
- Develop and evaluate mathematical arguments and proofs.
- Select and use various types of reasoning and methods of proof.

Connections

- Recognize and use connections among mathematical ideas.
- Understand how mathematical ideas interconnect and build on one another.
- Recognize and apply mathematics in contexts outside of mathematics.

Representation

- Create and use representations to organize, record, and communicate mathematical ideas.
- Select, apply, and translate among mathematical representations to solve problems.
- Use representations to model and interpret physical, social, and mathematical phenomena.

The description of the fifth process category as given in the *Mathematics: Content Knowledge (0061) Test at a Glance* is as follows:

Use of Technology

- Use technology appropriately as a tool for problem solving.
- Use technology as an aid to understanding mathematical ideas.

The process categories are integrated into the content questions. This means you will not be asked explicit questions about the process categories, but rather you will be expected to use one or more of the processes in answering questions on the test.

Scoring of the Test

Educational Testing Service (ETS) does not release the exact details of the way the Mathematics CK is scored. For each question you answer correctly you get 1 raw point, and your total raw score is the number of questions you answer correctly out of the 50 questions on the test.

Your raw point score is converted to a scaled score that adjusts for the difficulty level of the particular edition of the test that you took. Your score report for the test will show a scaled score ranging from 100 to 200. You can find additional information about the scoring of the test in *Understanding Your Praxis Scores* (available at www.ets.org/Media/Tests/PRAXIS/pdf/uyps_1011.pdf).

Note: For the practice tests in this study guide, you are provided a tabular guideline for converting your raw score to an estimated scaled score.

The Role of the Mathematics CK in Teacher Certification

The Mathematics CK is one of the PRAXIS II Series subject assessment tests designed by Educational Testing Service (ETS). The PRAXIS II tests are part of a national teacher assessment program and are used as part of the certification or licensing requirements in states across the U. S. This means you can transfer your score on the Mathematics CK from state to state for those states that use the PRAXIS II subject assessment tests.

If your state has selected the Mathematics CK to assess secondary teacher candidates' mathematical knowledge and skills, then this *CliffsNotes* book will be invaluable in helping you achieve the passing score for your state. Test scores needed to obtain certification vary from state to state because each state sets its own passing score. ETS maintains a listing by state of links to test requirements for those states that require the PRAXIS II subject assessment tests for certification at www.ets.org/praxis/prxstate.html. The following is a list of states that require the Mathematics CK along with the current (in 2011) score needed to obtain certification in each state:

Alabama—126	Maine—126	North Dakota—139
Alaska—146	Maryland—141	Ohio—139
Arkansas—125	Mississippi—123	Pennsylvania—~~136~~ 160
Colorado—156	Missouri—137	South Carolina—131
Connecticut—137	Nevada—133	South Dakota—124
Delaware—141	New Hampshire—127	Tennessee—136
District of Columbia—141	New Jersey—137	Utah—138
Hawaii—136	North Carolina—*license for Mathematics requires a combined score of 281 from Mathematics: Content Knowledge (0061) and Mathematics: Pedagogy (0065). There are no minimum scores.*	Vermont—141
Idaho—119		Virginia—147
Indiana—136		West Virginia—133
Kansas—137		Wisconsin—135
Kentucky—125		
Louisiana—135		

Questions Commonly Asked About the Mathematics CK

Q. What is the Mathematics CK?

A. The Mathematics CK is a PRAXIS II Series subject assessment test. It is used by 31 states and the District of Columbia as part of their teacher certification/licensure requirements.

Q. Who administers the Mathematics CK?

A. The Mathematics CK is administered by Educational Testing Service (ETS).

Q. When and where is the Mathematics CK given?

A. PRAXIS Series tests, including the Mathematics CK, are administered seven times a year (usually in September, November, January, March, April, June, and July or August) at locations throughout the United States. You can find information on test dates, site locations, fees, registration procedures, and policies in the current *The Praxis Series Information Bulletin (Information Bulletin),* available at www.ets.org/Media/Tests/PRAXIS/pdf/01361.pdf.

Q. How do I register to take to the test?

A. You can register online using a credit card at the PRAXIS Web site (www.ets.org/praxis), Monday through Friday from 7 a.m. to 1 a.m. (Eastern Time), and Saturday 7 a.m. to Sunday 8 p.m. (Eastern Time); or you can register by mail by downloading the registration form available on the PRAXIS Web site and then mailing the completed form to ETS-The Praxis Series, Box 382065, Pittsburgh, PA 15251–8065.

Q. Are special testing arrangements available?

A. If you have a disabling condition (visual, physical, hearing, etc.), special testing arrangements and test materials can be made available for you. Complete the registration form and follow the instructions at www.ets.org/praxis/prxdsabl.html.

If you are unable to take the test on Saturday because of your religious convictions or because of duties as a member of the U.S. armed forces, you can request a Monday testing day by following the instructions in the *Information Bulletin.* A copy of your military duties or a letter from your clergy on the clergy's letterhead, verifying the religious basis for your request, must be included with your registration application.

If your primary language is not English, you can request extended testing time by following the instructions in the *Information Bulletin.*

Don't forget to make copies of everything before you mail it.

Q. May I change my registration if I need to?

A. Yes, the fee (in 2011) for this service is $45. To reschedule, call PRAXIS Customer Service (800-772-9476) no later than three full days prior to your test date. You can also download a Test, Test Center, and Test Date Change Request form at www.ets.org/praxis and mail it to ETS along with the fee.

Q. What is the fee for the test?

A. The fee (in 2011) for regular registration for the Mathematics CK is $80 plus a nonrefundable $50 general registration fee that is charged once per testing year (September 1–August 31). The fee for late registration is an additional $45.

Q. What should I bring to the test site?

A. The day of the test, you should bring your admission ticket, a valid form of photo and signature identification (for example: driver's license or military identification), your graphing calculator, several sharpened Number 2 soft lead pencils, a good eraser, a blue or black ink pen, and a watch to help pace yourself during the exam. However, you are not permitted to use watch alarms, clocks on cell phones, or mechanical pencils. The testing center will not provide pencils, erasers, or pens.

No personal items such as handbags, cell phones, or study materials or other aids including paper of any kind are permitted in the testing room. The testing centers have secure storage in which you may store personal belongings, including prohibited items, during testing. You are not allowed to eat, drink, or smoke inside the testing room.

Q. Is the Mathematics CK divided into timed sections?

A. No, you have two hours to complete the 50 multiple-choice test items. You may work through the questions at your own pace as long as you stay within the two-hour time frame.

Q. What is the passing score?

A. The passing score varies from state to state (see "The Role of the Mathematics CK in Teacher Certification" in this chapter for a list by state of minimum passing scores). Your score report will show PASSED or NOT PASSED based on a comparison of your score to the passing score in your state.

Q. When will I get my score report?

A. You can check your score report online approximately four weeks after the test date. For a $30 fee, you can get your scores earlier by using the Scores-by-Phone service. See "Getting Your Praxis Scores" at www.ets.org/praxis/scores/get for additional information on score reporting dates and accessing your score.

Q. How should I prepare?

A. Now that you're ready to begin taking your certification exams, using this test-prep book is your best preparation. This study guide gives you insights, reviews, and strategies for the question types.

Q. How do I get more information about the Mathematics CK?

A. Check the PRAXIS Web site (www.ets.org/praxis). If new information on the Mathematics CK becomes available, it will be posted on this site.

Q. What is the ETS Recognition of Excellence Award (ROE)?

A. This award is a way ETS recognizes test-takers who demonstrate a high level of proficiency on any of 11 PRAXIS II tests. For the Mathematics CK, achieving a score of 165 or higher will earn you the ROE. You will receive a congratulatory letter and recognition certificate from ETS acknowledging your high score on the test. In addition, the award will be noted on your score report, and summary award data will be included on reports sent to institutions of higher education and state agencies.

How to Use This *CliffsNotes* Book

The review for the Mathematics CK in this *CliffsNotes* book is designed around the ten content categories assessed on the test: Algebra and Number Theory, Measurement, Geometry, Trigonometry, Functions, Calculus, Data Analysis and Statistics, Probability, Matrix Algebra, and Discrete Mathematics.

You have three full-length practice tests for assessing yourself periodically. The practice tests follow the review chapters in this book. Complete answer explanations are provided for each of the practice tests.

When you read through the list of content categories that are assessed on the Mathematics CK, you may feel overwhelmed by the task of preparing for the test. Here are some suggestions for developing an effective study program using this book.

1. Set up a regular schedule of study sessions. Try to set aside approximately two hours for each session. If you complete one session per day (including weekends), it should take you about four to six weeks to work your way through the review and practice material provided in this book. Of course, if your test date is coming up soon, you might need to lengthen your study time per day.

2. Reserve a place for studying where you will have few distractions, so you can concentrate. Make sure you have adequate lighting and a room temperature that is comfortable—not too warm or too cold. Be sure you have an ample supply of water to keep your brain hydrated, and you might also want to have some light snacks available. To improve mental alertness, choose snacks that are high in protein and low in carbohydrates (for example, nuts). Gather all the necessary study aids (paper, pencils, note cards, and so on) beforehand. Let your voicemail answer your phone during your study time.

3. Take Practice Test 1 before you begin reading the review material to help you discover your strengths and weaknesses. Read the answer explanations for all the questions, not just the ones you missed, because you might have gotten some of your correct answers by guessing. Make a list of the content categories with which you had the most problems. Plan your study program so you can spend more time on content categories that your Practice Test 1 results indicate are weak areas for you. For instance, if you did very well on algebra and number theory, but poorly in calculus, you should plan to spend more time studying the review material for calculus.

4. Carefully study the review of the test areas in Part I of this book to refresh your memory about the key ideas for each of the content categories, being sure to concentrate as you go through the material. Work through the examples and make sure you understand them thoroughly.

5. Make flashcards to aid you in memorizing key definitions and formulas and keep them with you at all times. When you have a few spare minutes, take out the flash cards and go over the information you've recorded on them.

6. Take several two- to three-minute breaks during your study sessions to give your mind time to absorb the review material you just read. According to brain research, you remember the first part and last part of something you've read more easily than you remember the middle part. Taking several breaks will allow you to create more beginnings and endings to maximize the amount of material you remember. It's best not to leave your study area during a break. Try stretching, closing your eyes for a few minutes, or getting a quick drink or snack.

7. Periodically review material you have already studied to reinforce what you have learned and to help you identify topics you might need to restudy.

8. When you complete your first review, take Practice Test 2. Use a timer and take the test under the same conditions you expect for the actual test, being sure to adhere to the two-hour time limit for the test. When you finish taking the test, as you did for Practice Test 1, carefully study the answer explanations for *all* the questions. Then, go back and review again any topics in which you performed unsatisfactorily.

9. When you complete your second review, take Practice Test 3 under the same conditions you expect for the actual test, adhering to the two-hour time limit again by using a timer. When you finish taking the test, carefully study the answer explanations for *all* the questions and do additional study, if needed.

10. Organize a study group, if possible. A good way of learning and reinforcing the material is to discuss it with others. If feasible, set up a regular time to study with one or more classmates or friends. Take turns explaining how to work problems to each other. This strategy will help you clarify your own understanding of the problems and, at the same time, help you discover new insights into how to approach various problems.

After completing your study program, you should find yourself prepared and confident to achieve a passing score on the Mathematics CK.

How to Prepare for the Day of the Test

There are several things you can do to prepare yourself for the day of the test.

1. Know how to get to the testing center and how to get into the room where you will be testing at the testing center.

2. Make sure you have dependable transportation to get to the test center and know where you should park (if you plan to go by car).

3. Keep all the materials you will need to bring to the test center—especially your admission ticket and identification—in a secure place so you easily can find them on the day of the test.

4. The night before the test, try to get a good night's rest. Avoid taking nonprescription drugs or consuming alcohol as the use of these products might impair your mental faculties on test day.

5. On the day of the test, get to the testing center early—at least 30 minutes before your test is scheduled to begin.

6. Dress in comfortable clothing and wear comfortable shoes. Even if it is warm outside, wear layers of clothing that can be removed or put on, depending on the temperature in the test center.

7. Eat a light meal. Select foods you have found that usually give you the most energy and stamina.

8. Drink plenty of water to make sure your brain remains hydrated during the test for optimal thinking.

9. Clear your calculator's memory before you leave for the testing center. Before you do, back up anything in your calculator's memory that you want to keep. Put fresh batteries in your calculator just before you leave for the testing center.

10. Make a copy of this list and post it in a strategic location. Check it before you leave for the testing center.

Test-Taking Strategies for the Mathematics CK

Here are some general test-taking strategies to help maximize your score on the test:

1. When you receive the test, take several deep, slow breaths before you begin, exhaling slowly while mentally visualizing yourself performing successfully on the test. Do not get upset if you feel nervous. Most of the people taking the test with you will be experiencing some measure of anxiety.

2. During the test, follow all the directions, including the test center administrator's (TCA) oral directions and the written directions in the test booklet. If you do not understand something in the directions, raise your hand and ask the TCA for clarification.

3. Move through the test at a steady pace. The test consists of 50 multiple-choice items. As you begin the test, skim through the booklet to find question 25 and mark this question as an approximate halfway point. When you get to question 25, check your watch to see how much time has passed. If more than one hour has gone by, you will need to pick up the pace. Otherwise, continue to work as rapidly as you can without being careless, but do not rush.

4. Try to answer the questions in order. Skipping around can waste time and might cause mistakes on your answer sheet. However, if a question is taking too much of your time, place a large check mark next to it in the test booklet (not on the answer booklet), mark your best guess in the answer booklet, and move on.

5. Read each question entirely. Skimming to save time can cause you to misread a question or miss important information.

6. Write in the test booklet. Mark on diagrams, draw figures, underline or circle key words or phrases, and do scratch work in the test booklet. Remember, however, to mark your answer choice in the separate answer booklet. Answers marked only in the test booklet are not scored.

7. Don't read too much into a question. For instance, don't presume a geometric figure is drawn accurately or to scale.

8. Refer to the notation, definitions, and formulas provided with the test as often as needed. Always double-check every formula after you write it down.

9. Use your calculator, but use it wisely. Keep in mind that graphing calculators are powerful tools, but they can make errors. See the discussion about graphing calculators that follows this section.

10. Be sure you are answering the right question. Circle or underline what you are being asked to find to help you stay focused on it.

11. Read all the answer choices before you select an answer. You might find an answer that immediately strikes you as correct, but this determination might have occurred because you jumped to a false conclusion or made an incorrect assumption.

12. Eliminate as many wrong choices as you can. When applicable, estimate the answer to help you decide which answers are unreasonable.

13. Change an answer only if you have a good reason to do so. Be sure to completely erase the old answer choice before marking the new one.

14. If you are trying to recall information during the test, close your eyes and try to visualize yourself in your study place. This may trigger your memory.

15. Remain calm during the test. If you find yourself getting anxious, stop and take several deep, slow breaths and exhale slowly, while mentally visualizing yourself in a peaceful place, to help you relax. Do not be upset if the student next to you finishes, gets up, and leaves before you do. Keep your mind focused on the task at hand—completing your exam. Trust yourself. You should not expect to know the correct response to every question on the test. Think only of doing your personal best.

16. Record your answers in the answer booklet carefully. The test is scored electronically, so it is critical that you mark your answer booklet accurately. As you go through the test questions, circle the letters of your answer choices in the test booklet. Then mark those answers in the answer booklet in bunches of five to ten (until the last minutes of the time allotted, when you should start marking answers one by one).

17. Before turning in your answer booklet, be sure you have marked an answer for every test question. You are not penalized for a wrong answer (you merely score a 0 for that test question), so even if you have no clue about the correct answer, make a guess. Also, erase any stray marks in the answer booklet and brush off any loose eraser dust.

18. As you work through the practice tests provided in this book, consciously use the strategies suggested in this section as preparation for the actual Mathematics CK. Try to reach a point where the strategies are automatic for you.

Graphing Calculators and the Mathematics CK

Because you are required to bring a graphing calculator to use when you take the Mathematics CK, you should have your calculator on hand and use it, when needed, to work problems in the review material and practice tests in this book. Select a calculator that you will feel comfortable using. Don't purchase a high-powered calculator that will require an investment of your time to learn while you are preparing for the test.

A word of caution: Graphing calculators are very powerful tools, but you should be aware that they can make errors!

One situation in which errors might occur is when the calculator is finding the roots or zeros of a high-degree polynomial (for example, a polynomial of degree eight). The algorithm that the calculator uses to find the roots of the polynomial forces the calculator to round numbers to a certain number of decimal places before the final result is obtained, thus yielding inaccurate answers.

Another situation in which errors commonly occur is when the calculator is drawing the graph of a function. Your choice of viewing window dimensions can give results that are visually very misleading. For instance, you can be led to believe that a function has only two zeros when, in fact, it has three zeros. Changing the dimensions for the viewing window can clear up the problem in most cases; however, not every time. Most notably, for some graphing calculators, the graph of $y = \sin(1/x)$ at values near $x = 0$ will never be correct no matter what window dimensions you select.

The point of this discussion is to make you aware that such mistakes can happen. Therefore, you should use your mathematical expertise to evaluate all your calculator's answers for reliability and accuracy.

You will benefit greatly from this *CliffsNotes* book. By using the recommendations in this chapter as you complete your study program, you will be prepared to walk into the testing room with confidence. Good luck on the test and on your new career as a mathematics teacher!

PART I

SUBJECT AREA REVIEWS

Chapter 1

Review for the Praxis Mathematics Content Knowledge (0061)

The review of the Mathematics CK in this *CliffsNotes* book is designed around the ten content categories assessed on the test: Algebra and Number Theory, Measurement, Geometry, Trigonometry, Functions, Calculus, Data Analysis and Statistics, Probability, Matrix Algebra, and Discrete Mathematics. Each content category is defined by a list of specific knowledge and skills. The review for each content category will discuss the key ideas and formulas that are most important for you to know for the Mathematics CK. Mathematical notation, definitions, and formulas like those that will be provided for you when you take the official test are included on the following three pages.

Notation, Definitions, and Formulas

Notation

(a, b)	$\{x: a < x < b\}$
$[a, b)$	$\{x: a \leq x < b\}$
$(a, b]$	$\{x: a < x \leq b\}$
$[a, b]$	$\{x: a \leq x \leq b\}$
gcd (m, n)	greatest common divisor of two integers m and n
lcm (m, n)	least common multiple of two integers m and n
$[x]$	greatest integer m such that $m \leq x$
$m \equiv k \pmod{n}$	m and k are congruent modulo n (m and k have the same remainder when divided by n, or equivalently, $m - k$ is a multiple of n)
f^{-1}	inverse of an invertible function f; (*not* to be read as $\frac{1}{f}$)
$\lim\limits_{x \to a^+} f(x)$	right-hand limit of $f(x)$; limit of $f(x)$ as x approaches a from the right (if it exists)
$\lim\limits_{x \to a^-} f(x)$	left-hand limit of $f(x)$; limit of $f(x)$ as x approaches a from the left (if it exists)
$\varnothing$	the empty set
$x \in S$	x is an element of set S
$S \subset T$	set S is a proper subset of set T
$S \subseteq T$	either set S is a proper subset of set T or $S = T$
$S \cup T$	union of sets S and T
$S \cap T$	intersection of sets S and T

Definitions

Discrete Mathematics

A relation $\Re$ on a set S is

reflexive if $x \Re x$ for all $x \in S$

symmetric $x \Re y \Rightarrow y \Re x$ for all $x, y \in S$

transitive if $(x \Re y$ and $y \Re z) \Rightarrow x \Re z$ for all $x, y, z \in S$

antisymmetric if $(x \Re y$ and $y \Re z) \Rightarrow x = y$ for all $x, y \in S$

An *equivalence* relation is a reflexive, symmetric, and transitive relation.

Formulas

Sum and Difference	$\sin(x \pm y) = \sin x \cos y \pm \cos x \sin y$ $\cos(x \pm y) = \cos x \cos y \mp \sin x \sin y$ $\tan(x \pm y) = \dfrac{\tan x \pm \tan y}{1 \mp \tan x \tan y}$
Half-Angle (sign depends on the quadrant of $\frac{\theta}{2}$)	$\sin\dfrac{\theta}{2} = \pm\sqrt{\dfrac{1-\cos\theta}{2}};$ $\qquad$ $\cos\dfrac{\theta}{2} = \pm\sqrt{\dfrac{1+\cos\theta}{2}}$
Range of Inverse Trigonometric Functions	$\sin^{-1}x \quad -\dfrac{\pi}{2}, \dfrac{\pi}{2}; \cos^{-1}x \quad 0, \pi; \tan^{-1}x \quad -\dfrac{\pi}{2}, \dfrac{\pi}{2}$
Law of Sines	$\dfrac{\sin A}{a} = \dfrac{\sin B}{b} = \dfrac{\sin C}{c}$
Law of Cosines	$c^2 = a^2 + b^2 - 2ab(\cos C)$
De Moivre's Theorem	$\left(\cos\theta + i\sin\theta\right)^k = \cos\left(k\theta\right) + i\sin\left(k\theta\right)$

Coordinate Transformation		
Rectangular (x, y) to polar (r, θ):	$r^2 = x^2 + y^2;$	$\tan\theta = \dfrac{y}{x}$ if $x \neq 0$
Polar (r, θ) to rectangular (x, y):	$x = r\cos\theta;$	$y = r\sin\theta$
Distance from point (x_1, y_1) to line $Ax + By + C = 0$	$d = \dfrac{\left|Ax_1 + By_1 + C\right|}{\sqrt{A^2 + B^2}}$	

Volume	
Sphere: radius r	$V = \dfrac{4}{3}\pi r^3$
Right circular cone: height h, base of radius r	$V = \dfrac{1}{3}\pi r^2 h$
Right circular cylinder: height h, base of radius r	$V = \pi r^2 h$
Pyramid: height h, base of area B	$V = \dfrac{1}{3}Bh$
Right Prism: height h, base of area B	$V = Bh$

Surface Area	
Sphere: radius r Right circular cone: radius r, slant height s	$A = 4\pi r^2$ $A = \pi r s + \pi r^2$

Differentiation	
$\left(f(x)g(x)\right)' = f(x)g'(x) + g(x)f'(x);$	$\left(\dfrac{f(x)}{g(x)}\right)' = \dfrac{g(x)f'(x) - f(x)g'(x)}{\left(g(x)\right)^2}$ provided $g(x) \neq 0;$ $(f(g(x)))' = f'(g(x))g'(x)$
Integration by Parts	$\int u\, du = uv - \int v\, du$

While you are practicing for the Mathematics CK, make sure you become very familiar with the information given to you on the Notation, Definitions, and Formulas pages included in this chapter and at the beginning of the Mathematics CK test booklet. You will need to know other common mathematical formulas not listed on the Notation, Definitions, and Formulas pages, such as the three formulas given here.

Simple Interest Formula $I = Prt$	where I = simple interest earned, P = principal invested or present value of investment, r = annual simple interest rate, and t = time in years.
Compound Interest Formula $P = P_0\left(1 + \dfrac{r}{n}\right)^{nt}$	where P is the total value of an initial investment of P_0 for t years at an annual rate r, compounded n times per year.
Distance Formula $d = rt$	where d = distance traveled, r = (uniform) rate of speed, and t = time.

In addition, you will need to know other familiar formulas relevant to the content categories, such as the formulas for the area and perimeter of common geometric shapes. The most important formulas for you to know are given in the reviews for the content categories.

Chapter 2

Algebra and Number Theory

According to the *Mathematics: Content Knowledge (0061) Test at a Glance* (www.ets.org/Media/Tests/PRAXIS/pdf/0061.pdf), the Algebra and Number Theory content category of the Mathematics CK tests your knowledge and skills in nine topic areas:

- The real and complex number systems
- Properties of number systems
- Properties of the counting numbers
- Ratio, proportion, percent, and average
- Algebraic expressions, formulas, and equations
- Systems of equations and inequalities
- Geometric interpretations of algebraic principles
- Algebraic representations of lines, planes, conic sections, and spheres
- Formulas used in two- and three-dimensional coordinate systems

This review discusses the key ideas and formulas in each topic area that are most important for you to know for the Mathematics CK.

The Real and Complex Number Systems

For this topic, you must understand the structure of the natural, integer, rational, real, and complex number systems and perform basic operations on numbers in these systems.

Important sets of numbers in algebra for you to know are

natural numbers or counting numbers = $\{1, 2, 3,...\}$

whole numbers = $\{0, 1, 2, 3,...\}$

integers = $\{..., -3, -2, -1, 0, 1, 2, 3,...\}$

rational numbers = $\left\{\dfrac{p}{q}, \text{where } p, \ q \text{ are integers with } q \neq 0\right\}$

irrational numbers = {nonterminating, nonrepeating decimals} = {numbers that *cannot* be written as $\dfrac{p}{q}$, where p, q are integers with $q \neq 0$}

real numbers = rational numbers $\cup$ irrational numbers. The natural numbers, whole numbers, integers, rational numbers, and irrational numbers are subsets of the real numbers. The real numbers can be represented on a number line. Every point on the number line corresponds to a real number.

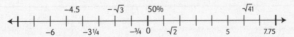

complex numbers = $\{x + yi, \text{where } x \text{ and } y \text{ are real numbers and } i^2 = -1\}$. For the complex number $z = x + yi$, the coefficients x and y are the real part and imaginary part, respectively, of z. When x is 0, the resulting set of numbers consists of pure imaginary numbers. When y is 0, the resulting set of numbers consists of the real numbers. Thus, the real numbers are a subset of the complex numbers. The complex numbers can be represented on the complex plane, where the horizontal axis is the *real* axis and the vertical axis is the *imaginary* axis. The complex numbers $z_1 = 2 + i$, $z_2 = 3 - 2i$, $z_3 = -3 + 2i$, and $z_4 = -2 - 4i$ are shown in the complex plane in the following figure.

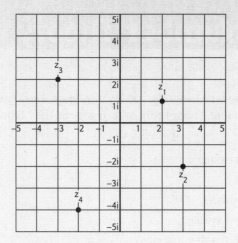

Intervals and Interval Notation

Intervals show sets of numbers on the real number line. Open intervals do not include the endpoints. Closed intervals include both endpoints. Half-open (or half-closed) intervals include only one endpoint. Finite intervals are bounded intervals. Intervals that extend indefinitely to the right or left are unbounded intervals.

To graph an interval on the number line, shade the number line to show the numbers included in the interval. Use a solid circle to indicate an endpoint is included and an open circle to indicate an endpoint is not included. The following table summarizes intervals and interval notation.

Interval	Notation and Type	Graph
$x < b$	$(-\infty, b)$, unbounded, open	
$x > a$	(a, ∞), unbounded, open	
$x \le b$	$(-\infty, b]$, unbounded, half-open	
$x \ge a$	$[a, \infty)$, unbounded, half-open	
$a < x < b$	(a, b), bounded, open	
$a \le x < b$	$[a, b)$, bounded, half-open	
$a < x \le b$	$(a, b]$, bounded, half-open	
$a \le x \le b$	$[a, b]$, bounded, closed	

Rules to Compute By

Computations using real numbers are performed by using the absolute values, which are always positive or 0, of the numbers. The absolute value of a real number is its distance from 0 on the real number line. The absolute value of a real number x is either x or $-x$, whichever of these is nonnegative.

For sums and differences of real numbers, use the following rules.

Rule 1. To add two numbers that have the same sign: Add their absolute values and give the sum their common sign.

Rule 2. To add two numbers that have opposite signs: Subtract the lesser absolute value from the greater absolute value and give the sum the sign of the number with the greater absolute value; if the two numbers have the same absolute value, their sum is 0.

Rule 3. The sum of 0 and any number is the number.

Rule 4. To find the difference of two real numbers: Keep the first number, and then add the opposite of the number that follows the minus sign. (In other words, "subtracting a number" and "adding the opposite of the number" give the same answer.)

For products and quotients of real numbers, use the following rules.

Rule 5. To find the product of two *nonzero* real numbers that have the same sign: Multiply their absolute values and keep the product positive (no sign is necessary).

Rule 6. To find the product of two *nonzero* real numbers that have opposite signs: Multiply their absolute values and indicate that the product is negative.

Rule 7. When 0 is one of the factors, the product is *always* 0; otherwise, products involving an *even* number of negative factors are positive, whereas those involving an *odd* number of negative factors are negative.

Rule 8. To find the quotient of two *nonzero* real numbers that have the same sign: Divide their absolute values and keep the quotient positive (no sign is necessary).

Rule 9. To find the quotient of two *nonzero* real numbers that have opposite signs: Divide their absolute values and indicate that the quotient is negative.

Rule 10. The quotient is 0 when the dividend is 0 and the divisor is a nonzero number. For example: $\frac{0}{10} = 0$, $\frac{0}{-8} = 0$.

Rule 11. A quotient is *undefined* when the divisor is 0. For example: $\frac{35}{0}$ = undefined; $\frac{0}{0}$ = undefined.

Order of Operations

When more than one operation is involved in a numerical expression, you must follow the order of operations to evaluate the expression. A commonly used mnemonic is "Please Excuse My Dear Aunt Sally"—abbreviated as **PE(MD)(AS).** The first letters of the words remind you of the following:

First, operations enclosed in <u>P</u>arentheses (or other grouping symbol, if present)

Next, <u>E</u>xponentiation

Then, <u>M</u>ultiplication and <u>D</u>ivision in the order in which they occur from left to right

Last, <u>A</u>ddition and <u>S</u>ubtraction in the order in which they occur from left to right

Tip: Note that multiplication does not have to be done before division, or addition before subtraction. You multiply and divide in the order they occur in the problem. Similarly, you add and subtract in the order they occur in the problem. That's why there are parentheses around MD and AS in PE(MD)(AS).

Grouping symbols such as parentheses ( ), brackets [ ], and braces { } are used to keep things together that belong together. Parentheses are used also to indicate multiplication as in (–2)(–5) or for clarity as in –(–15). Fraction bars, absolute value bars | |, and square root symbols $\sqrt{\ }$ are grouping symbols, too. When you are performing computations, perform operations in grouping symbols first. It is *very important* to do this when addition or subtraction is inside the grouping symbol. For instance: $(1 + 1)^3 = 2^3$, $|3-10| = |-7| = 7$, and $\sqrt{16+9} = \sqrt{25} = 5$.

The rules for performing operations with complex numbers follow. Keep in mind that because the coefficients x and y in a complex number $x + yi$ are *real* numbers, the computations involving these real number coefficients must adhere to Rules 1 through 11 given previously.

For sums and differences of complex numbers, use the following rules.

Rule 1. Addition of two complex numbers: $(x + yi) + (u + vi) = (x + u) + (y + v)i$

Tip: Add the real parts. Add the imaginary parts.

Rule 2. Subtraction of two complex numbers: $(x + yi) - (u + vi) = (x - u) + (y - v)i$

Tip: Subtract the real parts. Subtract the imaginary parts.

When multiplying complex numbers, it is important to remember that $i^2 = -1$.

For products of complex numbers, use the following rule.

Rule 3. Multiplication of two complex numbers: $(x + yi)(u + vi) = (xu - yv) + (xv + yu)i$

Tip: Use F.O.I.L. (First terms, Outer terms, Inner terms, and Last terms) to perform the multiplication.

The complex numbers $x + yi$ and $x - yi$ are complex conjugates of each other. The product of a complex number and its conjugate is a real number. Specifically, $(x + yi)(x - yi) = x^2 - xyi + xyi - y^2i^2 = x^2 - y^2(-1) = x^2 + y^2$.

This concept is used in the division of complex numbers.

For quotients of complex numbers, use the following rule using the complex conjugate.

Rule 4. Division of two complex numbers:

$$\frac{x+yi}{u+vi} = \frac{(x+yi)}{(u+vi)} \cdot \frac{(u-vi)}{(u-vi)} = \frac{xu - xvi + yui - yvi^2}{u^2 - uvi + uvi - v^2i^2} = \frac{xu + yv + yui - xvi}{u^2 + v^2} = \frac{xu + yv}{u^2 + v^2} + \frac{yu - xv}{u^2 + v^2}i$$

Tip: Multiply the numerator and denominator by the conjugate of the denominator.

You can use the definition of multiplication and the fact that $i^2 = -1$ to compute whole number powers of the imaginary unit i. For instance, $i^1 = i$; $i^2 = -1$; $i^3 = i \cdot i^2 = i \cdot -1 = -i$; $i^4 = i^2 \cdot i^2 = -1 \cdot -1 = 1$; $i^5 = i \cdot i^4 = i \cdot 1 = i$; $i^6 = i^2 \cdot i^4 = -1 \cdot 1 = -1$; $i^7 = i^3 \cdot i^4 = -i \cdot 1 = -i$; $i^8 = i^4 \cdot i^4 = 1 \cdot 1 = 1$. As you look at this list, you see a pattern of $i, -1, -i, 1, i, -1, -i, 1, \ldots$ This pattern will continue through higher powers of i. In general, $(i^4)^n = 1$ for any integer. Thus, for example: $i^{103} = (i^4)^{25} i^3 = 1 \cdot (-i) = -i$.

Properties of Number Systems

For this topic, you compare and contrast properties (such as closure, commutativity, associativity, and so forth) of number systems under various operations.

The set of real numbers has the following 11 field properties under the binary operations of addition and multiplication for all real numbers a, b, and c:

Field Properties of the Real Numbers	
Field Property	**Explanation**
Closure property:	$a + b$ and ab are real numbers. The sum or product of any two real numbers is a real number.
Commutative property:	$a + b = b + a$ and $ab = ba$. You can switch the order of any two numbers when you add or multiply without changing the answer.
Associative property:	$(a + b) + c = a + (b + c)$ and $(ab)c = a(bc)$. The way the addends or factors are grouped does not affect the final sum or product.
Additive identity property:	There exists a real number, denoted 0, such that $a + 0 = a$ and $0 + a = a$. This property ensures that 0 is a real number and that its sum with any real number is the number.
Multiplicative identity property:	There exists a real number, denoted 1, such that $a \cdot 1 = a$ and $1 \cdot a = a$. This property ensures that one is a real number and that its product with any real number is the number.
Additive inverse property:	For every real number a, there exists a real number, denoted $-a$, such that $a + (-a) = 0$ and $(-a) + a = 0$. This property ensures that for every real number, there is another real number, opposite to it in sign, which when added to the number gives 0.
Multiplicative inverse property:	For every nonzero real number a, there exists a real number, denoted a^{-1}, such that $a(a^{-1}) = 1$ and $(a^{-1})a = 1$. This property ensures that for every real number, except 0, there is another real number, which when multiplied by the number gives 1.
Distributive property:	$a(b + c) = ab + ac$ and $(b + c)a = ba + ca$. When you have a factor times a sum, you can either add first and then multiply, or multiply first and then add. Either way, the answer works out to be the same.

Similarly, for all complex numbers $x + yi$, $u + vi$, $a + bi$, and $c + di$, you have

Field Properties of the Complex Numbers	
Field Property	**Explanation**
Closure Property of Addition:	$(x + yi) + (u + vi) = (x + u) + (y + v)i$ is a complex number.
Closure Property of Multiplication:	$(x + yi)(u + vi) = (xu - yv) + (xv + yu)i$ is a complex number.
Commutative Property of Addition:	$(x + yi) + (u + vi) = (u + vi) + (x + yi)$.
Commutative Property of Multiplication:	$(x + yi)(u + vi) = (u + vi)(x + yi)$.
Associative Property of Addition:	$[(x + yi) + (u + vi)] + (a + bi) = (x + yi) + [(u + vi) + (a + bi)]$.
Associative Property of Multiplication:	$[(x + yi)(u + vi)](a + bi) = (x + yi)[(u + vi)(a + bi)]$.
Additive Identity Property:	There exists a complex number, 0, such that $(x + yi) + (0) = x + yi$ and $(0) + (x + yi) = x + yi$.
Multiplicative Identity Property:	There exists a complex number, 1, such that $(x + yi)(1) = x + yi$ and $(1)(x + yi) = x + yi$.
Additive Inverse Property:	For every complex number $x + yi$, there exists a complex number, $(-x) + (-y)i$, such that $(x + yi) + ((-x) + (-y)i) = 0$ and $((-x) + (-y)i) + (x + yi) = 0$.
Multiplicative Inverse Property:	For every nonzero complex number $x + yi$, there exists a complex number, $\left(\dfrac{x}{x^2 + y^2}\right) + \left(\dfrac{-y}{x^2 + y^2}\right)i$, such that $(x + yi)\left(\left(\dfrac{x}{x^2 + y^2}\right) + \left(\dfrac{-y}{x^2 + y^2}\right)i\right) = 1$ and $\left(\left(\dfrac{x}{x^2 + y^2}\right) + \left(\dfrac{-y}{x^2 + y^2}\right)i\right)(x + yi) = 1.$
Distributive Property:	$(x + yi)[(a + bi) + (c + di)] = (x + yi)(a + bi) + (x + yi)(c + di)$.

Note: Proof of each of these properties relies on the corresponding field property for the real numbers.

In general, a system consisting of a set S and two binary operations defined on S is a field if the 11 field properties are satisfied for S under the two operations.

Properties of the Counting Numbers

For this topic, you must understand properties of counting numbers (for example, prime, composite, prime factorization, even, odd, factors, multiples).

The counting numbers are the natural numbers. Counting numbers that are greater than 1 are either prime or composite. A prime number is a whole number greater than 1 that has exactly two distinct factors: itself and 1. Thus, the primes are 2, 3, 5, 7, 11, 13, . . .

The counting numbers greater than 1 that are *not* prime are the composite numbers. They are 4, 6, 8, 9, 10, 12, . . .

The counting number 1 is neither prime nor composite.

Counting numbers that are multiples of 2 are even. The even counting numbers are 2, 4, 6, 8, 10, . . .

Counting numbers that are *not* multiples of 2 are odd. The odd counting numbers are 1, 3, 5, 7, 9, . . .

The principle of mathematical induction states that any set of counting numbers that contains the number 1 and $k + 1$, whenever it contains the counting number k, contains all the counting numbers.

The Fundamental Theorem of Arithmetic states that every counting number greater than or equal to 2 is either a prime or can be factored into a product of primes in one and only one way, except for the order in which the factors appear.

Divisibility rules can help with factoring numbers. A counting number is divisible by another counting number if, after dividing by that number, the remainder is 0. You write $a|b$ to mean a divides b evenly or, equivalently, b "is divisible by" a (for example: 3|36, which means 36 is divisible by 3—therefore, 3 is a factor of 36). The following table shows some common divisibility rules that are useful to know.

Common Divisibility Rules		
Divisibility by	**Rule**	**Example**
2	A number is divisible by 2 if and only if the last digit of the number is even.	2|2,347,854 because 4 (the last digit) is even.
3	A number is divisible by 3 if and only if the sum of its digits is divisible by 3.	3|151,515 because 3 divides 1 + 5 + 1 + 5 + 1 + 5 = 18 (the sum of the digits).
4	A number is divisible by 4 if and only if the last two digits form a number that is divisible by 4.	4|47,816 because 4 divides 16 (the number formed by the last two digits).
5	A number is divisible by 5 if and only if the last digit of the number is 0 or 5.	5|42,115 because the last digit is 5.
6	A number is divisible by 6 if and only if it is divisible by both 2 and 3.	6|18,122,124 because 2|18,122,124 (the last digit is even) and 3|18,122,124 (21, the sum of the digits, is divisible by 3).
7	To test for divisibility by 7, double the last digit and subtract the product from the number formed by the remaining digits. If the result is a number divisible by 7, the original number is also divisible by 7.	7|875 because 7 divides 87 – 10 = 77 (87 minus 2 times 5).
8	A number is divisible by 8 if and only if the last 3 digits form a number that is divisible by 8.	8|55,864 because 8 divides 864 (the number formed by the last three digits).
9	A number is divisible by 9 if and only if the sum of its digits is divisible by 9.	9|151,515 because 9 divides 1 + 5 + 1 + 5 + 1 + 5 = 18 (the sum of the digits).

Divisibility by	Rule	Example
10	A number is divisible by 10 if and only if the last digit of the number is 0.	10|66660 because the last digit is 0.
11	To test for divisibility by 11, alternately add and subtract the digits. If the result is a number divisible by 11, the original number is also divisible by 11.	11|2574 because 11 divides $2 - 5 + 7 - 4 = 0$ (the sum of the digits).

The greatest common factor of two or more counting numbers is the greatest product that will divide evenly into each of the counting numbers. It can be obtained by writing the prime factorization of each counting number and building a product consisting of each factor the *highest* number of times it appears as a *common* factor of the counting numbers in the set. The greatest common factor of two counting numbers m and n is denoted gcf (m,n). For instance, gcf $(72, 48) = $ gcf $(2^3 \cdot 3^2, 2^4 \cdot 3) = 2^3 \cdot 3 = 24$.

The greatest common divisor of two counting numbers m and n, denoted gcd (m,n), is the greatest common factor of m and n.

The least common multiple of a set of counting numbers is the least product that is a multiple of each of the counting numbers. It can be obtained by factoring each counting number and building a product consisting of each factor the *most* number of times it appears as a factor in any *one* of the counting numbers in the set. The least common multiple of two counting numbers m and n is denoted lcm (m,n). For instance, lcm $(72, 48) = $ lcm $(2^3 \cdot 3^2, 2^4 \cdot 3) = 2^4 \cdot 3^2 = 144$.

Tip: The least common multiple of a set of numbers is the least number that is divisible by each of the numbers in the set.

Ratio, Proportion, Percent, and Average

For this topic, you solve ratio, proportion, percent, and arithmetic average (including weighted average) problems.

A ratio is the comparison of two quantities. You can express a ratio in three different forms: a to b, $a{:}b$, or $\frac{a}{b}$. The quantities a and b are the terms of the ratio. A ratio is a pure number—it does not have any units. When you find the ratio of two quantities, you must make sure they have the same units so that when you write the ratio, the units will divide out. If the two quantities cannot be converted to like units, then you must keep the units and write the quotient as a rate.

A proportion is a mathematical statement that two ratios are equal. The terms of the proportion are the four numbers that make up the two ratios. For example, the proportion $\frac{a}{b} = \frac{c}{d}$ has terms a, b, c, and d. In a proportion, cross products are equal. Cross products are the product of the numerator of the first ratio times the denominator of the second ratio, and the product of the denominator of the first ratio times the numerator of the second ratio. That is,

$$\frac{a}{b} = \frac{c}{d} \text{ if and only if } ad = bc$$

When you are given a proportion that has a missing term, you can use cross products to find the missing term. You can shorten the process by finding a cross product you can calculate and then dividing by the numerical term in the proportion you did not use. Because you are allowed to use a calculator on the Mathematics CK, this is the quickest and most reliable way to solve a proportion on the test. Here is an example.

Solve $\frac{d}{18} = \frac{20}{0.75}$.

Find a cross product you can calculate. You don't know the value of d, so the only cross product you can calculate is 18 times 20. Divide by 0.75, the numerical term you didn't use.

$$d = \frac{18 \cdot 20}{0.75} = 480$$

Percent means per hundred. When used in computations, percents are changed to fractions or decimals. Thus, $6\% = 0.06$. The key idea in percent problems is that a specified percent of an amount is that percent multiplied times the amount. The formula is $P = RB$, where

P is the percentage, the "part of the whole."

R is the rate, the number with "%" or the word "percent" attached.

B is the base, the "whole amount."

An effective strategy for solving percent problems is to first identify P, R, and B, and then do one of the following:

1. Write and solve an equation, written in the form $P = RB$, for the unknown quantity.
2. Write and solve a proportion that has the following form: $\frac{r}{100} = \frac{\text{part}}{\text{whole}}$, where $r\% = R$.

Tip: In application problems, a percent without a base is usually meaningless. Make sure you identify the base associated with each percent mentioned in a problem.

To calculate the arithmetic average of a set of numbers: first, sum the numbers and then divide by how many numbers are in the set. Thus, you have

$$\text{arithmetic average} = \frac{\text{sum of the numbers}}{\text{how many numbers you have}}$$

To find the weighted average of a set of n values $x_1, x_2, \ldots, x_n$ that have given respective weights $w_1, w_2, \ldots, w_n$, use the formula:

$$\text{weighted average} = \frac{w_1 x_1 + w_2 x_2 + \cdots + w_n x_n}{w_1 + w_2 + \cdots + w_n}$$

Note: The arithmetic average and weighted average are also known as the mean and weighted mean, respectively.

Algebraic Expressions, Formulas, and Equations

For this topic, you work with algebraic expressions, formulas, and equations; add, subtract, multiply, and divide polynomials; add, subtract, multiply, and divide algebraic fractions; and perform standard algebraic operations involving complex numbers, radicals, and exponents, including fractional and negative exponents.

Roots and Radicals

You square a number by multiplying the number by itself. The reverse of squaring is finding the square root. Every positive number has two square roots that are equal in absolute value, but opposite in sign. The positive square root is called the principal square root of the number. Zero has only one square root, namely 0. The principal square root of 0 is 0. In general, if x is a real number such that $x \cdot x = s$, then $\sqrt{s} = |x|$ (the absolute value of x), where $\sqrt{s}$ denotes the principal square root of s.

Tip: The $\sqrt{}$ symbol always gives one number as the answer and that number is nonnegative: positive or 0. For instance, $\sqrt{25} = 5$, not ±5. Also, $\sqrt{-3 \cdot -3} = |-3| = 3$, not –3.

A number that is an exact square of another number is a perfect square. For instance, the integers 4, 9, 16, and 25 are perfect squares.

A number x such that $x \cdot x \cdot x = c$ is a cube root of c. Finding the cube root of a number is the reverse of cubing a number. Every real number has exactly *one* real cube root, called its principal cube root. You use $\sqrt[3]{c}$ to indicate the principal cube root of c. The principal cube root of a negative number is negative, and the principal cube root of a positive number is positive. If x is a real number such that $x \cdot x \cdot x = c$, then $\sqrt[3]{c} = x$.

In general, if $\underbrace{x \cdot x \cdot x \cdot \cdots \cdot x}_{n \text{ factors of } x} = a$ where n is a natural number, x is called an nth root of a. The principal nth root of a is denoted $\sqrt[n]{a}$. The expression $\sqrt[n]{a}$ is a radical, a is called the radicand, n is called the index and indicates which root is desired. If no index is written, it is understood to be 2 and the radical expression indicates the principal square root of the radicand. A *positive* real number has exactly *one* real positive nth root whether n is even or odd; and *every* real number has exactly one real nth root when n is odd. Negative numbers do not have real nth roots when n is even. Finally, the nth root of 0 is 0, whether n is even or odd: $\sqrt[n]{0} = 0$ (always).

The following rules are for radicals when x and y are real numbers, m and n are positive integers, and the radical expression denotes a real number:

Rules for Radicals

$\sqrt[n]{x^n} = x$ if n is odd $\qquad$ $\sqrt[n]{x^n} = |x|$ if n is even $\qquad$ $\sqrt[n]{x^m} = \left(\sqrt[n]{x}\right)^m$ $\qquad$ $\left(\sqrt[n]{x}\right)\left(\sqrt[n]{y}\right) = \sqrt[n]{xy}$

$\dfrac{\sqrt[n]{x}}{\sqrt[n]{y}} = \sqrt[n]{\dfrac{x}{y}}, (y \neq 0)$ $\qquad$ $\sqrt[m]{\sqrt[n]{x}} = \sqrt[mn]{x}$ $\qquad$ $\sqrt[pn]{x^{pm}} = \sqrt[n]{x^m}$ $\qquad$ $a\left(\sqrt[n]{x}\right) + b\left(\sqrt[n]{x}\right) = (a + b)\left(\sqrt[n]{x}\right)$

These rules form the basis for simplifying radical expressions. (See Appendix B for a discussion on simplifying radicals.)

Exponents

In mathematical expressions, exponentiation is indicated by a small raised number, called the exponent, written to the upper right of a quantity, which is the base for the exponential expression. Common types of exponents are summarized in the following table.

Common Types of Exponents		
Type of Exponent	**Definition**	**Example**
Positive Integer	If x is any real number and n is a positive integer, then $x^n = \underbrace{x \cdot x \cdot x \cdot \cdots \cdot x}_{n \text{ factors of } x}$, where x^n is read "x to the nth power" or as "x to the n."	$2^5 = 2 \cdot 2 \cdot 2 \cdot 2 \cdot 2 = 32$
Zero	For any real number x (except 0), $x^0 = 1$.	$(-12.78)^0 = 1$
Rational Number	If x is any real number (except 0) and m and n are natural numbers, then $x^{\frac{1}{n}} = \sqrt[n]{x}$; and $x^{\frac{m}{n}} = \left(\sqrt[n]{x}\right)^m$ or $\sqrt[n]{x^m}$; provided, in all cases, that $x \geq 0$ when n is even.	$16^{\frac{1}{2}} = \sqrt{16} = 4$ and $64^{\frac{4}{3}} = \left(\sqrt[3]{64}\right)^4 = (4)^4 = 256$
Negative Number	If x is any real number (except 0) and $-n$ is a negative number, then $x^{-n} = \dfrac{1}{x^n}$ and $\dfrac{1}{x^{-n}} = x^n$.	$2^{-3} = \dfrac{1}{2^3} = \dfrac{1}{8}$ and $\dfrac{1}{2^{-3}} = 2^3 = 8$

Tip: The exponent 2 on a number is usually read "squared" rather than "to the second power." Likewise, the exponent 3 is usually read "cubed" rather than "to the third power."

The following rules for exponents hold

Rules for Exponents

For real numbers x and y and integers m, n, and p:

$$x^1 = x \qquad x^0 = 1, x \neq 0 \qquad 0^0 \text{ is undefined} \qquad x^{-n} = \frac{1}{x^n} \qquad \left(\frac{x}{y}\right)^{-1} = \left(\frac{y}{x}\right) \qquad \left(\frac{x}{y}\right)^{-n} = \left(\frac{y}{x}\right)^n$$

$$(x^n)^p = x^{np} \text{ (power of a power)} \qquad \left(\frac{x}{y}\right)^p = \frac{x^p}{y^p} \text{ (power of a quotient)} \qquad (xy)^p = x^p y^p \text{ (power of a product)}$$

$$x^m x^n = x^{m+n} \text{ (product rule)} \qquad \frac{x^m}{x^n} = x^{m-n} \text{ (quotient rule)},$$

provided, in all cases, that *neither even roots of negative quantities nor division by 0 occurs*.

For real numbers x and y and natural number n

$$(x+y)^n = \underbrace{(x+y)(x+y)\cdots(x+y)}_{n \text{ times}}, \text{ according to the rules for multiplying binomials.}$$

Many students have difficulty working with exponents. Here are some things to remember.

The product and quotient rules for exponential expressions can be used only when the exponential expressions have exactly *the same base*:

$x^2 x^3 = x^{2+3} = x^5$ and $\frac{x^5}{x^3} = x^{5-3} = x^2$; but $x^2 y^3$ and $\frac{x^5}{y^3}$ cannot be simplified further.

Exponentiation is not *"commutative"*: $2^5 \neq 5^2$.

Exponentiation does not *distribute over addition (or subtraction)*: $(3+2)^3 = 5^3 = 125$; $(3+2)^3 \neq 3^3 + 2^3 = 27 + 8 = 35$.

An exponent applies only to the base to which it is attached: $3 \cdot 5^2 = 3 \cdot 25 = 75$; $3 \cdot 5^2 \neq 3^2 \cdot 5^2 = 9 \cdot 25 = 225$; $-3^2 = -(3 \cdot 3) = -9$, $-3^2 \neq (-3)^2 = -3 \cdot -3 = 9$.

Use parentheses around the factors for which the exponent applies: $(3 \cdot 5)^2 = 3^2 \cdot 5^2 = 9 \cdot 25 = 225$.

A negative number raised to an even power yields a positive product: $(-2)^4 = -2 \cdot -2 \cdot -2 \cdot -2 = 16$.

A negative number raised to an odd power yields a negative product: $(-2)^5 = -2 \cdot -2 \cdot -2 \cdot -2 \cdot -2 = -32$.

A nonzero number or mathematical expression raised to the 0 power is 1: $\begin{pmatrix} \text{nonzero number} \\ \text{or mathematical} \\ \text{expression} \end{pmatrix}^0 = 1 \text{ ALWAYS!}$

Only exponential expressions that are factors *in the numerator or denominator of a fraction can be moved simply by changing the sign of the exponent*:

$$\frac{1}{2^{-1}3^{-1}} = \frac{2 \cdot 3}{1} = \frac{6}{1} = 6, \text{ but } \frac{1}{2^{-1}+3^{-1}} = \frac{1}{\frac{1}{2}+\frac{1}{3}} = \frac{1}{\frac{5}{6}} = \frac{6}{5} = 1\frac{1}{5}; \frac{1}{2^{-1}+3^{-1}} \neq \frac{2+3}{1} = \frac{5}{1} = 5$$

Algebraic Expressions

A variable holds a place open for a number (or numbers, in some cases) whose value may vary and is represented by a symbol (often a letter).

A constant is a quantity whose value remains fixed throughout a discussion. For example, all the real and complex numbers are constants. Each has a fixed, definite value. Thus, when a letter is used to name a constant, the letter has one fixed value. For instance, the Greek letter π stands for the number that equals the ratio of the circumference of a circle to its diameter, which is approximately 3.14159.

A numerical expression is any constant or combination of two or more constants joined by operational symbols.

An algebraic expression (or symbolic expression) is a symbol or combination of symbols that represents a number. Algebraic expressions consist of one or more variables joined by one or more operations with or without constants (explicitly) included.

In an algebraic expression, terms are the parts of the expression that are connected to the other parts by plus or minus symbols. If the algebraic expression has no plus or minus symbols, then the algebraic expression itself is a term. Quantities enclosed within grouping symbols are considered single terms, even though they may contain + or – symbols. Thus, the algebraic expression $10(x + 5) - 8$ has two terms.

In a term that is a product of two or more factors, the coefficient of a factor is the product of the other factors in that term. For instance, in the term $5y(x + 2)$, $5y$ is the coefficient of $(x + 2)$, and $5(x + 2)$ is the coefficient of y. The product of the numerical factors of a term is the numerical coefficient of the term. If no numerical coefficient is explicitly written, then the numerical coefficient is understood to be 1.

A monomial is a term that when simplified is a constant or a product of one or more variables raised to nonnegative integer powers, with or without an explicit coefficient. The degree of a monomial is the sum of the exponents of its variables. For instance, the degree of the monomial $8x^4y$ is 5. The degree of a nonzero constant c is 0 because $c = cx^0$ for any constant c. The degree of the monomial 0 is undefined.

Like terms are monomial terms that differ only in their numerical coefficients. For instance, $8x^4y$ and $-6x^4y$ are like terms; however, $8x^4y$ and $8xy^4$ are unlike terms. All constants are like terms.

A polynomial is an algebraic expression composed of one or more monomials. Thus, a monomial is a polynomial that has exactly one term, such as $8x^4y$. A binomial is a polynomial of exactly two terms, such as $8x^4y + 5$. A trinomial is a polynomial of three terms, such as $16x^2 + 8x + 1$.

Performing Operations with Polynomials

The following table summarizes rules for addition and subtraction of polynomials.

Addition and Subtraction of Polynomials		
Operation	Rule	Example
Addition	Combine like monomial terms by adding or subtracting their numerical coefficients, use the result as the coefficient of the common variable factor or factors, and simply indicate the sum or difference of unlike terms.	$(5x^2 + 10x - 6) + (3x^2 - 2x + 4) = 5x^2 + 10x - 6 + 3x^2 - 2x + 4 = 8x^2 + 8x - 2$
Subtraction	Keep the first polynomial, change the sign of every term in the second polynomial, and proceed as in addition.	$(5x^2 + 10x - 6) - (3x^2 - 2x + 4) = 5x^2 + 10x - 6 - 3x^2 + 2x - 4 = 2x^2 + 12x - 10$

Tip: When simple parentheses (or brackets or braces) are immediately preceded by a + symbol, they can be removed without changing the signs of the terms within, but if the parentheses are immediately preceded by a – symbol, the sign of every term within the grouping must be changed when the parentheses are removed.

The following table summarizes rules for multiplication of polynomials.

To multiply polynomials, multiply each term in the first polynomial by each term in the second polynomial.

Multiplication of Polynomials		
Operation	**Rule**	**Example**
Multiplication—Monomial by Monomial	Multiply both the numerical coefficients and the variable factors.	$(-5x^2y)(10xy) = -50x^3y^2$
Multiplication—Polynomial by Monomial	Use the distributive property to multiply each term of the polynomial by the monomial.	$2x^2(3x^2 - 5x + 1) = 6x^4 - 10x^3 + 2x^2$
Multiplication—Polynomial by Polynomial	Use the distributive property to multiply each term in the second polynomial by each term of the first polynomial, and then combine like terms.	$(x + 2)(x^2 - 2x + 4) = x^3 - 2x^2 + 4x + 2x^2 - 4x + 8 = x^3 + 8$
Multiplication—Binomial by Binomial	Use the distributive property to multiply each term in the second binomial by each term of the first binomial and then combine like terms.	$(2x - 3)(x + 4) = 2x^2 + 8x - 3x - 12 = 2x^2 + 5x - 12$

Tip: Use F.O.I.L. (First terms, Outer terms, Inner terms, and Last terms) to obtain the product of two binomials.

Tip: When multiplying polynomials, if possible, arrange the terms of the polynomials in descending or ascending powers of a common variable.

Special Products

Some special products are the following:

$(x + y)^2 = (x + y)(x + y) = x^2 + 2xy + y^2$ Perfect Trinomial Square

$(x - y)^2 = (x - y)(x - y) = x^2 - 2xy + y^2$ Perfect Trinomial Square

$(x + y)(x - y) = x^2 - y^2$ Difference of Two Squares

$(x + y)(x^2 - xy + y^2) = x^3 + y^3$ Sum of Two Cubes

$(x - y)(x^2 + xy + y^2) = x^3 - y^3$ Difference of Two Cubes

$(x + y)^3 = x^3 + 3x^2y + 3xy^2 + y^3$ Perfect Cube

$(x - y)^3 = x^3 - 3x^2y + 3xy^2 - y^3$ Perfect Cube

Division of Polynomials

Division of polynomials is analogous to division of real numbers. Because division by 0 is undefined, you must exclude values for the variable or variables that would make the divisor 0. For convenience, you can assume such values are excluded as you review the rules in this section.

The following table summarizes rules for division of polynomials by monomials.

Division by a Monomial		
Operation	**Rule**	**Example**
Division—Monomial by Monomial	Divide the numerical coefficients. Divide the variable factors that have a common base. Leave other variable factors alone. Use the quotient of the numerical coefficients as the coefficient for the answer.	$\dfrac{-50x^3y^2z}{-5x^2y} = 10xyz$

Operation	Rule	Example
Division—Polynomial by Monomial	Divide each term of the polynomial by the monomial.	$\dfrac{25x^5y^3 + 35x^3y^2 - 10x^2y}{-5x^2y} = -5x^3y^2 - 7xy + 2$

Tip: To avoid sign errors when you are doing division of polynomials, keep a – symbol with the number that follows it.

Long division of polynomials is performed like long division in arithmetic. The result is usually written as a mixed expression: quotient + $\dfrac{\text{remainder}}{\text{divisor}}$. Synthetic division is a shortcut method commonly used to divide a polynomial by a binomial of the form $x - r$. See Appendix A for examples of long division and a discussion of synthetic division.

Simplifying Polynomials

To simplify a polynomial expression, follow these steps:

1. Perform all operations within grouping symbols, starting with the innermost grouping symbol and working outward.
2. Perform all indicated multiplication, including exponentiation.
3. Combine like terms.

Tip: Remove parentheses preceded by a minus sign by changing the sign of every term within the parentheses.

Factoring Polynomials

Factoring a polynomial means to write the polynomial as a product of two or more polynomial factors, if possible. A polynomial that cannot be written as a product of two or more polynomial factors is said to be prime. To factor a polynomial that is not prime, you must find two or more polynomials whose product is the original polynomial. For example, $(2x - 3)(x + 4)$ is a factorization of $2x^2 + 5x - 12$ because $(2x - 3)(x + 4) = 2x^2 + 5x - 12$. The polynomials $(2x - 3)$ and $(x + 4)$ cannot be factored further, so they are prime polynomial factors of $2x^2 + 5x - 12$. Factoring a polynomial completely means writing it as a product of prime polynomial factors. When you factor polynomials, proceed systematically as follows.

1. Check for a greatest common monomial factor.
2. If a factor is a binomial, check for

    difference of two squares: $x^2 - y^2 = (x + y)(x - y)$

    sum of two cubes: $x^3 + y^3 = (x + y)(x^2 - xy + y^2)$

    difference of two cubes: $x^3 - y^3 = (x - y)(x^2 + xy + y^2)$

3. If a factor is a trinomial, check for

    perfect trinomial square: $x^2 + 2xy + y^2 = (x + y)^2$

    $x^2 - 2xy + y^2 = (x - y)^2$

    general factorable quadratic: $x^2 + (a + b)x + ab = (x + a)(x + b)$

    $acx^2 + (ad + bc)x + bd = (ax + b)(cx + d)$

4. If a factor has four terms, first try grouping some of the terms together and factoring the groups separately, and then factoring the entire expression.
5. Write the original polynomial as the product of all the factors obtained. Check to make sure that all polynomial factors except monomial factors are prime.
6. Check by multiplying the factors to obtain the original polynomial.

Rational Expressions

A rational expression is an algebraic fraction in which both the numerator and denominator are polynomials. Values for which the denominator sums to 0 are excluded. For instance, $\frac{2x}{5}$ (no excluded value); $\frac{5}{2x}, (x \neq 0)$; $\frac{10x}{x-1}, (x \neq 1)$; $\frac{x^2-4}{x^2-3x-4} = \frac{(x+2)(x-2)}{(x-4)(x+1)}, (x \neq 4, x \neq -1)$; and all polynomials (no excluded values) are rational expressions. Hereafter, whenever a rational expression is written, it will be understood that any values for which the expression is undefined are excluded.

To perform computations with algebraic fractions, often you will need to factor the polynomials used in the algebraic fractions. For instance, factoring is frequently necessary when reducing algebraic fractions to lowest terms and when finding a common denominator for algebraic fractions. The following table summarizes the process.

Reducing Algebraic Fractions to Lowest Terms		
Type of Algebraic Fraction	Rule	Example
$\dfrac{\text{monomial}}{\text{monomial}}$	Divide numerator and denominator by the greatest common factor of the two monomials.	$\dfrac{9x^5 y^2 z}{12x^2 y^3} = \dfrac{3x^2 y^2 \cdot 3x^3 z}{3x^2 y^2 \cdot 4y} = \dfrac{3x^3 z}{4y}$
$\dfrac{\text{monomial}}{\text{polynomial}}$ or $\dfrac{\text{polynomial}}{\text{monomial}}$	Factor out the greatest monomial factor, if any, from the polynomial, and then divide numerator and denominator by the greatest common factor. Then simplify the polynomial if possible.	$\dfrac{-9x^2 y}{12x^3 y - 36x^2 y - 48xy} = \dfrac{-9x^2 y}{12xy(x^2-3x-4)} = \dfrac{3xy \cdot -3x}{3xy \cdot 4(x^2-3x-4)} =;$ $\dfrac{3xy(-3x)}{3xy \cdot 4(x^2-3x-4)} = \dfrac{-3x}{4(x^2-3x-4)} = -\dfrac{3x}{4(x-4)(x+1)}$ $\dfrac{12x^3 y - 36x^2 y - 48xy}{9x^2 y} = \dfrac{12xy(x^2-3x-4)}{9x^2 y} = \dfrac{4(x^2-3x-4)}{3x} =$ $\dfrac{4(x-4)(x+1)}{3x}$
$\dfrac{\text{polynomial}}{\text{polynomial}}$	Factor the polynomials completely, and then divide numerator and denominator by the greatest common factor.	$\dfrac{9x^2 y - 9y}{12x^3 y - 36x^2 y - 48xy} = \dfrac{9y(x^2-1)}{12xy(x^2-3x-4)} = \dfrac{3y(x+1) \cdot 3(x-1)}{3y(x+1) \cdot 4x(x-4)} =$ $\dfrac{3y(x+1) \cdot 3(x-1)}{3y(x+1) \cdot 4x(x-4)} = \dfrac{3(x-1)}{4x(x-4)}$

Tip: When reducing algebraic fractions, make sure you divide by factors only. For instance, $\dfrac{x+2}{4}$ cannot be reduced further. Even though 2 is a factor of the denominator, it is not a factor of the numerator—it is a term of the numerator. Remember, divide numerator and denominator by common factors, not terms.

The following table summarizes computations with algebraic fractions.

Computations with Algebraic Fractions		
Operation	**Rule**	**Example**
Addition/Subtraction—Like Denominators	Add/subtract the numerators to find the numerator of the answer, which is placed over the common denominator. Simplify and reduce to lowest terms, if needed.	$\dfrac{x+2}{x-3}+\dfrac{2x-11}{x-3}=\dfrac{3x-9}{x-3}=\dfrac{3(x-3)}{x-3}=\dfrac{3}{1}=3$
	When subtracting, you must change the sign of every term of the numerator of the second fraction.	$\dfrac{5x^2}{3(x+1)}-\dfrac{4x^2+1}{3(x+1)}=\dfrac{5x^2-4x^2-1}{3(x+1)}=\dfrac{x^2-1}{3(x+1)}=$ $\dfrac{\cancel{(x+1)}(x-1)}{3\cancel{(x+1)}}=\dfrac{x-1}{3}$
Addition/Subtraction—Unlike Denominators	Factor each denominator completely. Find the common denominator, which is the product of each prime factor the highest number of times it is a factor in any one denominator. Write each algebraic fraction as an equivalent fraction having the common denominator as a denominator. Add/subtract the numerators to find the numerator of the answer, which is placed over the common denominator. Simplify and reduce to lowest terms, if needed.	$\dfrac{1}{x^2-3x-4}+\dfrac{2}{x^2-1}=\dfrac{1}{(x+1)(x-4)}+\dfrac{2}{(x+1)(x-1)}=$ $\dfrac{1(x-1)}{(x+1)(x-4)(x-1)}+\dfrac{2(x-4)}{(x+1)(x-1)(x-4)}=$ $\dfrac{x-1}{(x+1)(x-4)(x-1)}+\dfrac{2x-8}{(x+1)(x-1)(x-4)}=$ $\dfrac{3x-9}{(x+1)(x-1)(x-4)}=\dfrac{3(x-3)}{(x+1)(x-1)(x-4)}$
Multiplication	Factor all numerators and denominators completely and then divide numerators and denominators by their common factors (as in reducing). The product of the remaining numerator factors is the numerator of the answer, and the product of the remaining denominator factors is the denominator of the answer.	$\dfrac{a^2+4a+4}{a^2+a-2}\cdot\dfrac{a^2-2a+1}{a^2-4}=\dfrac{(a+2)(a+2)}{(a+2)(a-1)}\cdot\dfrac{(a-1)(a-1)}{(a+2)(a-2)}=$ $\dfrac{\cancel{(a+2)}\cancel{(a+2)}}{\cancel{(a+2)}\cancel{(a-1)}}\cdot\dfrac{\cancel{(a-1)}(a-1)}{\cancel{(a+2)}(a-2)}=\dfrac{a-1}{a-2}$
Division	Multiply the first algebraic fraction by the reciprocal of the second algebraic fraction.	$\dfrac{a^2+4a+4}{a^2+a-2}\div\dfrac{a^2-4}{a^2-2a+1}=\dfrac{a^2+4a+4}{a^2+a-2}\cdot\dfrac{a^2-2a+1}{a^2-4}$ $=\dfrac{(a+2)(a+2)}{(a+2)(a-1)}\cdot\dfrac{(a-1)(a-1)}{(a+2)(a-2)}$ $=\dfrac{\cancel{(a+2)}\cancel{(a+2)}}{\cancel{(a+2)}\cancel{(a-1)}}\cdot\dfrac{\cancel{(a-1)}(a-1)}{\cancel{(a+2)}(a-2)}$ $=\dfrac{a-1}{a-2}$

A complex fraction is a fraction that has fractions in its numerator, denominator, or both. One way to simplify a complex fraction is to interpret the fraction bar of the complex fraction as meaning division. For instance:

$$\frac{\dfrac{1}{x}+\dfrac{1}{y}}{\dfrac{1}{x}-\dfrac{1}{y}}=\frac{\dfrac{y}{xy}+\dfrac{x}{xy}}{\dfrac{y}{xy}-\dfrac{x}{xy}}=\frac{\dfrac{y+x}{xy}}{\dfrac{y-x}{xy}}=\frac{y+x}{xy}\div\frac{y-x}{xy}=\frac{y+x}{xy}\cdot\frac{xy}{y-x}=\frac{y+x}{y-x}$$

Another way to simplify a complex fraction is to multiply its numerator and denominator by the least common denominator of all the fractions used in its numerator and denominator. For instance:

$$\frac{\dfrac{1}{x}+\dfrac{1}{y}}{\dfrac{1}{x}-\dfrac{1}{y}}=\frac{xy\left(\dfrac{1}{x}+\dfrac{1}{y}\right)}{xy\left(\dfrac{1}{x}-\dfrac{1}{y}\right)}=\frac{xy\cdot\dfrac{1}{x}+xy\cdot\dfrac{1}{y}}{xy\cdot\dfrac{1}{x}-xy\cdot\dfrac{1}{y}}=\frac{y+x}{y-x}$$

Solving One-Variable Linear Equations

An equation is a mathematical sentence stating equality between two expressions. Equations containing only numerical expressions are either true or false. For instance, $1 + 2 = 3$ is true, but $1 + 2 = 5$ is false. An equation containing one or more variables is an open sentence. For instance, $x + 2 = 3$ and $x + 2y = 8$ are open sentences. Generally, you can determine whether an open sentence is true or false only after numerical quantities are substituted for the variables in the sentence.

A solution (or root) of a one-variable equation is a number that when substituted for the variable makes the equation true. To determine whether a number is a solution of a one-variable equation, replace the variable with the number and perform all operations indicated on each side of the equation. If the resulting statement is true, the number is a solution of the equation. This process is called checking a solution. The solution set of an equation is the set consisting of all the solutions of the equation. To solve an equation means to find its solution set.

An identity is an equation whose solution set is the set of all possible values of the variable. If the solution set is empty, the equation has no solution.

Equivalent equations are equations that have the same solution set.

A one-variable linear equation is an equation that can be written in the form $ax + b = 0$, where $a \neq 0$ and b is a constant in the discussion. For instance, $2x + 6 = 0$, $12x + 1 = 5(x - 4)$, and $\frac{2y}{3} - 45 = y$ are one-variable linear equations.

A one-variable equation is solved when the variable is by itself on one and only one side of the equation and has a coefficient of 1.

You use two main algebraic tools in solving equations:

1. Addition or subtraction of the same quantity on both sides of the equation.
2. Multiplication or division by the same *nonzero* quantity on both sides of the equation.

Tip: It is important to remember that when you are solving an equation, you must never multiply or divide both sides by 0.

When you use one of these tools, the resulting equation is equivalent to the original equation. The process of solving a one-variable linear equation uses a series of steps to produce an equivalent equation of the form: x = solution (or solution = x). To solve a one-variable linear equation, use the following steps.

> **Steps for Solving One-Variable Linear Equations**
>
> 1. Remove grouping symbols, if any, by applying the distributive property and then simplify.
> 2. *Eliminate fractions, if any, by multiplying both sides of the equation by the least common denominator of all the fractions in the equation, and then simplify.
> 3. Undo indicated addition or subtraction to isolate the variable on one side—that is, get all terms containing the variable on one side and all other terms on the other side—and then simplify.
> 4. If necessary, factor the side containing the variable so that one of the factors is the variable.
> 5. Divide both sides by the coefficient of the variable.
> 6. Check the solution in the original equation.
>
> *This step is optional, but when fractions are involved, it usually simplifies the process to include it.

An equation that expresses the relationship between two or more variables is a formula. The procedure for solving one-variable linear equations can be used to solve a formula for a specific variable when the value(s) of the other variable(s) are known. The procedure also can be used to solve a formula or literal equation (an equation with no numbers, only letters) for a specific variable in terms of the other variable(s). In general, isolate the specific variable and treat all other variable(s) as constants. This is called changing the subject of the formula or literal equation.

The procedure for solving one-variable linear equations can be used to solve a two-variable equation for one variable in terms of the other variable. Another common use for the procedure for solving one-variable linear equations is to transform equations of lines into the form: $y = mx + b$, where m and b are constants.

Solving One-Variable Linear Inequalities

If you replace the equal sign in a one-variable linear equation with either < (less than), > (greater than), ≤ (less than or equal), or ≥ (greater than or equal), the result is a one-variable linear inequality. The graph of the solution set of the inequality can be illustrated on a number line. When you solve one-variable linear inequalities, treat them just like one-variable linear equations *except* for one difference:

> If you multiply or divide both sides of the inequality by a negative number, reverse the direction of the inequality.

Sometimes two statements of inequality apply to a variable expression simultaneously and, thus, can be combined into a double inequality. For instance, $x > 0$ and $x < 3$ can be written as $0 < x < 3$.

Solving One-Variable Absolute Value Equations and Inequalities

You can solve one-variable absolute value equations using the procedure for solving one-variable linear equations and the following:

> $|ax + b| = 0$ if and only if $ax + b = 0$; or
> If c is any positive number, $|ax + b| = c$ if and only if either $ax + b = c$ or $ax + b = -c$.

Tip: Notice that for equations like $|ax + b| = c$, you must solve two linear equations. Don't forget the second equation!

One-variable absolute value inequalities can be solved using the procedure for solving one-variable linear equations and the following:

> If c is any positive number,
>
> $\quad |ax + b| < c$ if and only if $-c < ax + b < c$;
>
> $\quad |ax + b| > c$ if and only if either $ax + b < -c$ or $ax + b > c$.

Tip: Notice that for absolute value inequalities you must solve two linear inequalities.

Note: In the above discussion, you can replace < and > with ≤ and ≥, respectively, without loss of generality.

Solving One-Variable Quadratic Equations

A one-variable quadratic equation is an equation that can be written in the standard form $ax^2 + bx + c = 0$, where $a \neq 0$ and a, b, and c are real-valued constants in the discussion. Specifically, a is the numerical coefficient of x^2, b is the numerical coefficient of x, and c is the constant coefficient, or simply the constant term. The solutions of a quadratic equation are its roots. A quadratic equation may have exactly *one* real root, exactly *two* real unequal roots, or *no* real roots.

Quadratic equations that can be written in the form $x^2 = C$ have the solution $x = \pm\sqrt{C}$. If the quantity C is 0, there is *one* real root that has the value 0; if *positive*, there are *two* unequal real roots; and if *negative*, there are *no* real roots.

Three algebraic methods for solving quadratic equations of the form $ax^2 + bx + c = 0$ are (1) by factoring, (2) by completing the square, and (3) by using the quadratic formula.

Solving a Quadratic Equation by Factoring

To solve a quadratic equation by factoring, use the following procedure.

1. Express the equation in standard form: $ax^2 + bx + c = 0$.
2. Factor the left side of the equation.
3. Set each factor containing the variable equal to 0.
4. Solve each of the resulting linear equations.
5. Check each root by substituting it into the original equation.

Step 3 in this procedure is based on the *property of 0 products* for numbers: If the product of two quantities is 0, at least one of the quantities is 0.

Solving a Quadratic Equation by Completing the Square

To solve a quadratic equation by completing the square, use the following procedure:

1. Get all terms containing the variable on the left side, and all other terms on the right.
2. If the coefficient of the squared term is not 1, divide each term by it.
3. Add the square of half the coefficient of x (the first-degree term) to both sides.
4. Factor the left side as the square of a binomial.
5. Find the square root of both sides.
6. Solve for the variable.
7. Check each root by substituting it into the original equation.

Note: This method is not an efficient way to solve a quadratic equation on the Mathematics CK. Use the quadratic formula instead.

Solving a Quadratic Equation by Using the Quadratic Formula

To solve a quadratic equation by using the quadratic formula, use the following procedure:

1. Express the equation in standard form: $ax^2 + bx + c = 0$.
2. Determine the values of the coefficients a, b, and c.
3. Substitute into the quadratic formula: $x = \dfrac{-b \pm \sqrt{b^2 - 4ac}}{2a}$.
4. Evaluate and simplify.
5. Check each root by substituting it into the original equation.

Tip: When determining the values of coefficients for the quadratic formula, keep a – symbol with the number that follows it.

The quantity $b^2 - 4ac$ is the discriminant of the quadratic equation. The quadratic equation $ax^2 + bx + c = 0$ has exactly *one* real root if $b^2 - 4ac = 0$, *two* real unequal roots if $b^2 - 4ac > 0$, and *no* real roots if $b^2 - 4ac < 0$.

Tip: When solving quadratic equations, never divide both sides of the equation by the variable or by an expression containing the variable because you run the risk of unknowingly dividing by 0.

Note: This method is an efficient way to solve a quadratic equation on the Mathematics CK.

You also can solve linear and quadratic equations that have real zeros by using the graphing features of your graphing calculator. Check your owner's manual for instructions. For example, the Trace feature of a graphing calculator is one way to find the roots. When the trace cursor moves along the function, the y-value is calculated from the x-value. You can move the trace cursor to the point or points where the graph appears to cross the x-axis (that is, where $y = 0$). You might need to zoom in to obtain better resolution and more accurate results. Most likely, you will have to approximate the roots because you are limited by your viewing screen's pixel resolution. (Pixels are the small cells that light up when you graph an equation.)

Many equations involving fractions in which a denominator expression contains the variable can be transformed into linear or quadratic equations by multiplying both sides of the equation by the least common denominator of all the fractions. An *excluded value* for the variable *cannot* be in the solution set.

Many equations containing radicals or fractional exponents can be transformed into linear or quadratic equations by raising both sides to an appropriate power. Use caution when doing this because the solution set of the transformed equation may contain an extraneous root, a value that is *not* a solution of the original equation. Therefore, check all answers obtained in the *original* equation.

Equations that are not quadratic equations but that can be written in the form of a quadratic can be solved using the methods for solving quadratic equations. It naturally follows that equations that can be written so one side is a factorable higher degree polynomial and the other side contains only 0 can be solved by factoring completely, and then setting each factor equal to 0.

Solving One-Variable Quadratic Inequalities

Quadratic inequalities have the standard forms: $ax^2 + bx + c < 0$, $ax^2 + bx + c > 0$, $ax^2 + bx + c \le 0$, and $ax^2 + bx + c \ge 0$. The solution sets for quadratic inequalities in standard form are based on the rules for multiplying signed numbers: If two factors have the same sign, their product is positive; if they have opposite signs, their product is negative. To solve a quadratic inequality, put it in standard form with $a > 0$ and apply the following.

> If $ax^2 + bx + c = 0$ has no real roots, $ax^2 + bx + c$ is always positive.
>
> If $ax^2 + bx + c = 0$ has exactly one real root, $ax^2 + bx + c$ is 0 at that root.
>
> If $ax^2 + bx + c = 0$ has two real roots, $ax^2 + bx + c$ is negative between them, positive to the left of the leftmost root, positive to the right of the rightmost root, and 0 only at its roots.

For example, $x^2 + 2x - 24 = (x + 6)(x - 4) = 0$ has two real roots, –6 and 4. So $x^2 + 2x - 24$ is negative in the interval (–6, 4) and positive in the intervals (–∞, –6) and (4, ∞).

Note: If you have a quadratic inequality in which $a < 0$, to put the inequality in standard form with $a > 0$ multiply both sides of the inequality by –1 and reverse the direction of the inequality.

Systems of Equations and Inequalities

For this topic, you solve and graph systems of equations and inequalities including those involving absolute value.

A set of equations, each with the same set of variables, is called a system when all the equations in the set are considered simultaneously. The system possesses a solution when the equations in the system are all satisfied by at least one set of values of the variables. A system that has a solution is consistent. A system that has no solution is inconsistent.

A system of two linear equations in two variables consists of a pair of linear equations in the same two variables. To solve a system of linear equations in two variables means to find all pairs of values for the two variables that make *both* equations true simultaneously. A pair of values—for example, an x-value paired with a corresponding y-value—is called an ordered pair and is written as (x, y). An ordered pair that makes an equation true is said to satisfy the equation. When an ordered pair makes both equations in a system true, the ordered pair satisfies the system. The solution set is the collection of all solutions. There are three possibilities: the system has exactly *one solution*, *no solutions,* or *infinitely many solutions*.

Four methods commonly used to solve a system of linear equations are substitution, elimination, transformation of the augmented matrix (see the chapter titled "Matrix Algebra" for this method), and using the Trace feature of the graphing calculator.

Solving a System of Two Linear Equations by Substitution

To solve a system of linear equations by using substitution, use the following procedure:

1. Select the simpler equation and express one of the variables in terms of the other.
2. Substitute this expression into the other equation, simplify, and solve, if possible.
3. Check the solution in the original equations.

Solving a System of Two Linear Equations by Elimination (That Is, by Addition)

To solve a system of linear equations by using elimination, use the following procedure:

1. Write both equations in standard form: $Ax + By = C$.
2. If necessary, multiply one or both of the equations by a nonzero constant or constants to make the coefficients of one of the variables sum to 0.
3. Add the equations and solve.
4. Check the solution in the original equations.

Solving a System of Two Linear Equations by Using the Trace Feature

To solve a system of linear equations by using the Trace feature of the graphing calculator, use the following procedure:

1. Write both equations in the form: $y = mx + b$.
2. Enter the two functions into the graphing editor.
3. Plot the functions simultaneously.
4. If the two graphs appear to cross, move the trace cursor to their point of intersection. Adjust the viewing window, if needed. Zoom in to obtain better resolution and more accurate results. Most likely, you will have to approximate the solution because you are limited by your viewing screen's pixel resolution.
5. Check the solution by substituting it into the original equations.

The solution to a system of three equations with three or more variables can be solved using substitution, elimination, or transformation of the augmented matrix. In general, it is most efficient to solve such systems by using the augmented matrix. This method will be discussed in Chapter 10, "Matrix Algebra."

Graphing Two-Variable Linear Inequalities

The graph of a two-variable linear inequality is a half-plane.

To graph two-variable inequalities, follow these steps:

1. Graph the linear equation that results when the inequality symbol is replaced with an equal sign. Use a dashed line for < or > inequalities and a solid line for ≤ or ≥ inequalities. This is the boundary line.
2. Select and shade the correct portion of the plane by testing a point that is *not* on the boundary line (the origin is usually a good choice unless the boundary passes through it). If the coordinates of the point satisfy the inequality, shade the portion of the plane containing the test point; if not, shade the portion of the plane that does *not* contain the test point.

Geometric Interpretations of Algebraic Principles

For this topic, you interpret algebraic principles geometrically.

Many algebraic principles can be interpreted geometrically. For instance, in the previous discussion (see the section "Systems of Equations and Inequalities") of systems of two-linear equations, the two-linear equations can be represented as lines in the plane as shown below. For the two lines, there are three possibilities that can occur. If the system is consistent and has *exactly one solution*, then the two lines intersect in a unique point in the plane. If the system is consistent and has *infinitely many solutions*, then the two lines are coincident (that is, have all points in common). If the system is inconsistent and has *no solutions*, then the two lines are parallel in the plane.

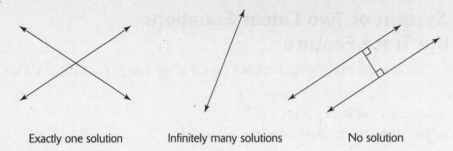

Exactly one solution   Infinitely many solutions   No solution

The distance d between two points (x_1, y_1) and (x_2, y_2) in a coordinate plane can be interpreted geometrically as the hypotenuse of a right triangle having legs of length $x_2 - x_1$ and $y_2 - y_1$. (See "Formulas Used in Two- and Three-Dimensional Coordinate Systems" for the formula.)

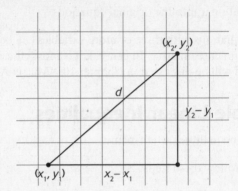

Algebraic Representations of Lines, Planes, Conic Sections, and Spheres

For this topic, you recognize and use algebraic representations of lines, planes, conic sections, and spheres.

If two copies of the real number line are placed perpendicular to each other, so that they intersect at the 0 point on each line, the lines form the axes of a rectangular coordinate system called the Cartesian coordinate plane. The horizontal real line with positive direction to the right is the horizontal axis, or the x-axis, and the vertical real line with positive direction upward is the vertical axis, or the y-axis. Their point of intersection is called the origin.

In the plane, you identify each point in the plane by an ordered pair (x, y) of real numbers x and y, called its coordinates. The ordered pair $(0, 0)$ names the origin. In an ordered pair, the first element is the abscissa and the second element, the ordinate. Two ordered pairs are equal if and only if they have *exactly* the same coordinates. That is, $(x, y) = (u, v)$ if and only if $x = u$ and $y = v$.

The plane in which the coordinate system lies is divided into four sections called quadrants. They are named with the Roman numerals I, II, III, and IV. The numbering process begins in the upper-right section and proceeds counterclockwise as shown here.

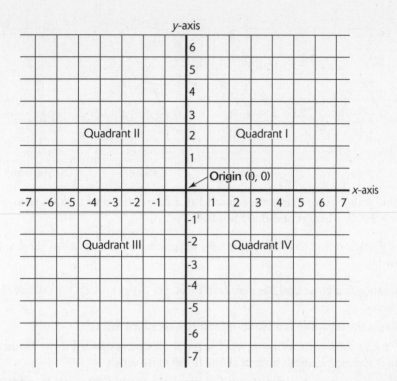

In Quadrant I, both coordinates are positive; in Quadrant II, the x-coordinate is negative and the y-coordinate is positive; in Quadrant III, both coordinates are negative; and in Quadrant IV, the x-coordinate is positive and the y-coordinate is negative. Points that have 0 as one or both of the coordinates are on the axes. If the x-coordinate is 0, the point lies on the y-axis. If the y-coordinate is 0, the point lies on the x-axis. If both coordinates of a point are 0, the point is at the origin.

Algebraic Representation of a Line

The equation of a line can be determined using one of the following:

- The slope-intercept form: $y = mx + b$, where the line determined by the equation has slope* $= m$ and y-intercept $= b$
- The standard form: $Ax + By = C$, where the line determined by the equation has slope $= -\dfrac{A}{B}$ and y-intercept $= \dfrac{C}{B}$, $(B \neq 0)$
- The point-slope form: $y - y_1 = m(x - x_1)$, where m is the slope of the line and (x_1, y_1) is a point on the line

*Note: See the section "Formulas Used in Two- and Three-Dimensional Coordinate Systems" for the formula for finding the slope of a line given two points on the line.

Algebraic Representation of Conic Sections

The four basic kinds of conics are the circle, parabola, ellipse, and hyperbola. Geometrically, these conic sections are two-dimensional figures realized as the result of cutting a double-napped right-circular cone with a plane. They are formed by altering the angle of the cutting plane as shown here.

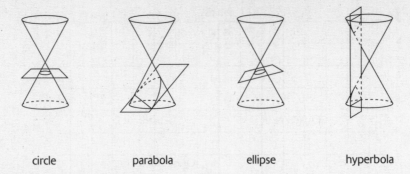

circle   parabola   ellipse   hyperbola

The equation of a conic with axis (or axes) on or parallel to a coordinate axis (or axes) can be written as $Ax^2 + By^2 + Cx + Dy + F = 0$, where A and B are not both 0.

This equation defines a relation that has different graphs depending on the values of the coefficients A, B, and C, according to the following:

a. If $A = B$, the equation is a circle and has standard form: $(x - h)^2 + (y - k)^2 = r^2$, where (h, k) is the center and the radius is $|r|$ units.

b. If either A or B is 0, the equation is a parabola and has standard forms:

(1) $y = a(x - h)^2 + k$, $(a \neq 0)$, with vertex (h, k). The parabola opens upward if $a > 0$ and downward if $a < 0$. The parabola is symmetric about a vertical line through its vertex.

(2) $x = a(y - k)^2 + h$, $(a \neq 0)$, with vertex (h, k). The parabola opens right if $a > 0$ and left if $a < 0$. The parabola is symmetric about a horizontal line through its vertex.

c. If $AB > 0$, the equation is an ellipse and has standard form: $\dfrac{(x-h)^2}{a^2} + \dfrac{(y-k)^2}{b^2} = 1$ with center at (h, k).

The ellipse has vertices $(h - a, k)$, $(h + a, k)$, $(h, k - b)$, and $(h, k + b)$. The line segment joining the vertices $(h - a, k)$ and $(h + a, k)$ is a horizontal axis of symmetry, and the line segment joining the vertices $(h, k - b)$ and $(h, k + b)$ is a vertical axis of symmetry. The longer axis is called the major axis and the shorter axis is called the minor axis. The lengths of the two axes are $2|a|$ and $2|b|$.

d. If $AB < 0$, the equation is a hyperbola and has standard forms:

(1) $\dfrac{(x-h)^2}{a^2} - \dfrac{(y-k)^2}{b^2} = 1$ with center at (h, k). It opens left and right along the line $y = k$, and it passes through the vertices $(h - a, k)$ and $(h + a, k)$. It has the intersecting lines $y = k + \dfrac{b}{a}(x - h)$ and $y = k - \dfrac{b}{a}(x - h)$ as (slanting) asymptotes. The asymptotes are the diagonals of a rectangle with dimensions $2|a|$ by $2|b|$ centered at (h, k).

(2) $\dfrac{(y-k)^2}{a^2} - \dfrac{(x-h)^2}{b^2} = 1$ with center at (h, k). It opens up and down along the line $x = h$, and it passes through the vertices $(h, k - a)$ and $(h, k + a)$. Similar to the previous case, it has the intersecting lines $y = k + \dfrac{a}{b}(x - h)$ and $y = k - \dfrac{a}{b}(x - h)$ as (slanting) asymptotes. The asymptotes are the diagonals of a rectangle with dimensions $2|a|$ by $2|b|$ centered at (h, k).

If the equation of a conic section is not in standard form, it can be put in standard form by completing the squares on the x and y terms.

The general equation for a sphere in a three-dimensional coordinate system is $(x - x_0)^2 + (y - y_0)^2 + (z - z_0)^2 = r^2$, with center (x_0, y_0, z_0) and radius $|r|$.

Formulas Used in Two- and Three-Dimensional Coordinate Systems

For this topic, you solve problems in two and three dimensions (for example, distance between two points, the coordinates of the midpoint of a line segment).

To find the slope m of the line that connects the points (x_1, y_1) and (x_2, y_2) on a coordinate graph, use the formula:

$$\text{Slope of line} = m = \frac{y_2 - y_1}{x_2 - x_1}, \ (x_1 \neq x_2)$$

When a line slopes *upward* to the right, its slope is *positive,* and when a line slopes *downward* to the right, its slope is *negative*. All horizontal lines have slope 0. Vertical lines have no slope. If two lines are parallel, their slopes are equal. If two lines are perpendicular, their slopes are negative reciprocals of each other.

To find the distance d between two points (x_1, y_1) and (x_2, y_2) on a coordinate graph, use the formula

$$\text{Distance between two points} = d = \sqrt{\left(x_2 - x_1\right)^2 + \left(y_2 - y_1\right)^2}$$

To find the midpoint between two points (x_1, y_1) and (x_2, y_2) on a coordinate graph, use the formula

$$\text{Midpoint between two points} = \left(\frac{x_1 + x_2}{2}, \frac{y_1 + y_2}{2}\right)$$

Tip: Notice that you add, not subtract, the coordinates in the numerator.

To find the distance d from point (x_1, y_1) to line $Ax + By + C = 0$, use the formula

$$d = \frac{\left|Ax_1 + By_1 + C\right|}{\sqrt{A^2 + B^2}}$$

Note: The formula to find the distance from a point to a line is given in the Notation, Definitions, and Formulas pages at the beginning of the Mathematics CK test booklet.

Tip: When substituting values into formulas, enclose in parentheses any negative substituted value to avoid making a sign error.

Chapter 3

Measurement

According to the *Mathematics: Content Knowledge (0061) Test at a Glance* (www.ets.org/Media/Tests/PRAXIS/pdf/0061.pdf), the Measurement content category of the Mathematics CK tests your knowledge and skills in three topic areas:

- Unit analysis
- Precision, accuracy, and approximate error
- Informal approximation concepts

This review will discuss the key ideas and formulas in each topic area that are most important for you to know for the Mathematics CK.

Unit Analysis

For this topic, you make decisions about units and scales that are appropriate for problem situations involving measurement and use unit analysis.

On the Mathematics CK, you will have to demonstrate your knowledge of measurement using the U.S. customary system and the metric system. Here are some common conversion facts you will be expected to know.

1 yard = 3 feet = 36 inches

1 mile = 1760 yards = 5280 feet

1 acre = 43,560 square feet

1 hour = 60 minutes

1 minute = 60 seconds

1 cup = 8 fluid ounces

1 pint = 2 cups

1 quart = 2 pints

1 gallon = 4 quarts

1 pound = 16 ounces

1 ton = 2000 pounds

1 liter = 1000 milliliters = 1000 cubic centimeters

1 meter = 100 centimeters = 1000 millimeters

1 kilometer = 1000 meters

1 gram = 1000 milligrams

1 kilogram = 1000 grams

You can convert from one measurement unit to another by using an appropriate "conversion fraction." You make conversion fractions by using a conversion fact, such as 1 gallon = 4 quarts. For each conversion fact, you can write *two* conversion fractions. For example, for the conversion fact given, you have $\frac{1\text{ gal}}{4\text{ qt}}$ and $\frac{4\text{ qt}}{1\text{ gal}}$ as your two conversion fractions.

Every conversion fraction is equivalent to the number 1 because the numerator and denominator are different names for measures of the same quantity. Therefore, if you multiply a quantity by a conversion fraction, you will not change the value of the quantity.

When you need to change one measurement unit to another unit, multiply by the conversion fraction whose *denominator is the same as the units of the quantity to be converted*. This strategy falls under unit analysis (or dimensional analysis), a powerful tool used by scientists (including mathematicians) and engineers to analyze units and to guide or check equations and calculations. When you do the multiplication, the units you started out with will "cancel" (divide) out, and you will be left with the desired new units. If this doesn't happen, then you used the wrong conversion fraction, so do it over again with the other conversion fraction.

Additionally, for some conversions you might need to make a "chain" of conversion fractions to obtain your desired units. Here is an example.

Convert 3 gallons to cups.

Start with your quantity to be converted and keep multiplying by conversion fractions until you obtain your desired units.

$$\frac{3 \text{ gal}}{1} \cdot \frac{4 \text{ qt}}{1 \text{ gal}} \cdot \frac{2 \text{ pt}}{1 \text{ qt}} \cdot \frac{2 \text{ c}}{1 \text{ pt}} = \frac{3 \text{ gal}}{1} \cdot \frac{4 \text{ qt}}{1 \text{ gal}} \cdot \frac{2 \text{ pt}}{1 \text{ qt}} \cdot \frac{2 \text{ c}}{1 \text{ pt}} = 48 \text{ c}$$

Tip: It is a good idea to assess your final answer to see if it makes sense. When you are converting from a larger unit to a smaller unit, you should expect that it will take more of the smaller units to equal the same amount. When you are converting from a smaller unit to a larger unit, you should expect that it will take less of the larger units to equal the same amount.

Precision, Accuracy, and Approximate Error

For this topic, you must be able to analyze precision, accuracy, and approximate error in measurement situations (*Mathematics: Content Knowledge (0061) Test at a Glance*, page 3).

In the physical world, measurement of continuous quantities is always approximate. The precision and accuracy of the measurement relate to the worthiness of the approximation.

Precision refers to the degree to which a measurement is repeatable and reliable; that is, consistently getting the same data each time the measurement is taken. A measurement's precision depends on the magnitude of the smallest measuring unit used to obtain the measurement (for example, to the nearest meter, to the nearest centimeter, to the nearest millimeter, and so on). In theory, the smaller the measurement unit used, the more precise the measurement.

Accuracy refers to the degree to which a measurement is true or correct. A measurement can be precise without being accurate. This can occur, for example, when a measuring instrument needs adjustment, so that the measurements obtained, no matter how precisely measured, are inaccurate.

The amount of error involved in a physical measurement is the approximate error of the measurement. A measurement's maximum possible error is half the magnitude of the smallest measurement unit used to obtain the measurement. For example, if the smallest measurement unit is 1 inch, the maximum possible error is 0.5 inch.

The most accurate way of expressing a measurement is as a tolerance interval. For instance, a measurement of 10 inches, to the nearest inch, should be reported as 10 inches ± 0.5 inches. In other words, the true measurement lies between 9.5 inches and 10.5 inches. Closer approximations can be obtained by refining the measurement to a higher degree of precision (for example, by measuring to the nearest half-inch).

Results of calculations with approximate measurement should not be reported with a degree of precision that would be misleading—that is, suggesting a degree of accuracy greater than the actual accuracy that could be obtained using the approximate measurements. Generally, such calculations should be rounded to have the same precision as the measurement with least precision in the calculation.

Informal Approximation Concepts

For this topic, you apply informal concepts of successive approximation, upper and lower bounds, and limit in measurement situations.

Methods of successive approximation can be used to approximate the area of plane regions. The region's area is approximated using the sum of the areas of a sequence of rectangles. One technique is to partition the region in two different ways—so that one partitioning overestimates the area, yielding an upper bound, and the other partitioning underestimates the area, yielding a lower bound. Sequences of increasingly accurate approximations are obtained by refining the precision of the partitioning. The upper and lower bounds get increasingly close to each other, and their average approaches the true area of the plane region. A solid's volume can be approximated in a similar manner using the sum of the volumes of a sequence of geometric solids.

Sigma notation is an abbreviated way to represent the sums of the areas of the rectangles or the sums of the volumes of the geometric solids. For instance, a Riemann sum for the area under the curve of a continuous function f defined on the closed interval $[a, b]$ is a limiting sum given by the following: $\lim\limits_{\max \Delta x_i \to 0} \sum\limits_{i=1}^{n} f(c_i) \Delta x_i$, where $[a, b]$ is divided into n subintervals (not necessarily equal), c_i is a point in the ith subinterval $[x_{i-1}, x_i]$, and $\Delta x_i = x_i - x_{i-1}$, provided this limit exists.

Chapter 4

Geometry

According to the *Mathematics: Content Knowledge (0061) Test at a Glance* (www.ets.org/Media/Tests/PRAXIS/pdf/0061.pdf), the Geometry content category of the Mathematics CK tests your knowledge and skills in seven topic areas:

- Relationships involving geometric figures
- Relationships among quadrilaterals
- Problems involving properties of plane figures
- The Pythagorean theorem
- Problems involving properties of circles
- Perimeter, area, and volume
- Geometric transformations

This review will discuss the key ideas and formulas in each topic area that are most important for you to know for the Mathematics CK.

Relationships Involving Geometric Figures

For this topic, you solve problems using relationships of parts of geometric figures (for example: medians of triangles, inscribed angles in circles) and among geometric figures (for example: congruence, similarity) in two and three dimensions.

General Geometric Relationships

Congruent (symbolized by ≅) geometric figures have exactly the same size and same shape. They are superimposable, meaning they will fit exactly on top of each other. Corresponding parts of congruent figures are congruent. Hash marks (as in the pair of congruent triangles shown) can be used to draw attention to corresponding congruent parts.

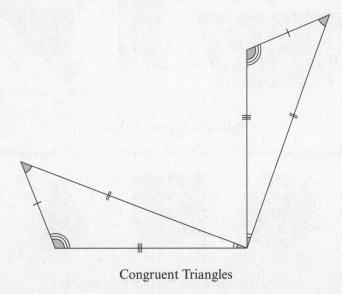

Congruent Triangles

Similar (symbolized by ~) geometric figures have the same shape, but not necessarily the same size. According to the 2008 *National Mathematics Advisory Panel Report of the Task Group on Learning Processes* (www.ed.gov/about/bdscomm/list/mathpanel/index.html), a more "mathematically correct" definition of similarity is to say that two geometric "figures are similar if one of the figures is congruent to a dilated version of the other" (page 95). (See "Geometric Transformations" in this chapter for a discussion of *dilation.*). Here are examples of similar figures. Notice that congruent figures are also similar figures.

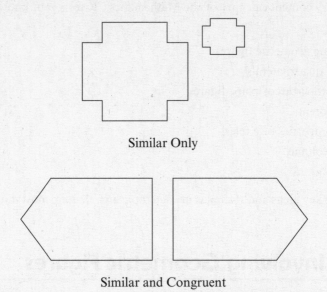

Similar Only

Similar and Congruent

Symmetry describes a characteristic of the shape of a figure or object. A figure has reflective (or bilateral) symmetry if it can be folded exactly in half and the resulting two parts are congruent. The line along the fold is the line of symmetry. A figure has rotational symmetry if it can be rotated onto an exact copy of itself before it comes back to its original position. The center of rotation is the center of symmetry. (See "Geometric Transformations" in this chapter for a discussion of *rotation* of geometric figures.) Here are examples.

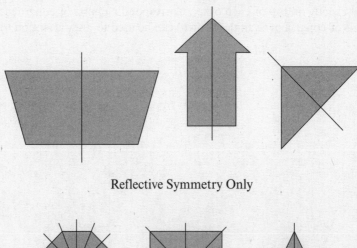

Reflective Symmetry Only

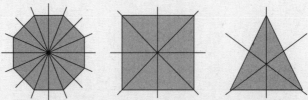

Both Reflective and Rotational Symmetry

Relationships of Parts of Triangles

A triangle's altitude is the line segment drawn from a vertex perpendicular to the side opposite that vertex (or to an extension of that side). Every triangle has three altitudes, one from each vertex. The lines containing a triangle's altitudes are concurrent, meaning they intersect in a point. This point of concurrency of a triangle's altitudes is the triangle's orthocenter.

A triangle's median is a line segment connecting a vertex of the triangle to the midpoint of the side opposite that vertex. The lines containing the triangle's medians are concurrent, and their point of concurrency, called the centroid, is two-thirds of the way along each median, from the vertex to the opposite side.

A perpendicular bisector of a triangle's side is a line perpendicular to that side at its midpoint. The perpendicular bisectors of a triangle's sides are concurrent, and the circumcenter, their point of concurrency, is equidistant from the triangle's vertices. Thus, if a circle is circumscribed about the triangle, the circumcenter is the center of the circumscribed circle.

An angle bisector in a triangle is a line that cuts in half an angle of the triangle. The angle bisectors of a triangle's interior angles are concurrent, and their point of concurrency, called the incenter, is equidistant from the three sides. Thus, if a circle is inscribed in a triangle, the incenter is the center of the inscribed circle.

Here are examples.

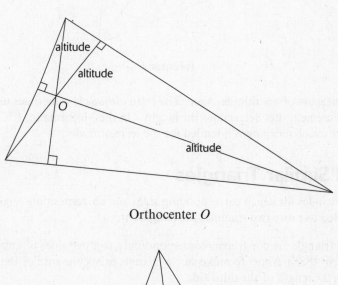

Orthocenter *O*

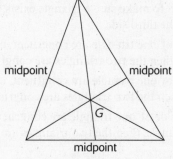

Centroid *G*

47

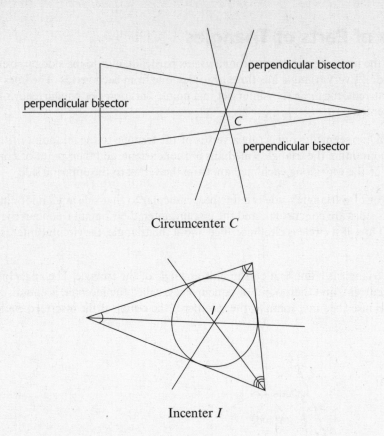

Circumcenter C

Incenter I

A triangle's height is the measure of an altitude. *Note:* The term *altitude* is sometimes used to mean the triangle's *height* rather than the line segment that determines the height. On the Mathematics CK, you will be able to tell from the problem's context which meaning is intended for the term *altitude*.

Congruent and Similar Triangles

Congruent triangles are triangles for which corresponding sides and corresponding angles are congruent. The following theorems can be used to prove two triangles are congruent.

- If three sides of one triangle are congruent, correspondingly, to three sides of another triangle, then the two triangles are congruent (SSS). *Note:* To make sure a triangle exists, the sum of the lengths of any two sides must be greater than the length of the third side.
- If two sides and the included angle of one triangle are congruent, correspondingly, to two sides and the included angle of another triangle, then the two triangles are congruent (SAS).
- If two angles and the included side of one triangle are congruent, correspondingly, to two angles and the included side of another triangle, then the two triangles are congruent (ASA).
- If two angles and the nonincluded side of one triangle are congruent, correspondingly, to two angles and the nonincluded side of another triangle, then the two triangles are congruent (AAS).

Tip: Two methods that do NOT work for proving congruence are AAA (three corresponding angles congruent) and SSA (two corresponding sides and the nonincluded angle congruent).

Similar triangles are triangles for which corresponding sides are proportional and corresponding angles are congruent. The following theorems can be used to prove two triangles are similar.

- If corresponding angles of two triangles are congruent, the two triangles are similar.
- If corresponding sides of two triangles are proportional, the two triangles are similar.

- If two angles of one triangle are congruent to two corresponding angles of another triangle, then the two triangles are similar.
- If two sides of one triangle are proportional to two corresponding sides of another triangle, and the included angles are congruent, then the two triangles are similar.

Relationships among Quadrilaterals

For this topic, you must be able to describe relationships among sets of special quadrilaterals, such as the square, rectangle, parallelogram, rhombus, and trapezoid (*Mathematics: Content Knowledge (0061) Test at a Glance*, page 3).

A quadrilateral is a closed two-dimensional geometric figure that is made up of four straight line segments. Quadrilaterals are subclassified as trapezoids or parallelograms.

A trapezoid has two definitions, both of which are widely accepted. One definition is that a trapezoid is a quadrilateral that has *exactly* one pair of opposite sides that are parallel. This definition would exclude parallelograms as a special case. The other definition is that a trapezoid is a quadrilateral that has *at least* one pair of parallel sides. This definition would allow any parallelogram to be considered a special kind of trapezoid. This situation is one of the few times that mathematicians do not agree on the definition of a term. For purposes of this *CliffsNotes* book, we will have to assume that answers to problems involving trapezoid(s) on the Mathematics CK will not hinge on the definition for trapezoid you choose to use during the test.

A parallelogram is a quadrilateral that has two pairs of opposite parallel sides. Some useful properties of parallelograms are the following: Opposite sides are congruent; the sum of the four interior angles is 360°; opposite interior angles are congruent; consecutive interior angles are supplementary; the diagonals bisect each other; and each diagonal divides the parallelogram into two congruent triangles.

Some parallelograms have special names because of their special properties. A rhombus is a parallelogram that has four congruent sides. A rectangle is a parallelogram that has four right angles. A square is a parallelogram that has four right angles and four congruent sides. These three figures have all the general properties of parallelograms. In addition, in rectangles and squares, the diagonals are congruent. In rhombuses and squares, the diagonals intersect at right angles.

Here are examples of quadrilaterals.

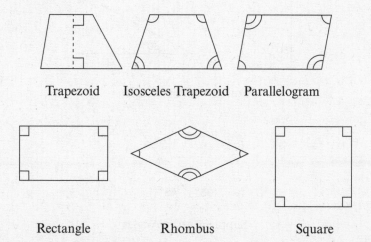

Trapezoid   Isosceles Trapezoid   Parallelogram

Rectangle   Rhombus   Square

Following are theorems about quadrilaterals that are useful to know.

- The sum of the angles of a quadrilateral is 360°.
- If the diagonals of a quadrilateral bisect each other, the quadrilateral is a parallelogram.

- If two sides of a quadrilateral are parallel and congruent, the quadrilateral is a parallelogram.
- If the diagonals of a quadrilateral are perpendicular bisectors of each other, the quadrilateral is a rhombus.
- If a parallelogram has one right angle, it has four right angles and is a rectangle.
- If a rhombus has one right angle, it has four right angles and is a square.

Problems Involving Properties of Plane Figures

For this topic, you must be able solve problems using the properties of triangles, quadrilaterals, polygons, circles, and parallel and perpendicular lines (*Mathematics: Content Knowledge (0061) Test at a Glance*, page 3).

In geometry, the terms *point*, *line*, and *plane* are undefined. You can think of a point as a location in space. You can think of a line as a set of points that extends infinitely in both directions. You can think of a plane as a set of points that forms a flat infinite surface. *Note:* For discussions in this chapter, unless specifically stated otherwise, all plane figures and objects are considered to lie in the same plane.

Lines and Angles

A ray is a line extending from a point. When two rays meet at a common point, they form an angle. The point where the rays meet is the angle's vertex.

The number of degrees in an angle is its measure. If there are k degrees in angle A, then you write $m\angle A = k°$. You can classify angles by the number of degrees in their measurement. An acute angle measures between 0° and 90°; that is, if angle A is acute, $0° < m\angle A < 90°$. A right angle measures exactly 90°; that is, if angle C is a right angle, $m\angle C = 90°$. An obtuse angle measures between 90° and 180°; that is, if angle B is obtuse, $90° < m\angle B < 180°$. A straight angle measures exactly 180°.

Two angles whose measures sum to 90° are complementary angles. Two angles whose measures sum to 180° are supplementary angles. Two angles with the same measure are congruent. Adjacent angles are angles that have a common vertex and a common side. Here are examples.

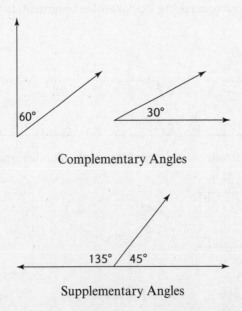

60°   30°

Complementary Angles

135° 45°

Supplementary Angles

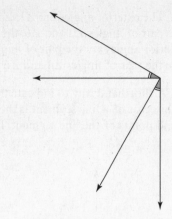

Congruent Angles

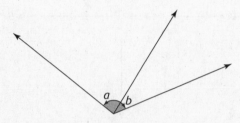

Adjacent Angles

Lines in a plane can be parallel or intersecting. Intersecting lines cross at a point in the plane. Two nonadjacent angles formed by intersecting lines are vertical angles. Vertical angles formed by two intersecting lines are congruent. In the figure shown, ∠1 and ∠2 are congruent vertical angles, and ∠3 and ∠4 are congruent vertical angles.

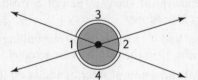

Parallel lines (in a plane) never meet. The distance between them is always the same. A shorthand way to indicate that a line *AB* is parallel to a line *CD* is to write *AB∥CD*. A transversal is a straight line that intersects two or more given lines. When two parallel lines are cut by a transversal, eight angles are formed. In the figure shown, parallel lines *l* and *m* are cut by a transversal *n*.

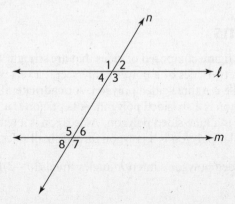

The interior angles are ∠3, ∠4, ∠5, and ∠6. The exterior angles are ∠1, ∠2, ∠7, and ∠8. The corresponding angles are the pair of angles ∠1 and ∠5, the pair of angles ∠2 and ∠6, the pair of angles ∠4 and ∠8, and the pair of angles ∠3 and ∠7. The alternate exterior angles are the pair of angles ∠1 and ∠7 and the pair of angles ∠2 and ∠8. The alternate interior angles are the pair of angles ∠4 and ∠6 and the pair of angles ∠3 and ∠5.

Perpendicular lines intersect at right angles. A shorthand way to indicate that a line AB is perpendicular to a line CD is to write $AB \perp CD$. The perpendicular bisector of a line segment is the set of all points in the plane of the line segment that are equidistant from the end points of the line segment. In the figure shown, line m is the perpendicular bisector of line segment $\overline{AB}$.

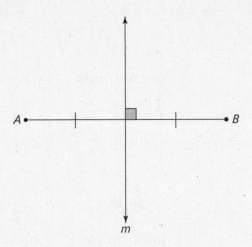

Following are theorems about lines that are useful to know.

- Euclid's Parallel Postulate: Given a line and a point in the same plane but not on the line, there is one and only one line through the given point that is parallel to the given line.
- If two parallel lines are cut by a transversal, then any pair of corresponding angles, alternate exterior angles, or alternate interior angles is congruent.
- If two lines are cut by a transversal and if any pair of corresponding angles, alternate exterior angles, or alternate interior angles is congruent, then the two lines are parallel.
- If two lines are cut by a transversal and a pair of interior angles on the same side of the transversal is supplementary, then the two lines are parallel.
- The shortest distance from a point to a line is the measure of the perpendicular line segment from the point to the line.
- Two distinct lines (in a plane) that are perpendicular to the same line are parallel.
- If a line in a plane is perpendicular to one of two parallel lines, it is perpendicular to the other parallel line.

Properties of Polygons

A polygon is a simple, closed-plane figure composed of sides that are straight line segments that meet only at their end points. The point at which two sides of a polygon intersect is a vertex. Polygons are classified by the number of sides they have. A triangle is a three-sided polygon. A quadrilateral is a four-sided polygon. A pentagon is a five-sided polygon. A hexagon is a six-sided polygon. A heptagon is a seven-sided polygon. An octagon is an eight-sided polygon. A nonagon is a nine-sided polygon. A decagon is a ten-sided polygon. In general, an n-gon is an n-sided polygon. A regular polygon is a polygon for which all sides and angles are congruent.

The sum of the measures of an n-sided polygon's interior angles equals $(n - 2)180°$.

A line segment that connects a polygon's two nonconsecutive vertices is a diagonal. The number of an n-sided polygon's diagonals is given by the formula: $\frac{n(n-3)}{2}$. Here are examples of regular polygons with the number of diagonals indicated below the name of the figure.

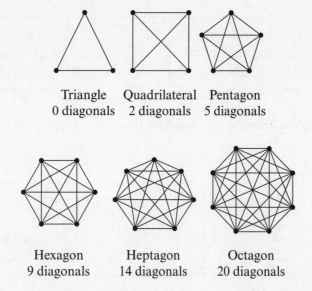

Triangle   Quadrilateral   Pentagon
0 diagonals   2 diagonals   5 diagonals

Hexagon   Heptagon   Octagon
9 diagonals   14 diagonals   20 diagonals

If all the diagonals of a polygon lie within the polygon's interior, the polygon is convex; otherwise, the polygon is concave. Here are examples.

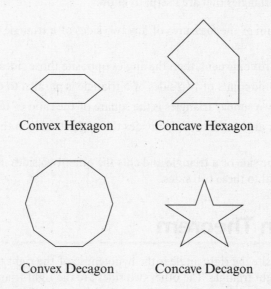

Convex Hexagon   Concave Hexagon

Convex Decagon   Concave Decagon

Properties of Triangles

Triangles can be classified in two ways. One way you can classify triangles is according to their sides—scalene, isosceles, or equilateral. A scalene triangle has no two sides congruent. An isosceles triangle has at least two congruent sides (and the angles opposite the congruent sides are congruent base angles). An equilateral triangle has three congruent sides (and three congruent angles).

A second way to classify triangles is according to the measures of their interior angles. The sum of the measures of a triangle's interior angles is 180°. An acute triangle has three acute interior angles. A right triangle has exactly one right interior angle. An obtuse triangle has exactly one obtuse interior angle. Here are examples.

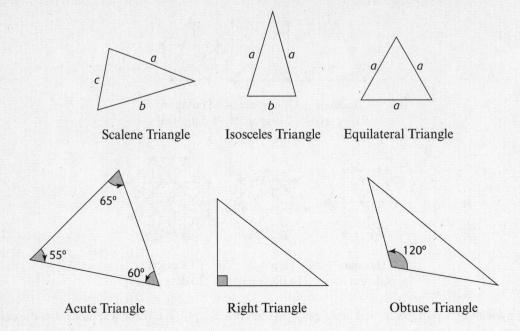

Scalene Triangle   Isosceles Triangle   Equilateral Triangle

Acute Triangle   Right Triangle   Obtuse Triangle

Here are other theorems about triangles that are useful to know.

- Triangle inequality: The sum of the measures of any two sides of a triangle must be greater than the measure of the third side.
- If two sides of a triangle are congruent, then the angles opposite those sides are congruent, and conversely.
- The segment between the midpoints of two sides of a triangle is parallel to the third side and half as long.
- The ratio of the areas of two similar triangles is the square of the ratio of any two corresponding sides.
- The bisector of an interior angle of a triangle divides the opposite side in the ratio of the sides that form the angle bisected.
- A line that is parallel to one side of a triangle and cuts the other two sides in distinct points cuts off segments that are proportional to these two sides.

The Pythagorean Theorem

In a right triangle the side opposite the right angle is the hypotenuse of the right triangle. The hypotenuse is *always* the longest side of the right triangle. The other two sides are the right triangle's legs. Commonly, the letter c is used to represent the hypotenuse of a right triangle and the letters a and b to represent the legs. Here is an illustration.

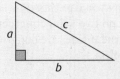

A special relationship, named after the famous Greek mathematician Pythagoras, exists between a right triangle's sides. This special relationship is the Pythagorean theorem, which states that $c^2 = a^2 + b^2$. The Pythagorean relationship applies only to right triangles. If you know any two sides of a right triangle, you can find the third side by using the formula $c^2 = a^2 + b^2$. Here is an example.

Find the hypotenuse of a right triangle that has legs 9 cm and 12 cm.

Substituting into the formula and omitting units for convenience, you have

$$c^2 = a^2 + b^2$$
$$c^2 = 9^2 + 12^2$$
$$c^2 = 81 + 144$$
$$c^2 = 225$$
$$c = \sqrt{225} = 15$$

Thus, $c = 15$ cm.

If the measures of a triangle's three sides satisfy the Pythagorean relationship, the triangle is a right triangle. Numbers such as 3, 4, and 5 that satisfy the Pythagorean relationship are Pythagorean triples. After you identify a Pythagorean triple, any multiple of the three numbers is also a Pythagorean triple. For example, because 3, 4, and 5 is a Pythagorean triple, then so is 30, 40, and 50.

The altitude to a right triangle's hypotenuse divides the triangle into two right triangles that are similar to each other and to the original right triangle. Furthermore, the altitude's length is the geometric mean of the lengths of the two segments into which it separates the hypotenuse. In the figure shown, $\triangle ACB \sim \triangle AHC \sim \triangle CHB$; and $\dfrac{\overline{AH}}{h} = \dfrac{h}{\overline{HB}}$.

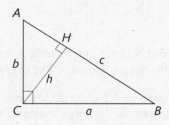

Here are additional theorems about right triangles that are useful to know.

- The sides of a 45°-45°-90° right triangle are in the ratio $1 : 1 : \sqrt{2}$.
- The sides of a 30°-60°-90° right triangle are in the ratio $1 : \sqrt{3} : 2$, where the shortest side is opposite the 30-degree angle.
- Given two right triangles, if the hypotenuse and one leg of one triangle are congruent to the hypotenuse and the corresponding leg of the other triangle, then the two right triangles are congruent.

Problems Involving Properties of Circles

For this topic, you must be able to solve problems using the properties of circles, including those involving inscribed angles, central angles, chords, radii, tangents, secants, arcs, and sectors (*Mathematics: Content Knowledge (0061) Test at a Glance*, page 3).

A circle is a closed-plane figure for which all points are the same distance from a point within, called the center. A circle's radius is a line segment joining the circle's center to any point on the circle. A circle's chord is a line segment with both endpoints on the circle. A diameter is a chord that passes through the circle's center. A circle's diameter is twice the radius. Conversely, a circle's radius is half the diameter. Here is an illustration.

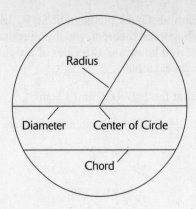

In a circle, a radius perpendicular to a chord bisects the chord. Consequently, a chord's perpendicular bisector passes through the circle's center. Here is an illustration.

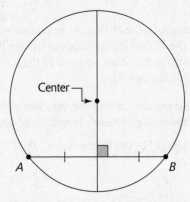

An arc is part of a circle; it is the set of points between and including two points on the circle. A semicircle is an arc whose endpoints are the endpoints of the circle's diameter. The degree measure of a semicircle is 180°.

A central angle of a circle is an angle that has its vertex at the circle's center. A central angle determines two arcs on the circle. If the two arcs are of unequal measure, the arc with the smaller measure is the minor arc and the arc with the greater measure is the major arc. Arcs are measured in degrees. The measure of a minor arc is equal to the measure of its central angle. The measure of a major arc equals 360° minus the measure of the minor arc's central angle. In the circle shown, the measure of minor arc $\overarc{AB}$ is 80°, and the measure of major arc $\overarc{AB}$ is 360° – 80° = 280°.

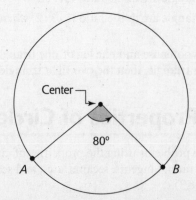

An inscribed angle is an angle whose vertex is on a circle and whose sides are chords of the circle. The arc of the circle that is in the inscribed angle's interior and whose endpoints are on the angle's sides is its intercepted arc. The measure of an inscribed angle is half the measure of its intercepted arc. An angle inscribed in a semicircle is a right angle. Look at these examples.

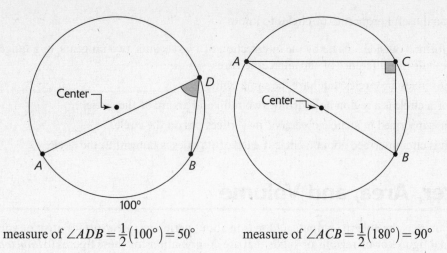

$$\text{measure of } \angle ADB = \frac{1}{2}(100°) = 50° \qquad \text{measure of } \angle ACB = \frac{1}{2}(180°) = 90°$$

If two chords intersect within a circle, each of the angles formed equals one-half the sum of its intercepted arcs. Furthermore, the product of the lengths of the segments formed for one chord equals the product of the lengths of the segments formed for the other chord. In the circle shown, $\angle SVT = \frac{1}{2}(70° + 50°) = \frac{1}{2}(120°) = 60°$; and $\overline{RV} \cdot \overline{VS} = \overline{UV} \cdot \overline{VT}$.

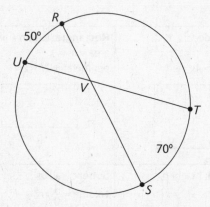

A secant to a circle is a line that contains a chord. A tangent to a circle is a line in the circle's plane that intersects the circle in only one point. The point of contact is the point of tangency. If a straight line is tangent to a circle, then the radius drawn to the point of tangency will be perpendicular to the tangent. Here is an illustration.

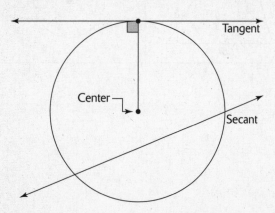

Here are additional useful properties of circles to know.

- An angle formed outside a circle by the intersection of two secants, two tangents, or a tangent and a secant equals one-half the difference of the intercepted arcs.
- Concentric circles are circles that have the same center.
- A sector of a circle is a region bounded by two radii and an arc of the circle.
- A polygon is inscribed in a circle if each of its vertices lies on the circle.
- A polygon is circumscribed about a circle if each of its sides is tangent to the circle.

Perimeter, Area, and Volume

For this topic, you must be able to compute and reason about perimeter, area/surface area, or volume of two- or three-dimensional figures or of regions or solids that are combinations of these figures (*Mathematics: Content Knowledge (0061) Test at a Glance*, page 3).

Geometric Formulas

Here are the most important formulas for perimeter, area/surface area, and volume that you need to know for the Mathematics CK.

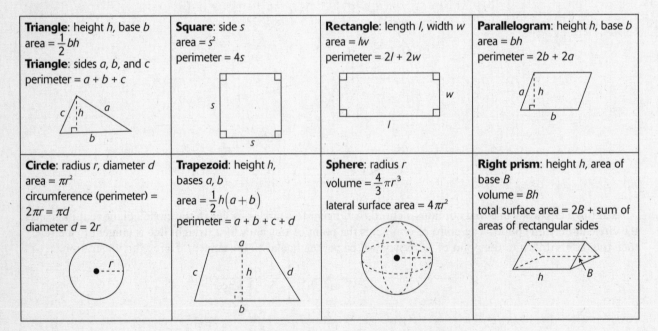

Triangle: height h, base b area $= \frac{1}{2}bh$ **Triangle**: sides a, b, and c perimeter $= a + b + c$	**Square**: side s area $= s^2$ perimeter $= 4s$	**Rectangle**: length l, width w area $= lw$ perimeter $= 2l + 2w$	**Parallelogram**: height h, base b area $= bh$ perimeter $= 2b + 2a$
Circle: radius r, diameter d area $= \pi r^2$ circumference (perimeter) $=$ $2\pi r = \pi d$ diameter $d = 2r$	**Trapezoid**: height h, bases a, b area $= \frac{1}{2}h(a+b)$ perimeter $= a + b + c + d$	**Sphere**: radius r volume $= \frac{4}{3}\pi r^3$ lateral surface area $= 4\pi r^2$	**Right prism**: height h, area of base B volume $= Bh$ total surface area $= 2B +$ sum of areas of rectangular sides

Rectangular prism:
length l, width w, height h
volume $= lwh$
total surface area $= 2hl + 2hw + 2lw$

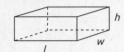

Cube: edge s
volume $= s^3$
total surface area $= 6s^2$

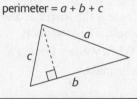

Right circular cylinder:
height h, radius of base r
volume $= \pi r^2 h$
lateral surface area $= (2\pi r)h$
total surface area $= (2\pi r)h + 2(\pi r^2)$

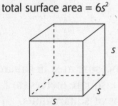

Pyramid: height h, area of base B
volume $= \frac{1}{3}Bh$
total surface area $= B +$ sum of areas of triangular sides

Right circular cone: height h, radius of base r
volume $= \frac{1}{3}\pi r^2 h$
lateral surface area $=$
$\pi r\sqrt{r^2 + h^2} = \pi rs$, where s is the slant height $= \sqrt{r^2 + h^2}$
total surface area $=$
$\pi r\sqrt{r^2 + h^2} + \pi r^2 = \pi rs + \pi r^2$

Here are additional formulas that you might need to know for the Mathematics CK.

Scalene triangle: sides a, b, and c
area $= \sqrt{s(s-a)(s-b)(s-c)}$
where $s = \dfrac{a+b+c}{2}$
perimeter $= a + b + c$

Equilateral triangle: side a
area $= \dfrac{\sqrt{3}}{4}a^2$
Perimeter $= 3a$

Isosceles triangle: sides a, a, and b
area $= \dfrac{1}{2}b\sqrt{a^2 - \dfrac{b^2}{4}}$
Perimeter $= 2a + b$

Sector of circle: radius r, θ measure of subtended central angle in radians
area $= \dfrac{\theta r^2}{2}$
arc length $= s = r\theta$

Tip: Rather than memorizing the formulas for the areas of equilateral and isosceles triangles, you likely will find it easier to construct a suitable altitude and then use the Pythagorean theorem to determine its length so that you can compute the area of the triangle.

Tip: In the radian system of angular measurement, $360° = 2\pi$ radians. Thus, you have: $1° = \dfrac{\pi}{180°}$ radians and 1 radian $= \dfrac{180°}{\pi}$. See Chapter 5 "Trigonometry" for an additional discussion of radian measurement.

Perimeter and Circumference

A figure's perimeter is the distance around it. A circle's perimeter is called its circumference. You measure perimeter in units of length, such as inches, feet, yards, miles, kilometers, meters, centimeters, and millimeters. Here is an example of finding the perimeter of a figure that is a combination of figures.

The figure shown consists of a semicircle of radius r and an attached rectangle whose longer side is $2r$ and whose shorter side is r. What is the perimeter of the figure in terms of r?

The perimeter = circumference of the semicircle + 2 times shorter side and 1 times the longer side of the attached rectangle = $\frac{1}{2}(2\pi r) + 2 \cdot r + 2r = \pi r + 4r$.

Area

The area of a plane figure is the amount of surface enclosed by the figure's boundary. You measure area in square units, such as square inches (in^2), square feet (ft^2), square miles (mi^2), square kilometers (km^2), square meters (m^2), square centimeters (cm^2), and square millimeters (mm^2). The area is always described in terms of square units, regardless of the figure's shape.

A figure's boundary measurements are measured in two dimensions (for example: length and width, base and height). The units for the boundary measurements are linear units (for example: inches, feet, miles, meters, and so on). You obtain the square units needed to describe area when you multiply the unit by itself. For example, (1 in) (1 in) = 1 in^2 = 1 square inch. Here is an example of finding the area of a triangle.

Find the area of the triangle whose base measures 8 feet and whose height to that base measures 7 feet.

From the list of formulas, you know that to find the area of a triangle you must know the measure of the triangle's base and height. The base can be any of the triangle's three sides. The height for the base is the length of the line drawn from the opposite vertex that meets the base (or an extension of it) at a right angle. The formula is $A = \frac{1}{2}bh$, where b is the length of a base of the triangle, and h is the height for that base. When you are finding a triangle's area, you can pick any convenient side of the triangle to serve as the base in the formula.

Tip: When you work problems involving geometric figures, sketch a diagram if no diagram is given.

Sketch a figure.

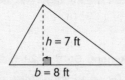

Apply the formula to your figure and compute the area.

$$A = \frac{1}{2}(8 \text{ ft})(7 \text{ ft}) = 28 \text{ ft}^2$$

Surface Area

When you have a solid figure such as a rectangular prism (a box), a cylinder, or a pyramid, you can find the area of every face (surface) and add the areas together. The sum is the solid figure's surface area.

Here is an example of finding the surface area of a rectangular box.

What is the surface area of the box shown?

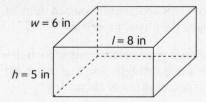

The box is composed of six faces, all of which are rectangles. Use the length and height to find the areas of the front and back faces. Use the length and width to find the areas of the top and bottom faces. Use the width and height to find the areas of the two side faces.

Surface Area = 2(8 in)(5 in) + 2(8 in)(6 in) + 2(6 in)(5 in) = 80 in² + 96 in² + 60 in² = 236 in²

Volume

A solid figure's volume is the amount of space inside the solid. Solid figures have three dimensions (for example: length, width, and height of a box). When you use the dimensions of a solid to find its volume, the units for the volume are cubic units, such as cubic inches (in³), cubic feet (ft³), cubic miles (mi³), cubic kilometers (km³), cubic meters (m³), cubic centimeters (cm³), and cubic millimeters (mm³).

Here is an example of finding the volume of a sphere.

Find the volume of a sphere of radius 6 centimeters. (Round your answer to the nearest whole number.)

Sketch a figure.

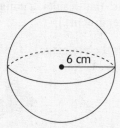

From the list of formulas, you know that the formula for a sphere's volume is $V = \frac{4}{3}\pi r^3$.

Apply the formula to the problem and compute the volume.

$$V = \frac{4}{3}(\pi)(6 \text{ cm})^3 \approx 905 \text{ cm}^3$$

Note: In the context of rounding, the symbol "≈" is read "is approximately equal to."

Geometric Transformations

For this topic, you must be able to solve problems involving translations, reflections, rotations, and dilations of geometric figures in the plane (*Mathematics: Content Knowledge (0061) Test at a Glance*, page 3).

A geometric transformation is a mapping between two sets of points such that each point in the preimage has a unique image and each point in the image has exactly one preimage. The four geometric transformations are translations, reflections, rotations, and dilations. Translations, reflections, and rotations are rigid motions, meaning that the transformation preserves size and shape. Thus, the image and the preimage of translations, reflections, and rotations are congruent. The situation is different for dilations. In general, a dilation is not a rigid motion. A dilation preserves shape, but in only one special circumstance does a dilation preserve size. Thus, the image and preimage of a dilation are similar, but not necessarily congruent. You can think of geometric transformations as ways to change geometric figures without changing their basic properties.

A *translation* of a plane geometric figure is a geometric transformation in which every point P is "moved" the same distance and in the same direction along a straight line to a new point P'. Informally, a translation is a *slide* in a horizontal or vertical direction (or a combination of these two).

A *reflection* of a plane geometric figure is a geometric transformation in which every point P is "moved" to a new point P' that is the same distance from a fixed line, but on the opposite side of the line. The fixed line is the line of reflection. Informally, a reflection is a *flip* across a line, so that the new figure is a mirror image of the original.

A *rotation* of a plane geometric figure is a geometric transformation in which every point P is "rotated" through an angle around a fixed point, called the center of rotation. Informally, a rotation is a *turn* around a point. A figure has rotational symmetry if there is a rotation of less than 360° in which the image and its preimage coincide under the rotation.

A *dilation* of a plane geometric figure is a geometric transformation in which every point P is mapped to a new point P', where the point P' lies on a ray through a fixed point O and the point P, so that the $\overline{OP'} = |k|\overline{OP}$, where k is a nonzero real number, called the scale factor. Informally, a dilation is an expanding ($|k| > 1$) or contracting ($|k| < 1$) of a geometric shape using a scale factor, while its shape, location, and orientation remain the same. In the case that $|k| = 1$, the dilated image is congruent to the original geometric shape, and the dilation is a rigid motion.

[*Note:* Some sources insist that a dilation must change a figure's size. This requirement would exclude the scale factor k, where $|k| = 1$. However, to be consistent with the 2008 *National Mathematics Advisory Panel Report of the Task Group on Learning Processes* (www.ed.gov/about/bdscomm/list/mathpanel/index.html), which suggests the use of dilation in defining similarity, the case that results in congruency between the image and preimage must be included (given that similar figures can be congruent).]

Here are examples in which the shaded figure is the preimage.

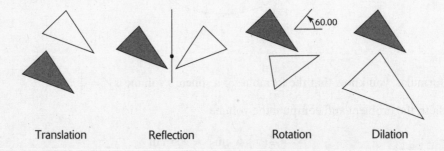

| Translation | Reflection | Rotation | Dilation |

Note: See the section "Representation of Geometric Transformations" in Chapter 10, "Matrix Algebra," for an additional discussion of geometric transformation.

Chapter 5

Trigonometry

According to the *Mathematics: Content Knowledge (0061) Test at a Glance* (www.ets.org/Media/Tests/PRAXIS/pdf/0061.pdf), the Trigonometry content category of the Mathematics CK tests your knowledge and skills in five topic areas:

- The six basic trigonometric functions
- The law of sines and the law of cosines
- Special angle formulas and identities
- Trigonometric equations and inequalities
- Rectangular and polar coordinate systems

This review discusses the key ideas and formulas in each topic area that are most important for you to know for the Mathematics CK.

The Six Basic Trigonometric Functions

For this topic, you must be able to define and use the six basic trigonometric functions using the degree or radian measure of angles and know their graphs and be able to identify their periods, amplitudes, phase displacements or shifts, and asymptotes (*Mathematics: Content Knowledge (0061) Test at a Glance*, page 4).

Right Triangle Ratios

To define the six basic trigonometric ratios, begin with a right triangle ABC and label its parts as follows:

Right triangle ABC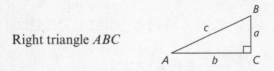

A = measure of $\angle A$
B = measure of $\angle B = 90° - A$
C = measure of $\angle C = 90°$
a = side opposite $\angle A$
b = side adjacent to $\angle A$
c = side opposite the right angle = hypotenuse

The ratios relative to angle A in the right triangle ABC are as follows:

sine of $\angle A = \sin A = \dfrac{\text{side opposite}}{\text{hypotenuse}} = \dfrac{a}{c}$ 　　　 cosecant of $\angle A = \csc A = \dfrac{\text{hypotenuse}}{\text{side opposite}} = \dfrac{c}{a}$

cosine of $\angle A = \cos A = \dfrac{\text{side adjacent}}{\text{hypotenuse}} = \dfrac{b}{c}$ 　　　 secant of $\angle A = \sec A = \dfrac{\text{hypotenuse}}{\text{side adjacent}} = \dfrac{c}{b}$

tangent of $\angle A = \tan A = \dfrac{\text{side opposite}}{\text{side adjacent}} = \dfrac{a}{b}$ 　　　 cotangent of $\angle A = \cot A = \dfrac{\text{side adjacent}}{\text{side opposite}} = \dfrac{b}{a}$

From the preceding formulas, you can see that sine and cosecant are reciprocals of each other, that cosine and secant are reciprocals of each other, and that tangent and cotangent are reciprocals of each other. Therefore, it is necessary to remember only the sine, cosine, and tangent ratios because the other ratios can be determined by using the reciprocal relationships.

Tip: The mnemonic SOH-CAH-TOA (soh-kuh-toh-uh) can help you remember that S (sine) is O (opposite) over H (hypotenuse), that C (cosine) is A (adjacent) over H (hypotenuse), and T (tangent) is O (opposite) over A (adjacent).

Typically, when working with right triangles on the Mathematics CK, you need to find a missing angle or a missing side of a right triangle. If you are given two sides of the right triangle, you should use the Pythagorean theorem to find the missing side. (See the chapter titled "Geometry" for a discussion of the Pythagorean theorem.) If you are given a side and one of the acute angles, label the sides as follows: opposite side (the side across from the given angle), the hypotenuse (across from the right angle), and the adjacent side (the leftover side). Then select the trigonometric ratio that best fits the information you are given.

Tip: When solving a right triangle in which the angles are given in degrees, be sure to set the mode of your calculator to degree mode.

Two special right triangles of trigonometry that are useful to know are the 30°–60°–90° right triangle and the 45°–45°–90° right triangle shown here.

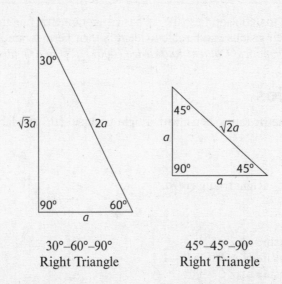

30°–60°–90°
Right Triangle

45°–45°–90°
Right Triangle

The trigonometric ratios associated with these triangles are given in the following table.

Special Trigonometric Ratios			
Angle	30°	45°	60°
Sine	$\dfrac{1}{2}$	$\dfrac{1}{\sqrt{2}} = \dfrac{\sqrt{2}}{2}$	$\dfrac{\sqrt{3}}{2}$
Cosine	$\dfrac{\sqrt{3}}{2}$	$\dfrac{\sqrt{2}}{2}$	$\dfrac{1}{2}$
Tangent	$\dfrac{1}{\sqrt{3}} = \dfrac{\sqrt{3}}{3}$	1	$\sqrt{3}$

Rather than trying to memorize this table, it is better to remember the triangles and how the ratios are defined. All triangles similar to these two have the same ratio values. Here is an example of using the special trigonometric ratios.

Given $\angle C = 90°$, $\angle A = 60°$, and $b = 5$, find the lengths of sides a and c for the following triangle:

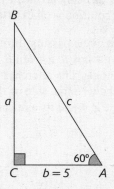

Given $\angle A = 60°$, then $\angle B = 90° - 60° = 30°$. The triangle is similar to the basic 30°–60°–90° right triangle, thus, $\cos A = \dfrac{b}{c} = \dfrac{5}{c} = \dfrac{1}{2}$. Hence, $c = 10$. Also, $\sin A = \dfrac{a}{c} = \dfrac{a}{10} = \dfrac{\sqrt{3}}{2}$. Hence, $a = 5\sqrt{3}$.

The Unit Circle and Trigonometric Functions

The unit circle is a circle centered at (0, 0) with radius equal to 1. If the unit circle is plotted on the Cartesian coordinate system, then the sine and cosine trig functions are associated with the circle in the manner shown.

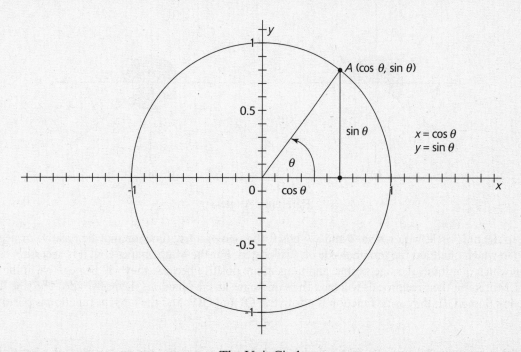

The Unit Circle

Because the radius is 1, $\cos \theta$ is the x-coordinate and $\sin \theta$ is the y-coordinate of the point on the circle intercepted by the ray determined by the central angle θ.

If the point on the circle is rotated counterclockwise to the y-axis, then $\sin \theta = 1$ and $\cos \theta = 0$. Thus, $\sin(90°) = 1$ and $\cos(90°) = 0$. By the same token, $\sin(0°) = 0$ and $\cos(0°) = 1$.

If an angle θ is placed on the Cartesian coordinate plane such that the vertex is at the origin and one side is along the x-axis, then θ is said to be in standard position. The side along the x-axis is the initial side, and the other side is the terminal side. An angle can be thought of as being formed by a rotation of the terminal side. If the rotation is counterclockwise, the angle is positive; if the rotation is clockwise, the angle is negative.

As the terminal side of θ moves around the unit circle passing through the four quadrants of the coordinate plane, the value of the trig functions $y = \sin \theta$, $y = \cos \theta$, $y = \tan \theta$, $y = \csc \theta$, $y = \sec \theta$, and $y = \cot \theta$ can be determined by using the appropriate reference angle. The reference angle for an angle in standard position is the positive acute angle formed by the x-axis and the terminal side of the angle. For example, the reference angle for 120° is 60°. The following figure illustrates angle $\angle A$ and its associated reference angle $\angle A_r$ in the four quadrants.

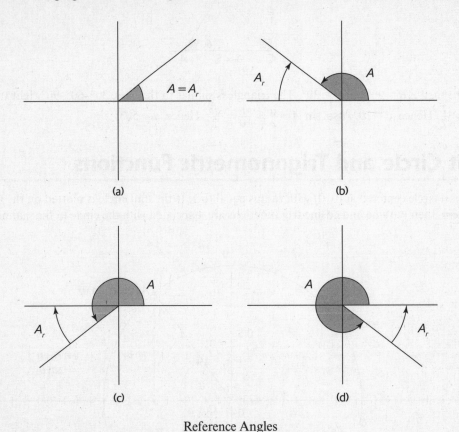

Reference Angles

Referring to the unit circle, with $y = \sin \theta$ and $x = \cos \theta$, the sign of a trig function may be positive or negative depending in which quadrant the terminal side of θ is located. For the Mathematics CK, it is necessary to remember only in which quadrants the sine, cosine, and tangent are positive because they will be negative in the other quadrants. Moreover, their reciprocals will have the same signs as the functions themselves do. The sine function is positive in QI and QII; the cosine function is positive in QI and QIV; and the tangent function is positive in QI and QIII.

Tip: Use the mnemonic "<u>A</u>ll <u>S</u>tudents <u>T</u>ake <u>C</u>alculus" to help you remember the correct sign of a function as you move in a counterclockwise direction from QI to QIV. The initial letters A-S-T-C in the mnemonic remind you that <u>A</u>ll the functions are positive in QI; the <u>S</u>ine function is positive in QII; the <u>T</u>angent function is positive in QIII; and the <u>C</u>osine function is positive in QIV.

Here is an example of determining the values of trig functions using reference angles.

Determine $\sin\theta$, $\cos\theta$, and $\tan\theta$ for $\theta = 315°$.

The angle $\theta = 315°$ is in Quadrant IV. The reference angle is $360° - 315° = 45°$. Thus, $\sin 315° = -\sin 45° = -\frac{\sqrt{2}}{2}$, $\cos 315° = \cos 45° = \frac{\sqrt{2}}{2}$, and $\tan 315° = -\tan 45° = -1$.

The trig functions, of course, can be associated with any circle of radius r. The ratios then take on the forms $\sin\theta = \frac{y}{r}$, $\cos\theta = \frac{x}{r}$, and $\tan\theta = \frac{y}{x}$. Note that $y = r\sin\theta$ and $x = r\cos\theta$. These connections will be used later in this chapter in the discussion on polar coordinates.

The angle θ can be expressed in degrees or radians. In the radian system of angular measurement, $360° = 2\pi$ radians. Thus, you have: $1° = \frac{\pi}{180}$ radians and 1 radian $= \frac{180}{\pi}°$. If $\theta = x$ radians, where x is a real number, the six basic trigonometric functions of x are $y = \sin x$, $y = \cos x$, $y = \tan x$, $y = \csc x$, $y = \sec x$, and $y = \cot x$.

Trigonometric Function	Domain	Range	Asymptotes
	Let k be any integer		Let k be any integer
$y = \sin x$	all reals	$-1 \leq y \leq 1$	none
$y = \cos x$	all reals	$-1 \leq y \leq 1$	none
$y = \tan x$	$\left\{ x \in \text{reals}, x \neq \frac{\pi}{2} + k\pi \right\}$	all reals	$x = \frac{\pi}{2} + k\pi$
$y = \csc x$	$\{x \in \text{reals}, x \neq k\pi\}$	$(-\infty, -1] \cup [1, \infty)$	$x = k\pi$
$y = \sec x$	$\left\{ x \in \text{reals}, x \neq \frac{\pi}{2} + k\pi \right\}$	$(-\infty, -1] \cup [1, \infty)$	$x = \frac{\pi}{2} + k\pi$
$y = \cot x$	$\{x \in \text{reals}, x \neq k\pi\}$	all reals	$x = k\pi$

Tip: Switch to radian mode when the argument of the trigonometric function is a real number.

The following table summarizes the values of the trigonometric functions for some special angles.

angle (°)	angle (radians)	sine	cosine	tangent	cotangent	secant	cosecant
0°	0	0	1	0	undefined	1	undefined
30°	$\frac{\pi}{6}$	$\frac{1}{2}$	$\frac{\sqrt{3}}{2}$	$\frac{1}{\sqrt{3}}$	$\sqrt{3}$	$\frac{2}{\sqrt{3}}$	2
45°	$\frac{\pi}{4}$	$\frac{1}{\sqrt{2}}$	$\frac{1}{\sqrt{2}}$	1	1	$\sqrt{2}$	$\sqrt{2}$
60°	$\frac{\pi}{3}$	$\frac{\sqrt{3}}{2}$	$\frac{1}{2}$	$\sqrt{3}$	$\frac{1}{\sqrt{3}}$	2	$\frac{2}{\sqrt{3}}$
90°	$\frac{\pi}{2}$	1	0	undefined	0	undefined	1

Graphs of the Trigonometric Functions

Referring to the unit circle, as the angle increases from 0° to 360°, the sine function begins at 0, then to 1, back to 0, then to –1, then back to 0 and repeats itself. The cosine starts at 1, then to 0, then to –1, then to 0, and back to 1 and then repeats. This repetition reflects the periodic behavior of both functions. Because the tangent function is the quotient of the sine function over the cosine function, it has vertical asymptotes at angles where the cosine is 0. The tangent function is also periodic.

A function f is periodic if there is a positive number P such that $f(x + P) = f(x)$ for all x in the domain. The least number P for which this is true is the period of f. The sine and cosine functions are periodic with period 2π. The tangent function is periodic with period π.

Note: In graphing the trig functions, commonly the radian measure for angles is used.

The graphs of $y = \sin x$, $y = \cos x$, and $y = \tan x$—the three main trigonometric functions—are shown in the following figures.

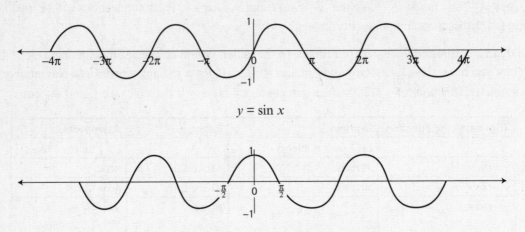

$$y = \sin x$$

$$y = \cos x$$

Graphs of the Sine and Cosine Functions

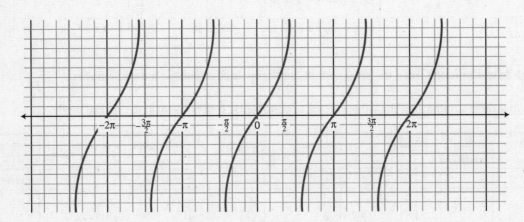

Graph of the Tangent Function

The graphs of the other three trig functions are shown in the following figures.

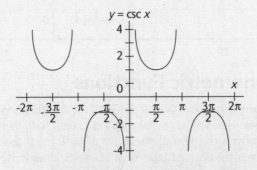

Graph of the Cosecant Function

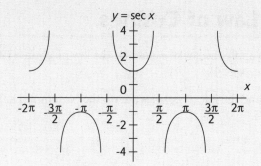

Graph of the Secant Function

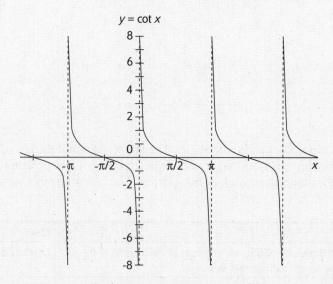

Graph of the Cotangent Function

Knowing the shapes of the graphs of the basic trig functions will help you graph functions that are similar but are variations of the basic graphs.

Transformations of the Trigonometric Functions

If $b > 0$, the general forms for the sine and cosine functions, $y = a \sin(bx + c) + k$ and $y = a \cos(bx + c) + k$, have graphs with amplitude $= |a|$, period $= \frac{2\pi}{b}$, a horizontal or phase shift of $\frac{|c|}{b}$ units (to the left of the origin if $\frac{c}{b}$ is positive; to the right of the origin if $\frac{c}{b}$ is negative), and a vertical shift of $|k|$ units (up from the origin if k is positive; down from the origin if k is negative). Graphically, the coefficient a causes the function to be "stretched" *away* from the x-axis or "compressed" *toward* the x-axis in the vertical direction by the multiple $|a|$. For the sine and cosine functions, the maximum height of the graph is $|a| + k$, and the minimum height is $-|a| + k$.

If $b > 0$, the general form for the tangent function, $y = a \tan(bx + c) + k$, has a graph with period $= \frac{\pi}{b}$, a horizontal or phase shift of $\frac{|c|}{b}$ units (to the left of the origin if $\frac{c}{b}$ is positive; to the right of the origin if $\frac{c}{b}$ is negative), and a vertical shift of $|k|$ units (up from the origin if k is positive; down from the origin if k is negative). Graphically, the coefficient a causes the function to be "stretched" *away* from the x-axis or "compressed" *toward* the x-axis in the vertical direction by the multiple $|a|$; however, unlike the sine and cosine functions, the tangent function has neither a maximum nor a minimum value.

Law of Sines and Law of Cosines

For this topic, you must be able to apply the law of sines and the law of cosines (*Mathematics: Content Knowledge (0061) Test at a Glance*, page 4).

The formulas for the law of sines and the law of cosines are on the Notation, Definitions, and Formulas pages that will be provided.

Law of Sines: $\dfrac{\sin A}{a} = \dfrac{\sin B}{b} = \dfrac{\sin C}{c}$

Law of Cosines: $c^2 = a^2 + b^2 - 2ab \cos C$
$a^2 = b^2 + c^2 - 2bc \cos A$
$b^2 = a^2 + c^2 - 2ac \cos B$

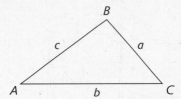

Every triangle has six parts: three sides and three angles. The law of sines and the law of cosines are used to find missing parts of oblique triangles (triangles that are not right triangles). Three possibilities can result: one solution, two solutions (called the ambiguous case), or no solution. The following table summarizes when to use the two laws.

Situation in the Problem:	Use:	No. of solutions:
You are given the measures of three sides (SSS), and the sum of the lengths of the two smaller sides is greater than the length of the larger side.	Law of Cosines	one
You are given the measures of three sides (SSS), and the sum of the lengths of the two smaller sides is less than or equal to the length of the larger side.	Neither	no solution
You are given the measures of two sides and the included angle (SAS).	Law of Cosines	one solution
You are given the measures of two angles and the included side (ASA), and the sum of the given angles is less than 180°.	Law of Sines	one solution
You are given the measures of two angles and a nonincluded side (AAS), and the sum of the given angles is less than 180°.	Law of Sines	one solution
You are given the measures of two angles and either the included side (ASA) or a non-included side (AAS), and the sum of the given angles is greater than or equal to 180°.	Neither	no solution
You are given the measures of two sides and a nonincluded obtuse angle (SSA), and the length of the side opposite the given angle is greater than the length of the side adjacent to the given angle.	Law of Sines	one solution
You are given the measures of two sides and a nonincluded obtuse angle, and the length of the side opposite the given angle is less than or equal to the length of the side adjacent to the given angle.	Neither	no solution
You are given the measures of two sides and a nonincluded acute angle (SSA), and the length of the side opposite the given angle is greater than or equal to the length of the side adjacent to the given angle.	Law of Sines	one solution
You are given the measures of two sides and a nonincluded acute angle (SSA), and the length of one side falls between the length of the altitude from the vertex where the two given sides meet and the length of the other side.	Law of Sines	two solutions

Situation in the Problem:	Use:	No. of solutions:
You are given the measures of two sides and a nonincluded acute angle (SSA), and the length of the altitude from the vertex where the two given sides meet falls between the lengths of the two given sides.	Neither	no solution
You are given the measures of three angles (AAA).	Neither	no unique solution

Here is an example of using the law of sines.

Solve the triangle, given $\angle A = 40°$, $a = 50$, and $b = 30$.

Sketch a figure.

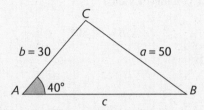

You are given the measures of two sides and a nonincluded acute angle (SSA), and the length of the side opposite the given angle is greater than the length of the side adjacent to the given angle, so there is one solution. Using the law of sines, you have $\frac{\sin B}{30} = \frac{\sin 40°}{50}$. Thus, $\sin B = \frac{30 \sin 40°}{50} \approx 0.3857$. Using the inverse sine function on the calculator yields $\angle B_r \approx 22.7°$. Thus, $\angle B \approx 22.7°$ or $\angle B \approx 180° - 22.7° = 157.3°$. The latter value will not work because $40° + 157.3° > 180°$. It follows that $\angle C \approx 180° - 40° - 22.7° = 117.3°$. Using this result and again applying the law of sines gives $\frac{\sin 40°}{50} = \frac{\sin 117.3°}{c}$, so $c = \frac{50 \sin 117.3°}{\sin 40°} \approx 69.1$. Therefore, the triangle is solved.

Here is an example of using the law of cosines.

Solve the triangle ABC given $a = 15$, $b = 25$, and $c = 28$.

Sketch a figure.

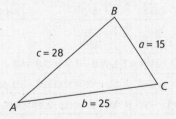

You are given the measures of three sides (SSS), and the sum of the lengths of the two smaller sides is greater than the length of the larger side, so there is one solution. Applying the law of cosines, solve for $\angle A$:

$$15^2 = 25^2 + 28^2 - 2(25)(28) \cos A$$
$$225 = 625 + 784 - 1400 \cos A$$
$$225 = 1409 - 1400 \cos A$$
$$-1184 = -1400 \cos A$$
$$\cos A \approx 0.8457$$

Using the inverse cosine function on the calculator yields

$$\angle A \approx 32.25°$$

Applying the law of cosines a second time, solve for $\angle B$:

$$25^2 = 15^2 + 28^2 - 2(15)(28) \cos B$$
$$625 = 225 + 784 - 840 \cos B$$
$$625 = 1009 - 840 \cos B$$
$$-384 = -840 \cos B$$
$$\cos B \approx 0.4571$$

Using the inverse cosine function on the calculator yields

$$\angle B \approx 62.80°$$

Then $\angle C \approx 180° - 32.25° - 62.8° \approx 84.95°$.

Therefore, the triangle is solved.

> **Tip: When solving an oblique triangle, be sure to set the mode of your calculator to degree mode if the angle measurements are in degrees and to radian mode if the angle measurements are given in radians.**

Special Angle Formulas and Identities

For this topic you must be able to apply the formulas for the trigonometric functions of $\frac{x}{2}$, $2x$, $x + y$, and $x - y$, and prove trigonometric identities (*Mathematics: Content Knowledge (0061) Test at a Glance*, page 4).

For the Mathematics CK you need to know certain fundamental identities and formulas that can be used to simplify or change trigonometric expressions. Following is a list of the most important identities to commit to memory before the test.

Reciprocal Identities:	$\sec\theta = \dfrac{1}{\cos\theta}$, $\csc\theta = \dfrac{1}{\sin\theta}$, and $\cot\theta = \dfrac{1}{\tan\theta}$
Ratio Identities:	$\tan\theta = \dfrac{\sin\theta}{\cos\theta}$, $\cot\theta = \dfrac{\cos\theta}{\sin\theta}$
Pythagorean Identities:	$\sin^2\theta + \cos^2\theta = 1$, $\tan^2\theta + 1 = \sec^2\theta$, and $1 + \cot^2\theta = \csc^2\theta$
Cofunction Identities:	$\cos\theta = \sin(90° - \theta)$, $\csc\theta = \sec(90° - \theta)$, and $\cot\theta = \tan(90° - \theta)$
Even-Odd Identities:	$\sin(-\theta) = -\sin\theta$, $\cos(-\theta) = \cos\theta$, and $\tan(-\theta) = -\tan\theta$

The following formulas are given on the Notation, Definitions, and Formulas pages that are provided.

Addition Formulas:	$\sin(x \pm y) = \sin x \cos y \pm \cos x \sin y$, $\cos(x \pm y) = \cos x \cos y \mp \sin x \sin y$, and $\tan(x \pm y) = \dfrac{\tan x \pm \tan y}{1 \mp \tan x \tan y}$
Half-Angle Formulas:	$\sin\dfrac{\theta}{2} = \pm\sqrt{\dfrac{1 - \cos\theta}{2}}$, $\cos\dfrac{\theta}{2} = \pm\sqrt{\dfrac{1 + \cos\theta}{2}}$ from which you can obtain $\tan\dfrac{\theta}{2} = \pm\sqrt{\dfrac{1 - \cos\theta}{1 + \cos\theta}}$ or $\tan\dfrac{\theta}{2} = \dfrac{\sin\theta}{1 + \cos\theta} = \dfrac{1 - \cos\theta}{\sin\theta}$

Note: Sign of function depends on the quadrant of $\frac{\theta}{2}$.

Even though you can derive the following formulas from the addition formulas, it is a good idea to be familiar with them.

Double Angle Formulas:	$\sin(2\theta) = 2\sin\theta\cos\theta$, $\cos(2\theta) = \cos^2\theta - \sin^2\theta = 2\cos^2\theta - 1 = 1 - 2\sin^2\theta$, and $\tan 2\theta = \dfrac{2\tan\theta}{1 - \tan^2\theta}$

Given that the Mathematics CK is a multiple-choice test, you will not have to prove identities per se on the test; however, you likely will have to select which trigonometric expression is an identity for a given trigonometric expression. Here are some strategies you might find helpful.

- Change all the trigonometric functions in the given expression to sines and cosines and simplify.
- Combine fractions and simplify.
- If the numerator or denominator of a fraction has the form $f(x) + 1$, multiply the numerator and denominator by $f(x) - 1$ to obtain the difference of two squares, and then look for a Pythagorean identity; for $f(x) - 1$ multiply by $f(x) + 1$.
- Evaluate the given trigonometric expression for a convenient value of the angle, and then evaluate each of the answer choices for the same value of the angle to find one that evaluates to be the same value as you obtained for the given trigonometric expression.

Trigonometric Equations and Inequalities

For this topic, you must be able to solve trigonometric equations and inequalities (*Mathematics: Content Knowledge (0061) Test at a Glance*, page 4).

Trigonometric equations and inequalities are solved in a manner similar to the way that algebraic equations and inequalities are solved. (See the chapter titled "Algebra and Number Theory" for a discussion on solving algebraic equations/inequalities). The main difference is that because of the periodic nature of the trigonometric functions, there might be multiple solutions to the equation, depending on the specifications in the problem. For instance, to solve $\cos\theta = \dfrac{1}{2}$, you must find all values for θ that make the equation true. For simplicity, suppose you want to express the answer in radians. Because $\dfrac{1}{2}$ is the cosine of a special angle (see the section in this chapter titled "The Six Basic Trigonometric Functions" for a summary of special angles), you know that $\dfrac{\pi}{3}$ is a value for θ that makes the equation true. However, the cosine function is also positive in QIV. The angle in QIV with reference angle $\dfrac{\pi}{3}$ is $\dfrac{5\pi}{3}$, which is also a value for θ that makes the equation true. Because you know that the cosine function is periodic with period 2π, you have many more values for θ that satisfy $\cos\theta = \dfrac{1}{2}$. To list all of them, add multiples of 2π to each of the values $\dfrac{\pi}{3}$ and $\dfrac{5\pi}{3}$. Thus, the solutions are $\theta = \dfrac{\pi}{3} + k \cdot 2\pi$ and $\dfrac{5\pi}{3} + k \cdot 2\pi$, where k is any integer. If the problem specifies that you are to find only values in a particular interval, then you omit any values outside the given interval.

Solving equations frequently involves using the concept and properties of inverse functions. (See the chapter titled "Functions" for a discussion of inverses of functions). For trigonometric equations, some restrictions must be made to allow you to use inverses. The restrictions in this case are on the domains, so that the inverse will be a function. The restricted domains on the three basic functions are shown in the table that follows.

Restricted Domains of Trig Functions	
$\sin\theta$	$-\dfrac{\pi}{2} \leq \theta \leq \dfrac{\pi}{2}$
$\cos\theta$	$0 \leq \theta \leq \pi$
$\tan\theta$	$-\dfrac{\pi}{2} < \theta < \dfrac{\pi}{2}$

On the restricted domains, the functions are one-to-one and have inverses. The graphs of each function and its inverse are shown in the following figure. Three common notations for the inverse functions are $\sin^{-1} x$, arcsin x, and arcsin x.

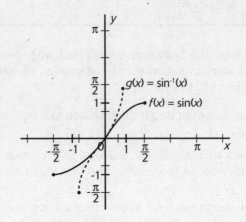

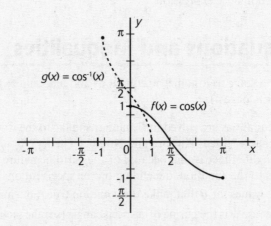

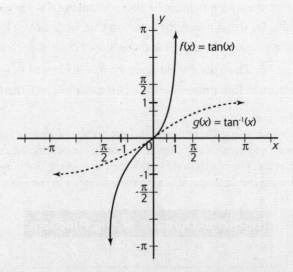

Graphs of Trig Functions and their Inverses over their Restricted Domains

Observe that the domain of both $\sin^{-1}x$ and $\cos^{-1}x$ is the interval $[-1,1]$, and the domain of $\tan^{-1}x$ is $(-\infty,\infty)$.

You can use your graphing calculator to solve trigonometric equations by using the keys for the inverse trigonometric functions, $y = \sin^{-1}x$, $y = \cos^{-1}x$, and $y = \tan^{-1}x$. The range for an inverse trigonometric function is restricted. When you use the keys for the inverse functions, the values returned will be in the restricted ranges. You will have to use your knowledge of reference angles and the periodicity of the functions to determine other values in the solution set if needed.

> **Tip:** If the answer choices are given as radians expressed in terms of π, you might set your calculator to degree mode when obtaining the angle's value, and then convert the angle into radians using the relationship that $1° = \dfrac{\pi}{180}$ radians. If you set your calculator to radian mode, the solution's value will be displayed as a real number. You will have to convert the answer choices to real numbers to decide which answer is the same as your solution.

Here is an example of solving a trig equation.

Solve $2\sin\theta - \sqrt{2} = 0$ for all solutions in $[0,3\pi]$.

$$2\sin\theta - \sqrt{2} = 0$$

$$\sin\theta = \frac{\sqrt{2}}{2}$$

$$\sin^{-1}(\sin\theta) = \sin^{-1}\left(\frac{\sqrt{2}}{2}\right)$$

$$\theta = \frac{\pi}{4}$$

All solutions are $\dfrac{\pi}{4}$, $\dfrac{3\pi}{4}$, $\dfrac{9\pi}{4}$, and $\dfrac{11\pi}{4}$.

> **Tip:** You will find that visualizing the unit circle and the algebraic sign of the given function in the various quadrants is helpful when you are determining all solutions for trig equations.

Rectangular and Polar Coordinate Systems

For this topic, you must be able to convert between rectangular and polar coordinate systems (*Mathematics: Content Knowledge (0061) Test at a Glance*, page 4).

Polar Coordinates

Polar coordinates are based on a directed distance and an angle relative to a fixed point. As illustrated in the following figure, a fixed ray, called the polar axis, emanating from a fixed point O, the origin, is the basis for the coordinate system. A point in the plane is then located by polar coordinates (r,θ).

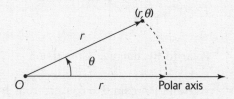

Polar Coordinates

The quadrant in which a point lies is determined by the sign of r and the magnitude of θ. If r is positive, the point is in the same quadrant as θ; if r is negative, the point is in the opposite quadrant.

Here is an example of plotting polar coordinates.

Plot the points $\left(3, \frac{\pi}{4}\right)$, (2, 30°), (4, 75°), (−3, π), and (3, −60°) on the polar plane.

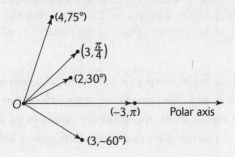

One feature of this coordinate system is that, unlike rectangular coordinates in which the coordinates are unique, a point has an unlimited number of representations in polar coordinates. For instance, $(r, \theta) = (r, \theta + 2n\pi)$, for n an integer. Also, $(r, \theta) = (-r, \pi + \theta) = (-r, -\pi + \theta)$ (see the following illustration).

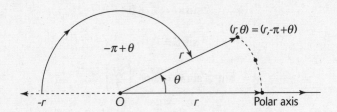

Nonunique Representation of Polar Coordinates

Converting Between Coordinate Systems

The right triangle trigonometric relationships are central to converting between coordinate systems, as shown in the following figure.

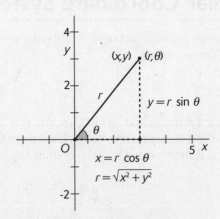

Polar-to-Rectangular Conversion

You use the conversion equations $x = r \cos \theta$ and $y = r \sin \theta$ to convert from polar coordinates to rectangular coordinates.

On the other hand, the conversion equations from rectangular to polar coordinates are $r = \sqrt{x^2 + y^2}$ and $\theta = \tan^{-1} \frac{y}{x}$, $x \neq 0$.

Here is an example of converting from polar coordinates to rectangular form.

Convert the polar coordinates (6, 240°) to rectangular form.

$x = r\cos\theta = 6\cos 240° = 6\left(-\dfrac{1}{2}\right) = -3$ and $y = r\sin\theta = 6\sin 240° = 6\left(-\dfrac{\sqrt{3}}{2}\right) = -3\sqrt{3}$.

Thus, $(6, 240°) = (-3, -3\sqrt{3})$.

Here is an example of converting from rectangular coordinates to polar form.

Convert the rectangular coordinates (–2, 6) to polar form.

The point (–2, 6) is in Quadrant II. $r = \sqrt{(-2)^2 + 6^2} = \sqrt{40} \approx 6.3$. $\theta_r = \tan^{-1}\left(\dfrac{6}{-2}\right) = \tan^{-1}(-3) \approx -71.6°$.

$\theta \approx 180° - 71.6° = 108.4°$. Thus, (–2, 6) ≈ (6.3, 108.4°).

The trigonometric form of a complex number $z = x + yi$ is $r\cos\theta + ir\sin\theta = r(\cos\theta + i\sin\theta)$, where $r = \sqrt{x^2 + y^2}$ and $\tan\theta = \dfrac{y}{x}$, provided $x \neq 0$. Because z also can be represented by the ordered pair (x, y), the similarity to formulas for polar coordinates is not surprising.

De Moivre's theorem is stated as follows: $(\cos\theta + i\sin\theta)^k = \cos(k\theta) + i\sin(k\theta)$. It is useful for finding powers and roots of complex numbers. Here is an example.

$\left(-3 - i3\sqrt{3}\right)^3 = \left(6\cos 240° + i6\sin 240°\right)^3 = 6^3\left(\cos 240° + i\sin 240°\right)^3 = 216(\cos 720° + i\sin 720°) = 216(1 + 0) = 216$.

Chapter 6

Functions

According to the *Mathematics: Content Knowledge (0061) Test at a Glance* (www.ets.org/Media/Tests/PRAXIS/pdf/0061.pdf), the Functions content category of the Mathematics CK tests your knowledge and skills in six topic areas:

- Representation of functions
- Properties of functions
- Solving problems involving functions
- Composition and inverses of functions
- Modeling with functions
- Functions of two variables

This review discusses the key ideas and formulas in each topic area that are most important for you to know for the Mathematics CK.

Representation of Functions

For this topic, you must demonstrate an understanding of and ability to work with functions in various representations (for example: graphs, tables, symbolic expressions, and verbal narratives) and to convert flexibly among them (*Mathematics: Content Knowledge (0061) Test at a Glance*, page 4).

Relations

An ordered pair of numbers, denoted (x, y), is a pair of numbers expressed in a specific order so that one number is written first in the ordered pair, and the other number is written second. In the ordered pair (x, y), x is the first component and y is the second component. Two ordered pairs are equal if and only if they have *exactly* the same coordinates; that is, $(a, b) = (c, d)$ if and only if $a = c$, and $b = d$. The set consisting of all possible ordered pairs of real numbers is denoted $R \times R$, or simply R^2. A relation $\Re$ in R^2 is any subset of R^2. The set consisting of all the first components in the ordered pairs contained in $\Re$ is the domain of $\Re$, and the set of all second components is the range of $\Re$.

Graphically, R^2 is represented by the Cartesian coordinate plane. Here is an illustration.

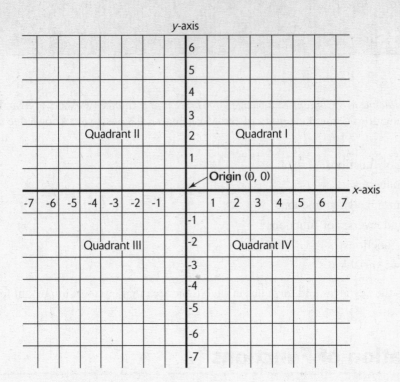

Two intersecting real number lines form the axes of the Cartesian coordinate plane. The horizontal axis with positive direction to the right is commonly designated the *x*–axis, and the vertical axis with positive direction upward is commonly designated the *y*–axis. Their point of intersection is the origin. The axes divide the coordinate plane into four quadrants. The Roman numerals I, II, III, and IV name the quadrants. The numbering process starts in the upper right quadrant and proceeds counterclockwise. Every point in the coordinate plane has a location defined by an ordered pair, (x, y), of real numbers. The numbers x and y are the coordinates of the point.

Definition of a Function

A function is a set of ordered pairs for which each first component is paired with *one and only one* second component. In other words, a function is a relation in which no two ordered pairs have the same first component but different second components, that is, if (a, b) and (a, d) are ordered pairs in the function, then $b = d$. Thus, the set of ordered pairs $\{(1, 2), (2, 3)\}$ is a function, but the set of ordered pairs $\{(1, 2), (1, 3)\}$ is *not* a function.

Single letters, such as f and g, are commonly used as names for functions. For the function f, the ordered pairs are written $(x, f(x))$ or (x, y), where $y = f(x)$. You read the function notation $f(x)$ as "f of x."

In the function defined by $y = f(x)$, x is the independent variable, and y is the dependent variable. The variable y is "dependent" on x in the sense that you substitute a value of x, called an argument of f, into $y = f(x)$ to find y, the value of f at x (also called the image of x under f). The notation D_f indicates the domain of f, and the notation R_f indicates the range of f. You can think of a function as a process f that takes a number $x \in D_f$ and produces from it the number $f(x) \in R_f$.

Note: On the Mathematics CK, unless a problem clearly indicates otherwise, the functions on the test are real-valued functions. This means that both the domains and ranges of the functions consist of real numbers.

Functions are represented in various ways. If a function consists of a *finite* number of ordered pairs, you can define the function by listing or showing its ordered pairs in a set, in a table, as an arrow diagram, or as a graph in a coordinate plane. You also might define the function by giving a rule or an equation. When the number of ordered pairs is *infinite*, more often than not the function is defined by either an equation or a graph. Note: In this book, equations that define functions will use only real numbers as coefficients or constants.

Two functions f and g are equal, written $f = g$, if and only if their domains are equal and they contain exactly the same set of ordered pairs; that is, $D_f = D_g$ and $f(x) = g(x)$ for all x in their common domain.

Properties of Functions

For this topic, you must be able to find properties of a function such as domain, range, intercepts, symmetries, intervals of increase or decrease, discontinuities, and asymptotes (*Mathematics: Content Knowledge (0061) Test at a Glance*, page 4).

Determining Domain and Range

The domain, D_f, of a function $f = \{(x, y) | y = f(x)\}$, where no domain is specified, is the largest possible subset of the real numbers for which each x value gives a corresponding y value that is a *real* number.

To determine the domain of a function f, start with the set of real numbers and exclude all values for x, if any, that would make the equation undefined over the real numbers. If $y = f(x)$ contains a rational expression, to avoid division by 0, exclude values for x, if any, which would make a denominator 0. If $y = f(x)$ contains a radical with an *even* index, to avoid even roots of negative numbers exclude all values for x, if any, that would cause the expression under the radical to be negative.

> **Tip:** Division by 0 and even roots of negative numbers are the two types of domain problems you are most likely to encounter on the Mathematics CK; however, you should be aware that other problems can arise. For instance, the domain for the logarithm function, which will be discussed later in this chapter, cannot include 0 or negative values for x.

The range, denoted R_f, of a function f defined by $y = f(x)$ is the set of all real numbers y for which y is the image of at least one x value in the domain. When you can solve the equation $y = f(x)$ explicitly for x, you can determine the range of f in a manner similar to that used to find the domain of f. Otherwise, you can examine $y = f(x)$ for insight into the possible values for y.

Here are examples of finding D_f and R_f for a function f.

Determine the domain, D_f, and the range, R_f, for the function f defined by $y = \dfrac{1}{x-3}$.

For every real number x, except 3, the quantity $\dfrac{1}{x-3}$ is a real number; thus, the domain of f consists of all real numbers except 3, written $D_f = \{x | x \neq 3\}$. To determine the range of f, solve $y = \dfrac{1}{x-3}$ explicitly for x to obtain $x = \dfrac{1+3y}{y}$. Since for every real number y, except 0, the quantity $\dfrac{1+3y}{y}$ is a real number, the range of f consists of all real numbers except 0, written $R_f = \{y | y \neq 0\}$.

Determine the domain and range of the function f defined by $f(x) = \sqrt{x-5} + 2$.

The domain of f is all real numbers such that $x - 5 \geq 0$; therefore, $D_f = \{x | x \geq 5\}$. For all real numbers x, $y = f(x) = \sqrt{x-5}$ is nonnegative, so $f(x) = \sqrt{x-5} + 2 \geq 2$. Therefore, $R_f = \{y | y \geq 2\}$.

> **Tip:** You will find your graphing calculator very helpful when you need to determine a function's domain and/or range. When using your graphing calculator to explore a function, use trial and error and the Zoom feature to find a good viewing window of its graph; otherwise, you might be misled by the graph displayed.

Characteristics Associated with Graphs of Functions

Because a function is a set of ordered pairs, its graph can be determined in a coordinate plane. Each ordered pair is represented by a point in the plane. The graph of a function f is the set of all ordered pairs (x, y) for which x is in the domain of f and $y = f(x)$; in other words, the graph of a function is a visual representation of its solutions, the set of ordered pairs that satisfy the equation $y = f(x)$.

> **Tip:** A graphing calculator is an indispensable tool when you are exploring graphs of functions. Most graphing calculators require that you enter the equation of the graph in the form $y = f(x)$. This form excludes graphs of relations that are not functions (such as graphs of circles, ellipses, and so on). For such relations, break the equation into two parts, so that each part defines a function, and then graph the two parts on the same coordinate grid.

Vertical line test: By definition, each element in the domain of a function is paired with exactly one element in the range; thus, if a vertical line can be drawn so that it cuts the graph of a relation in more than one point, the relation is not a function This fact is known as the vertical line test: A relation is a function if any vertical line in the plane intersects the graph of the relation in no more than one point. Here is an example of a relation that does *not* pass the vertical line test, so it is *not* a function. There are two points on the graph that correspond to $x = 2$, namely $(2, 1.7)$ and $(2, -1.7)$.

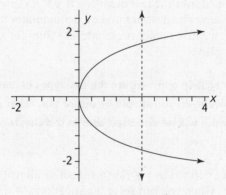

Vertical Line Test

One-to-one function and horizontal line test: A function f is one-to-one if and only if $f(a) = f(b)$ implies that $a = b$; that is, if (a, c) and (b, c) are elements of f, then $a = b$. In a one-to-one function, each first component is paired with *exactly one* second component *and* each second component is paired with *exactly one* first component. Therefore, you have the horizontal line test: A function is one-to-one if any horizontal line in the plane intersects the graph of the function in no more than one point. Here is an example of a function that does *not* pass the horizontal line test, so it is *not* a one-to-one function.

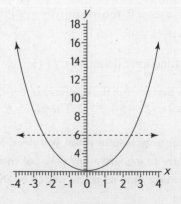

Horizontal Line Test

Increasing-decreasing-constant behavior: Suppose a function f is defined over an interval. Then f is increasing on the interval if, for every pair of numbers x_1 and x_2 in the interval, $f(x_1) < f(x_2)$ whenever $x_1 < x_2$; f is decreasing on the interval if, for every pair of numbers x_1 and x_2 in the interval, $f(x_1) > f(x_2)$ whenever $x_1 < x_2$; f is constant on the interval if $f(x_1) = f(x_2)$ for every pair of numbers x_1 and x_2 in the interval.

Thus, a function is increasing on an interval if its graph moves upward from left to right as the independent variable assumes values from left to right in the interval. A function is decreasing on an interval if its graph moves downward from left to right as the independent variable assumes values from left to right in the interval. A function is constant on an interval if the function value stays the same as the independent variable assumes values from left to right in the interval.

Monotonic function: A function is monotonic if, on its entire domain, the function is either only increasing or only decreasing. A monotonic increasing or decreasing function is one-to-one. Here is an example.

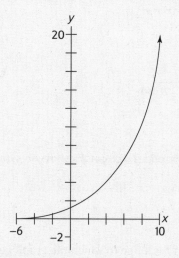

Monotonic Increasing Function

Positive and negative behavior: A function f is positive on an interval if its graph lies above the x-axis for all x-values in the interval; similarly, a function f is negative on an interval if its graph lies below the x-axis for all x values in the interval. Here is an example.

Describe the positive and negative behavior of the function f shown that crosses the x-axis at $(-1, 0)$, $(0, 0)$, $(2, 0)$, and $(3, 0)$.

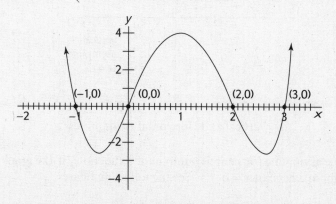

Positive and Negative Behavior of the Function f

The function f is positive in the intervals $(-\infty, -1)$, $(0, 2)$, and $(3, \infty)$, and negative in the intervals $(-1, 0)$ and $(2, 3)$.

Even and odd functions: A function is even if for every x in D_f, $-x$ is in D_f and $f(-x) = f(x)$. A function is odd if for every x in D_f, $-x$ is in D_f and $f(-x) = -f(x)$. The graphs of even functions are symmetric about the y-axis. The graphs of odd functions are symmetric about the origin. Here are examples.

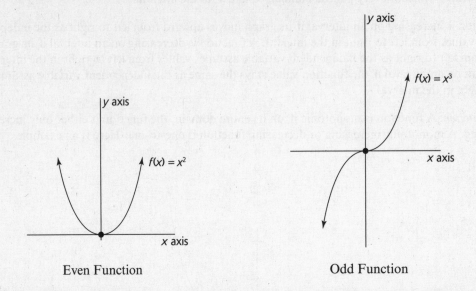

Even Function   Odd Function

Note: Many functions are neither even nor odd. Their graphs show no symmetry with respect to either the *y*-axis or the origin.

Asymptotes

An asymptote of the graph of a function f is a line to which the graph gets closer and closer in at least one direction along the line. The vertical line $x = a$ is a vertical asymptote of the graph of a function f if as x draws close to a from the left or right, the graph goes toward either $-\infty$ or ∞. A horizontal line $y = b$ is a horizontal asymptote of the graph of f if $f(x)$ approaches b as x approaches either $-\infty$ or ∞. See the following figure.

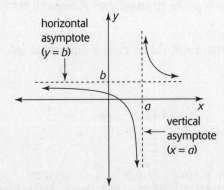

Vertical and Horizontal Asymptotes

A line $y = g(x)$ is an oblique asymptote (or slant asymptote) of a function f if the graph of the function approaches $y = g(x)$ as x approaches either ∞ or $-\infty$. See the following figure.

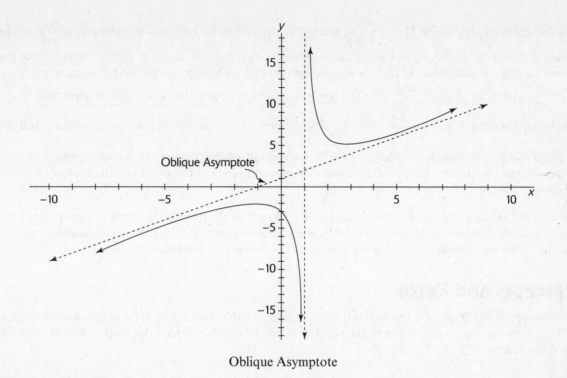

Oblique Asymptote

Commonly, asymptotes are associated with rational functions (see "Rational functions" later in this chapter for a fuller discussion of rational functions).

For a rational function f, defined by $f(x) = \dfrac{p(x)}{q(x)}$, you find vertical asymptotes by setting the denominator $q(x)$ equal to 0 and solving for x (provided the rational function is in simplified form and the degree of $q(x)$ is at least 1). You find horizontal asymptotes by determining the value that $y = f(x)$ approaches as x approaches either ∞ or $-\infty$ (again, provided the rational function is in simplified form and the degree of $q(x)$ is at least 1).

A rational function will have at most one horizontal asymptote. The following guidelines will help you identify a horizontal asymptote for a rational function defined by $f(x) = \dfrac{p(x)}{q(x)}$, where $f(x)$ is in simplified form and the degree of $q(x)$ is at least 1:

- If the degree of $p(x)$ is less than the degree of $q(x)$, then the x-axis ($y = 0$) is a horizontal asymptote. For example, the x-axis is a horizontal asymptote of $f(x) = \dfrac{1}{x-3}$.

- If the degree of $p(x)$ equals the degree of $q(x)$, then the graph will have a horizontal asymptote at $y = \dfrac{a_n}{b_n}$, where a_n is the leading coefficient of $p(x)$ and b_n is the leading coefficient of $q(x)$. For example, $y = \dfrac{3}{4}$ is a horizontal asymptote of $g(x) = \dfrac{3x^2 - 4}{4x^2 - 1}$.

- If the degree of $p(x)$ exceeds the degree of $q(x)$ by more than 1, the graph will *not* have a horizontal asymptote. For example, $g(x) = \dfrac{x^6 - 64}{x^2 - 2x - 15}$ has no horizontal asymptote.

Here is an example of finding vertical and horizontal asymptotes.

Find the vertical and horizontal asymptotes for the function defined by the equation $y = \dfrac{1}{x-3} + 5$.

The denominator $x - 3$ equals 0 when $x = 3$. Thus, the vertical asymptote is $x = 3$.

As x approaches either ∞ or $-\infty$, $\dfrac{1}{x-3}$ approaches 0. Thus, as x approaches ∞ or $-\infty$, $\dfrac{1}{x-3} + 5$ approaches $0 + 5 = 5$, so $y = 5$ is a horizontal asymptote.

A rational function, defined by $f(x) = \dfrac{p(x)}{q(x)}$, where $f(x)$ is in simplified form and the degree of $q(x)$ is at least 1, will have at most one oblique asymptote. If the degree of $p(x)$ exceeds the degree of $q(x)$ by *exactly* 1, the graph will have an oblique asymptote. To find the equation of the oblique asymptote, use long division to rewrite $f(x) = \dfrac{p(x)}{q(x)}$ as quotient plus $\dfrac{\text{remainder}}{q(x)}$. The line with equation $y = $ quotient is an oblique asymptote. For example, suppose that $f(x) = \dfrac{x^2 + 3}{x - 1} = x + 1 + \dfrac{4}{x - 1}$; then $y = x + 1$ is an oblique asymptote of the graph of f.

The graph of a function can *never* intersect a vertical asymptote of the function. However, the graph of a function may cross a line that is a horizontal or oblique asymptote as long as the graph eventually draws asymptotically close to the line.

In an informal sense, a function has discontinuities if the graph of the function has vertical asymptotes, holes, or jumps that make it impossible to sketch the graph of the function without lifting the pencil. See the chapter "Calculus" for a mathematically rigorous discussion of continuity and discontinuity.

Intercepts and Zeros

An x-intercept of the graph of a function is the x-coordinate of the point at which the graph intersects the x-axis, and the y-intercept is the y-coordinate of the point at which the graph intersects the y-axis. The following figure shows illustrations.

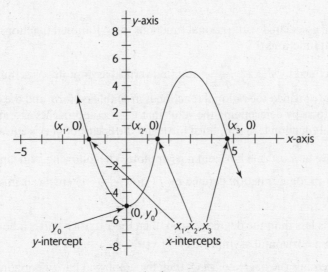

x- and *y*-intercepts

The graph of a function has at most *one* y-intercept. A function f cannot have more than one y-intercept because, by definition, each x value in the domain of f is paired with *exactly one* y value in the range. If 0 is in the domain of f, then $f(0)$ is the y-intercept of the graph of f.

To determine the x-intercept(s), if any, for a function f, set $f(x) = 0$ and then solve for x. Similarly, provided that 0 is in the domain of f, to determine the y-intercept, if any, let $x = 0$, and then solve $f(0) = y$ for y.

A graph can have many x-intercepts, or it might not have any. The x-intercepts, if any, are the real zeros of f. The zeros are determined by finding all values x for which $f(x) = 0$. You can describe a real zero of a function as one of the following: an x-intercept for the graph of $y = f(x)$, an x-value for which $f(x) = 0$, or a real root of the equation $f(x) = 0$. See "Polynomial Functions" in this chapter for an illustration of the zeros of a function.

Note: It is important that you understand the distinction between x-intercepts and zeros. To clarify the relationship in general: For any function f, x-intercepts (if any) of the graph of f are *always* zeros of f; however, only *real* zeros (if any) of *f* are *x*-intercepts of its graph. Some functions have zeros that are not real numbers, so these zeros do not correspond to *x*-intercepts because these values do not lie on the *x*-axis.

Horizontal and Vertical Translations

A translation, or shift, is a geometric transformation of the graph of a function *f* that results in a new graph congruent to the graph of *f*, but for which every point *P* (preimage) on the graph of *f* is "moved" the same distance and in the same direction along a straight line to a new point *P'* (image). Informally, a translation is a slide of the graph of a function in a horizontal or vertical direction.

You perform a horizontal shift by adding or subtracting a positive constant *h* to or from the independent variable *x*. You perform a vertical shift by adding or subtracting a positive constant *k* to or from *f(x)*. Table 6.1 contains a summary of vertical and horizontal shifts.

Table 6.1 Horizontal and Vertical Shifts	
Type of translation	**Effect on graph of *f***
(*h*, *k* both positive)	
$y = f(x + h)$	horizontal shift: *h* units to left
$y = f(x - h)$	horizontal shift: *h* units to right
$y = f(x) + k$	vertical shift: *k* units up
$y = f(x) - k$	vertical shift: *k* units down

Here is an example.

The graph of the function *g* is the result of a horizontal shift of 1 unit to the right and a vertical shift of 2 units down of the graph of the function *f* defined by $y = x^2$. Write the equation for the graph of the function *g*.

To shift the graph of *f* 1 unit to the right, subtract 1 from *x* and to shift the graph down 2 units, subtract 2 from *f(x)* to obtain $g(x) = f(x - 1) - 2 = (x - 1)^2 - 2$. The graphs of *f* and *g* are shown here.

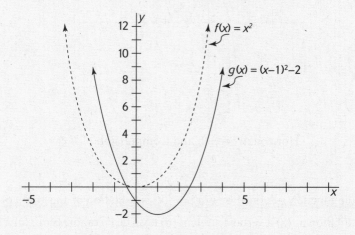

Graphs of $y = x^2$ and $g(x) = (x - 1)^2 - 2$

Dilations

A dilation is a geometric transformation of the graph of a function *f* that results in a new graph that is geometrically similar in shape to the graph of *f*, but for which the graph of *f* has undergone a vertical stretch or compression or a horizontal stretch or compression.

When $a > 1$, the graph defined by $g(x) = af(x)$ is a vertical stretch *away* from the horizontal axis of the graph defined by $y = f(x)$; and when $0 < a < 1$, the graph defined by $g(x) = af(x)$ is a vertical compression *toward* the horizontal axis of the graph defined by $y = f(x)$. In either case, if (x, y) is on the graph defined by $y = f(x)$, then (x, ay) is on the graph defined by $g(x) = af(x)$. See the following figure for illustrations.

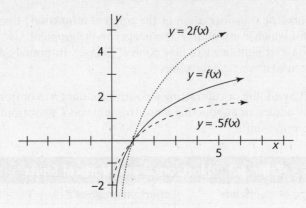

Vertical Stretch and Compression of $f(x)$

When $b > 1$, the graph defined by $g(x) = f(bx)$ is a horizontal compression *toward* the vertical axis of the graph defined by $y = f(x)$; and when $0 < b < 1$, the graph defined by $g(x) = f(bx)$ is a horizontal stretch *away* from the vertical axis of the graph defined by $y = f(x)$. In either case, if (x, y) is on the graph defined by $y = f(x)$, then $\left(\dfrac{x}{b}, y\right)$ is on the graph defined by $g(x) = f(bx)$. See the following figure for illustrations.

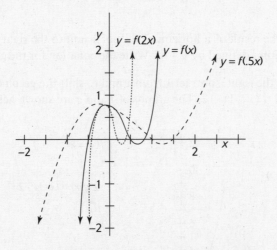

Horizontal Stretch and Compression of $f(x)$

Here are examples.

Given that the graph of the function g defined by $g(x) = \dfrac{3}{4}x^3$ is a dilation of the graph of the function f defined by $f(x) = x^3$, describe the dilation as (a) a vertical stretch, (b) a vertical compression, (c) a horizontal stretch, or (d) a horizontal compression.

Given that $g(x) = \dfrac{3}{4}x^3 = \dfrac{3}{4}f(x)$ and that $0 < \dfrac{3}{4} < 1$, the function g is a vertical compression of the function f.

For the function f, defined by $f(x) = x^3$, (a) write an equation for a function g whose graph is a dilation of the graph of f satisfying the condition that $g(x) = f(3x)$ (do not simplify the equation) and (b) for the point $(-5, -125)$ on the graph defined by $f(x) = x^3$, give the coordinates of the corresponding point on the graph defined by $g(x) = f(3x)$.

(a) $g(x) = f(3x) = (3x)^3$ (b) Given $(-5, -125)$ is on the graph defined by $f(x) = x^3$, then $\left(-\dfrac{5}{3}, -125\right)$ is its corresponding point on the graph defined by $g(x) = (3x)^3$.

Reflections

A reflection is a mirror image of a function. The function $-f(x)$ reflects $f(x)$ over the x-axis; and $f(-x)$ reflects $f(x)$ over the y-axis. Here are illustrations.

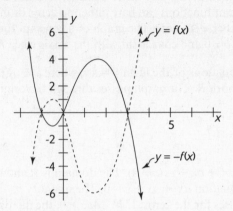

Reflection about the x-axis

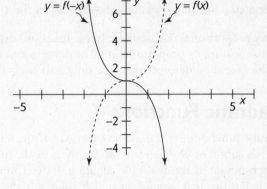

Reflection about the y-axis

Solving Problems Involving Functions

For this topic, you must be able to use the properties of trigonometric, exponential, logarithmic, polynomial, and rational functions to solve problems (*Mathematics: Content Knowledge (0061) Test at a Glance*, page 4).

Linear Functions

Linear functions are defined by equations of the form $f(x) = mx + b$. The domain for all linear functions is R, the set of real numbers. When $m \neq 0$, the range is R. When $m = 0$, the range is the set $\{b\}$, containing the single value b. The equation $y = mx + b$ is the slope-intercept form of the equation of a line.

The graph of a linear function f defined by $f(x) = mx + b$ is always a nonvertical line with slope m and y-intercept b. When $m \neq 0$, the graph has exactly one y-intercept b and exactly one x-intercept $-\frac{b}{m}$. Thus, the points $(0, b)$ and $\left(-\frac{b}{m}, 0\right)$ are contained in the graph. The only zero is the real number $x = -\frac{b}{m}$; thus, the graph crosses the x-axis at the point $\left(\frac{b}{m}, 0\right)$. If $m > 0$, f is increasing; if $m < 0$, f is decreasing. The following figure shows the graph of the linear function $y = -\frac{1}{2}x + 6$ that has slope $-\frac{1}{2}$, y-intercept 6, and x-intercept 12.

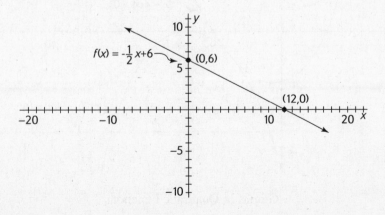

The identity function is the linear function defined by the equation $f(x) = x$. This function maps each x value to an identical y value. The domain and range are both R. The graph has slope 1. The graph passes through the origin, so both the x- and y-intercept are 0. The only zero is $x = 0$.

Constant functions are linear functions defined by equations of the form $f(x) = b$, where $b \in R$. The domain is R, and the range is the set $\{b\}$ containing the single element b. Constant functions can have either no zeros or infinitely many zeros: If $b \neq 0$, it has no zeros; if $b = 0$, every real number x is a zero. The graph of a constant function is a horizontal line that is $|b|$ units above or below the x-axis when $b \neq 0$ and coincident with the x axis when $b = 0$.

Directly proportional functions are linear functions defined by equations of the form $y = kx$, where $k \in R$ is the nonzero constant of proportionality. The domain and range are both R. The graph passes through the origin, so both the x- and y-intercept are 0. The only zero is $x = 0$.

Quadratic Functions

Quadratic functions are defined by equations of the form $f(x) = ax^2 + bx + c$, $(a \neq 0)$. The domain is R and the range is a subset of R. The zeros are the roots of the quadratic equation $ax^2 + bx + c = 0$. The quantity $b^2 - 4ac$ is the discriminant of the quadratic equation. It determines three cases for the zeros: If $b^2 - 4ac > 0$, the quadratic function has two real *unequal* zeros; if $b^2 - 4ac = 0$, the quadratic function has one real zero (double root); and if $b^2 - 4ac < 0$, the quadratic function has no real zeros.

The graph of $f(x) = ax^2 + bx + c$ is a parabola. The vertex is $\left(-\dfrac{b}{2a}, f\left(-\dfrac{b}{2a}\right)\right)$. When $a > 0$, the parabola opens upward and the y-coordinate of the vertex is an absolute minimum of f. When $a < 0$, the parabola opens downward and the y-coordinate of the vertex is an absolute maximum of f. The parabola is symmetric about its axis of symmetry, a vertical line through its vertex that is parallel to the y-axis.

Depending on the solution set of $ax^2 + bx + c = 0$, the parabola might or might not intersect the x-axis. Three cases occur: If $ax^2 + bx + c = 0$ has *two* real *unequal* roots, the parabola will intersect the x-axis at those *two* points; if $ax^2 + bx + c = 0$ has exactly *one* real root, the parabola will be tangent to the x-axis at only that *one* point; and if $ax^2 + bx + c = 0$ has *no* real roots, the parabola will *not* intersect the x-axis. The following figure shows illustrations.

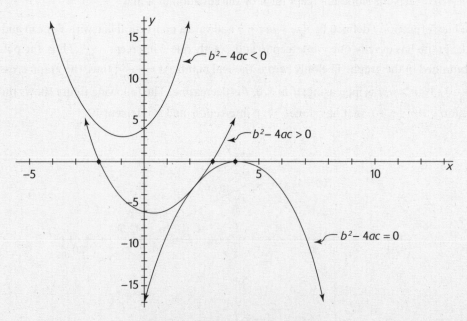

Graphs of Quadratic Functions

The standard form for the equation of a parabola that opens upward or downward is $f(x) = y = a(x - h)^2 + k$, $(a \neq 0)$ with vertex (h, k). Any quadratic function can be put in standard form by using the process of completing the square. (See "Solving a Quadratic Equation by Completing the Square" in the chapter titled "Algebra and Number Theory" for a discussion on completing the square.) When $a < 0$, the range of f is $(-\infty, k]$. The function is increasing on $(-\infty, h]$ and decreasing on $[h, \infty)$. When $a > 0$, the range of f is $[k, \infty)$. The function is decreasing on $(-\infty, h]$ and increasing on $[h, \infty)$.

Polynomial Functions

Polynomial functions are defined by equations of the form $P(x) = a_n x^n + a_{n-1} x^{n-1} + \cdots + a_2 x^2 + a_1 x + a_0$, with leading coefficient $a_n \neq 0$. The degree of the polynomial is n, a nonnegative integer. Linear and quadratic functions are polynomial functions of degree one and two, respectively. The domain for any polynomial function is R. When n is odd, the range is R. When n is even, the range is a subset of R. The zeros are the solutions of the equation $P(x) = 0$.

A number r is a zero of $y = P(x)$ if and only if $P(r) = 0$. If $r \in R$, the graph of $y = P(x)$ crosses the x-axis at the point $(r, 0)$ and has x-intercept r. The graph has y-intercept $P(0)$. The graph of a polynomial function P is a continuous smooth curve (or line) without breaks of any kind; furthermore, it has no cusps (sharp corners). The y-intercept of the graph is $P(0)$. The x-intercepts correspond to the real zeros (if any) of P. As the degree of polynomial functions increases, their graphs become more complex. The graph below shows a polynomial function that has zeros (and x-intercepts) -1, 0, 2, and 3, and y-intercept 0.

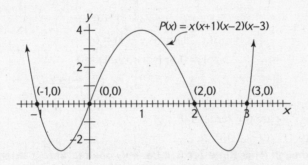

Graph of $P(x) = x(x + 1)(x - 2)(x - 3)$

The graph of a polynomial function will have a turning point (x, y) whenever the graph changes from increasing to decreasing or from decreasing to increasing. The y-value of a turning point is either a relative maximum or relative minimum value for the function. An nth-degree polynomial will have at most $(n - 1)$ turning points.

Note: A turning point is an ordered pair (x, y) that identifies a point on the graph where the graph changes from increasing to decreasing or conversely. A maximum or minimum value is a value of the function, not a point on the graph.

Some useful theorems to know about polynomial functions are the following:

If $a, b \in R$ such that $P(a)$ and $P(b)$ have opposite signs, then P has at least one zero between a and b.

Factor Theorem: $P(r) = 0$ if and only if $x - r$ is a factor of $P(x) = a_n x^n + a_{n-1} x^{n-1} + \cdots + a_2 x^2 + a_1 x + a_0$. Thus, you can factor $P(x)$ by finding the zeros of P; and, conversely, you can determine the zeros of P by factoring $P(x)$. In general, a zero r of a polynomial function P has multiplicity k if $(x - r)^k$ is a factor of $P(x)$ and $(x - r)^{k+1}$ is not a factor of $P(x)$.

Remainder Theorem: If $P(x) = a_n x^n + a_{n-1} x^{n-1} + \cdots + a_2 x^2 + a_1 x + a_0$ is divided by $x - r$, the remainder is $P(r)$.

Rational Root Theorem: If $P(x) = a_n x^n + a_{n-1} x^{n-1} + \cdots + a_2 x^2 + a_1 x + a_0$ with integral coefficients ($a_n \neq 0$ and $a_0 \neq 0$) and $\frac{p}{q}$ is a rational root of $P(x)$ in simplified form, then p is a factor of a_0 and q is a factor of a_n.

Descartes' Rule of Signs: If $P(x)$ has real coefficients and is written in descending (or ascending) powers of x, then the number of positive real roots of $P(x) = 0$ is either the number of sign changes, from left to right, occurring in the coefficients of $P(x)$, or it is less than this number by an even number. Similarly, the number of negative real roots of $P(x) = 0$ is either the number of sign changes, from left to right, occurring in the coefficients of $P(-x)$, or it is less than this number by an even number. Note: When using this rule, ignore missing powers of x.

Fundamental Theorem of Algebra: Over the complex numbers, every polynomial of degree $n \geq 1$ has at least one zero. It follows that if you allow complex roots and count a root again each time it occurs more than once, a polynomial of degree n has exactly n roots. This theorem guarantees that for every polynomial $P(x)$ of degree $n \geq 1$ there exist complex roots $r_1, r_2, \ldots, r_n$, so you can factor $P(x)$ completely as $P(x) = a_n(x - r_1)(x - r_2) \ldots (x - r_n)$, where a_n is the leading coefficient of $P(x)$.

Complex Conjugate Rule: If $P(x)$ has real coefficients, and $a + bi$, $(b \neq 0)$, is a complex root of $P(x)$, then its complex conjugate $a - bi$ is also a root of $P(x)$.

Here is an example of finding the zeros of a polynomial.

Find the zeros of the polynomial function P defined by $P(x) = x^3 - 1$.

The zeros of P are the roots of $x^3 - 1 = 0$. Since $P(x)$ has degree 3, the equation $x^3 - 1 = 0$ has exactly three roots. Solving, you have:

$$x^3 - 1 = 0$$
$$(x - 1)(x^2 + x + 1) = 0$$
$$x - 1 = 0 \text{ or } (x^2 + x + 1) = 0$$
$$x = 1 \text{ or } x = \frac{-1 \pm i\sqrt{3}}{2}$$

Thus, 1, $-\frac{1}{2} + \frac{\sqrt{3}}{2}i$, and $-\frac{1}{2} - \frac{\sqrt{3}}{2}i$ are the zeros of P.

> **Note: In this problem, even though P has three zeros, it has only one real zero, namely, 1, so its graph will intersect the x-axis only once—at $x = 1$, as shown in the following figure.**

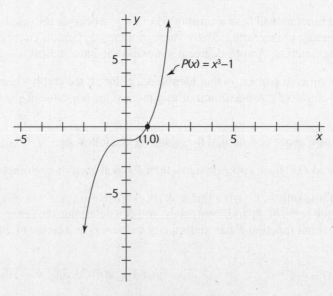

Graph of $P(x) = x^3 - 1$

Rational Functions

Rational functions are defined by equations of the form $f(x) = \dfrac{P(x)}{Q(x)} = \dfrac{a_n x^n + a_{n-1} x^{n-1} + \cdots + a_1 x + a_0}{b_m x^m + b_{m-1} x^{m-1} + \cdots + b_1 x + b_0}$, where $P(x)$ and $Q(x)$ are polynomials and $Q(x) \neq 0$. The domain is $\{x \in R | Q(x) \neq 0\}$. The range is a subset of R. When $f(x)$ is in simplified form (that is, when the numerator and denominator polynomials have no common factors), the zeros, if any, occur at x values for which $P(x) = 0$. If 0 is in the domain of f, the y-intercept is $f(0)$. When $f(x) = \dfrac{P(x)}{Q(x)}$ is in simplified form, the x-intercepts occur at real values for which $P(x) = 0$.

To graph $f(x) = \dfrac{P(x)}{Q(x)}$, first factor $P(x)$ and $Q(x)$ to identify possible "holes" in the graph of f. If $P(x)$ and $Q(x)$ have a common factor, $(x - h)$, that will divide out completely from the denominator when $f(x)$ is simplified, then the graph will have a hole at $(h, f(h))$, where $f(h)$ is calculated after $f(x)$ is simplified. Here is an example.

Let $f(x) = \dfrac{x+2}{x^2 - 4} = \dfrac{x+2}{(x+2)(x-2)}$. The common factor, $(x + 2)$, will divide out completely from the denominator when $f(x)$ is simplified to $f(x) = \dfrac{1}{x-2}$. Therefore, the graph of f has a hole at $\left(-2, -\dfrac{1}{4}\right)$. See the following figure.

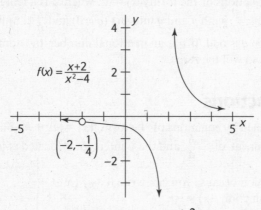

$$f(x) = \frac{x+2}{x^2 - 4}$$

$$\left(-2, -\frac{1}{4}\right)$$

Graph of $f(x) = \dfrac{x+2}{x^2 - 4}$

After identifying possible holes, next you use the simplified form of $f(x)$ to determine asymptotes of the graph. See "Asymptotes" earlier in this chapter for a discussion of this topic.

To determine the behavior of $f(x) = \dfrac{P(x)}{Q(x)} = \dfrac{a_n x^n + a_{n-1} x^{n-1} + \cdots + a_1 x + a_0}{b_m x^m + b_{m-1} x^{m-1} + \cdots + b_1 x + b_0}$, as x approaches ∞ or $-\infty$, separately factor out $a_n x^n$, the term with highest degree in the numerator, and $b_m x^m$, the term with highest degree in the denominator; then $f(x) = \dfrac{P(x)}{Q(x)}$ behaves as $\dfrac{a_n x^n}{b_m x^m}$ does.

Square Root Functions

Square root functions are defined by equations of the form $f(x) = \sqrt{ax + b}$. The domain is $\{x \in R \mid ax + b \geq 0\}$. The range is $\{y \in R \mid y \geq 0\}$. The graph is nonnegative with the only zero at $x = -\dfrac{b}{a}$. The following figure shows the square root function $f(x) = \sqrt{x}$.

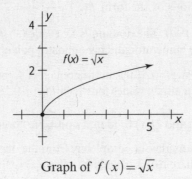

Graph of $f(x) = \sqrt{x}$

Power Functions

Power functions are defined by equations of the form $f(x) = x^a$, where a is a real number (provided that 0^0 does not occur). If a is a rational number $\dfrac{p}{q}$ [with p and q integers ($q \neq 0$) and $\dfrac{p}{q}$ simplified], then the domain is $[0, \infty)$ when q is even and is $(-\infty, \infty)$ when q is odd. If a is an irrational number, the domain is $[0, \infty)$. The range will vary depending on the value of a, and so will the zeros.

Absolute Value Functions

Absolute value functions are defined by equations of the form $f(x) = |ax + b|$. The domain is R, and the range is $\{y \in R \mid y \geq 0\}$. The only zero occurs at $x = -\dfrac{b}{a}$, and the y-intercept is located at $|b|$. The absolute value function $f(x) = |ax + b|$ is a piecewise function because you can write it as $f(x) = \begin{cases} ax + b & \text{if } x \geq -\dfrac{b}{a} \\ -(ax + b) & \text{if } x < -\dfrac{b}{a} \end{cases}$. The following figure shows the absolute value function $f(x) = |x|$.

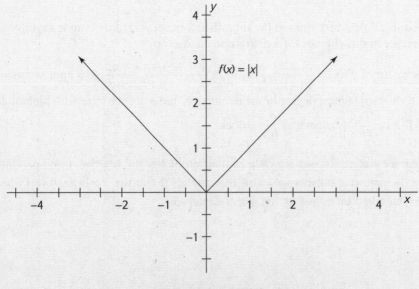

Graph of $f(x) = |x|$

The absolute value function has the following properties.

$$|x| \geq 0$$
$$|x| = |-x|$$
$$|xy| = |x||y|$$
$$\left|\frac{x}{y}\right| = \frac{|x|}{|y|}, \, y \neq 0$$
$$|u + v| \leq |u| + |v|$$
$$\sqrt{x^2} = |x|$$

Note: Always perform computations inside absolute value bars *before* you evaluate the absolute value.

For $c > 0$,

$|x| = c$ if and only if either $x = c$ or $x = -c$

$|x| < c$ if and only if $-c < x < c$

$|x| > c$ if and only if either $x < -c$ or $x > c$

Note: Properties involving $<$ and $>$ hold if you replace $<$ with $\leq$ and $>$ with $\geq$.

Greatest Integer Functions

The greatest integer function (also called the *step function*) is defined by $f(x) = [\![x]\!]$, where the brackets denote finding the greatest integer n such that $n \leq x$. The domain is R, and the range is the integers. The zeros lie in the interval $[0, 1)$. The y-intercept is 0. The x-intercepts lie in the interval $[0, 1)$. The graph of the function is constant between the integers, but "jumps" at each integer. The following figure shows the greatest integer function.

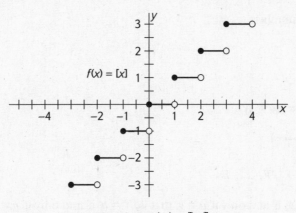

Graph of $f(x) = [\![x]\!]$

Exponential Functions

Exponential functions are defined by equations of the form $f(x) = b^x (b > 0, b \neq 1)$, where b, a constant, is the base of the exponential function. The domain is R, and the range is $(0, \infty)$, which is to say that $b^x > 0$ for every real number x. Because $f(x) = b^x = 0$ has no solution, there are no zeros.

The graph of $f(x) = b^x (b > 0, b \neq 1)$ is a smooth, continuous curve. The graph passes through the points (0, 1) and (1, b) and is located in the first and second quadrants only. The y-intercept is 1. The graph of the function does not cross the x-axis, so it has no x-intercepts. The x-axis is a horizontal asymptote.

If $b > 1$, the function is increasing. As x approaches ∞, $f(x) = b^x$ approaches ∞. As x approaches $-\infty$, $f(x) = b^x$ approaches 0, but never reaches 0. If $0 < b < 1$, the function is decreasing. As x approaches ∞, $f(x) = b^x$ approaches 0, but never reaches 0. As x approaches $-\infty$, $f(x) = b^x$ approaches ∞.

The following figure shows the graph of the exponential function $f(x) = 2^x$.

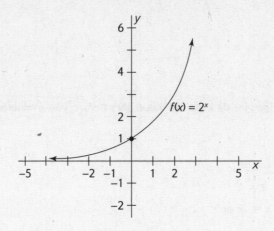

Graph of $f(x) = 2^x$

The natural exponential function is defined by $f(x) = e^x$, where the base e is the irrational number whose rational decimal approximation is 2.718281828 (to nine digits).

The base-10 exponential function is defined by $f(x) = 10^x$.

Exponential functions have the following properties.

For the function f defined by $f(x) = b^x$ ($b > 0$, $b \neq 1$),

$f(x) = b^x > 0$, for all real numbers

$f(0) = b^0 = 1$

$f(1) = b^1 = b$

$f(-x) = b^{-x} = \dfrac{1}{b^x}$

$f(u) \cdot f(v) = b^u \cdot b^v = b^{u+v} = f(u + v)$

$\dfrac{f(u)}{f(v)} = \dfrac{b^u}{b^v} = b^{u-v} = f(u - v)$

$\left(f(x)\right)^p = \left(b^x\right)^p = b^{xp} = f(xp)$

One-to-one property: $f(u) = f(v)$ if and only if $u = v$; that is, $b^u = b^v$ if and only if $u = v$.

> **Tip: Do not confuse exponential functions with power functions. The exponents in exponential functions are *variables,* whereas the exponents in power functions are *constants*. For instance, $f(x) = 3^x$ defines an exponential function and $g(x) = x^3$ defines a power function.**

Logarithmic Functions

Logarithmic functions are defined by equations of the form $f(x) = \log_b x$, where $\log_b x = y$ if and only if $x = b^y$ ($b > 0$, $b \neq 1$). The constant b is the base of the logarithmic function. The domain is $(0, \infty)$, and the range is R. The function has one zero at $x = 1$.

The graph of $f(x) = \log_b x$ $(b > 0, b \neq 1)$ is a smooth, continuous curve. The graph passes through $(1, 0)$ and $(b, 1)$ and is located in the first and fourth quadrants only. The graph of the function does not cross the y-axis, so it does not have a y-intercept. The y-axis is a vertical asymptote.

If $b > 1$, the function is increasing. As x approaches ∞, $f(x) = \log_b x$ approaches ∞. As x approaches 0, $f(x) = \log_b x$ approaches $-\infty$. If $0 < b < 1$, the function is decreasing. As x approaches ∞, $f(x) = \log_b x$ approaches $-\infty$. As x approaches 0, $f(x) = \log_b x$ approaches ∞. The natural logarithmic function is defined by $f(x) = \log_e x$. This function is denoted $f(x) = \ln x$. The common logarithmic function is defined by $f(x) = \log_{10} x$.

For a given base, the logarithmic function is the inverse of the corresponding exponential function, and conversely. The logarithm function $f(x) = \log_{10} x$ (common logarithmic function) is the inverse of the exponential function $g(x) = 10^x$. The logarithm function $g(x) = \ln x$ (natural logarithmic function) is the inverse of the exponential function $f(x) = e^x$.

The following figure shows the graphs of the logarithmic function defined by $g(x) = \ln x$ and its mutually inverse exponential function defined by $f(x) = e^x$.

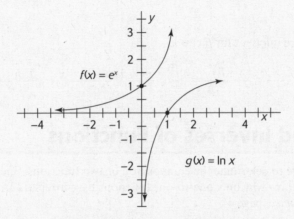

Graphs of $f(x) = e^x$ and $g(x) = \ln x$

Logarithmic functions have the following properties.

For the function f defined by $f(x) = \log_b x$ $(b > 0, b \neq 1)$,

$$f(1) = \log_b 1 = 0$$
$$f(b) = \log_b b = 1$$
$$f(b^x) = \log_b b^x = x$$
$$f\left(\frac{1}{u}\right) = \log_b \frac{1}{u} = -\log_b u$$
$$f(uv) = \log_b(uv) = \log_b u + \log_b v$$
$$f\left(\frac{u}{v}\right) = \log_b\left(\frac{u}{v}\right) = \log_b u - \log_b v$$
$$f(u^p) = \log_b(u^p) = p\log_b u$$

Change-of-base formula: $f(x) = \log_b x = \dfrac{\log_a x}{\log_a b} = \dfrac{\ln x}{\ln b} = \dfrac{\log_{10} x}{\log_{10} b}$ $(a > 0, a \neq 1)$

One-to-one property: $f(u) = f(v)$ if and only if $u = v$; that is, $\log_b u = \log_b v$ if and only if $u = v$

Tip: Logarithms are exponents, so think about the rules for exponents when you are working with logarithms.

Note: See the chapter titled "Trigonometry" for a discussion of the trigonometric functions.

Average rate of change and difference quotient

If (x_1, y_1) and (x_2, y_2) are two distinct points on the graph of a function f, the average rate of change of f as x goes from x_1 to x_2 is given by $\dfrac{\Delta y}{\Delta x} = \dfrac{y_2 - y_1}{x_2 - x_1} = \dfrac{f(x_2) - f(x_1)}{x_2 - x_1}$, where Δy is the change in y values and Δx is the change in x values. The average rate of change measures the "speed," *on average*, at which a function is changing over an interval of its domain. Here is an example.

Find the average rate of change of $f(x) = x^2$ on the interval $[1, 4]$.

$$\frac{\Delta y}{\Delta x} = \frac{f(x_2) - f(x_1)}{x_2 - x_1} = \frac{f(4) - f(1)}{4 - 1} = \frac{4^2 - 1^2}{3} = \frac{15}{3} = 5$$

If $(x + h, f(x + h))$ and $(x, f(x))$ are two ordered pairs in a function f, the difference quotient is the expression $\dfrac{f(x+h) - f(x)}{(x+h) - (x)} = \dfrac{f(x+h) - f(x)}{h}$, where $h \neq 0$. The difference quotient is the average rate of change of f as x goes from x to $x + h$.

Find and simplify the difference quotient for $f(x) = x^2$.

$$\frac{f(x+h) - f(x)}{h} = \frac{(x+h)^2 - (x)^2}{h} = \frac{x^2 + 2xh + h^2 - x^2}{h} = \frac{2xh + h^2}{h} = 2x + h$$

Composition and Inverses of Functions

For this topic, you must be able to determine the composition of two functions, find the inverse of a one-to-one function in simple cases, and know why only one-to-one functions have inverses (*Mathematics: Content Knowledge (0061) Test at a Glance*, page 4).

Arithmetic of Functions and Composition

Suppose that both $f(x)$ and $g(x)$ exist. For all real numbers x such that $x \in D_f \cap D_g$, the following definitions for the arithmetic of functions hold:

> the sum of f and g is the function $f + g$, defined by $(f + g)(x) = f(x) + g(x)$;
>
> the difference of f and g is the function $f - g$, defined by $(f - g)(x) = f(x) - g(x)$;
>
> the product of f and g is the function fg, defined by $(fg)(x) = f(x) \cdot g(x)$; and
>
> the quotient of f and g is the function $\dfrac{f}{g}$, defined by $\dfrac{f}{g}(x) = \dfrac{f(x)}{g(x)}$, where $g(x) \neq 0$.

Here is an example.

Let $f(x) = x^2 + 1$ and $g(x) = \sqrt{x} - 3$. (a) Find the domain of $\dfrac{f}{g}$, and (b) write a simplified expression for $\left(\dfrac{f}{g}\right)(x)$.

(a) The domain of $\dfrac{f}{g}$ must exclude negative values of x and also values of x for which $g(x) = \sqrt{x} - 3 = 0$. Solving $\sqrt{x} - 3 = 0$ yields $x = 9$, so the domain of $\dfrac{f}{g}$ is $\{x | x \geq 0, x \neq 9\}$.

(b) $\left(\dfrac{f}{g}\right)(x) = \dfrac{f(x)}{g(x)} = \dfrac{x^2 + 1}{\sqrt{x} - 3}$

The composition of f and g is the function $f \circ g$ defined by $(f \circ g)(x) = f(g(x))$, provided that $g(x) \in D_f$. (Note: Read $f(g(x))$ as "f of g of x.") The domain of $f \circ g$ is all x in the domain of g such that $g(x)$ is defined and $g(x)$ is in the domain of f. Here are examples.

If $f = \{(-3, -5), (-2, -4), (0, -5), (1, 3), (2, 0), (4, 7)\}$ and $g = \{(-4, 8), (-3, -8), (-2, -3), (0, 1), (1, 4)\}$ find (a) $f \circ g$ and (b) $g \circ f$ and, if possible, evaluate (c) $(f \circ g)(1)$ and (d) $(g \circ f)(-3)$.

> (a) $f \circ g = \{(-2, -5), (0, 3), (1, 7)\}$
>
> (b) $g \circ f = \{(-2, 8), (2, 1)\}$
>
> (c) $(f \circ g)(1) = f(g(1)) = f(4) = 7$
>
> (d) $(g \circ f)(-3) = g(f(-3)) = g(-5) =$ undefined because -5 is not in the domain of g.

Let $f(x) = x^2$ and $g(x) = \sqrt{x+3}$. (a) Determine the domain of $f \circ g$, (b) write a simplified expression for $(f \circ g)(x)$, and (c) if possible, evaluate $(f \circ g)(6)$, $(f \circ g)(-1)$, and $(f \circ g)(-6)$.

> (a) The domain of $f \circ g$ is all x in the domain of g such that $g(x)$ is defined and $g(x)$ is in the domain of f. The function g defined by $g(x) = \sqrt{x+3}$ has the domain $D_g = \{x | x \geq -3\}$. In the composition, $g(x)$ must be in the domain of f. The domain of f is all real numbers, so $g(x)$ is definitely in the domain of f. Therefore, the domain of $f \circ g$ is the same as the domain of g; that is, the domain of $f \circ g = \{x | x \geq -3\}$.
>
> (b) $(f \circ g)(x) = f(g(x)) = f(\sqrt{x+3}) = (\sqrt{x+3})^2 = x+3, \; x \geq -3$
>
> (c) $(f \circ g)(6) = f(g(6)) = f(\sqrt{6+3}) = f(\sqrt{9}) = f(3) = 3^2 = 9$
>
> $(f \circ g)(-1) = f(g(-1)) = f(\sqrt{-1+3}) = f(\sqrt{2}) = (\sqrt{2})^2 = 2$
>
> $(f \circ g)(-6)$ is undefined because -6 is not in the domain of $f \circ g$.

Note: Composition of functions is not commutative; that is, in general, $(f \circ g)(x) \neq (g \circ f)(x)$.

Also, the product function fg is fundamentally different from the composition function $f \circ g$. For instance, if $f(x) = 3x$ and $g(x) = x^2$, $fg(x) = f(x) \cdot g(x) = (3x) \cdot (x^2) = 3x^3$; but $(f \circ g)(x) = f(g(x)) = f(x^2) = 3(x^2) = 3x^2$.

Inverses of Functions

If f is a one-to-one function, its inverse, denoted f^{-1} (read "f inverse"), is the function such that $(f^{-1} \circ f)(x) = x$ for all x in the domain of f and $(f \circ f^{-1})(x) = x$ for all x in the domain of f^{-1}, and $R_{f^{-1}} = D_f$ and $R_f = D_{f^{-1}}$. Graphically, f^{-1} is a reflection of f over the line $y = x$.

Tip: Do not interpret f^{-1} to mean $\dfrac{1}{f}$. The $^{-1}$ that is attached to f is not an exponent; it is a notation that denotes the inverse of a function.

If a function f defined by a set of ordered pairs is one-to-one, then you can find f^{-1} by interchanging x and y in each of the ordered pairs of f. Here is an example.

Given $f = \{(-1, 2), (3, 5), (6, -1)\}$, find f^{-1}.

$$f^{-1} = \{(2, -1), (5, 3), (-1, 6)\}$$

If a function is one-to-one, its inverse exists. When a one-to-one function f is defined by an equation, two ways you can find the equation of f^{-1} are the following.

Method 1. Set $(f \circ f^{-1})(x) = x$ and solve for $f^{-1}(x)$. Here is an example.

Given $y = f(x) = 3x$, find $f^{-1}(x)$.

$$(f \circ f^{-1})(x) = x$$
$$f(f^{-1}(x)) = x$$
$$3f^{-1}(x) = x$$
$$f^{-1}(x) = \frac{x}{3}$$

Method 2. First, interchange x and y in $y = f(x)$, and then solve $x = f(y)$ for y. Here is an example.

Given $y = f(x) = 3x$, find $f^{-1}(x)$.

First, interchanging x and y gives $x = 3y$. Next, solving for y gives $\frac{x}{3} = y$ or $y = \frac{x}{3}$. Thus, $y = f^{-1}(x) = \frac{x}{3}$, the same as obtained through Method 1.

Only one-to-one functions have inverses that are functions. However, when a function f is not one-to-one, it might be possible to restrict its domain so that f is one-to-one in the restricted domain. Then, f will have an inverse function in the restricted domain.

Modeling with Functions

For this topic you must be able to find an appropriate family of functions to model particular phenomena (for example: population growth, cooling, simple harmonic motion) (*Mathematics: Content Knowledge (0061) Test at a Glance*, page 4).

Some common families of functions that are used to model phenomena in the real world are the families of linear functions, quadratic functions, exponential functions, and trigonometric functions.

Linear functions model processes in which the rate of change is constant. For instance, a linear function can be used to describe the distance a moving object travels at a constant rate of speed.

Quadratic functions are used to model processes that involve a maximum or a minimum value. For instance, in business a quadratic function can be used to model a company's profit or revenue, which depends on the number of units sold.

Exponential functions are used to model physical phenomena such as population growth and population decay. This family of functions is also used in business for determining the growth of money when interest is compounded.

Trigonometric functions are used to model periodic processes. For example, physical phenomena such as light waves, sound waves, and the movement of a pendulum or a weight attached to a coiled spring can be modeled using the trigonometric sine or cosine function.

Here is an example of modeling with functions.

A homeowner has 100 feet of fencing to enclose a rectangular region for a small garden. The homeowner will use a portion of the side of a large shed as one side of the rectangle, as shown in the following figure.

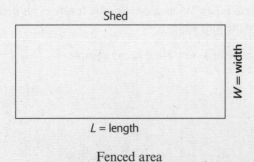

Fenced area

Let $f(W)$ be the area of the rectangular region expressed in terms of its width, W.

(a) Write a formula for $f(W)$.

(b) Find the dimensions of the rectangle that give the maximum area for the garden.

(c) The fence does not go along the shed, so (omitting units)

$100 = 2W + L$; thus, $L = 100 - 2W$.

The area of the rectangular region equals length times width, thus,

$$f(W) = (100 - 2W)W = 100W - 2W^2 = -2W^2 + 100W, \text{ a quadratic function.}$$

The graph of $f(W)$ is a parabola opening downward. The vertex formula is $\left(-\dfrac{b}{2a}, f\left(-\dfrac{b}{2a}\right)\right)$, so the maximum value for $f(W)$ occurs when $W = -\dfrac{b}{2a} = -\dfrac{100}{2(-2)} = 25$ feet. The corresponding length is $L = 100 - 2W = 100 - 2 \cdot 25 = 100 - 50 = 50$ feet. The dimensions that maximize the area are 50 feet by 25 feet.

Functions of Two Variables

For this topic, you must be able to interpret representations of functions of two variables, such as three-dimensional graphs, level curves, and tables (*Mathematics: Content Knowledge (0061) Test at a Glance*, page 4).

A real-valued function of two variables is a function f that associates with each pair (x, y) of real numbers of a set $D_f \subseteq R^2$ one and only one real number $z = f(x, y)$. The set D_f is the domain of f, and the set of all real numbers $z = f(x, y)$ is D_f, the range of f.

As with functions of one variable, functions of two variables can be represented numerically (using a table of values), algebraically (using a formula), and sometimes graphically (using a graph).

The graph of the function f of two variables is the set of all points $(x, y, f(x, y))$ defining a region or curved surface in three-dimensional space, where we restrict the values of (x, y) to lie in the domain of f. In other words, the graph is the set of all points (x, y, z) with $z = f(x, y)$.

Chapter 7

Calculus

According to the *Mathematics Content Knowledge Test at a Glance,* (www.ets.org/Media/Tests/PRAXIS/pdf/0061. pdf), the Calculus content category of the Mathematics CK tests your knowledge and skills in nine topic areas:

- Limits
- Derivatives
- Continuity
- Analyzing the behavior of a function
- The Mean Value Theorem and the Fundamental Theorem of Calculus
- Integration as a limiting sum
- Differentiation and integration techniques
- Numerical approximation of derivatives and integrals
- Limits of sequences and series

This review will discuss the key ideas and formulas in each topic area that are most important for you to know for the Mathematics CK.

Limits

For this topic, you must demonstrate an understanding of what it means for a function to have a limit at a point, calculate limits of functions or determine that the limit does not exist, and solve problems using the properties of limits (*Mathematics: Content Knowledge (0061) Test at a Glance*, page 4).

The study of calculus begins with the study of limits. For the Mathematics CK, the following definitions and properties of limit are essential to know.

Definition of Limit

Let f be a function defined on an open interval containing a, except possibly at a, then the $\lim_{x \to a} f(x) = L$ (read "the limit of f as x approaches a equals L") if for every number $\varepsilon > 0$, there exists a number $\delta > 0$ such that if $0 < |x - a| < \delta$, then $|f(x) - L| < \varepsilon$ for every x in the domain of f. That is, a function f has a limit L as x approaches a, written, $\lim_{x \to a} f(x) = L$, provided the error between $f(x)$ and L, written $|f(x) = L|$, can be made less than any pre-assigned positive number ε whenever x is close to, but not equal to, a.

The limit $\lim_{x \to a} f(x) = L$ *exists* only if the following conditions are satisfied: (i) the limit L is a single finite real number; and (ii) the limit as x approaches a from the left equals the limit as x approaches a from the right; that is, $\lim_{x \to a^-} f(x) = \lim_{x \to a^+} f(x)$. If no such L exists, then the $\lim_{x \to a} f(x)$ *does not exist*. Common situations that occur when the limit of a function f as x approaches a does *not* exist are (i) $\lim_{x \to a^-} f(x) \ne \lim_{x \to a^+} f(x)$, (ii) $f(x)$ increases or decreases without bound as x approaches a, or (iii) $f(x)$ oscillates between two fixed values as x approaches a. Here is an example.

Determine $\lim_{x \to 5} \dfrac{10}{x - 5}$.

From the limit definition you know that $\lim_{x \to 5} \dfrac{10}{x - 5}$ can exist only if $\dfrac{10}{x - 5}$ approaches a single finite value as x approaches 5 from either the left or right. As x approaches 5 from the left, the number $\dfrac{10}{x - 5}$ is decreasing without bound; symbolically, you indicate this behavior as $\lim_{x \to 5^-} \dfrac{10}{x - 5} = -\infty$. As x approaches 5 from the right, the number $\dfrac{10}{x-5}$ is increasing without bound, indicated as $\lim\limits_{x\to 5^+}\dfrac{10}{x-5}=\infty$. Since $\dfrac{10}{x-5}$ does not approach a single finite value as x approaches 5 from either the left or right of 5, $\lim\limits_{x\to 5}\dfrac{10}{x-5}$ does not exist.

Intuitively, the "$\varepsilon-\delta$" definition of limit means that if the values of $f(x)$ get arbitrarily close to a single value L as x approaches a from either side, then $\lim\limits_{x\to a}f(x)=L$. When $\lim\limits_{x\to a}f(x)$ exists, the limit is unique. Furthermore, its value is independent of the value of f at a. When $\lim\limits_{x\to a}f(x)$ exists, three situations might occur at a: (i) $f(a)=\lim\limits_{x\to a}f(x)$, (ii) $f(a)$ is undefined, or (iii) $f(a)$ is defined, but $f(a)\neq\lim\limits_{x\to a}f(x)$. Here is an example.

Determine $\lim\limits_{x\to 5}(x^2+3)$ using an intuitive approach.

If x gets very close to but unequal to 5 in value, either from the left or right, x^2+3 is very close to 28 in value. (For instance, when $x=4.99$, $x^2+3=27.9001$; and when $x=5.01$, $x^2+3=28.1001$.) Thus, x^2+3 approaches a single finite value, namely 28, as x approaches 5 from either the left or right. Therefore, $\lim\limits_{x\to 5}(x^2+3)=28$.

Limits of Continuous Functions

Notice that in the limit concept, x *cannot* take on the value of a. Therefore, you must be cautious about assuming that $\lim\limits_{x\to a}f(x)=f(a)$; that is, that you determine the limit by substituting $x=a$ into the expression that defines $f(x)$ and then evaluating. However, when a function is continuous at a point a, you have the situation whereby the limit *can* be calculated by actually evaluating the function at the point a. Thus, when a function f is *continuous* at $x=a$, then $\lim\limits_{x\to a}f(x)=f(a)$, so you can find the limit by direct substitution (see "Continuity" in this chapter for a discussion of the term *continuous*). Here are some common limits that can be evaluated using direct substitution.

$$\lim_{x\to a}b=b$$

$$\lim_{x\to a}x=a$$

$$\lim_{x\to a}\frac{1}{x}=\frac{1}{a},\ a\neq 0$$

$$\lim_{x\to a}x^2=a^2$$

$$\lim_{x\to a}x^n=a^n,\text{ for }n\text{ a positive integer}$$

$$\lim_{x\to a}\sqrt{x}=\sqrt{a},\ a\geq 0$$

$$\lim_{x\to a}\sqrt[n]{x}=\sqrt[n]{a},\text{ for }n\text{ a positive integer with the restriction that if }n\text{ is even, }a\geq 0$$

$$\lim_{x\to a}|x|=|a|$$

If f is a polynomial function given by $f(x)=c_n x^n+c_{n-1}x^{n-1}+c_{n-2}x^{n-2}+\cdots+c_2 x^2+c_1 x+c_0$, then $\lim\limits_{x\to a}f(x)=c_n a^n+c_{n-1}a^{n-1}+c_{n-2}a^{n-2}+\cdots+c_2 a^2+c_1 a+c_0$.

If f is a rational function given by $f(x)=\dfrac{p(x)}{q(x)}$, $\lim\limits_{x\to a}f(x)=\dfrac{p(a)}{q(a)}$, provided $q(a)\neq 0$.

$\lim\limits_{x\to a}e^x=e^a$ and $\lim\limits_{x\to a}b^x=b^a$, $b>0$, $b\neq 1$

$\lim\limits_{x\to a}\ln x=\ln a$ and $\lim\limits_{x\to a}\log_b x=\log_b a$, $b>0$, $b\neq 1$

For a in the domain of the function,

$$\lim_{x\to a}\sin x=\sin a \qquad \lim_{x\to a}\csc x=\csc a$$

$$\lim_{x\to a}\cos x=\cos a \qquad \lim_{x\to a}\sec x=\sec a$$

$$\lim_{x\to a}\tan x=\tan a \qquad \lim_{x\to a}\cot x=\cot a$$

Here are examples.

$$\lim_{x \to 5} \frac{1}{x} = \frac{1}{5}$$

$$\lim_{x \to 3} x^4 = 3^4 = 81$$

$$\lim_{x \to 36} \sqrt{x} = \sqrt{36} = 6$$

$$\lim_{x \to 32} \log_2 x = \log_2 32 = 5$$

$$\lim_{x \to 3} 4^x = 4^3 = 64$$

$$\lim_{x \to \frac{\pi}{6}} \sin x = \sin\left(\frac{\pi}{6}\right) = \frac{1}{2}$$

Limit of a composite function: If f and g are functions such that g is continuous at a and f is continuous at $g(a)$, then $\lim_{x \to a} f \circ g(x) = \lim_{x \to a} f(g(x)) = f\left(\lim_{x \to a} g(x)\right) = f(g(a))$.

Here is an example with $f(x) = |x|$ and $g(x) = \tan x$.

$$\lim_{x \to \frac{7\pi}{4}} |\tan x| = \left|\lim_{x \to \frac{7\pi}{4}} \tan x\right| = |-1| = 1$$

L'Hôpital's Rule

If $\lim_{x \to a} p(x) = 0$ and $\lim_{x \to a} q(x) = 0$, then direct substitution into $\lim_{x \to a} \frac{p(x)}{q(x)}$ yields $\frac{0}{0}$, which is an indeterminate form. When this problem occurs, try factoring $x - a$ from $p(x)$ and $q(x)$, reducing the algebraic fraction $\frac{p(x)}{q(x)}$, and then finding the limit of the resulting expression, if it exists. Here is an example.

$$\lim_{x \to 4} \frac{x^2 - 16}{x - 4} = \lim_{x \to 4} \frac{(x+4)(x-4)}{(x-4)} = \lim_{x \to 4} (x + 4) = 8$$

Another way to approach problems of this type is to apply L'Hôpital's rule, which says that if p and q are differentiable (see "Derivatives" in this chapter for a discussion of derivatives and the term *differentiable*) at every number x in an open interval I, except possibly at a, and $\lim_{x \to a} p(x) = 0 = \lim_{x \to a} q(x) = 0$, then $\lim_{x \to a} \frac{p(x)}{q(x)} = \lim_{x \to a} \frac{p'(x)}{q'(x)}$, provided $q'(x) \neq 0$ for all $x \neq a$ in I and $\lim_{x \to a} \frac{p'(x)}{q'(x)}$ exists. (Note: $p'(x)$ and $q'(x)$ are the derivatives of p and q, respectively. The term *derivative* is explained in the next section, "Derivatives.") L'Hôpital's rule also applies when $\lim_{x \to a} p(x) = \pm\infty$ and $\lim_{x \to a} q(x) = \pm\infty$.

Here are examples (refer to "Differentiation Formulas" in this chapter).

$$\lim_{x \to 4} \frac{x^2 - 16}{x - 4} = \lim_{x \to 4} \frac{D_x(x^2 - 16)}{D_x(x - 4)} = \lim_{x \to 4} \frac{2x}{1} = 8$$

$$\lim_{x \to 0} \frac{\sin x}{6x} = \lim_{x \to 0} \frac{D_x(\sin x)}{D_x(6x)} = \lim_{x \to 0} \frac{\cos x}{6} = \frac{1}{6}$$

Note: $D_x f(x) = f'(x)$

A word of caution: If you use your graphing calculator to help you evaluate a limit as the variable approaches a particular value, you run the risk of obtaining an incorrect answer. Remember, you cannot always trust the sketch of a function produced by your graphing calculator. For instance, for some graphing calculators, the graph of $y = \sin\left(\dfrac{1}{x}\right)$ at values near x equal 0 is incorrect. Thus, using your graphing calculator to aid in finding $\lim\limits_{x \to 0} \sin\left(\dfrac{1}{x}\right)$ likely would lead you to a completely wrong conclusion.

Assuming that the functions f and g have limits that exist as x approaches a, the following fundamental properties have to do with the limits of various combinations of f and g.

Properties of Limits

Sum or Difference:	$\lim\limits_{x \to a}\left[f(x) \pm g(x)\right] = \lim\limits_{x \to a} f(x) \pm \lim\limits_{x \to a} g(x)$
Product:	$\lim\limits_{x \to a}\left[f(x) \cdot g(x)\right] = \lim\limits_{x \to a} f(x) \cdot \lim\limits_{x \to a} g(x)$
Quotient:	$\lim\limits_{x \to a} \dfrac{f(x)}{g(x)} = \dfrac{\lim\limits_{x \to a} f(x)}{\lim\limits_{x \to a} g(x)}$, provided $g(x) \ne 0$ and $\lim\limits_{x \to a} g(x) \ne 0$
Power:	$\left[\lim\limits_{x \to a} f(x)\right]^n = \left[\lim\limits_{x \to a} f(x)\right]^n$
Root:	$\lim\limits_{x \to a} \sqrt[n]{f(x)} = \sqrt[n]{\lim\limits_{x \to a} f(x)}$ for n a positive integer, provided $\lim\limits_{x \to a} f(x) \ge 0$ when n is even
Scalar Multiplication:	$\lim\limits_{x \to a} k\, f(x) = k \lim\limits_{x \to a} f(x)$, for any real number k

Here are examples:

$$\lim_{x \to 2} \frac{3x-5}{5x+2} = \frac{\lim\limits_{x \to 2}(3x-5)}{\lim\limits_{x \to 2}(5x+2)} = \frac{\lim\limits_{x \to 2} 3x - \lim\limits_{x \to 2} 5}{\lim\limits_{x \to 2} 5x + \lim\limits_{x \to 2} 2} = \frac{3\lim\limits_{x \to 2} x - \lim\limits_{x \to 2} 5}{5\lim\limits_{x \to 2} x + \lim\limits_{x \to 2} 2} = \frac{3 \cdot 2 - 5}{5 \cdot 2 + 2} = \frac{1}{12}$$

$$\lim_{x \to 4}\left(3x + \sqrt{16x}\right) = \lim_{x \to 4} 3x + \lim_{x \to 4} \sqrt{16x} = 3\lim_{x \to 4} x + \sqrt{\lim_{x \to 4} 16x} = 3\lim_{x \to 4} x + \sqrt{16\lim_{x \to 4} x} =$$

$$3 \cdot 4 + \sqrt{16 \cdot 4} = 12 + \sqrt{64} = 20$$

Derivatives

For this topic, you must demonstrate an understanding of the derivative of a function as a limit, as the slope of a curve, and as a rate of change (for example: velocity, acceleration, growth, decay) (*Mathematics: Content Knowledge (0061) Test at a Glance*, page 4).

Definition of Derivative

The derivative f' (read "f prime") of the function f at the number x is defined as $f'(x) = \lim\limits_{x \to 0} \dfrac{f(x+h) - f(x)}{h}$, if this limit exists. If this limit does not exist, then f does not have a derivative at x. Here is an example.

Given the function f defined by $f(x) = -2x + 3$, use the definition of the derivative to find $f'(x)$.

$$f'(x) = \lim_{h \to 0} \frac{f(x+h) - f(x)}{h} = \lim_{h \to 0} \frac{(-2(x+h)+3) - (-2x+3)}{h} =$$

$$\lim_{h \to 0} \frac{(-2x-2h+3)+2x-3}{h} = \lim_{h \to 0} \frac{-2x-2h+3+2x-3}{h} = \lim_{h \to 0} \frac{-2h}{h} = \lim_{h \to 0}(-2) = -2$$

A *differentiable* function is a function that has a derivative. If $f'(c)$ exists, then f is differentiable at c; otherwise, f does not have a derivative at c. Various symbols are used to represent the derivative of a function f. For the notation $y = f(x)$, you can symbolize the derivative of f by $f'(x)$, $\frac{dy}{dx}$, $D_x f(x)$, y', $D_x y$, or $\frac{d}{dx} f(x)$.

The derivative $f'(x)$ is the first derivative of f. The derivative of $f'(x)$ is the second derivative of f and is denoted $f''(x)$. Similarly, the derivative of $f''(x)$ is the third derivative of f and is denoted $f'''(x)$. In general, the nth derivative of f is denoted $f^{(n)}(x)$.

Slope of Tangent Line and Instantaneous Rate of Change

If $f'(a)$ exists, then the slope of the tangent line to the graph of the function f at the point $P(a, f(a))$ is the line through P that has slope $m = f'(a)$. Here is an example.

Find the slope of the tangent line to the parabola $y = f(x) = x^2 + 1$ at the point $(2, 5)$.

Given that $f(x) = x^2 + 1$, then $f'(x) = 2x$.

Therefore, the slope at point $(2, 5) = m = f'(2) = 4$. See figure.

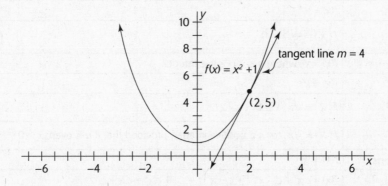

Slope of Tangent Line to $f(x) = x^2 + 1$ at $(2, 5)$

If $f'(t)$ exists, then the (instantaneous) rate of change of f at t is $f'(t)$. For example, if $s(t)$ is the position function of a moving object, then the velocity (the instantaneous rate of change) of the object at time t is $s'(t)$. Additionally, the acceleration of the object at time t is $s''(t)$. Here is an example (refer to "Differentiation Formulas" in this chapter).

Suppose $s(t) = 100t^2 + 100t$ describes the motion (in feet) of a moving object as a function of time t (in seconds). Find the velocity (in feet per second) and acceleration (in feet per second^2) of the object at time $t = 2$ seconds.

Velocity $= s'(t) = 200t + 100$, so at time $t = 2$ seconds, velocity $= s'(2) = 200(2) + 100 = 500$ feet per second.

Acceleration $= s''(t) = 200$, so at time $t = 2$ seconds, acceleration $= 200$ feet per second^2.

Continuity

For this topic, you must be able to show that a particular function is continuous and demonstrate an understanding of the relationship between continuity and differentiability (*Mathematics: Content Knowledge (0061) Test at a Glance*, page 4).

Definition of Continuous Function

The function f is continuous at the point $x = a$ in the domain of f if *all three* of the following conditions are met: (i) $f(a)$ is defined; (ii) $\lim_{x \to a} f(x)$ exists; and (iii) $\lim_{x \to a} f(x) = f(a)$; otherwise, the function f is discontinuous at x. Here are examples.

Given $f(x) = \sqrt{2x+17}$, is f continuous at $x = 4$?

$\lim_{x \to 4} \sqrt{2x+17} = \sqrt{\lim_{x \to 4}(2x+17)} = \sqrt{25} = 5$ exists and is equal to $f(4) = \sqrt{2 \cdot 4 + 17} = \sqrt{25} = 5$; therefore, f is continuous at 4.

Given $g(x) = \dfrac{15}{x-2}$, is g continuous at $x = 2$?

$\lim_{x \to 2} \dfrac{15}{x-2}$ does not exist; thus, g is discontinuous at 2.

A function f is continuous in an open interval if it is continuous at each point in the interval. If a function is continuous on the entire real line, the function is everywhere continuous; that is to say, its graph has no holes, jumps, or gaps in it.

Common Continuous Functions

The following types of functions are continuous at every point in their domains.

Constant functions:	$f(x) = k$, where k is a constant
Identity function:	$f(x) = x$
Reciprocal functions:	$f(x) = \dfrac{1}{x}, x \neq 0$
Power functions:	$f(x) = x^n$, where n is a positive integer
Quadratic functions:	$f(x) = x^2$
Square root functions:	$f(x) = \sqrt{x}, x \geq 0$
Radical functions:	$f(x) = \sqrt[n]{x}$, for n a positive integer, provided that if n is even, $x \geq 0$
Absolute value functions:	$f(x) = |x|$
Polynomial functions:	$f(x) = c_n x^n + c_{n-1} x^{n-1} + c_{n-2} x^{n-2} + \ldots + c_2 x^2 + c_1 x + c_0$
Rational functions:	$f(x) = \dfrac{p(x)}{q(x)}, q(x) \neq 0$
Exponential functions:	$f(x) = b^x, b > 0, b \neq 1$
Logarithmic functions:	$f(x) = \log_b x, b > 0, b \neq 1$
Trigonometric functions:	$f(x) = \sin x$, $f(x) = \cos x$, $f(x) = \tan x$, $f(x) = \csc x$, $f(x) = \cot x$, and $f(x) = \sec x$

Properties of Continuity

If f and g are continuous at $x = a$, then the following functions are also continuous at $x = a$.

Sum and difference:	$f \pm g$
Product:	fg
Scalar multiple:	kf, for k a real number
Quotient:	$\dfrac{f}{g}, g(a) \neq 0$
Composition:	If g is continuous at a and f is continuous at $g(a)$, then $f \circ g(x) = f(g(x))$ is continuous at a.

If a function f is differentiable at $x = a$, then f is continuous at $x = a$; in other words, *differentiability implies continuity*. Therefore, if f is *not* continuous at $x = a$, then f is also *not* differentiable at $x = a$. Caution: Continuity does *not* imply differentiability. A function can be continuous at a point $x = a$ even though $f'(x)$ does not exist at $x = a$. This circumstance occurs when there is a cusp (a sharp corner) or a vertical tangent line at a. For instance, the absolute value function (shown below) is continuous at $x = 0$, however $f'(x)$ does not exist at $x = 0$.

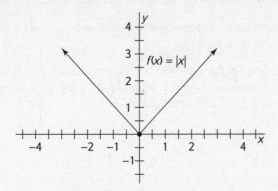

Absolute Value Function

Analyzing the Behavior of a Function

For this topic, you must be able to analyze the behavior of a function (for example: find relative maxima and minima, concavity), solve problems involving related rates, and solve applied minima-maxima problems (*Mathematics: Content Knowledge (0061) Test at a Glance*, page 4).

Increasing and Decreasing Behavior

If f is continuous on a closed interval $[a, b]$ and differentiable on the open interval (a, b), then (i) f is increasing on $[a, b]$ if $f'(x) > 0$ on (a, b), (ii) f is decreasing on $[a, b]$ if $f'(x) < 0$ on (a, b), and (iii) f is constant on $[a, b]$ if $f'(x) = 0$ on (a, b). Here is an example.

Describe the behavior of the function f defined by $f(x) = x^2 + 1$ in the interval $[-3, 3]$.

The function f defined by $f(x) = x^2 + 1$ is a quadratic function, so it is everywhere continuous. Given $f(x) = x^2 + 1$, then $f'(x) = 2x$. For any $x \in (-3, 0)$, $f'(x) = 2x < 0$; and for any $x \in (0, 3)$, $f'(x) = 2x > 0$. Therefore, f is decreasing on $(-3, 0)$ and increasing on $(0, 3)$.

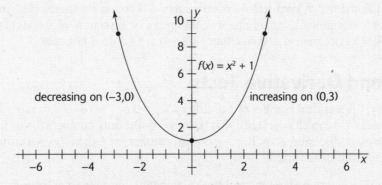

Increasing and Decreasing Behavior of $f(x) = x^2 + 1$

Extrema and the Extreme Value Theorem

Let f be defined on an interval containing c. The value $f(c)$ is a minimum (also called the absolute minimum) of f in the interval if $f(c) \leq f(x)$ for every number x in the interval; similarly, $f(c)$ is a maximum (also called the absolute maximum) of f in the interval if $f(c) \geq f(x)$ for every number x in the interval. The minimum and maximum values of a function in an interval are the extreme values, or extrema, of the function in the interval.

The Extreme Value Theorem states that if f is continuous on a closed interval $[a, b]$, then f has both a minimum and a maximum value in $[a, b]$. Here is an example.

Describe the extrema for the function f defined by $f(x) = x^3$ on the interval $[-2, 2]$. The function f defined by $f(x) = x^3$ is everywhere continuous, so it is continuous in the interval $[-2, 2]$. By the Extreme Value Theorem, f has a minimum and a maximum value in $[-2, 2]$. The minimum value is $f(-2) = (-2)^3 = -8$ and the maximum value is $f(2) = (2)^3 = 8$. See the figure.

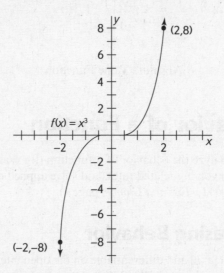

Minimum and Maximum Behavior of $f(x) = x^3$ on the interval $[-2, 2]$

> **Tip:** The Extreme Value Theorem tells you when the minimum and maximum of a function exist, but not how to find these values. You can use your graphing calculator's minimum-maximum feature to find the extreme values of a function.

The number $f(c)$ is a relative minimum of a function f if there exists an open interval containing c in which $f(c)$ is a minimum; similarly, the number $f(c)$ is a relative maximum of a function f if there exists an open interval containing c in which $f(c)$ is a maximum. If $f(c)$ is a relative minimum or maximum of f, it is called a relative extremum of f. If f has a relative extremum at c, then either $f'(c) = 0$ or $f'(c)$ does not exist.

First and Second Derivative Tests

If c is in the domain of f, c is a critical number of f if either $f'(c) = 0$ or $f'(c)$ does not exist. The critical numbers determine points at which $f'(x)$ can change signs; that is, these are the only numbers for which the graph of f can have turning points, cusps, or discontinuities. If c is a critical number for f, then $f(c)$ is a critical value of f and the point $(c, f(c))$ is a critical point of the graph.

A sign diagram for $f'(x)$ is a diagram along the real line showing the signs for $f'(x)$ between critical numbers for f. You can use a sign diagram to predict the shape of the graph of f.

The First Derivative Test provides that if c is a critical number of a function f that is continuous on an open interval I containing c, then (i) if $f'(x)$ changes sign at c from negative (for x values in I less than c) to positive (for x values in I greater than c), then $f(c)$ is a relative minimum of f; and (ii) if $f'(x)$ changes sign at c from positive (for x values in I less than c) to negative (for x values in I greater than c), then $f(c)$ is a relative maximum of f.

The Second Derivative Test provides that if c is a critical number of f and $f''(c)$ exists on an open interval containing c, then (i) $f(c)$ is a relative minimum of f if $f''(c) > 0$, and (ii) $f(c)$ is a relative maximum of f if $f''(c) < 0$. If $f''(c) = 0$, the test is inconclusive.

Concavity

If f is a function whose first and second derivatives exist on some open interval containing the number c, then (i) the graph of f is concave upward at $(c, f(c))$ if $f''(c) > 0$, and (ii) the graph of f is concave downward at $(c, f(c))$ if $f''(c) < 0$. The point $(c, f(c))$ is a point of inflection if the concavity of the graph of f changes at $(c, f(c))$. If a graph has an inflection point at $x = c$, then either $f''(c)$ is 0 or does not exist.

A methodical way to analyze the behavior of a function is to proceed as follows: First, find the critical number(s) of f by solving $f'(c) = 0$; next, use the First Derivative Test, a sign diagram, and, if applicable, the Second Derivative Test to find relative extrema; and then use $f''(c)$, if it exists, to investigate concavity and identify points of inflection. Here is an example.

Given $f(x) = 2x^3 - 9x^2 + 2$, discuss critical points, the sign diagram, turning points, extrema, concavity, and points of inflection with regard to f.

Given $f(x) = 2x^3 - 9x^2 + 2$, then $f'(x) = 6x^2 - 18x$. Set $f'(x) = 6x^2 - 18x = 6x(x - 3) = 0$ to obtain $x = 0$ and $x = 3$ as critical numbers. The sign diagram for f is shown here.

	$x < 0$	$x = 0$	$0 < x < 3$	$x = 3$	$x > 3$
$f'(x)$	+	0	−	0	+
$f(x)$	increasing	2	decreasing	−25	increasing

Next, evaluate the second derivative $f''(x) = 12x - 18$ at the critical numbers to obtain $f''(0) = 12(0) - 18 = -18$ and $f''(3) = 12(3) - 18 = 18$. Thus, by the Second Derivative test, $f(0) = 2(0)^3 - 9(0)^2 + 2 = 2$ is a relative maximum because $f''(0) = -18 < 0$, and $f(3) = 2(3)^3 - 9(3)^2 + 2 = -25$ is a relative minimum because $f''(3) = 18 > 0$. For $x < 0$, $f''(x) = 12x - 18 < 0$, so the graph of f is concave downward in that interval. For $x > 3$, $f''(x) = 12x - 18 > 0$, so the graph of f is concave upward in that interval. Solving $f''(x) = 12x - 18 = 0$ yields $x = 1.5$ as a possible point of inflection. For $0 < x < 1.5$, $f''(x) = 12x - 18 < 0$, so the graph of f is concave downward from 0 to 1.5. From $1.5 < x < 3$, $f''(x) = 12x - 18 > 0$, so the graph of f is concave upward from 1.5 to 3. The concavity of the graph changes at $(1.5, -11.5)$, so $(1.5, -11.5)$ is a point of inflection. See the graph shown.

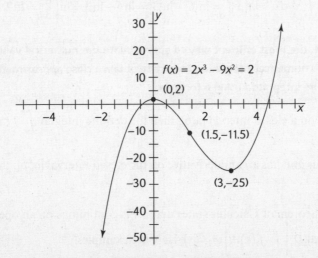

Graph of $f(x) = 2x^3 - 9x^2 + 2$

The Mean Value Theorem and the Fundamental Theorem of Calculus

For this topic, you must demonstrate an understanding of and ability to use the Mean Value Theorem and the Fundamental Theorem of Calculus (*Mathematics: Content Knowledge (0061) Test at a Glance*, page 4).

The Mean Value Theorem

The Mean Value Theorem states that if the function f is continuous in the closed interval $[a, b]$ and $f'(x)$ exists on the open interval (a, b), then there exists a number c in (a, b) such that $f(b) - f(a) = (b - a)f'(c)$. Here is an example.

Find the value of c, if any, in the interval $1 \le x \le 3$ that satisfies the Mean Value Theorem for the function f defined by $f(x) = x^2$.

Find c such that $f(3) - f(1) = (3 - 1)f'(c)$. Thus, $f'(c) = \dfrac{f(3) - f(1)}{3 - 1} = \dfrac{9 - 1}{3 - 1} = 4$. Because $f'(x) = 2x$, you have $2c = 4$, which yields $c = 2$.

Fundamental Theorems of Calculus

The function F is called an antiderivative (or indefinite integral) of the function f if $F'(x) = f(x)$.

The Fundamental Theorem of Calculus states that if f is continuous on the closed interval $[a, b]$ and F is an antiderivative of f on $[a, b]$, then the evaluation of the definite integral $\int_a^b f(x)\,dx$ is given by $\int_a^b f(x)\,dx = F(b) - F(a)$. (Note: See the next section titled "Integration as a Limiting Sum" for a discussion of definite integrals.)

The following notations are used when applying the Fundamental Theorem of Calculus:
$$\int_a^b f(x)\,dx = F(b) - F(a) = F(x)\Big|_a^b = F(x)\Big]_a^b = \Big[F(x)\Big]_a^b = \Big[F(x)\Big]_{x=a}^{x=b}$$

Thus, to find the numerical value of the integral $\int_a^b f(x)\,dx$, you first find an antiderivative, say $F(x)$, for $f(x)$, evaluate that antiderivative at a and b, and then find the difference, $F(b) - F(a)$.

Here are examples (refer to "Integration Formulas" in this chapter).

$$\int_1^4 15x^2\,dx = 5x^3\Big|_1^4 = 5(4)^3 - 5(1)^3 = 320 - 5 = 315$$

$$\int_3^6 \frac{1}{x}\,dx = \ln|x|\Big|_3^6 = \ln|6| - \ln|3| = \ln 6 - \ln 3 = \ln\left(\frac{6}{3}\right) = \ln 2$$

Tip: For the Mathematics CK, the most efficient way to approximate the numerical value of a definite integral is to use your graphing calculator's numerical integration feature to obtain a close approximation of the answer—provided you are confident that f can be integrated using a formula.

If a function f is continuous on a closed interval [a,b], then the definite integral $\int_a^b f(x)\,dx$ is a unique number that always exists.

If the function f is continuous and has an antiderivative on the closed interval $[a, b]$, then the average value of f on $[a, b]$ is $\dfrac{1}{b-a}\int_a^b f(x)\,dx$.

The Second Fundamental Theorem of Calculus states that if f is continuous on an open interval containing c, then for every x in the interval $D_x\left[\int_c^x f(t)\,dt\right] = f(x)$. Here are examples.

$$D_x \int_3^x \left(3t^2 - 7\right) dt = 3x^2 - 7$$

$$D_x \int_0^x \sin t \, dt = \sin x$$

Suppose f is a continuous function in the closed interval $[0, 3]$ and $F(x) = \int_0^x f(t)\,dt$, where $0 \leq x \leq 3$, then $F'(x) = D_x \int_0^x f(t)\,dt = f(x)$. If f has the graph shown, at which of the labeled points is F increasing?

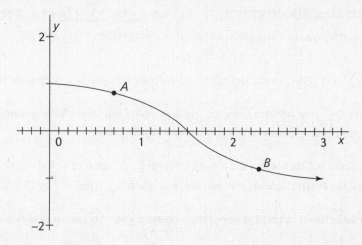

Given f is the first derivative of F, its graph tracks the slope of the tangent line to F at any point $x \in [0, 3]$. Thus, F is increasing when the graph of f is positive and decreasing when the graph of f is negative. Therefore, F is increasing at the point A.

Note: The expression $\int_c^x f(t)\,dt$ is an integral with a variable upper limit. The t appearing in this expression is called a "dummy variable" and can be replaced with any other letter not already being used.

Properties of the Definite Integral

If f is defined at $x = a$, then $\int_a^a f(x)\,dx = 0$.

If f is integrable on $[a, b]$, then $\int_a^b f(x)\,dx = -\int_b^a f(x)\,dx$.

If f is integrable on $[a, b]$ and k is a constant, then the function kf is integrable on $[a, b]$ and $\int_a^b kf(x)\,dx = k\int_a^b f(x)\,dx$.

If f and g are integrable on $[a, b]$, then the functions $f \pm g$ are integrable on $[a, b]$ and $\int_a^b \left(f(x) \pm g(x)\right) dx = \int_a^b f(x)\,dx \pm \int_a^b g(x)\,dx$.

If f is integrable on $[a, b]$, $[a, c]$, and $[c, b]$, then $\int_a^b f(x)\,dx = \int_a^c f(x)\,dx + \int_c^b f(x)\,dx$.

If f is integrable and nonnegative on $[a, b]$, then $\int_a^b f(x)\,dx \geq 0$.

If f and g are integrable on $[a, b]$, and $f(x) \leq g(x)$ for $a \leq x \leq b$, then $\int_a^b f(x)\,dx \leq \int_a^b g(x)\,dx$.

If f is integrable on $[-a, a]$ and f is even, then $\int_{-a}^a f(x)\,dx = 2\int_0^a f(x)\,dx$.

If f is integrable on $[-a, a]$ and f is odd, then $\int_{-a}^a f(x)\,dx = 0$.

If k is a constant, then $\int_a^b k \, dx = k(b - a)$.

Integration as a Limiting Sum

For this topic, you must demonstrate an intuitive understanding of integration as a limiting sum that can be used to compute area, volume, distance, or other accumulation processes (*Mathematics: Content Knowledge (0061) Test at a Glance*, page 5).

If a function f is a continuous function defined on the closed interval $[a, b]$, then the definite integral of f from $x = a$ to $x = b$ is defined as a limiting sum given by: $\int_a^b f(x)dx = \lim_{\max \Delta x_i \to 0} \sum_{i=1}^n f(c_i) \Delta x_i$, where $[a, b]$ is divided into n subintervals (not necessarily equal), c_i is a point in the ith subinterval $[x_{i-1}, x_i]$ and $\Delta x_i = x_i - x_{i-1}$, provided this limit exists.

The limiting sum, $\lim_{\max \Delta x_i \to 0} \sum_{i=1}^n f(c_i) \Delta x_i$, in the definition of definite integral is a Riemann Sum.

> **Tip: For the Mathematics CK, you will not have to use the definition of definite integral to evaluate integrals; however, it is important that you understand integration as a limiting sum.**

If f is a nonnegative, continuous function on the closed interval $[a, b]$, then the area of the region bounded by the graph of f, the x-axis, and the vertical lines $x = a$ and $x = b$ is given by: Area $= \int_a^b f(x)dx$.

> **Tip: Your graphing calculator has a numerical integration feature you can use to find the area under a curve to a close approximation.**

If f and g are continuous functions on the closed interval $[a, b]$ and $f(x) \geq g(x)$ on $[a, b]$, then the area of the region bounded by $y = f(x)$, $y = g(x)$, and the vertical lines $x = a$ and $x = b$ is given by: Area $= \int_a^b (f(x) - g(x))dx$.

Here is an example (refer to "Integration Formulas" in this chapter).

Find the area in the first quadrant enclosed by the curves $y = x^2$ and $y = x^3$.

The graphs of $y = x^2$ and $y = x^3$ intersect when $x^2 = x^3$ (see figure below).

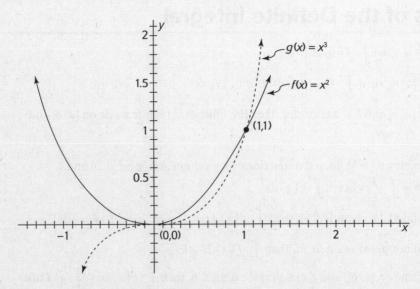

Solving this equation for x yields

$$x^2 = x^3$$
$$x^3 - x^2 = 0$$
$$x^2(x - 1) = 0$$
$$x = 0 \text{ or } x = 1$$

Since $x^2 \geq x^3$ on the interval from $x = 0$ to $x = 1$, the area enclosed by the two curves is given by

$$\int_0^1 (x^2 - x^3)\,dx = \left(\frac{x^3}{3} - \frac{x^4}{4}\right)\Bigg|_0^1 = \frac{1}{3} - \frac{1}{4} = \frac{1}{12}$$

> **Tip:** For the Mathematics CK, if asked to find the area enclosed by two curves, first, you might need to find the points of intersection of the two curves to determine a and b. Your graphing calculator has features that will allow you to find where the curves intersect, or you might elect to find the points of intersection algebraically. After determining a and b, you can numerically evaluate the integral using your calculator's numerical integration feature.

The definite integral can be used to compute area under a curve or between two curves as shown in this section. It can also be used to compute the volume of three-dimensional figures, accumulated distance, accumulated production, the total of a continuous income stream, and the results of other limiting sum processes.

Approximation of Derivatives and Integrals

For this topic, you must be able to numerically approximate derivatives and integrals (*Mathematics: Content Knowledge (0061) Test at a Glance*, page 4).

If $f'(x)$ exists, then the numerical value of f at c is $f'(c)$. Analytically, this means that to find the numerical value of the derivative of a function at a point c, you must first find the derivative of the function, and then evaluate the function at the point c. For the Mathematics CK, the most efficient way to approximate the numerical value of the derivative of a function at a point c is to use your graphing calculator's numerical derivative feature to obtain a close approximation of the answer. Check your calculator's user's guide for instructions.

For $\int_a^b f(x)\,dx = F(x)\Big]_a^b = F(b) - F(a)$, on the Mathematics CK, the most efficient way to approximate the numerical value of a definite integral is to use your graphing calculator's numerical integration feature to obtain a close approximation of the answer—provided you are confident that f can be integrated using a formula. If f is a function that cannot be integrated using a formula, a graphing calculator might give an approximation that is totally incorrect. (See the Trapezoid Rule and Simpson's Rule later in this chapter for two techniques for dealing with integrals containing functions that cannot be integrated using a formula.)

> **Tip:** For the Mathematics CK, you are expected to bring a graphing calculator that can compute both derivatives of functions numerically and definite integrals numerically. The time limitations for the test have been determined based on the assumption that you will be using such a calculator. Therefore, it is vital that you practice using your calculator's time-saving numerical derivative and numerical integration features as you encounter such problems in the practice tests in this *CliffsNotes* book so you will become adept at using these features before you take the official Mathematics CK.

You should be aware that some functions cannot be integrated by using a formula. In addition to the Riemann sum formula, the following two techniques are numerical integration methods that can be used to approximate a definite integral for a function f that is continuous on a closed interval $[a, b]$.

Trapezoid Rule: $\int_a^b f(x)dx \approx \dfrac{b-a}{2n}\Big[f(x_0)+2f(x_1)+2f(x_2)+\cdots+2f(x_{n-1})+f(x_n)\Big]$ where $[a, b]$ is divided into n subdivisions.

Simpson's Rule: $\int_a^b f(x)dx \approx \dfrac{b-a}{3n}\Big[f(x_0)+4f(x_1)+2f(x_2)+4f(x_3)+\cdots+2f(x_{n-2})+4f(x_{n-1})+f(x_n)\Big]$, where $[a, b]$ is divided into an even number n of equal subdivisions.

Differentiation and Integration Techniques

For this topic, you must be able to use standard differentiation and integration techniques (*Mathematics: Content Knowledge (0061) Test at a Glance*, page 4).

The process of finding a derivative is called differentiation. You will need to know the following differentiation formulas for the Mathematics CK test.

Differentiation Formulas

$D_x k = 0$, for k a real number $\qquad D_x x = 1 \qquad\qquad D_x x^n = nx^{n-1}$, for n a rational number

$D_x \sin x = \cos x \qquad\qquad D_x \cos x = \sin x \qquad D_x \tan x = \sec^2 x$

$D_x \sec x = \sec x \tan x \qquad\quad D_x \csc x = -\csc x \cot x \qquad D_x \cot x = -\csc^2 x$

$D_x \ln x = \dfrac{1}{x}, x > 0 \qquad\qquad D_x e^x = e^x$

If f and g are differentiable at x,

Scalar Multiplication: $D_x kf(x) = k \cdot f'(x)$ for k a real number

Sum and Difference: $D_x(f(x) \pm g(x)) = f'(x) \pm g'(x)$

Product: $D_x(f(x)g(x)) = f(x) \cdot g'(x) + g(x) \cdot f'(x)$

Quotient: $D_x \dfrac{f(x)}{g(x)} = \dfrac{g(x)\cdot f'(x) - f(x)\cdot g'(x)}{\left(g(x)\right)^2}, g(x) \neq 0$

Chain Rule: $D_x f(g(x)) = f'(g(x)) \cdot g'(x)$

Here are examples.

$D_x(-2x + 3) = -2 + 0 = -2$

$D_x(x^2 + 1) = 2x$

$D_t(100t^2 + 100t) = 200t + 100$

$D_t(200t + 100) = 200$

$D_x(2x^3 - 9x^2 + 2) = 6x^2 - 18x + 0 = 6x^2 - 18x$

$D_x(6x^2 - 18x) = 12x - 18$

$\dfrac{D_x(\sin x)}{D_x(6x)} = \dfrac{\cos x}{6} = \dfrac{1}{6}$

$D_x \ln x = \dfrac{1}{x}$

$D_x(x^2 \sin x) = x^2 \cdot \cos x + \sin x \cdot 2x = x^2 \cos x + 2x \sin x$

$D_x\left(\dfrac{1}{\sqrt{x}}\right) = \dfrac{\sqrt{x} \cdot 0 - 1 \cdot D_x x^{\frac{1}{2}}}{\left(\sqrt{x}\right)^2} = \dfrac{-1 \cdot \frac{1}{2}x^{-\frac{1}{2}}}{x} = -\dfrac{1}{2x^{\frac{3}{2}}}$

$D_x(x^2 - 1)^3 = 3(x^2 - 1)^2 \cdot 2x = 6x(x^2 - 1)^2$

Note: The formulas for $D_x(f(x)g(x))$, $D_x\left(\dfrac{f(x)}{g(x)}\right)$, and $D_x f(g(x))$ are given in the Notation, Definitions, and Formulas pages provided.

Integration Formulas

The process of integrating a function is called integration. You will need to know the following integration formulas for the Mathematics CK test. The constant C in the formulas is the constant of integration.

$$\int dx = x + C \qquad \int k\,dx = kx + C \qquad \int x^n\,dx = \frac{x^{n+1}}{n+1} + C,\, n \neq -1$$

$$\int \cos x\,dx = \sin x + C \qquad \int \sin x\,dx = -\cos x + C \qquad \int \sec^2 x\,dx = \tan x + C$$

$$\int \sec x \tan x\,dx = \sec x + C \qquad \int \csc x \cot x\,dx = -\csc x + C \qquad \int \csc^2 x\,dx = -\cot x + C$$

$$\int \frac{1}{x}\,dx = \ln x + C,\, x > 0 \qquad \int e^x\,dx = e^x + C$$

Change of Variable: $\int_a^b f\big(g(x)\big)g'(x)\,dx = \int_{g(a)}^{g(b)} f(u)\,du$, where $u = g(x)$ and $du = g'(x)dx$

Integration by Parts: $\int u\,dv = u \bullet v - \int v\,du$

Here are examples.

$$\int \left(x^e + e^x\right)dx = \int x^e\,dx + \int e^x\,dx = \frac{x^{e+1}}{e+1} + e^x + C$$

$$\int \left(x^2+1\right)\sqrt{x}\,dx = \int \left(x^2+1\right)x^{\frac{1}{2}}\,dx = \int \left(x^{\frac{5}{2}} + x^{\frac{1}{2}}\right)dx = \int x^{\frac{5}{2}}\,dx + \int x^{\frac{1}{2}}\,dx = \frac{x^{\frac{7}{2}}}{\frac{7}{2}} + \frac{x^{\frac{3}{2}}}{\frac{3}{2}} + C = \frac{2}{7}x^{\frac{7}{2}} + \frac{2}{3}x^{\frac{3}{2}} + C$$

Find $\int x \sin 3x\,dx$.

Let $u = x$ and $dv = \sin 3x\,dx$

Then $du = dx$ and $v = \int \sin 3x\,dx = -\frac{1}{3}\cos 3x$.

Note: The constant of integration is added at the end of the process.

Now, using the integration by parts equation, you have

$$\int u\,dv = u \bullet v - \int v\,du = \int x \sin 3x\,dx = (x)\left(-\frac{1}{3}\cos 3x\right) - \int \left(-\frac{1}{3}\cos 3x\right) \bullet dx = -\frac{1}{3}x\cos 3x + \frac{1}{3}\int \cos 3x\,dx =$$

$$-\frac{1}{3}x\cos 3x + \frac{1}{3} \bullet \frac{1}{3}\sin 3x = -\frac{1}{3}x\cos 3x + \frac{1}{9}\sin 3x + C$$

Note: The formula for integration by parts is given in the Notation, Definitions, and Formulas pages at the beginning of the Mathematics CK test booklet.

Limits of Sequences and Series

For this topic, you must be able to determine the limits of sequences and simple infinite series (*Mathematics: Content Knowledge (0061) Test at a Glance*, page 5).

A sequence is a function whose domain is the set of positive integers. The notation a_n denotes the image of the integer n, and a_n is the nth term (or element) of the sequence. You use $\{a_n\}$ to denote the sequence $a_1, a_2, \ldots, a_n, \ldots$

The sequence $a_1, a_2, \ldots, a_n, \ldots$ has limit L, written $\lim_{n \to \infty} a_n = L$ if for every number $\varepsilon > 0$, there exists a number M such that $|a_n - L| < \varepsilon$ whenever $n > M$. A sequence that has a limit is said to converge to that limit. Sequences that do not converge are said to diverge.

Three important limits of sequences you need to know for the Mathematics CK are the following:

$$\lim_{n \to \infty} k = k, \text{ for } k \text{ a real number}$$

$$\lim_{n \to \infty} \frac{1}{n} = 0$$

$$\lim_{n \to \infty} \frac{k}{n^p} = 0, \text{ for } k \text{ a real number and } p \text{ any positive rational number}$$

Properties of Limits of Sequences

Assuming that the sequences $\{a_n\}$ and $\{b_n\}$ have limits that exist, the following fundamental properties hold.

Sum or Difference:	$\lim_{n \to \infty} \left[a_n \pm b_n \right] = \lim_{n \to \infty} a_n \pm \lim_{n \to \infty} b_n$
Product:	$\lim_{n \to \infty} \left[a_n \cdot b_n \right] = \lim_{n \to \infty} a_n \cdot \lim_{n \to \infty} b_n$
Quotient:	$\lim_{n \to \infty} \dfrac{a_n}{b_n} = \dfrac{\lim_{n \to \infty} a_n}{\lim_{n \to \infty} b_n}$, provided $b_n \neq 0$ and $\lim_{n \to \infty} b_n \neq 0$
Scalar Multiplication:	$\lim_{n \to \infty} k a_n = k \lim_{n \to \infty} a_n$, for any real number k

Some useful theorems about limits of sequences are the following:

Squeeze Theorem: If $a_n \leq c_n \leq b_n$ for each integer n and if $\lim_{n \to \infty} a_n = \lim_{n \to \infty} b_n = L$, then $\lim_{n \to \infty} c_n = L$.

If $\lim_{n \to \infty} a_n = L$, then $\lim_{n \to \infty} |a_n| = |L|$.

If $\lim_{n \to \infty} |a_n| = 0$, then $\lim_{n \to \infty} a_n = 0$.

A sequence $\{a_n\}$ is monotonic if either (i) its terms are nondecreasing $a_1 \leq a_2 \leq a_3 \ldots \leq a_n \leq \ldots$ or (ii) its terms are nonincreasing $a_1 \geq a_2 \geq a_3 \ldots \geq a_n \geq \ldots$

A sequence $\{a_n\}$ is bounded above if there is a real number b_{upper} such that $a_n \leq b_{upper}$ for all n. A sequence $\{a_n\}$ is bounded below if there is a real number b_{lower} such that $b_{lower} \leq a_n$ for all n. A sequence is bounded if it is bounded above and bounded below.

If a sequence is monotonic and bounded, then it converges.

If $\{a_n\}$ is an infinite sequence, then $\sum_{n=1}^{\infty} a_n = a_1 + a_2 + a_3 + \cdots + a_n + \cdots$ is an infinite series (also called series). The notation a_n denotes the nth term of the series. You also can represent the series $\sum_{n=1}^{\infty} a_n$ as $\sum a_n$.

Associated with each infinite series is its sequence of partial sums: $S_1 = a_1$, $S_2 = a_1 + a_2$, $S_3 = a_1 + a_2 + a_3, \ldots, S_n = a_1 + a_2 + a_3 + \ldots + a_n, \ldots$ An infinite series with partial sums $S_1, S_2, S_3, \ldots, S_n, \ldots$ converges if and only if $\lim_{n \to \infty} S_n$ exists. If the limit does not exist, then the infinite series diverges. For a convergent series, if $\lim_{n \to \infty} S_n = S$, the number S is called the sum of the series.

Properties of Convergent Series

If $\sum_{n=1}^{\infty} a_n$ and $\sum_{n=1}^{\infty} b_n$ converge, then the following properties hold:

Sum or Difference:	$\sum_{n=1}^{\infty}(a_n \pm b_n) = \sum_{n=1}^{\infty} a_n \pm \sum_{n=1}^{\infty} b_n$
Scalar Multiplication:	$\sum_{n=1}^{\infty} ka_n = k\sum_{n=1}^{\infty} a_n$, for any real number k.

An infinite series of the form $\sum_{n=1}^{\infty} ar^{n-1} = a_1 + a_2 r + a_3 r^2 + \cdots + a_n r^{n-1} + \cdots$ is called an infinite geometric series with ratio r. This series diverges if $|r| \geq 1$ and converges if $0 < |r| < 1$. The sum of a geometric series that converges is given by: $\sum_{n=1}^{\infty} ar^{n-1} = \frac{a}{1-r}$, where $0 < |r| < 1$.

If the series $\sum a_n$ converges, then the sequence $\{a_n\}$ converges to 0. Thus, if the sequence $\{a_n\}$ does *not* converge to 0, then $\sum a_n$ diverges. This latter statement is sometimes called "the nth term test for divergence." That is, if the limit of the nth term of the series does *not* converge to 0, then the series diverges. Caution: Do not interpret this result to mean that if the nth term of the series does converge to 0, that the series converges. When the limit of the nth term of a series converges to 0, you can draw no conclusions about convergence or divergence of the series based solely on that information.

Tip: Sometimes it is convenient to begin an infinite sequence or series at $n = 0$ instead of $n = 1$, so be sure to check for the starting value of n when you work problems involving sequences or series on the Mathematics CK.

Note: See the section titled "Arithmetic and Geometric Sequences and Series" in the chapter titled "Discrete Mathematics" for an additional discussion of sequences and series.

Chapter 8

Data Analysis and Statistics

According to the Mathematics Content Knowledge (0061) Test at a Glance (www.ets.org/Media/Tests/PRAXIS/pdf/0061.pdf), the Data Analysis and Statistics content category of the Mathematics CK tests your knowledge and skills in seven topic areas:

- Organizing data
- Measures of central tendency and dispersion
- Regression
- Normal distributions
- Informal inference
- Types of studies
- Characteristics of well-designed studies

This review discusses the key ideas and formulas in each topic area that are most important for you to know for the Mathematics CK.

Organizing Data

For this topic, you must be able to organize data into a suitable form (for example, construct a histogram and use it in the calculation of probabilities) (*Mathematics: Content Knowledge (0061) Test at a Glance*, page 5).

There are several ways to record, organize, and present data. For the Mathematics CK, you should be able to perform data analysis by reading and interpreting information from charts and tables, pictographs, circle graphs, line graphs, dotplots, stem-and-leaf plots, bar graphs, and histograms.

Charts and tables organize information as entries in rows and columns. Row and column labels explain the data recorded in the chart or table. A frequency table is a tabular representation of data that shows the frequency of each value in the data set. A relative frequency table shows the frequency of each value as a proportion or percentage of the whole data set. The total of all relative frequencies should be 1.00 or 100 percent, but instead might be very close to 1.00 or 100 percent due to round-off error. Here is an example.

Grade Distribution for Test 1		
Grade	**Frequency**	**Relative Frequency**
A	5	0.20
B	8	0.32
C	9	0.36
D	2	0.08
F	1	0.04
Total	**25**	**1.00**

Pictographs use symbols or pictures to represent numbers. Each symbol stands for a definite number of a specific item. This information should be stated on the graph. To read a pictograph, you count the number of symbols shown and then multiply by the number it represents. Fractional portions of symbols are approximated and used accordingly. Here is an example.

A circle graph, or pie chart, is a graph in the shape of a circle. Circle graphs are used to visually display the relative contribution of each category of data within a set of data to the whole set. It is also called a "pie" chart because it looks like a pie cut into wedges. The wedges are labeled to show the categories for the graph. Usually the portion of the graph that corresponds to each category is shown as a percent. The total amount of percentage on the graph is 100 percent. The graph is made by dividing the 360 degrees of the circle into portions that correspond to the percentages for each category. You read a circle graph by reading the percents displayed on the graph for the different categories. Here is an example.

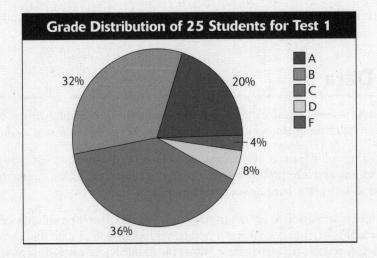

Line graphs use connected line segments to show information from a data set. The data values are plotted as ordered pairs on a grid that has horizontal and vertical scales. Consecutive points are connected by line segments. The slants of the line segments between points show trends in the data. Upward slants from left to right indicate increasing data values, downward slants from left to right indicate decreasing data values, and line segments with no slant (horizontal line) indicate that the data values are remaining constant. Line graphs are particularly suitable for showing change over time. You can plot two or more sets of data on the same graph, a display that facilitates comparisons between the data sets. Here is an example of a line graph.

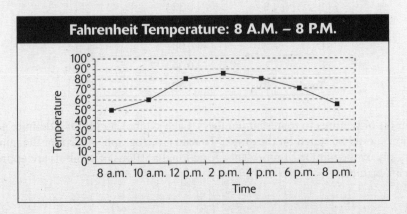

A dotplot (or line plot) is a graph in which the data's possible values are indicated along the horizontal axis, and dots (or other similar symbols) are placed above each value to indicate the number of times that particular value occurs in the data set. Here is an example.

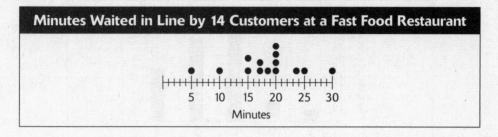

Minutes Waited in Line by 14 Customers at a Fast Food Restaurant

Minutes

A stem-and-leaf plot is a graphical display of data in which each data value is separated into two parts: a stem and a leaf. For a given data value, the leaf is commonly the last digit, and the stem is the remaining digits. For example, for the data value 198, 19 is the stem and 8 is the leaf. A stem-and-leaf plot includes a legend that explains what the stem and leaf represent so the reader can interpret the information in the plot; for example, $19|8 = 198$. Usually, the stems are listed vertically, from smallest to largest, in a column labeled "Stem." The leaves are listed horizontally, from smallest to largest, in the row of their corresponding stem under a column labeled "Leaves." Each leaf is listed to the right of its corresponding stem as many times as it occurs in the original data set. A feature of a stem-and-leaf plot is that the original data are retained and displayed in the plot. Reading information from a stem-and-leaf plot is a matter of interpreting the plot's stems and leaves. Here is an example of a stem-and-leaf plot.

Ages of 39 U.S. Presidents at Death	
Stem	**Leaves**
4	6 9
5	3 6 7 7 8
6	0 0 3 3 4 4 5 6 7 7 7 8
7	0 1 1 1 2 3 4 7 8 8 9
8	0 1 3 5 8
9	0 0 3 3
Legend: 4|6 = 46	

A bar graph uses rectangular bars of the same width to show the frequency, relative frequency, or amount of different categories of a data set. Labels at the base of the bars specify the categories. The bars are equally spaced from each other and may be displayed vertically or horizontally. A bar's length or height indicates the frequency, relative frequency, or amount for the category represented by that particular bar. A scale, marked in intervals, for measuring the bar's height (or length) will be shown on the graph. To read a bar graph, examine the scale to determine the units and the amount corresponding to each interval. Then determine where the bars' heights or lengths fall relative to the scale.

Here is an example.

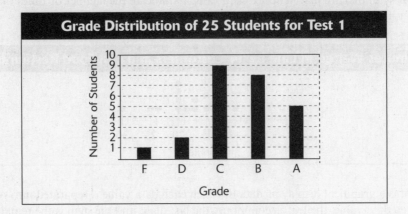

Two or more sets of data can be displayed on the same graph to facilitate comparison of the data sets to each other. Here is an example.

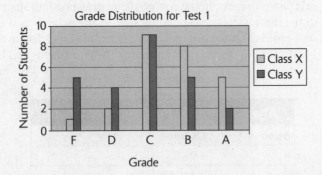

A histogram is a special type of bar graph that summarizes data by displaying the data's frequencies or relative frequencies within specified intervals, called class intervals. Class intervals are of equal width and cover from the lowest to the highest data value. The left and right endpoints for the class intervals are selected so that each data value clearly falls within one and only one class interval. The frequency or relative frequency of the data values' occurrence within a class interval is represented by a rectangular (or vertical) column. The height (or length) of the column is proportional to the data values' frequency or relative frequency within that interval. In a frequency histogram, the scale for measuring the bars' heights (or lengths) is marked with actual frequencies (or counts). In a relative frequency histogram, the scale is marked with relative frequencies instead of actual frequencies. The total of the relative frequencies corresponding to the class intervals should be 1.00 or 100 percent, but might instead be very close to 1.00 or 100 percent due to round-off error.

Here is an example of a frequency histogram.

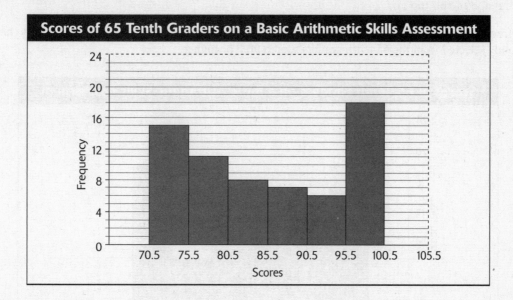

Drawing valid conclusions from graphical representations of data requires that you have read the graph accurately and analyzed the graphical information correctly. Sometimes a graphical representation will distort the data in some way, leading you to draw an invalid conclusion. Here is an example.

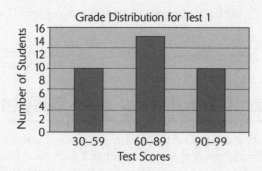

At first glance, the data for this graph look evenly distributed. Upon closer examination, you can see that each of the first two intervals covers a 30-point spread, but the last interval covers only a 10-point spread, making it difficult to draw conclusions from the graph.

When you interpret graphical information on the Mathematics CK, follow these suggestions:

- Make sure you understand the graph's title.
- Read the labels on the graph's parts to understand what is being represented.
- Make sure you know what each symbol in a pictograph represents.
- Examine carefully the scale of bar graphs, line graphs, histograms, and scatterplots.
- Look for trends such as rising values (upward slanting line segments), falling values (downward slanting line segments), and periods of inactivity (horizontal line segments) in line graphs.
- Look for concentrations of data values and note the general shape for dotplots, stem-and-leaf plots, bar graphs, histograms, and scatterplots.
- Mark or draw on graphs.
- Be ready to do simple arithmetic computations.
- Make sure the numbers add up correctly.
- Use only the information in the graph. Do not answer based on your personal knowledge or opinion.

Here is an example of using graphical information to determine a probability (see Chapter 9 "Probability" for a further discussion of this topic).

Given the frequency histogram for the scores of 65 tenth graders (shown below), find the probability that a student randomly selected from the 65 tenth graders scored 90.5 or higher.

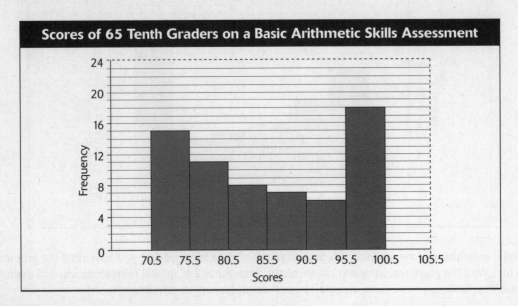

According to the graph, 6 + 18 = 24 of the 65 students scored 90.5 or higher. Thus, since the student is randomly selected:

$$P(\text{score is 90.5 or higher}) = \frac{\text{Number of outcomes favorable}}{\text{Total number of outcomes}} = \frac{24}{65}$$

Measures of Central Tendency and Dispersion

For this topic, you must know and be able to find the appropriate uses of common measures of central tendency (for example: population mean, sample mean, median, mode) and dispersion (for example: range, population standard deviation, sample standard deviation, population variance, sample variance) (*Mathematics: Content Knowledge (0061) Test at a Glance*, page 5).

Measures of Central Tendency

A measure of central tendency is a numerical value that describes a data set by attempting to provide a "central" or "typical" value of the data set. Three common measures of central tendency are the mean, median, and mode. Each of these measures is a way to describe a set of data's central value. Measures of central tendency should have the same units as those of the data values from which they are determined. If no units are specified for the data values, no units are specified for the measures of central tendency.

A data set's mean is another name for the data values' arithmetic average. Thus, the mean $= \frac{\text{sum of the data values}}{\text{number of data values}}$.

Here is an example.

Find the mean of the following data set: 21, 35, 34, 30, 32, 36, 24, 35, 28, 35.

$$\text{Mean} = \frac{\text{sum of the data values}}{\text{number of data values}} = \frac{21+24+28+30+32+34+35+35+35+36}{10} = \frac{310}{10} = 31$$

Tip: Using the statistical features of your graphing calculator is the most efficient way to calculate the mean of a data set. For the TI-83, press 2nd STAT to access the LIST menu. Select MATH (see below), then press 3 to choose 3:mean (.

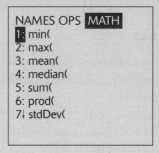

NAMES OPS **MATH**
1: min(
2: max(
3: mean(
4: median(
5: sum(
6: prod(
7↓ stdDev(

Enter the data inside braces and close the parentheses as shown here: mean({21, 35, 34, 30, 32, 36, 24, 35, 28, 35}). Press ENTER. The display will show the mean, which in this case is 31.

A weighted mean is a mean computed by assigning weights to the data values. To find a weighted mean, do the following: First, multiply each data value by its assigned weight and then sum the results. Next, divide the sum obtained by the sum of the weights. Thus, for data values $x_1, x_2, \ldots, x_n$ with respective assigned weights $w_1, w_2, \ldots, w_n$, weighted average $= \dfrac{\sum w_i x_i}{\sum w_i}$. Here is an example.

A student scores 80, 60, and 50 on three exams. Find the weighted mean of the student's three scores, where the score of 80 counts 20 percent, the score of 60 counts 20 percent, and the score of 50 counts 60 percent.

$$\text{weighted mean} = \frac{\sum w_i x_i}{\sum w_i} = \frac{20\%(80) + 20\%(60) + 60\%(50)}{20\% + 20\% + 60\%} = \frac{16 + 16 + 30}{100\%} = \frac{62}{1} = 62$$

The median is the middle value or the mean of the two middle values in an *ordered* set of data. For a small data set, you easily can determine a data set's median using a two-step process: First, put the data values in order from least to greatest (or greatest to least). Next, find the middle data value. If there is no single middle data value, find the mean of the two middle data values. Here is an example.

Find the median of the following data set: 21, 35, 34, 30, 32, 36, 24, 35, 28, 35.

Step 1. Put the data values in order: 21, 24, 28, 30, 32, 34, 35, 35, 35, 36.

Step 2. Find the mean of the two middle values: $\dfrac{32 + 34}{2} = 33$. Thus, the median is 33.

Note: In terms of position, the median is the $\left(\dfrac{n+1}{2}\right)$th data value in an ordered set of discrete values.

Tip: Using the statistical features of your graphing calculator is the most efficient way to calculate the median of a data set. For the TI-83, press 2nd STAT to access the LIST menu. Select MATH, then press 4 to choose 4:median (. Enter the data inside braces and close the parentheses as shown here: median({21, 35, 34, 30, 32, 36, 24, 35, 28, 35}). Press ENTER. The display will show the median, which in this case is 33.

The mode is the data value or values that occur with the highest frequency in a data set. A data set can have one mode, more than one mode, or no mode. If exactly two data values occur with the same frequency that is more often than that of any of the other data values, then the data set is bimodal. If three or more data values occur with the same frequency that is more often than that of any of the other data values, then the data is multimodal. A data set in which each data value occurs the same number of times has no mode. Here is an example.

Find the mode of the following data set: 21, 35, 34, 30, 32, 36, 24, 35, 28, 35.

The value 35 occurs 3 times, which is the highest frequency of occurrence for any one value in the data set. Thus, the mode is 35.

The mean, median, and mode are ways to describe a data set's central value. To know which of these measures of central tendency you should use to describe a data set, consider their characteristics.

The mean has several important characteristics.

- Although the mean represents a data set's central or typical value, the mean does not necessarily have the same value as one of the numbers in the set. For instance, the mean of 50, 50, 87, 78, and 95 is 72, yet none of the five numbers in this data set equals 72.

- The actual data values are used in the computation of the mean. If any one number is changed, the mean's value will change. For example, the mean of the data set consisting of 50, 50, 87, 78, and 95 is 72. If the 95 in this set is changed to 100, the new data set's mean is 73.

- A disadvantage of the mean is that it is influenced by outliers, especially in a small data set. An outlier is a data value that is extremely high or extremely low in comparison to most of the other data values. If a data set contains extremely high values that are not balanced by corresponding low values, the mean will be misleadingly high. For example, the mean of the data set consisting of 15, 15, 20, 25, and 25 is 20. If the 20 in this set is changed to 100, the mean of the new data set is 36. The value 36 does not represent the data set consisting of 15, 15, 100, 25, and 25 very well, since four of the data values are less than 30. Similarly, if a data set contains extremely low values that are not balanced by corresponding high values, the mean will be misleadingly low. For example, the mean of the data set consisting of 100, 100, 130, and 150 is 120. If the 150 in this set is changed to 10, the mean of the new data set is 85. The value 85 does not represent the data set consisting of 100, 100, 130, and 10 very well, since three of the data values are greater than or equal to 100.

The median is the most useful alternative to the mean as a measure of central tendency.

- Like the mean, the median does not necessarily have the same value as one of the numbers in the set. If the data set contains an odd number of data values, the median will be the middle number; however, for an even number of data values, the median is the arithmetic average of the two middle numbers.

- The median is not influenced by outliers. For instance, the median of the data set consisting of 10, 15, 20, 25, and 30 is 20. If the 30 in this set is changed to 100, the new data set's median remains 20.

- A disadvantage of the median as an indicator of a central value is that it is based on relative size rather than on the actual numbers in the set. For instance, a student who has test scores of 44, 47, and 98 shows improved performance that would not be reflected if the median of 47, rather than the mean of 63, was reported as the representative grade.

The mode is the least commonly used measure of central tendency.

- The mode is the simplest measure of central tendency to calculate.

- If a data set has a mode, the mode (or modes) is one of the data values.

- The mode is the only appropriate measure of central tendency for data that are strictly nonnumeric, like data on ice cream flavor preferences (vanilla, chocolate, strawberry, and so on). Although it makes no sense to determine a mean or median ice cream flavor for the data, the ice cream flavor that was named most frequently would be the modal flavor.

- A disadvantage of the mode as an indicator of a central value is that it is based on relative frequency than on all the values in the set. For instance, a student who has test scores of 45, 45, and 99 shows improved performance that would not be reflected if the mode of 45, rather than the mean of 63, was reported as the representative grade.

When you are summarizing data, you might want to report more than one measure of central tendency, if appropriate. For numeric data if you select only one measure, the mean is preferred for data sets in which outliers are not present. The median is the preferred measure when outliers are present. The mode is the preferred measure for nonnumeric categorical data.

Measures of Dispersion

A measure of dispersion is a value that describes the variability of a data set about its central value. The interpretation of measures of central tendency of a data set is enhanced when the variability about the central value is known. For the Mathematics CK, measures of dispersion you need to know are the range, standard deviation, and variance.

The range for a data set is the difference between the maximum value (the greatest value) and the minimum value (least value) in the data set: range = maximum value – minimum value. The range should have the same units as those of the data values from which it is computed. If no units are specified, then the range will not specify units. Here is an example.

Find the range of the following data set: 21, 35, 34, 30, 32, 36, 24, 35, 28, 35.

Range = maximum value – minimum value = 36 – 21 = 15.

The range gives an indication of the spread of the values in a data set, but its value is determined by only two of the data values. The extent of spread of the other data values is not considered. A measure of dispersion that takes into account all the data values is the standard deviation.

The formula for the standard deviation, σ (sig-muh), of a population (see the section titled "Informal Inference" in this chapter for a definition of the term *population*) with mean μ (mew) is given by: $\sigma = \sqrt{\dfrac{\sum (x-\mu)^2}{N}}$, where the x's are the data values and N is the number of elements in the population. The formula for the standard deviation, s, of a sample (see the section titled "Informal Inference" in this chapter for a definition of the term *sample*) with mean $\bar{x}$ (eks-bar) is given by: $s = \sqrt{\dfrac{\sum (x-\bar{x})^2}{n-1}}$, where n is the number of elements in the sample.

The standard deviation is a measure of the dispersion of a set of data values about the mean of the data set. If there is no dispersion in a data set, each data value equals the mean, giving a standard deviation of 0. The more the data values vary from the mean, the greater the standard deviation, meaning the data set has more spread. The standard deviation should have the same units as those of the data values from which it is computed. If no units are specified, then the standard deviation will not specify units.

The variance of a population, σ^2, is the square of the standard deviation of the population. The variance of a sample, s^2, is the square of the standard deviation of the sample.

Tip: Your graphing calculator will calculate the standard deviation and variance for a sample. For the Mathematics CK, if a problem requires that you calculate a standard deviation or variance, assume that you are calculating values for a sample unless you are told specifically otherwise.

You can use your understanding of standard deviation to assess a data value based on its location relative to the mean. The z-score for a data value is its distance in standard deviations from the mean of the data values. Computing a z-score is given by the formula:

$$z\text{-score} = \frac{\text{data value} - \text{mean}}{\text{standard deviation}}$$

If a z-score is positive, the data value is greater than the mean; if a z-score is negative, the data value is less than the mean. The mean has a z-score 0. Here is an example.

Suppose a student scored 80 on a chemistry test and 90 on a biology test. The mean and standard deviations of the scores from the entire class on the two tests are shown in the following table:

Course	Mean	Standard Deviation
Chemistry	70	5
Biology	84	6

On which test did the student perform better relative to the mean performance of the class on the test?

The student's z-score for the chemistry test is $\dfrac{\text{score} - \text{mean}}{\text{standard deviation}} = \dfrac{80 - 70}{5} = 2$; thus, the student scored two standard deviations above the mean on the chemistry test. The student's z-score for the biology test is $\dfrac{\text{score} - \text{mean}}{\text{standard deviation}} = \dfrac{90 - 84}{6} = 1$; thus, the student scored one standard deviation above the mean on the biology test. Therefore, relative to the mean performance of the class, the student performed better on the chemistry test.

Other Descriptive Measures

Other measures that are used to describe a data set are percentiles and quartiles. The Pth percentile is a value at or below which P percent of the data fall. For example, the median is the 50th percentile because 50 percent of the data fall at or below the median. Quartiles are values that divide an ordered data set into four portions, each of which contains approximately one-fourth of the data. Twenty-five percent of the data values are at or below the first quartile (also called the 25th percentile); 50 percent of the data values are at or below the second quartile (also called the 50th percentile), which is the same as the median; and 75 percent of the data values are at or below the third quartile (also called the 75th percentile).

For a set of data, the five-number summary consists of the minimum value (Min), the first quartile (Q_1), the median, the third quartile (Q_3), and the maximum value (Max) of the data set. A box-and-whiskers plot (shown here) is a graphical representation of the five-number summary for a data set.

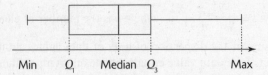

The interquartile range (IQR) is Q_3–Q_1. Fifty percent of the data fall in this range.

A data set can be described in terms of the skewness of its distribution. Skewness describes the "lopsidedness" of the distribution. A distribution that is symmetric has no skew. A distribution that has a longer tail to the right is positively skewed. A distribution that has a longer tail to the left is negatively skewed. In a positively skewed distribution, the mean lies to the right of the median. In a negatively skewed distribution, the mean lies to the left of the median. The mean and median coincide for a symmetric distribution (no skew).

Here are examples.

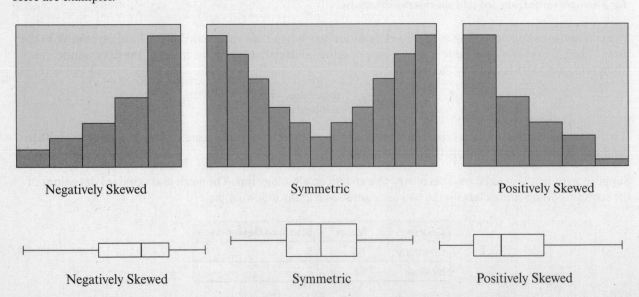

Regression

For this topic, you must be able to analyze data from specific situations to determine what type of function (for example: linear, quadratic, exponential) would most likely model that particular phenomenon, use the regression feature of the calculator to determine curve of best fit, and interpret the regression coefficients, correlation, and residuals in context (*Mathematics: Content Knowledge (0061) Test at a Glance*, page 5).

Simple Linear Regression is an area of statistics in which a relation between an independent variable X (also called the predictor or explanatory variable) and a dependent variable Y (also called the response variable) is explained through a regression equation.

A scatterplot is a graph of the bivariate data—paired values of data from the independent and dependent variables—plotted on a coordinate grid. The data are paired in a way that matches each value from one variable with a corresponding value from the other variable. The plot's pattern can be useful in determining whether there is a relationship between the two variables; and, if there is, the nature of that relationship. For the Mathematics CK, you should be able to examine scatterplots and distinguish between those indicating linear and those indicating nonlinear relationships between two variables. For linear relationships, a scatterplot that slants upward from left to right indicates a positive linear relationship, and one that slants downward from left to right indicates a negative linear relationship.

Here are examples of scatter plots.

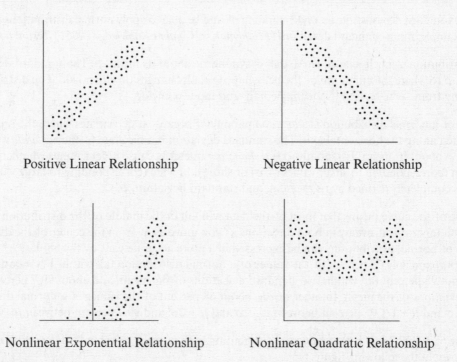

Positive Linear Relationship   Negative Linear Relationship

Nonlinear Exponential Relationship   Nonlinear Quadratic Relationship

If the data's scatterplot seems approximately linear, the line of best fit is the line that fits the data best and is given by the regression equation $\widehat{Y} = a + bx$, where $\widehat{Y}$ is the predicted value on the dependent variable, Y, a is a constant (corresponding to $X = 0$), and b is the regression coefficient. The coefficient b is the slope of the regression line and indicates the expected change in Y associated with a unit change in X.

The residuals are the differences between the actual y-values in the scatterplot and the $\widehat{Y}$-values predicted by the regression equation. The line of best fit minimizes the sum of squares of the residuals and is the least-squares regression line. The closer the plotted data points are to the regression line, the smaller the residual sum of squares.

For the Mathematics CK, you will be expected to use your graphing calculator to compute the equation of the least-squares regression line and the correlation coefficient r between the x and y values. Consult your owner's manual for details on how to use the regression features of your graphing calculator. Note: Most calculators will use y instead of $\widehat{Y}$ in the regression equation.

The correlation coefficient is a numerical measure that describes the strength of the linear relationship between the two variables under consideration. Correlation coefficients range from –1 to +1, with –1 indicating a "perfect" negative correlation and +1 indicating a "perfect" positive correlation. Correlation values very close to either –1 or +1 indicate very strong correlations. If the two variables have no relationship to each other, then the correlation coefficient will be 0. The further the correlation coefficient is from 0, the stronger the relationship. (Remember, however, that you cannot have correlation coefficients below –1 or above +1.) Nevertheless, the existence of a recognizable correlation between two variables does not imply a causative relationship between the variables. The correlation might be a reflection of outside variables that affect both variables under study.

Since the correlation coefficient is a measure of the strength of the linear relationship between the independent and dependent variables of the linear regression equation, it can be used as an estimate of the regression line's "goodness of fit." The closer $|r|$ is to 1, the more perfect the linear relationship is between x and y. If r is close to 0, there is little or no linear relationship, so the line is not a good fit for the data.

Normal Distributions

For this topic, you must demonstrate an understanding of and be able to apply normal distributions and their characteristics (for example: mean, standard deviation) (*Mathematics: Content Knowledge (0061) Test at a Glance*, page 5).

A normal distribution is a bell-shaped curve that is symmetric about its mean, μ. The standard deviation, σ, is the distance from μ to where the curvature of the bell-shaped graph changes on either side. The distribution is continuous, extending from $-\infty$ to ∞, and its mean, median, and mode coincide.

The mean, μ, of a normal distribution is a *location* parameter because it determines where the *center* of the distribution is located along the horizontal axis. The standard deviation is a measure of the *variability* (or spread) of the distribution about its mean. Essentially, σ is a *shape* parameter because it determines whether the distribution is tall and thin (corresponding to small values of σ) or short and wide (corresponding to large values of σ). The distribution is completely defined by its mean, μ, and standard deviation, σ.

The bell-shape of the curve means that most of the data will fall in the middle of the distribution with the amount of data tapering off evenly in both directions as you move away from the center of the distribution. This characteristic of normal distributions can be expressed in a more accurate way, by the 68-95-99.7 rule. According to this rule, approximately 68 percent of the values of a normal distribution fall within 1 standard deviation of the mean, about 95 percent fall within two standard deviations of the mean, and about 99.7 percent fall within 3 standard deviations of the mean. In other words, about 68 percent of the values of a normal distribution fall between $\mu - 1\sigma$ and $\mu + 1\sigma$, 95 percent between $\mu - 2\sigma$ and $\mu + 2\sigma$, and 99.7 percent between $\mu - 3\sigma$ and $\mu + 3\sigma$.

A result of the 68-95-99.7 rule is that a normal distribution with mean μ and standard deviation σ can be subdivided as shown in the following figure.

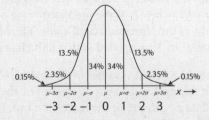

The numbers written horizontally along the bottom of the figure are measures of standard deviations from the mean, called z-scores.

Here is an example of using the 68-95-99.7 rule.

Express the 68-95-99.7 rule in terms of a normal distribution with mean, $\mu = 100$, and standard deviation, $\sigma = 15$.

According to the 68-95-99.7 rule, about 68 percent of the values will fall between $100 - 1(15)$ and $100 + 1(15)$, 95 percent between $100 - 2(15)$ and $100 + 2(15)$, and 99.7 percent between $100 - 3(15)$ and $100 + 3(15)$. Thus, for a normal distribution with mean, $\mu = 100$, and standard deviation, $\sigma = 15$: About 68 percent of the values fall between 85 and 115, about 95 percent fall between 70 and 130, and about 99.7 percent fall between 55 and 145.

In working problems involving normal distributions, you often will find it necessary to convert data values into z-scores using the formula $z\text{-score} = \dfrac{\text{data value} - \text{mean}}{\text{standard deviation}} = \dfrac{\text{data value} - \mu}{\sigma}$. The z-score expresses the position of the data value *relative to the mean*. Those with negative z-scores lie to the left of the mean, and those with positive z-scores lie to the right of the mean. The z-score for the mean is 0. Furthermore, z-scores are in terms of standard deviations. For instance, a data value that has a z-score of -1 is one standard deviation below the mean, and a data value that has a z-score of 1 is one standard deviation above the mean.

Here is an example.

Suppose that scores on a national exam are normally distributed with mean, $\mu = 500$, and standard deviation, $\sigma = 100$, find the z-score for a score of 800. Interpret the z-score in terms of standard deviations relative to the mean.

$z\text{-score for }800 = \dfrac{\text{data value} - \mu}{\sigma} = \dfrac{800 - 500}{100} = 3$. Thus, 800 is three standard deviations above the mean.

> **Tip: Using the statistical features of your graphing calculator is an efficient and time-saving way to work problems involving the normal distribution. Consult your owner's manual for detailed instructions on how to find percentages and probabilities using areas under a normal curve and how to find a z-score corresponding to a known probability obtained from a normal distribution.**

Informal Inference

For this topic, you must demonstrate an understanding of how sample statistics reflect the values of population parameters and use sampling distributions as the basis for informal inference (*Mathematics: Content Knowledge (0061) Test at a Glance*, page 5).

A population is the set of all elements (subjects, experimental units) under investigation. A parameter is a numerical measurement that describes a population. Customary symbols for the two population parameters, mean and standard deviation, are μ and σ, respectively.

A sample is a subset of the population. A statistic is a numerical measurement that describes a sample. Customary symbols for the two sample statistics, mean and standard deviation, are $\bar{x}$ and s, respectively.

In inferential statistics, information from samples is used to make estimates, predictions, decisions, or generalizations about a population.

A sampling distribution is the probability distribution of the values of a sample statistic obtained from all possible samples of the same size.

The sampling distribution of the mean $(\bar{x})$ has the following properties:

    (i) the mean of the sampling distribution of $\bar{x} =$ the mean of the sampled population;

    (ii) the standard deviation of the sampling distribution of $\bar{x} = \dfrac{\text{Standard deviation of the sampled population}}{\text{Square root of the sample size}}$ (provided the standard deviation is positive); and

    (iii) the sampling distribution of $\bar{x}$ approaches the normal distribution as the sample size increases (Central Limit Theorem).

Types of Studies

For this topic, you must demonstrate an understanding of the differences among various kinds of studies and which types of inferences can legitimately be drawn from each (*Mathematics: Content Knowledge (0061) Test at a Glance*, page 5).

Quantitative studies fall into four broad categories: survey, correlational, experimental, or observational.

In survey studies, the purpose is to gather information from a representative sample in order to generalize to a population of interest. Examples of this type of study include opinion surveys, fact-finding surveys, and questionnaire and interview studies. Results are summarized and reported. Generalization of the survey results to the population would be appropriate only when the sample has been randomly chosen from the population and is of adequate size.

In correlational studies, the purpose is to investigate the extent to which variations in one variable correspond with variations in another variable. Examples of such studies include investigating the relationship between performance on a standardized reading test and time spent reading independently, between college grades and high school GPA, and between income and years of education. It is very important to note that correlational studies *cannot* show causation. In other words, if two variables are correlated, it does not mean that one causes the other.

In experimental studies, the purpose is to investigate possible cause-and-effect relationships by exposing an experimental group to a treatment condition and comparing the results to a control group not receiving the treatment. The study is set up in such a way that one group of experimental units gets the treatment (the experimental group) and another group (the control group) does not, and then comparisons are made to see whether the treatment had an influence on the variable of interest. For such comparisons to be valid, other sources of variation must be controlled. Examples of such studies include investigating the effectiveness of a new method of teaching reading on reading ability, the effect of a new drug on cancer patients, and the effect of a type of fertilizer on plant growth. In a well-designed experimental study, experimental units are randomly assigned to either the treatment or control group to assure that groups are similar in all respects *except* for the treatment. Therefore, any difference in the two groups can be attributed to the treatment. Only when investigators conduct a well-designed experimental study would a cause-and-effect conclusion be valid.

Observational studies involve collecting and analyzing data without changing existing conditions. Observational studies are conducted when it is not possible (or, perhaps, not appropriate) to randomly assign experimental units to some treatment condition (for example, being a smoker). Such studies are conducted in a setting that does not permit the investigator to manipulate or control all relevant variables. The nonrandomness in sampling and the constraint imposed by observing a predetermined condition limit drawing cause-and-effect conclusions from observational studies because there is a possibility that results are due to some variables other than the variables being studied.

Characteristics of Well-Designed Studies

For this topic, you must know the characteristics of well-designed studies, including the role of randomization in surveys and experiments (*Mathematics: Content Knowledge (0061) Test at a Glance*, page 5).

A sample is a portion of a population that is examined to gain information about the whole population. A random sample is one in which the members of the sample are randomly selected from the population. A representative sample is one in which the characteristics of the sample entities mirror the characteristics of the population under investigation. The sample size is the number of entities in the sample. Statistical formulas or guidelines are available for determining adequate sample size for various types of studies. In general, increasing the sample size leads to more accurate results. A sample is most likely to be a representative sample when it has been chosen randomly from the population, and it is of adequate size.

Tip: Conclusions from a study should not be based on samples that are far too small (for example, a survey that uses fewer than 10 subjects). For the Mathematics CK, consider this aspect if you are asked to critique a study's results.

Bias in a study is a type of systematic error that favors particular results.

Extraneous variables are unwanted variables that are not themselves being studied but, nevertheless, might influence study outcomes.

To provide results worthy of consideration, carefully plan well-designed studies, investigate issues that are clear and unambiguous, clearly identify populations of study, use randomization in selecting representative samples of adequate size, use well-defined variables of interest, avoid bias of various types, and control for outside factors, such as extraneous variables, that could jeopardize the validity of conclusions. Only when investigators use well-designed studies can reliable and valid conclusions be drawn.

Chapter 9

Probability

According to the *Mathematics: Content Knowledge (0061) Test at a Glance* (www.ets.org/Media/Tests/PRAXIS/pdf/0061.pdf), the Probability content category of the Mathematics CK tests your knowledge and skills in four topic areas:

- Sample spaces and probability distributions
- Conditional probability and independent and dependent events
- Expected value
- Empirical probability

This review discusses the key ideas and formulas in each topic area that are most important for you to know for the Mathematics CK.

Sample Spaces and Probability Distributions

For this topic, you must demonstrate an understanding of concepts of sample space and probability distribution and be able to construct sample spaces and distributions in simple cases (*Mathematics: Content Knowledge (0061) Test at a Glance*, page 5).

Sample Spaces and Probability

A random experiment is a process that returns a single outcome that cannot be determined beforehand. For instance, a simple random experiment is flipping a coin one time and observing the up face on the coin.

A sample space, S, is the set of all possible outcomes of a random experiment. Each member of S is called an outcome (or simple event, sample point, or elementary outcome).

Note: A sample space can be finite or infinite. For the Mathematics CK, only finite sample spaces are considered.

An event, E, is a collection of outcomes from S; that is, an event E is a subset of the sample space S. An event E is said to occur if a member of E occurs when the experiment is performed.

Note: By convention, capital letters are used to designate events, with the word *event* being omitted in cases where the meaning is clear.

Here is an example.

For the experiment of drawing one tile (without looking) from a box containing five wooden, one-inch square tiles numbered 1 through 5, list the sample space S and let E represent the event that the tile drawn shows an odd number.

The sample space is $S = \{1, 2, 3, 4, 5\}$ and $E = \{1, 3, 5\}$, where "1" represents the outcome "the tile drawn shows a 1," "2" represents the outcome "the tile drawn shows a 2," and so on.

A probability measure on a sample space, S, is a function that assigns to each outcome in S a real number between 0 and 1, inclusive, so that the values assigned to the outcomes in S sum to 1. The value assigned to an outcome in S is called the probability of that outcome. For instance, for $S = \{1, 2, 3, 4, 5\}$, the sample space for the tile-drawing experiment, the probability of each outcome in S is $\frac{1}{5}$. Since the tiles are physically identical and the drawing is performed without looking (that is, randomly), each tile has a 1 in 5 chance of being drawn. The sum of the probabilities of the outcomes in S is $P(1) + P(2) + P(3) + P(4) + P(5) = \frac{1}{5} + \frac{1}{5} + \frac{1}{5} + \frac{1}{5} + \frac{1}{5} = \frac{5}{5} = 1$.

The probability of an event E, denoted $P(E)$, is the sum of the probabilities of the individual outcomes that are members of the event E. The probability of an event is a numerical value between 0 and 1, inclusive, that quantifies the chance or likelihood that the event will occur.

Here is an example.

Given the sample space $S = \{1, 2, 3, 4, 5\}$, the set of outcomes from the tile-drawing experiment, and $E = \{1, 3, 5\}$, the event that the tile drawn shows an odd number, then $P(E) = P(1) + P(3) + P(5) = \frac{1}{5} + \frac{1}{5} + \frac{1}{5} = \frac{3}{5}$.

Outcomes are equally likely if each outcome is as likely to occur as any other outcome.

If all outcomes in the sample space are equally likely, the probability of an event E is given by

$$P(E) = \frac{\text{Number of outcomes favorable to } E}{\text{Total number of outcomes in the sample space}}$$

For example, if the sample space is $S = \{1, 2, 3, 4, 5\}$, the set of outcomes from the tile-drawing experiment, and E is the event that the tile drawn shows an odd number, then $P(E) = \frac{\text{Number of outcomes favorable to } E}{\text{Total number of outcomes in the sample space}} = \frac{3}{5}$.

Tip: In a probability problem involving equally likely outcomes, the number of total outcomes possible will always be greater than or equal to the number of outcomes favorable to the event, so check to make sure that the denominator is *larger than* or *equal to* the numerator when you plug into the formula.

Probabilities can be expressed as fractions, decimals, or percents. In the example given, the probability of drawing an odd-numbered tile can be expressed as $\frac{3}{5}$, 0.6, or 60 percent.

Keep in mind that the formula for probability in which the outcomes are equally likely will *not* apply to sample spaces in which the events are not equally likely. For instance, the sample space for spinning the spinner shown is $S = \{green, red, yellow\}$.

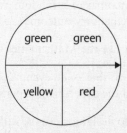

The probabilities for the different outcomes are the following: $P(\text{red}) = \frac{1}{4}$, $P(\text{yellow}) = \frac{1}{4}$, and $P(\text{green}) = \frac{1}{2}$. The three outcomes are not equally likely because the green section is larger than the other two sections.

Tip: Always remember to check whether the outcomes are equally likely before using the formula for probability.

An event is certain to occur if and only if the probability of the event is 1. An event is impossible if and only if the probability of the event is 0. The probability of any event is a number between 0 and 1, inclusive. For example, suppose the sample space is $S = \{1, 2, 3, 4, 5\}$, the set of outcomes from the tile-drawing experiment; W is the event that the tile drawn shows a whole number; and Z is the event that the tile drawn shows the number 6. Then $P(W) = 1$ and $P(Z) = 0$.

Thus, the lowest probability you can have is 0, and the highest probability you can have is 1. All other probabilities fall between 0 and 1. You can express this relationship symbolically this way: $0 \leq P(X) \leq 1$, for any event X. The closer the probability of an event is to 1, the more likely the event is to occur; the closer the probability of an event is to 0, the less likely the event is to occur.

Tip: If you work a probability problem and your answer is greater than 1 or your answer is negative, you've made a mistake! Go back and check your work.

Determining the outcomes in a sample space is a critical step in solving a probability problem. For simple experiments, counting techniques such as making a tree diagram or an organized chart are two useful ways to generate a list of the outcomes. More sophisticated techniques, which include the fundamental counting principle, permutations, and combinations, are needed for problems that are less straightforward. See the topic "Counting Techniques" in Chapter 11, "Discrete Mathematics," for a discussion of these methods.

Here is an example of using a tree diagram to determine the outcomes in a sample space.

Find the sample space for the experiment of recording the up faces when a fair coin is tossed, and then a fair six-sided die is rolled. The tree starts with the possibilities for the coin toss and then branches to the possibilities for the roll of the die as shown, where "H" stands for "heads appears on the up face of the coin," "T" stands for "tails appears on the up face of the coin," "1" stands for "the number 1 appears on the up face of the die," "2" stands for "the number 2 appears on the up face of the die," and so on.

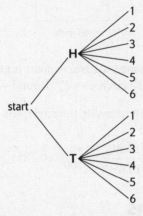

By following the different paths, you can determine that the sample space is {H1, H2, H3, H4, H5, H6, T1, T2, T3, T4, T5, T6} and that there are 12 total possible (equally likely) outcomes for the experiment.

Here is an example of using an organized chart to determine the outcomes of a sample space.

Finding the sample space for tossing a coin and observing the up face three times.

The table is constructed using the labels "1st toss," "2nd toss," and "3rd toss" as headings and then listing all possibilities under the headings.

1st Toss	2nd Toss	3rd Toss
H	H	H
H	H	T
H	T	H
H	T	T
T	H	H
T	H	T
T	T	H
T	T	T

From the table, you can determine that the sample space is {HHH, HHT, HTH, HTT, THH, THT, TTH, TTT} and that there are eight total possible (equally likely) outcomes for the experiment.

> **Tip: When you use a chart to list the outcomes for an experiment, proceed systematically so that you don't overcount or undercount the outcomes.**

Geometric Probability

Geometric probability involves determining probabilities associated with geometric objects.

Here is an example.

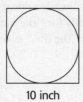

10 inch

The figure shown is a circle inscribed in a 10-inch square. A point is randomly selected within the square. What is the probability that the point will be inside the circle as well? Round your answer to three decimal places.

To calculate the probability that the point will be inside the circle, you calculate the ratio of the area of the circle to the area of the square.

$$P(\text{point is inside circle}) = \frac{\text{area of circle}}{\text{area of square}} = \frac{\pi(5 \text{ in})^2}{(10 \text{ in})^2} = \frac{25\pi}{100} \approx 0.785$$

Probability Distributions

A random variable is a function X that assigns a real number x, determined by chance, to each outcome in a sample space. The number x is referred to as a value of the random variable.

> **Note: Random variables can be discrete or continuous. This chapter deals only with discrete random variables.**

A probability distribution is a graph, chart, table, or formula that gives the probability for each of the random variable's values.

Suppose in the experiment (given previously) of drawing one tile (without looking) from a box containing five wooden, one-inch square tiles numbered 1 through 5 that the random variable X assigns the value 6 to the outcomes that show an odd number on the drawn tile and the value 1 to the outcomes that show an even number on the drawn tile. Then, the following table is the probability distribution for X:

x	6	1
$P(x)$	$\frac{3}{5}$	$\frac{2}{5}$

Conditional Probability and Independent and Dependent Events

For this topic, you must demonstrate an understanding of concepts of conditional probability and independent and dependent events and be able to compute the probability of a compound event (*Mathematics: Content Knowledge (0061) Test at a Glance*, page 5).

Compound Events

A compound event is any event combining two or more given events.

The complement of an event A, denoted $\overline{A}$ (or A^c), is the event that A does not occur. The probability of the complement of an event A is given by $P(\overline{A}) = 1 - P(A)$. For example, if $P(A) = 0.06$, then $P(\overline{A}) = 1 - P(A) = 1 - 0.06 = 0.94$.

In probability, the word *or* is used in the inclusive sense. Thus, $P(A \text{ or } B)$ is the probability that event A occurs or event B occurs or that both events occur simultaneously on one trial of an experiment.

Tip: You will find it helpful to know that *P(A or B)* is the probability that at least one of the events *A* or *B* occurs.

Addition Rule and Mutually Exclusive Events

The Addition Rule states that $P(A \text{ or } B) = P(A) + P(B) - P(A \text{ and } B)$. This rule applies to *one* trial of an experiment.

Here is an example.

A standard deck of 52 playing cards consists of four suits: clubs (♣), spades (♠), hearts (♥), and diamonds (♦). Clubs and spades are black-colored suits; hearts and diamonds are red-colored suits. Each suit has 13 cards consisting of three face cards (king, queen, and jack) and number cards from one (ace) to 10 as shown here.

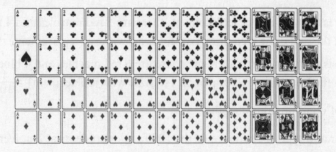

Standard Deck of 52 Playing Cards

Suppose a card is drawn at random from a standard deck of 52 playing cards—find the probability that the card is a face card or a diamond.

There are 12 face cards so $P(\text{face card}) = \frac{12}{52}$. There are 13 diamonds, so $P(\text{diamond}) = \frac{13}{52}$. There are 3 diamond face cards, so $P(\text{face card and diamond}) = \frac{3}{52}$. Thus, $P(\text{face card or diamond}) = P(\text{face card}) + P(\text{diamond}) - P(\text{face card and diamond}) = \frac{12}{52} + \frac{13}{52} - \frac{3}{52} = \frac{22}{52} = \frac{11}{26}$.

Usually the most efficient and straightforward way to find $P(A \text{ or } B)$ is to sum the number of ways that event A can occur and the number of ways that event B can occur, *being sure to add in such a way that no outcome is counted twice*, and then to divide by the total number of outcomes in the sample space.

Applying this strategy for the example given, you have the following.

There are 12 face cards. There are 10 diamonds that are *not* face cards. Thus, there are 12 + 10 = 22 distinct cards favorable to the event "face card or diamond." Therefore, $P(\text{face card or diamond}) = \frac{12+10}{52} = \frac{22}{52} = \frac{11}{26}$.

Two events are mutually exclusive if they cannot occur at the same time; that is, they have no outcomes in common. For example, suppose you draw one card from a deck of cards, the event of drawing a king and the event of drawing an ace are mutually exclusive.

When two events A and B are mutually exclusive, $P(A \text{ or } B) = P(A) + P(B)$. Here is an example.

One card is randomly drawn from a well-shuffled standard deck of 52 playing cards. Find the probability that the card drawn is a king or an ace.

There are 4 kings in the deck, so $P(\text{king}) = \frac{4}{52}$. There are 4 aces in the deck, so $P(\text{ace}) = \frac{4}{52}$. The event of drawing a king and the event of drawing an ace are mutually exclusive (since you cannot draw both at the same time on one draw from the deck), so you have:

$$P(\text{king or ace}) = P(\text{king}) + P(\text{ace}) = \frac{4}{52} + \frac{4}{52} = \frac{8}{52} = \frac{2}{13}$$

Conditional Probability

The probability of an event B, given that an event A has occurred, is a conditional probability, denoted $P(B|A)$ (said as "Probability of B given A"). In other words, you compute the probability of event B by taking into account that the event A has already occurred. Here is an example.

Suppose you draw two marbles, one after the other, from a box containing 6 red marbles and 4 blue marbles—find the probability of drawing a blue marble on the second draw given that (a) a red marble was drawn *without replacement* on the first draw and (b) a red marble was drawn *with replacement* on the first draw. Note: "With replacement" means that the first marble drawn is put back in the box before the second drawing takes place. "Without replacement" means that the first marble is not put back before the second drawing takes place.

(a) After the red marble is drawn without replacement, there are 5 red marbles and 4 blue marbles in the box. Therefore, $P(\text{blue on the 2nd draw} \mid \text{red drawn on 1st draw without replacement}) = \frac{4}{9}$.

(b) After the red marble is drawn with replacement, there are 6 red marbles and 4 blue marbles in the box. Therefore, $P(\text{blue on the 2nd draw} \mid \text{red drawn on 1st draw with replacement}) = \frac{4}{10} = \frac{2}{5}$.

Here is another example of conditional probability.

The table shows the gender and type of residence of the 2000 senior students at a university.

Gender and Type of Residence of Senior Students ($n = 2000$)		
	Females	**Males**
Apartment	229	180
Dorm	203	118
House	200	272
With Parent(s)	258	201
Sorority/Fraternity House	241	98

What is the probability that a senior selected at random (a) lives in a dorm given that the senior is female? (b) is a female senior given that the senior lives in a dorm?

(a) The total number of female seniors is 229 + 203 + 200 + 258 + 241 = 1131. Of that total, 203 live in a dorm. Thus,
$$P(\text{Dorm} \mid \text{Female}) = \frac{203}{1131}.$$

(b) The total number of seniors living in a dorm is 203 + 118 = 321. Of that total, 203 are female. Thus,
$$P(\text{Female} \mid \text{Dorm}) = \frac{203}{321}.$$

Tip: Notice that, generally, in a conditional probability situation, the total number of outcomes under consideration is "reduced" to a fewer number than with which the original problem began.

Multiplication Rule and Independent and Dependent Events

The Multiplication Rule states that $P(A \text{ and } B) = P(A)P(B|A)$. This rule applies when *two* trials are performed. Here is an example.

Two cards are drawn at random, one after the other, without replacement from a standard deck of 52 playing cards. What is the probability of drawing a jack on the first draw and a king on the second draw?

There are 4 jacks in the deck of 52 cards, so the probability of a jack on the first draw is $\frac{4}{52}$. After the jack is drawn without replacement, there are 4 kings in the remaining deck of 51 cards. Therefore, $P(\text{jack on 1st draw}$ and king on 2nd draw) = $P(\text{jack on 1st draw}) \, P(\text{king on 2nd draw} \mid \text{jack on 1st draw}) = \frac{4}{52} \cdot \frac{4}{51} = \frac{1}{13} \cdot \frac{4}{51} = \frac{4}{13 \cdot 51}$.

Note: In the Mathematics CK, sometimes the computations are indicated, as in this example.

If $P(A \text{ and } B) = P(A)P(B)$, then the events A and B are independent. Here is an example.

Two cards are drawn at random with replacement from a standard deck of 52 playing cards. What is the probability of drawing a club on the first draw and a king on the second draw?

There are 13 clubs in the deck of 52 cards, so the probability of a club on the first draw is $\frac{13}{52}$. After the club is drawn and replaced in the deck, there are 4 kings in the deck of 52 cards. Therefore,

$P(\text{club on 1st draw and king on 2nd draw}) = P(\text{club on 1st draw}) \, P(\text{king on 2nd draw} \mid \text{club on 1st draw}) = \frac{13}{52} \cdot \frac{4}{52} = \frac{1}{52}$.

Notice that in this case, that $P(\text{club on 1st draw and king on 2nd draw}) = \frac{13}{52} \cdot \frac{4}{52} = P(\text{club}) \, P(\text{king})$, so the event of drawing a club on the first draw with replacement and the event of drawing a king on the second draw are independent.

Tip: For the Mathematics CK, to find the probability that event *A* occurs on the first trial and event *B* occurs on the second trial, multiply the probability of event *A* times the probability of event *B*, where you have determined the probability of *B* by taking into account that the event *A* has already occurred.

Two events A and B are independent if the occurrence of one does not affect the probability of the occurrence of the other. Here is an example.

Suppose you flip a coin, and then toss a fair die. The event of obtaining a head on the up face of the fair coin and the event of obtaining a five on the up face of the fair die are independent.

If events A and B are not independent, they are said to be dependent. Here is an example.

Suppose you draw two marbles, one after the other, from a box containing 6 red marbles and 4 blue marbles. The event of drawing a red marble without replacement on the first draw and the event of drawing a blue marble on the second draw are dependent.

For some problems, you might find it convenient to determine the probability that at least one of something of interest occurs by using the multiplication rule and the rule of complements as follows: $P(\text{at least one}) = 1 - P(\text{none})$.

Here is an example.

A fair coin is tossed three times. Find the probability that at least one head occurs. The sample space is {HHH, HHT, HTH, HTT, THH, THT, TTH, TTT}, where "H" indicates "heads" and "T" indicates "tails." Thus, P(at least one head) $= 1 - P(\text{no heads}) = 1 - P(\text{TTT}) = 1 - \frac{1}{8} = \frac{7}{8}$. By looking at the sample space, you can see that this answer is correct because there are seven outcomes in which a head occurs. In fact, you could have worked the problem directly as follows: P(at least one head) $= \frac{7}{8}$. With larger sample spaces, it is often more convenient to determine the probability of at least one by using $1 - P(\text{none})$.

Odds

The odds in favor of an event A are given by $\dfrac{P(A)}{1-P(A)}$, usually expressed in the form $p: q$ (or p to q), where

p and q are integers with no common factors and $\dfrac{P(A)}{1-P(A)} = \dfrac{p}{q}$. The odds against an event A are given by

$\dfrac{1-P(A)}{P(A)}$, usually expressed in the form $q: p$ (or q to p), where p and q are integers with no common factors

and $\dfrac{1-P(A)}{P(A)} = \dfrac{q}{p}$. Here is an example.

Find the odds in favor of and the odds against getting a two on the up face when a fair die is rolled one time.

$P(\text{two}) = \frac{1}{6}$. Thus, the odds in favor of getting a two are given by $\dfrac{\frac{1}{6}}{1-\frac{1}{6}} = \dfrac{\frac{1}{6}}{\frac{5}{6}} = \dfrac{1}{5}$ or 1 to 5, and the odds against getting a two are 5 to 1.

Expected Value

For this topic, you must be able to compute and interpret the expected value of random variables in simple cases (for example: fair coins, expected winnings, expected profit) (*Mathematics: Content Knowledge (0061) Test at a Glance*, page 5).

If X is a discrete random variable that takes on values $x_1, x_2,...,x_n$, with respective probabilities $P(x_1), P(x_2),...P(x_n)$, the expected value, denoted $E(X)$, is the theoretical mean μ of X and is given by

$$\mu = E(X) = x_1 P(x_1) + x_2 P(x_2) + \cdots + x_n P(x_n).$$

For the random variable X (see "Probability Distributions" earlier in this chapter), developed from the experiment of drawing one tile (without looking) from a box containing five wooden, one-inch square tiles numbered 1 through 5, where the random variable X assigns the value 6 to the outcomes that show an odd number on the drawn tile and the value 1 to the outcomes that show an even number on the drawn tile, you have the following probability distribution and expected value:

x	6	1
$P(x)$	$\frac{3}{5}$	$\frac{2}{5}$

$$\mu = E(X) = x_1 P(x_1) + x_2 P(x_2) = 6 \cdot \frac{3}{5} + 1 \cdot \frac{2}{5} = 4$$

You can use your understanding of probability distributions and expected value to decide whether a game is fair. For instance, suppose you pay 5 chips to play a game with the numbered tiles. You receive 6 chips if the tile drawn shows an odd number and 1 chip if the tile drawn shows an even number. Your expected value for the game is 4 chips. Because you are paying a 5-chip fee to play the game, on average, you lose 1 chip per play. The game is not fair, since you, the player, can expect to lose.

Empirical Probability

In empirical probability, the probability of an event E is defined by conducting the experiment a large number of times, called trials, and counting the number of times that event E actually occurred. Based on these results, the probability of E is *estimated* as follows:

$$\text{Empirical Probability of } E = P(E) = \frac{\text{Number of times } E \text{ occurred}}{\text{Total number of trials}}$$

As the numbers of trials increase, the empirical probability approaches the event's true probability. An event's empirical probability is also called its relative frequency probability or experimental probability.

Here is an example.

Out of 100 light bulbs tested at Company X, two are defective. What is the empirical probability that a Company X light bulb is defective?

Empirical P(Company X light bulb is defective) $= \frac{2}{100} = 0.02 = 2\%$

In some situations, empirical probability is the only feasible way to assign a probability to an event. For instance, insurance companies set premiums based on empirical probabilities.

Chapter 10

Matrix Algebra

According to the *Mathematics: Content Knowledge Test (0061) at a Glance* (www.ets.org/Media/Tests/PRAXIS/pdf/0061.pdf), the Matrix Algebra content category of the Mathematics CK tests your knowledge and skills in five topic areas:

- Vectors and matrices
- Operations with matrices
- Solving systems of linear equations
- Determinants
- Representation of geometric transformations

This review discusses the key ideas and formulas in each topic area that are most important for you to know for the Mathematics CK.

Vectors and Matrices

For this topic, you must demonstrate an understanding of vectors and matrices as systems that have some of the same properties as the real number system (for example: identity, inverse, and commutativity under addition and multiplication) (*Mathematics: Content Knowledge (0061) Test at a Glance*, page 5).

A matrix is a rectangular array of elements. For the Mathematics CK, the elements of a matrix are real or complex numbers or expressions representing real or complex numbers. A matrix with m rows and n columns is an $m \times n$ matrix. Matrices are commonly denoted by uppercase letters and their elements by the corresponding lowercase letters, which are subscripted to indicate the location of the elements in the matrix. For a matrix A, the notation a_{ij} denotes the element in the ith row and jth column of the matrix. It is also customary to denote an $m \times n$ matrix A by $\left[a_{ij} \right]_{(m, n)}$ or simply by $\left[a_{ij} \right]$, if the order is clear.

> **Tip:** Your graphing calculator has a matrix menu that allows you to define, edit, or display a matrix. Most graphing calculators will allow up to ninety-nine rows or columns, depending on available memory.

The order of a matrix is the number of rows and columns it contains; thus, an $m \times n$ matrix has order $m \times n$. A $1 \times n$ matrix is a row vector of order n. An $m \times 1$ matrix is a column vector of order m. If $m = n$, the matrix is a square matrix of order n. Here is an example of a 2×3 matrix.

$$\begin{bmatrix} 5 & 0 & 4 \\ 6 & -2 & 9 \end{bmatrix}_{2 \times 3}$$

The main diagonal of a square matrix of order n is the diagonal of elements $a_{11}, a_{22}, \ldots, a_{nn}$ from the top-left corner to the bottom-right corner of the matrix.

A diagonal matrix is a square matrix whose only nonzero elements are on the main diagonal. A diagonal matrix that has only ones on the main diagonal is an identity matrix. The identity matrix of order n is denoted I_n. Here is an example.

$$I_2 = \begin{bmatrix} 1 & 0 \\ 0 & 1 \end{bmatrix}$$

A zero matrix, denoted 0 (or $0_{m \times n}$), is a matrix containing only 0 elements.

The negative of a matrix $A = \begin{bmatrix} a_{ij} \end{bmatrix}$ is the matrix $-A = \begin{bmatrix} -a_{ij} \end{bmatrix}$, whose elements are the negatives of their corresponding elements in A.

Two matrices A and B are equal if and only if they have the same order and their corresponding elements are equal. Therefore, if two matrices $A = \begin{bmatrix} a_{ij} \end{bmatrix}$ and $B = \begin{bmatrix} b_{ij} \end{bmatrix}$ are equal, then $a_{ij} = b_{ij}$, for $1 \leq i \leq m$ and $1 \leq j \leq n$.

The transpose of an $m \times n$ matrix A is an $n \times m$ matrix, denoted A^T (read as "A transpose"), obtained by interchanging the rows and columns of A. The transpose of a matrix A is also denoted A'. Here is an example.

Given $A = \begin{bmatrix} 5 & 0 & 4 \\ 6 & -2 & 9 \end{bmatrix}_{2 \times 3}$, then $A^T = \begin{bmatrix} 5 & 6 \\ 0 & -2 \\ 4 & 9 \end{bmatrix}_{3 \times 2}$

Tip: Your graphing calculator has a matrix feature that will return the transpose of a matrix.

A square matrix A is said to be symmetric if $A = A^T$. Here is an example.

$$A = \begin{bmatrix} 1 & 2 & 0 \\ 2 & 0 & -3 \\ 0 & -3 & 5 \end{bmatrix}_{3 \times 3} = A^T$$

With respect to arithmetic operations with matrices (which will be defined in the next section, "Operations with Matrices"), matrices *that contain elements that are complex numbers or real numbers* have some properties in common with the properties of their elements. With respect to the operation of matrix addition, the set of $m \times n$ matrices is closed, commutative, and associative, and has an additive identity and an additive inverse for each $m \times n$ matrix. For the operation of matrix multiplication, certain restrictions on the order of the matrices involved in the multiplication must be met before the operation is defined. For situations in which matrix multiplication is defined, matrix multiplication is closed, associative, has a multiplicative identity, and distributes over addition. In general, matrix multiplication is *not* commutative, nor does there always exist multiplicative inverses.

Operations with Matrices

For this topic, you must be able to perform scalar multiplication and add, subtract, and multiply vectors and matrices and find inverses of matrices (*Mathematics: Content Knowledge (0061) Test at a Glance*, page 5).

A scalar is a number or numerical quantity.

The scalar product, *kA,* of an $m \times n$ matrix $A = \begin{bmatrix} a_{ij} \end{bmatrix}$ and a scalar k is the $m \times n$ matrix $R = kA$, where $[r_{ij}] = [ka_{ij}]$. *Note:* Any size matrix can be multiplied by a scalar. Here are examples.

$$3 \begin{bmatrix} 5 & 2 \\ 0 & -1 \end{bmatrix} = \begin{bmatrix} 15 & 6 \\ 0 & -3 \end{bmatrix}$$

Tip: You can use the multiplication key on your graphing calculator's keyboard to find a scalar product.

Two matrices are conformable for matrix addition or subtraction if they have the same order. *Addition or subtraction of matrices with unlike orders is not defined.*

The sum, *A + B,* of two $m \times n$ matrices $A = \begin{bmatrix} a_{ij} \end{bmatrix}$ and $B = \begin{bmatrix} b_{ij} \end{bmatrix}$ is the $m \times n$ matrix $S = A + B$, where $[s_{ij}] = [a_{ij} + b_{ij}]$. Here is an example.

Given $A = \begin{bmatrix} 4 & 1 \\ -3 & 6 \end{bmatrix}$ and $B = \begin{bmatrix} 2 & -5 \\ 0 & 3 \end{bmatrix}$, find $A + B$.

$$A + B = \begin{bmatrix} 4 & 1 \\ -3 & 6 \end{bmatrix} + \begin{bmatrix} 2 & -5 \\ 0 & 3 \end{bmatrix} = \begin{bmatrix} 6 & -4 \\ -3 & 9 \end{bmatrix}$$

With respect to matrix addition, the 0 matrix is the additive identity element and $-A$ is the additive inverse for the matrix A. That is, if A and 0 have the same order, then $A + 0 = 0 + A = A$ and $A + -A = -A + A = 0$.

The difference, $A - B$, of two matrices is defined to be $A + (-B)$.

Tip: Provided the matrices have the same order, you can use the addition key on your graphing calculator's keyboard to perform matrix addition. Practice using this helpful calculator feature before you take the Mathematics CK.

The inner product (also called the dot product), $A \cdot B$, *in that order* of a $1 \times m$ row vector $A = [a_{11}, a_{12}, \ldots a_{1m}]$ and

an $m \times 1$ column vector $B = \begin{bmatrix} b_{11} \\ b_{21} \\ \vdots \\ b_{m1} \end{bmatrix}$ is the scalar $a_{11}b_{11} + a_{12}b_{21} + \ldots + a_{1m}b_{m1}$. Notice that you multiply *row by column*:

multiply each element of the row times the corresponding element of the column and then sum the products. Here is an example.

Find the inner product of $A = [1\ \ 0\ \ 5\ \ -2]$ and $B = \begin{bmatrix} 3 \\ -1 \\ 0 \\ 4 \end{bmatrix}$.

$$A \cdot B = \begin{bmatrix} 1 & 0 & 5 & -2 \end{bmatrix} \cdot \begin{bmatrix} 3 \\ -1 \\ 0 \\ 4 \end{bmatrix} = 1 \cdot 3 + 0 \cdot (-1) + 5 \cdot 0 + -2 \cdot 4 = -5$$

Two matrices, A and B, are conformable for matrix multiplication in the order AB, only if the number of columns of matrix A is equal to the number of rows of matrix B. In the product, AB, we say B is premultiplied by A and A is postmultiplied by B. *Multiplication of matrices that are not conformable is not defined.*

The product, AB, *in that order* of an $m \times k$ matrix $A = \begin{bmatrix} a_{ij} \end{bmatrix}$ and a $k \times n$ matrix $B = \begin{bmatrix} b_{ij} \end{bmatrix}$ is the $m \times n$ matrix $C = \begin{bmatrix} c_{ij} \end{bmatrix} = \begin{bmatrix} a_{i1}b_{1j} + a_{i2}b_{2j} + \cdots + a_{ik}b_{kj} \end{bmatrix}$, for $1 \le i \le m$ and $1 \le j \le n$. Notice that the element c_{ij} is the inner product of the ith row of A and the jth column of B. Here is an example.

Given $A = \begin{bmatrix} 1 & 5 \\ 3 & -5 \end{bmatrix}$ and $B = \begin{bmatrix} 0 & 4 & 2 \\ -5 & 3 & 1 \end{bmatrix}$, compute AB.

$$AB = \begin{bmatrix} 1 & 5 \\ 3 & -5 \end{bmatrix} \begin{bmatrix} 0 & 4 & 2 \\ -5 & 3 & 1 \end{bmatrix} = \begin{bmatrix} 1 \cdot 0 + 5 \cdot (-5) & 1 \cdot 4 + 5 \cdot 3 & 1 \cdot 2 + 5 \cdot 1 \\ 3 \cdot 0 + (-5) \cdot (-5) & 3 \cdot 4 + (-5) \cdot 3 & 3 \cdot 2 + (-5) \cdot 1 \end{bmatrix} =$$

$$\begin{bmatrix} -25 & 19 & 7 \\ 25 & -3 & 1 \end{bmatrix}$$

Tip: Provided the matrices are conformable for multiplication, you can use the multiplication key on your graphing calculator's keyboard to perform matrix multiplication. However, because of the distinctive way that matrix multiplication is defined, in general, matrix multiplication is not commutative, not even for square matrices of the same order. Because of this noncommutative feature of matrix arithmetic, you must pay careful attention to the order of the factors in any product of matrices when you are taking the Mathematics CK.

With respect to matrix multiplication, the matrix I is the multiplicative identity element; that is, if A is an $m \times n$ matrix, then $AI_n = A$ and $I_m A = A$.

If A is a square matrix of order n and there exists a square matrix B of order n such that $AB = BA = I$, then B is called the inverse of A. A matrix A that has an inverse is said to be invertible (or nonsingular). If no such matrix B exists, then A is singular.

Not all square matrices have inverses, but when the inverse for a square matrix exists, the inverse is unique and is designated A^{-1}. Thus, $AA^{-1} = A^{-1}A = I$.

The inverse of a 2×2 nonsingular matrix $A = \begin{bmatrix} a_{11} & a_{12} \\ a_{21} & a_{22} \end{bmatrix}$ is given by $A^{-1} = \frac{1}{\det(A)} \begin{bmatrix} a_{22} & -a_{12} \\ -a_{21} & a_{11} \end{bmatrix}$, where $\det(A) =$

$a_{11}a_{22} - a_{12}a_{21} \neq 0$. The scalar $\det(A) = a_{11}a_{22} - a_{12}a_{21}$ is the determinant of A. (See the section "Determinants" in this chapter for an additional discussion on determinants.) The matrix $A = \begin{bmatrix} a_{11} & a_{12} \\ a_{21} & a_{22} \end{bmatrix}$ has an inverse if and only if $\det(A) = a_{11}a_{22} - a_{12}a_{21} \neq 0$. Here is an example.

Let $A = \begin{bmatrix} 1 & 1 \\ 4 & 2 \end{bmatrix}$, find A^{-1}.

$$A^{-1} = \frac{1}{\det(A)} \begin{bmatrix} 2 & -1 \\ -4 & 1 \end{bmatrix} = \frac{1}{-2} \cdot \begin{bmatrix} 2 & -1 \\ -4 & 1 \end{bmatrix} = \begin{bmatrix} -1 & 1/2 \\ 2 & -1/2 \end{bmatrix}$$

If you use a graphing calculator, finding the inverse of a nonsingular 2×2 matrix is relatively easy. However, it is important that you know and understand how to find the inverse of a 2×2 matrix *without the use of a graphing calculator*. The procedure, which works *only* for nonsingular 2×2 matrices, can be stated in four steps: (1) Compute $\det(A) = a_{11}a_{22} - a_{12}a_{21}$, (2) switch a_{11} and a_{22}, (3) Change the signs of a_{12} and a_{21} (but don't switch them!), (4) divide each element by $\det(A)$. The reason you must understand the process is that a question might ask about the process rather than for you to find the inverse.

Another process for finding the inverse of a nonsingular 2×2 matrix $A = \begin{bmatrix} a_{11} & a_{12} \\ a_{21} & a_{22} \end{bmatrix}$ is to (1) create the 2×4 partitioned matrix $= \begin{bmatrix} a_{11} & a_{12} & \vdots & 1 & 0 \\ a_{21} & a_{22} & \vdots & 0 & 1 \end{bmatrix}$, which contains A as a submatrix on the left and I as a submatrix on the right, and (2) through a series of elementary row operations (interchanging two rows, multiplying a row by a nonzero scalar, adding two rows, multiplying a row by a scalar and adding the result to a row—all of which can be performed using the matrix menu of your graphing calculator), convert the submatrix A into an identity matrix. This process will yield the matrix $\begin{bmatrix} 1 & 0 & \vdots & \frac{a_{22}}{a_{11}a_{22} - a_{12}a_{21}} & \frac{-a_{12}}{a_{11}a_{22} - a_{12}a_{21}} \\ 0 & 1 & \vdots & \frac{-a_{21}}{a_{11}a_{22} - a_{12}a_{21}} & \frac{a_{11}}{a_{11}a_{22} - a_{12}a_{21}} \end{bmatrix}$, which shows I on the left

and A^{-1} on the right. This latter process will also work for higher-order matrices. Again, it's more important that you understand the process rather than how to actually use it to find the inverse of a matrix when you are taking the Mathematics CK. If you need to find the inverse of a matrix on the test, you should use the reciprocal key on your graphing calculator's keyboard to obtain the inverse so as to avoid tedious calculations that can waste valuable time.

Tip: When you determine an inverse for a matrix using your graphing calculator, if the entries in the inverse matrix are in decimal form, use the feature of your calculator that changes decimals to fractions to display the matrix entries as their fractional equivalents. If the answer cannot be simplified or the resulting denominator is more than three digits, most graphing calculators will return the decimal equivalent.

Solving Systems of Linear Equations

For this topic, you must be able to use matrix techniques to solve systems of linear equations (*Mathematics: Content Knowledge (0061) Test at a Glance*, page 5).

$$a_{11}x + a_{12}y + a_{13}z = c_1$$

A system of three equations with three unknowns is given by: $a_{21}x + a_{22}y + a_{23}z = c_2$

$$a_{31}x + a_{32}y + a_{33}z = c_3$$

This system can be solved using the algebraic methods of substitution and elimination (which are presented in the section "Systems of Equations and Inequalities" in Chapter 1, titled "Algebra and Number Theory") or the system can be solved using a technique called "transformation of the augmented matrix," which will be presented in this section. The system is said to be consistent if it has a solution; otherwise, the system is said to be inconsistent.

The augmented matrix for the system is the matrix $\begin{bmatrix} a_{11} & a_{12} & a_{13} & c_1 \\ a_{21} & a_{22} & a_{23} & c_2 \\ a_{31} & a_{32} & a_{33} & c_3 \end{bmatrix}$.

To solve the system, you use elementary row operations (interchanging two rows, multiplying a row by a nonzero scalar, adding two rows, multiplying a row by a scalar, and adding the result to a row) to transform the submatrix of coefficients a_{ij} as close as possible into the identity matrix. When the system is consistent, the results will be one of the following reduced row-echelon forms:

$\begin{bmatrix} 1 & 0 & 0 & x_0 \\ 0 & 1 & 0 & y_0 \\ 0 & 0 & 1 & z_0 \end{bmatrix}$, which yields the unique solution $x = x_0, y = y_0, z = z_0$;

$\begin{bmatrix} 1 & 0 & k_1 & x_0 \\ 0 & 1 & k_2 & y_0 \\ 0 & 0 & 0 & 0 \end{bmatrix}$, which yields the nonunique solution $x = x_0 - k_1 t, y = y_0 - k_2 t, z = t$, where t is an

arbitrarily chosen value for the "free" variable z; or

$\begin{bmatrix} 1 & j_1 & k_1 & x_0 \\ 0 & 0 & 0 & 0 \\ 0 & 0 & 0 & 0 \end{bmatrix}$, which yields the nonunique solution $x = x_0 - j_1 s - k_1 t, y = s, z = t$, where s and t are

arbitrarily chosen values for the free variables y and z.

Here is an example

$$x - 2y + 3z = 1$$

Solve the system: $x + 3y - z = 4$

$$2x + y - 2z = 13$$

The augmented matrix for the system is the matrix $\begin{bmatrix} 1 & -2 & 3 & 1 \\ 1 & 3 & -1 & 4 \\ 2 & 1 & -2 & 13 \end{bmatrix}$

$$\begin{bmatrix} 1 & -2 & 3 & 1 \\ 1 & 3 & -1 & 4 \\ 2 & 1 & -2 & 13 \end{bmatrix} \xrightarrow{\text{Multiply row 1 by } -1 \text{ and add to row 2}} \begin{bmatrix} 1 & -2 & 3 & 1 \\ 0 & 5 & -4 & 3 \\ 2 & 1 & -2 & 13 \end{bmatrix}$$

$$\xrightarrow{\text{Multiply row 1 by } -2 \text{ and add to row 3}} \begin{bmatrix} 1 & -2 & 3 & 1 \\ 0 & 5 & -4 & 3 \\ 0 & 5 & -8 & 11 \end{bmatrix}$$

$$\xrightarrow{\text{Multiply row 2 by } -1 \text{ and add to row 3}} \begin{bmatrix} 1 & -2 & 3 & 1 \\ 0 & 5 & -4 & 3 \\ 0 & 0 & -4 & 8 \end{bmatrix}$$

$$\xrightarrow{\text{Multiply row 3 by} -1 \text{ and add to row 2}} \begin{bmatrix} 1 & -2 & 3 & 1 \\ 0 & 5 & 0 & -5 \\ 0 & 0 & -4 & 8 \end{bmatrix}$$

$$\xrightarrow{\text{Multiply row 2 by } \frac{1}{5} \text{ and row 3 by } -\frac{1}{4}} \begin{bmatrix} 1 & -2 & 3 & 1 \\ 0 & 1 & 0 & -1 \\ 0 & 0 & 1 & -2 \end{bmatrix}$$

$$\xrightarrow{\text{Multiply row 2 by 2 and add to row 1}} \begin{bmatrix} 1 & 0 & 3 & -1 \\ 0 & 1 & 0 & -1 \\ 0 & 0 & 1 & -2 \end{bmatrix}$$

$$\xrightarrow{\text{Multiply row 3 by } -3 \text{ and add to row 1}} \begin{bmatrix} 1 & 0 & 0 & 5 \\ 0 & 1 & 0 & -1 \\ 0 & 0 & 1 & -2 \end{bmatrix}$$

The solution is $x = 5$, $y = -1$, $z = -2$.

The process of reducing the augmented matrix to reduced row-echelon form can be very time-consuming and tedious. Since the Mathematics CK is a timed test, you should use your graphing calculator to find the solution. Enter the elements of the augmented matrix into the calculator, have the calculator produce the reduced row-echelon form of the augmented matrix, and then "read" the solution from the display.

The technique of solving a system of linear equations by transformation of the augmented matrix can be applied to a system of n equations with n unknowns such as
$$\begin{array}{l} a_{11}x_1 + a_{12}x_2 + \cdots + a_{1n}x_n = c_1 \\ a_{21}x_1 + a_{22}x_2 + \cdots + a_{2n}x_n = c_2 \\ \cdots \quad \cdots \quad \cdots \quad \cdots \quad \cdots \\ a_{n1}x_1 + a_{n2}x_2 + \cdots + a_{nn}x_n = c_n \end{array}.$$

You would proceed in the same manner as shown for systems with three equations and three unknowns.

Determinants

For this topic, you must be able to use determinants to reason about inverses of matrices and solutions to systems of equations (*Mathematics: Content Knowledge (0061) Test at a Glance*, page 5).

For every square matrix A there is a unique corresponding scalar called the determinant of A, denoted $\det(A)$ (or $|a_{ij}|$), which is a well-defined combination of products of the elements of A. Notice that only square matrices have determinants.

The determinant of a 2×2 matrix $A = \begin{bmatrix} a_{11} & a_{12} \\ a_{21} & a_{22} \end{bmatrix}$ is given by $\det(A) = \begin{vmatrix} a_{11} & a_{12} \\ a_{21} & a_{22} \end{vmatrix} = a_{11}a_{22} - a_{12}a_{21}.$

One way to obtain the determinant of a 3×3 matrix $A = \begin{bmatrix} a_{11} & a_{12} & a_{13} \\ a_{21} & a_{22} & a_{23} \\ a_{31} & a_{32} & a_{33} \end{bmatrix}$ is given by

$$\det(A) = \begin{vmatrix} a_{11} & a_{12} & a_{13} \\ a_{21} & a_{22} & a_{23} \\ a_{31} & a_{32} & a_{33} \end{vmatrix} = a_{11} \begin{vmatrix} a_{22} & a_{23} \\ a_{32} & a_{33} \end{vmatrix} - a_{12} \begin{vmatrix} a_{21} & a_{23} \\ a_{31} & a_{33} \end{vmatrix} + a_{13} \begin{vmatrix} a_{21} & a_{22} \\ a_{31} & a_{32} \end{vmatrix} =$$

$$a_{11}(a_{22}a_{33} - a_{23}a_{32}) - a_{12}(a_{21}a_{33} - a_{23}a_{31}) + a_{13}(a_{21}a_{32} - a_{22}a_{31}).$$

Tip: A common error in applying this definition is to forget the negative sign on the second term.

Here is an example of finding the determinant of a 3×3 matrix.

Find the determinants of $B = \begin{bmatrix} 3 & 0 & 4 \\ -1 & 6 & 2 \\ 5 & -3 & 6 \end{bmatrix}.$

$$\det(B) = \begin{vmatrix} 3 & 0 & 4 \\ -1 & 6 & 2 \\ 5 & -3 & 6 \end{vmatrix} = 3 \begin{vmatrix} 6 & 2 \\ -3 & 6 \end{vmatrix} - 0 \begin{vmatrix} -1 & 2 \\ 5 & 6 \end{vmatrix} + 4 \begin{vmatrix} -1 & 6 \\ 5 & -3 \end{vmatrix} =$$

$$3(36 + 6) - 0(-6 - 10) + 4(3 - 30) = 126 - 108 = 18.$$

If a square matrix has a row or column consisting of only 0s, the determinant of the matrix equals 0.

If A is a square matrix, then $|ka_{ij}| = k|a_{ij}|$.

A matrix has an inverse if and only if its determinant does *not* equal 0.

If the coefficient matrix $A = [a_{ij}]$ of the system of n linear equations with n unknowns given by:

$$a_{11}x_1 + a_{12}x_2 + \cdots + a_{1n}x_n = c_1$$
$$a_{21}x_1 + a_{22}x_2 + \cdots + a_{2n}x_n = c_2$$
$$\cdots \quad \cdots \quad \cdots \quad \cdots \quad \cdots$$
$$a_{n1}x_1 + a_{n2}x_2 + \cdots + a_{nn}x_n = c_n$$

has a nonzero determinant (that is, if $\det(A) \neq 0$), then the system has exactly one solution. If $\det(A) = 0$, then the system might have no solution or infinitely many solutions.

Tip: You can calculate determinants for 2×2, 3×3, and higher-order matrices using your graphing calculator. Always double-check your entries to make sure you have entered the matrix correctly before finding the determinant.

Representation of Geometric Transformations

For this topic, you must be able to represent translations, reflections, rotations, and dilations of objects in the plane by using sketches, coordinates, vectors, and matrices (*Mathematics: Content Knowledge (0061) Test at a Glance*, page 5).

The four geometric transformations are translations, reflections, rotations, and dilations. You can think of geometric transformations as ways to change geometric figures without changing their basic properties. (See "Geometric Transformations" in Chapter 4, titled "Geometry" for an additional discussion of geometric transformations.)

A convenient way to represent geometric transformations is by using matrices. A geometric figure in the plane can be represented by a $2 \times n$ matrix whose columns' elements are the n vertices of the figure. For instance, the triangle T with vertices (x_1, y_1), (x_2, y_2), and (x_3, y_3) shown in the following figure can be represented as $T = \begin{bmatrix} x_1 & x_2 & x_3 \\ y_1 & y_2 & y_3 \end{bmatrix}$.

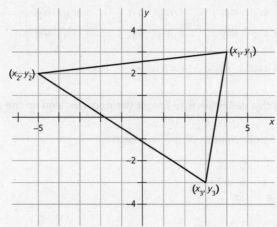

A translation h units horizontally and k units vertically is accomplished by adding the 2×3 translation matrix $\begin{bmatrix} h & h & h \\ k & k & k \end{bmatrix}$ to T: $\begin{bmatrix} h & h & h \\ k & k & k \end{bmatrix} + \begin{bmatrix} x_1 & x_2 & x_3 \\ y_1 & y_2 & y_3 \end{bmatrix} = \begin{bmatrix} h+x_1 & h+x_2 & h+x_3 \\ k+y_1 & k+y_2 & k+y_3 \end{bmatrix}$.

A reflection over the line $y = x$ is accomplished by premultiplying T by the 2×2 matrix $\begin{bmatrix} 0 & 1 \\ 1 & 0 \end{bmatrix}$: $\begin{bmatrix} 0 & 1 \\ 1 & 0 \end{bmatrix}\begin{bmatrix} x_1 & x_2 & x_3 \\ y_1 & y_2 & y_3 \end{bmatrix} = \begin{bmatrix} y_1 & y_2 & y_3 \\ x_1 & x_2 & x_3 \end{bmatrix}$. A reflection over the y-axis is accomplished by premultiplying T by the 2×2 matrix $\begin{bmatrix} -1 & 0 \\ 0 & 1 \end{bmatrix}$: $\begin{bmatrix} -1 & 0 \\ 0 & 1 \end{bmatrix}\begin{bmatrix} x_1 & x_2 & x_3 \\ y_1 & y_2 & y_3 \end{bmatrix} = \begin{bmatrix} -x_1 & -x_2 & -x_3 \\ y_1 & y_2 & y_3 \end{bmatrix}$. A reflection over the x-axis is accomplished by premultiplying T by the 2×2 matrix $\begin{bmatrix} 1 & 0 \\ 0 & -1 \end{bmatrix}$: $\begin{bmatrix} 1 & 0 \\ 0 & -1 \end{bmatrix}\begin{bmatrix} x_1 & x_2 & x_3 \\ y_1 & y_2 & y_3 \end{bmatrix} = \begin{bmatrix} x_1 & x_2 & x_3 \\ -y_1 & -y_2 & -y_3 \end{bmatrix}$.

A rotation of θ degrees about the origin is accomplished by premultiplying T by the 2×2 matrix $\begin{bmatrix} \cos\theta & -\sin\theta \\ \sin\theta & \cos\theta \end{bmatrix}$. For instance, for a 90° clockwise rotation ($\theta = -90°$), premultiply T by $\begin{bmatrix} 0 & 1 \\ -1 & 0 \end{bmatrix}$: $\begin{bmatrix} 0 & 1 \\ -1 & 0 \end{bmatrix}\begin{bmatrix} x_1 & x_2 & x_3 \\ y_1 & y_2 & y_3 \end{bmatrix} = \begin{bmatrix} y_1 & y_2 & y_3 \\ -x_1 & -x_2 & -x_3 \end{bmatrix}$.

A dilation by a scale factor k is accomplished by premultiplying T by the 2×2 matrix $\begin{bmatrix} k & 0 \\ 0 & k \end{bmatrix}$:

$$\begin{bmatrix} k & 0 \\ 0 & k \end{bmatrix} \begin{bmatrix} x_1 & x_2 & x_3 \\ y_1 & y_2 & y_3 \end{bmatrix} = \begin{bmatrix} kx_1 & kx_2 & kx_3 \\ ky_1 & ky_2 & ky_3 \end{bmatrix}.$$

To accomplish translations in combination with rotations, reflections, or dilations using one transformation matrix, write the vertex matrix as a $3 \times n$ matrix with ones as the elements in the third row. Then, for example, to reflect over the line $y = x$, and then translate h units horizontally and k units vertically, premultiply by the 3×3

$$\text{matrix} \begin{bmatrix} 0 & 1 & h \\ 1 & 0 & k \\ 0 & 0 & 1 \end{bmatrix} : \begin{bmatrix} 0 & 1 & h \\ 1 & 0 & k \\ 0 & 0 & 1 \end{bmatrix} \begin{bmatrix} x_1 & x_2 & x_3 \\ y_1 & y_2 & y_3 \\ 1 & 1 & 1 \end{bmatrix} = \begin{bmatrix} y_1+h & y_2+h & y_3+h \\ x_1+k & x_2+k & x_3+k \\ 1 & 1 & 1 \end{bmatrix}.$$

The technique of premultiplying the vertex matrix by either a 2×2 or a 3×3 transformation matrix can be applied when the number of vertices is extended to $n > 3$. You would proceed in the same manner as shown for a figure with three vertices.

Tip: When you are working problems involving geometric transformations on the Mathematics CK, sketch a figure to help you visualize the situation, in conjunction with using your graphing calculator to check the results of premultiplying by the transformation matrix.

Chapter 11

Discrete Mathematics

According to the *Mathematics: Content Knowledge (0061) Test at a Glance* (www.ets.org/Media/Tests/PRAXIS/pdf/0061.pdf), the Discrete Mathematics content category of the Mathematics CK tests your knowledge and skills in six topic areas:

- Counting techniques
- Recursive functions
- Equivalence relations
- Arithmetic and geometric sequences and series
- Discrete and continuous representations
- Modeling and solving problems

This review discusses the key ideas and formulas in each topic area that are most important for you to know for the Mathematics CK.

Counting Techniques

For this topic, you must be able to solve basic problems that involve counting techniques, including the multiplication principle, permutations, and combinations, and use counting techniques to understand various situations (for example: number of ways to order a set of objects, to choose a subcommittee from a committee, to visit n cities) (*Mathematics: Content Knowledge (0061) Test at a Glance*, page 6).

The Fundamental Counting Principle

The Fundamental Counting Principle (FCP) states that if one event can occur in any one of m ways, and, after it has occurred, a second event can occur in any one of n ways, then the first event *and* the second event can both occur, in the order given, in $m \cdot n$ ways. This counting principle can be extended to any number of events. Thus, in general, for a sequence of k events, if a first event can occur in any one of n_1 different ways, and, after that event is completed, a second event can occur in any one of n_2 different ways, and, after the first two events have been completed, a third event can occur in any one of n_3 different ways, and so on to the kth event, which can occur in any one of n_k different ways, then the total number of different ways the sequence of k events can occur is $n_1 \cdot n_2 \cdot n_3 \cdot \ \cdot n_k$. Note: This counting technique produces results in which *order determines different outcomes*. Here are examples.

How many different 10-digit telephone numbers can begin with area code 510 and prefix 569?

Four additional digits are needed to complete telephone numbers that begin (510) 569-. Therefore, in this problem, there are four events: determining each of the four digits. You can think of each of the positions of the four digits as a slot to fill. In this example, you make your selection for each slot from the same set, the digits 0 to 9. Since digits in a telephone number can repeat, you say that "repetitions are allowed." There are 10 ways to fill the first slot, 10 ways to fill the second slot, 10 ways to fill the third slot, and 10 ways to fill the fourth slot; so the total number of different telephone numbers that begin (510) 569- is $10 \cdot 10 \cdot 10 \cdot 10 = 10,000$.

In how many possible ways can a president, vice president, secretary, and membership chairperson be selected from 25 members of a club if all members are eligible for each position and no member can hold more than one office?

In this problem, there are four events: electing each of the four officers. You can think of each of the officer positions as a slot to fill. Since the officers must all be different, repetitions are not allowed in the selection process. There are 25 ways to fill the president's slot; after that, there are 24 ways remaining to fill the vice president's slot;

after that, there are 23 ways remaining to fill the secretary's slot; and, finally, there are 22 ways remaining to fill the membership chairperson's slot. Thus, there are 25×24×23×22 = 303,600 possible ways to select a president, vice president, secretary, and membership chairperson from the 25 members of the club.

The Addition Principle

The Addition Principle states that if one task can be done in any one of m ways and a second task can be done in any one of n ways and if the two tasks *cannot* be done at the same time, then the number of ways to do the first *or* the second task is $m + n$ ways. This principle can be extended to more than one task. Here is an example.

A student must select one elective from a list of 3 art classes, 10 kinesiology classes, and 2 music classes. How many possible classes are there from which to choose?

The student can choose an elective from the art classes in 3 ways, from the kinesiology classes in 10 ways, and from the music classes in 2 ways. Therefore, there are 3 + 10 + 2 = 15 classes from which to choose.

The Addition Principle can be modified in the following way for situations in which two tasks overlap; that is, when the two tasks can be done at the same time: If one task can be done in any one of m ways and a second task can be done in any one of n ways and if the two tasks *can* be done at the same time, then the number of ways to do the first or the second task is $m + n - $ (the number of ways the two tasks can be done at the same time). Here is an example.

A person selects one card at random from a standard deck of 52 playing cards. In how many ways can a king or a diamond be selected? (See the figure below.)

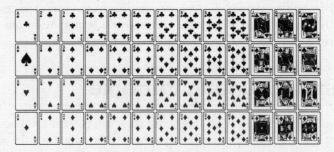

Standard Deck of 52 Playing Cards

There are 4 ways to select a king, 13 ways to select a diamond, and 1 way to select a king and a diamond at the same time (the king of diamonds). Therefore, there are 4 + 13 − 1 = 16 ways to select a king or a diamond.

Permutations

A *permutation* is an ordered arrangement of a set of distinctly different items. For permutations, different orderings of the same items are counted as different permutations. For instance, two different permutations of the numbers one through four are 1234 and 4213. Thus, when the order of the items in an arrangement is an important factor in a problem, you are working with permutations.

Through a direct application of the FCP, the number of permutations of n distinct items is given by $n! = n(n - 1)(n - 2) \ldots (2)(1)$.

Note: The notation $n!$ is read "n factorial." A factorial is the product of all positive integers less than or equal to a given positive integer. By definition $0! = 1$.

Here is an example of a permutation problem.

In how many different ways can five people be seated in a row of five seats?

You can work this problem using the FCP, or you can recognize that the seating arrangement is the permutation of five distinct items (people). Thus, there are $5! = 5 \cdot 4 \cdot 3 \cdot 2 \cdot 1 = 120$ ways for the five people to be seated in the five chairs.

Tip: For the TI-83, the factorial function is item 4 under PRB in the MATH menu.

The number of permutations of r items selected from n distinct items is $_nP_r = \dfrac{n!}{(n-r)!}$. When you apply the formula, $_nP_r$, it is important that you make sure the following conditions are met: the n items must be n *distinct* items, the r items must be selected *without repetition* from the same set, and you must count different orderings of the same items as *different* outcomes. Here is an example.

In how many possible ways can a president, vice president, secretary, and membership chairperson be selected from 25 members of a club if all members are eligible for each position and no member can hold more than one office?

You can work this problem using the FCP, or you can recognize that this problem satisfies the conditions for a permutation; that is, the 25 members of the club are distinct, the four officers are selected without repetition from the same set of 25 members, and different orderings of the same people are counted as a different slate of officers. Thus, the number of permutations of 4 items selected from 25 items is

$_{25}P_4 = \dfrac{25!}{(25-4)!} = \dfrac{25!}{(21)!} = \dfrac{25 \cdot 24 \cdot 23 \cdot 22 \cdot 21!}{21!} = 25 \cdot 24 \cdot 23 \cdot 22 = 303{,}600$ possible ways to select a president,

vice president, secretary, and membership chairperson from the 25 members of the club.

Tip: You can use your graphing calculator to compute $_nP_r$. For the TI-83, the $_nP_r$ function is item 2 under PRB in the MATH menu.

The number of permutations of n items for which n_1 of the n items are identical, n_2 of the n items are identical, $\ldots$, n_k of the n items are identical is $\dfrac{n!}{n_1! n_2! \cdots n_k!}$. Here is an example.

How many different "words" can you make using the eleven letters in the word *MISSISSIPPI* if you use all eleven letters each time?

Because the order in which different letters appear results in different words, this is a permutation problem. The word *MISSISSIPPI* consists of eleven letters: one M, four I's, four S's, and two P's. Since the eleven items (that is, the letters) to be arranged are not all mutually different items, the number of different words is given by:

$$\frac{n!}{n_1! n_2! \cdots n_k!} = \frac{11!}{4!4!2!} = 34{,}650$$

Tip: For the Mathematics CK, you should be able to work most, if not all, the permutation problems you might encounter by using the FCP rather than the formula $_nP_r$.

Some situations that (likely) indicate that you have a permutation problem are the following: creating passwords, license plates, words, or codes; assigning roles; filling positions; making ordered arrangements of things (colors, books, numbers, people, and so on); selecting first, second, third place, and such; distributing items among several people or objects; and similar situations.

Combinations

A combination is an arrangement of a set of distinct items in which different orderings of the same items are considered to be the same. For example, the set of three coins quarter, dime, and nickel is the same as the set nickel, dime, and quarter. That is, in a combination problem different orderings of the same items are *not* counted as separate results. Thus, when the order in which the items are arranged does *not* determine different outcomes, you are working with combinations. The number of combinations of r items selected from n distinct items is $_nC_r = \dfrac{n!}{r!(n-r)!}$.

> **Note: The notation $_nC_r$ is also written** $\begin{pmatrix} n \\ r \end{pmatrix}$.

When you apply the formula $_nC_r$, it is important that you make sure the following conditions are met: the n items must be n *different* items, the r items must be selected *without repetition* from the same set, and you must consider different orderings of the same items to be *the same*. Here is an example.

How many ways can a four-member committee be formed from the 25 members of a club?

Since the order in which committee members are arranged does not change the makeup of the committee, you would *not* try to work this problem using the FCP because it produces results in which order determines different outcomes. This example satisfies the conditions for a combination problem; that is, the 25 members of the club are distinct, the four committee members are selected without repetition from the same set of 25 members, and different orderings of the same people are counted as the same committee. Thus, the number of combinations of 4 items selected from 25 items is $_{25}C_4 = \dfrac{25!}{4!(25-4)!} = \dfrac{25!}{4!(21)!} = \dfrac{25\cdot24\cdot23\cdot22\cdot21!}{4!21!} = \dfrac{25\cdot24\cdot23\cdot22}{4\cdot3\cdot2\cdot1} = 12{,}650$

possible ways to form a four-member committee from the 25 members of the club.

> **Tip: You can use your graphing calculator to compute $_nC_r$. For the TI-83, the $_nC_r$ function is item 3 under PRB in the MATH menu.**

You can use the combination formula in conjunction with the FCP to determine the number of possible outcomes. Here is an example.

A party planner chooses 3 toy trucks, 7 toy cars, and 10 action figures from a selection of 8 different toy trucks, 10 different toy cars, and 12 action figures. How many different ways can the party planner make the selection?

Thinking in terms of the FCP, the party planner has three tasks to do: Select 3 of the 8 toy trucks, select 7 of the 10 toy cars, and select 10 of the 12 action figures. Since the arrangement of the toy items is not an important factor in the problem, you can determine the number of ways to select each of the toy items using the combination formula. Then, following those calculations, you can use the FCP to determine the total number of different ways the party planner can make the selection. Thus, the number of different ways the party planner can make the selection is given by:

(number of ways to select 3 of 8 toy trucks)(number of ways to select 7 of 10 toy cars)(number of ways to select 10 of 12 action figures) $= {_8C_3} \cdot {_{10}C_7} \cdot {_{12}C_{10}} = \dfrac{8!}{3!(8-3)!} \cdot \dfrac{10!}{7!(10-7)!} \cdot \dfrac{12!}{10!(12-10)!} = \dfrac{8!}{3!5!} \cdot \dfrac{10!}{7!3!} \cdot \dfrac{12!}{10!2!} =$

$56\cdot120\cdot66 = 443{,}520$

As you can see, the one important way that combinations differ from permutations is that different orderings of the same items are counted as separate results for permutation problems, but not for combination problems. Here are some situations that (likely) indicate a combination problem: forming a committee, making a collection of things (coins, books, and so on), counting the number of subsets of a given size from a set, dealing hands from a deck of cards, listing the combinations from a set of items, selecting questions from a test, selecting group members, and similar situations. For these situations, you will need to use $_nC_r$.

> **Tip: Your graphing calculator is designed to numerically evaluate both $_nP_r$ and $_nC_r$. Make a point to practice using this time-saving feature of your graphing calculator before you take the Mathematics CK.**

Recursive Functions

For this topic, you must be able to find values of functions defined recursively and understand how recursion can be used to model various phenomena and translate between recursive and closed-form expressions for a function (*Mathematics: Content Knowledge (0061) Test at a Glance*, page 6).

A sequence is a function whose domain is a subset of the integers, usually the natural numbers $N = \{1, 2, 3, ...\}$ or the whole numbers $W = \{0, 1, 2, ...\}$. (For this section, sequences are restricted, without loss of generality, to domains equal to N.) The notation a_n denotes the image of the integer n; that is, a_n is the nth term (or element) of the sequence. The initial term of the sequence is denoted a_1. When a_n can be expressed as a formula that can be used to generate any term of the sequence, it is conventional to call a_n the general term of the sequence. Even though a sequence is a function (a set of ordered pairs), it is customary to describe a sequence by listing the terms in the order in which they correspond to the natural numbers. For example, the list of terms of the sequence with initial term a_1 is $a_1, a_2, a_3, ..., a_n, ...$. (See Chapter 6, "Functions" for a discussion of functions in general.)

Note: The ellipsis (. . .) indicates that the sequence continues in the same manner.

A recursive definition for a sequence is a definition that includes the value of one or more initial terms of the sequence and a formula that tells you how to find each term from previous terms. Here is an example.

List the first four terms of the sequence defined as follows: $f(1) = 1$ and $f(n) = 3f(n - 1) + 1$ for $n \geq 2$.

For the recursive formula given in the problem, you will need to find the previous term before you can find the next term. You proceed as shown here.

$f(1) = 1$

$f(2) = 3f(1) + 1 = 3 \cdot 1 + 1 = 4$

$f(3) = 3f(2) + 1 = 3 \cdot 4 + 1 = 13$

$f(4) = 3f(3) + 1 = 3 \cdot 13 + 1 = 40$

Thus, the first four terms are 1, 4, 13, and 40.

A Fibonacci sequence begins with two repeating terms; and, thereafter, each term is the sum of the two preceding terms. For instance, the first seven terms of the Fibonacci sequence defined by the recursive definition $a_1 = 1$, $a_2 = 1$, and $a_n = a_{n-1} + a_{n-2}$, for $n \geq 3$, are 1, 1, 2, 3, 5, 8, 13, ...

A closed-form expression for the general term a_n of a recursive sequence is a formula that can be used to find a_n using only n and without knowing any of the previous terms. Note: Not all recursive sequences have an easily obtainable closed-form expression for the general term.

Tip: Sometimes it is convenient to begin a recursive sequence at $n = 0$ instead of $n = 1$, so be sure to check for the starting value of n when you work problems involving sequences on the Mathematics CK.

Equivalence Relations

For this topic, you must be able to determine whether a binary relation on a set is reflexive, symmetric, or transitive and determine whether a relation is an equivalence relation (*Mathematics: Content Knowledge (0061) Test at a Glance*, page 6).

The Cartesian product of two sets A and B, denoted $A \times B$, is the set of all ordered pairs (x, y) such that $x \in A$ and $y \in B$.

A binary relation (also called simply relation) from a set A to a set B is a subset of $A \times B$. If $A = B$, then we say the relation is on A. In other words, a relation on the set A is a subset of $A \times A$.

For a relation $\Re$, the notation $x \, \Re \, y$ (read "x is related to y") is used to denote that the ordered pair $(x, y) \in \Re$.

A relation $\Re$ on a set S is

> reflexive if $x \Re x$ for all $x \in S$,
> symmetric if $x \Re y \Rightarrow y \Re x$ for all $x, y \in S$,
> transitive if $(x \Re y \text{ and } y \Re z) \Rightarrow x \Re z$ for all $x, y, z \in S$, or
> antisymmetric if $(x \Re y \text{ and } y \Re x) \Rightarrow x = y$ for all $x, y \in S$.

An equivalence relation is a reflexive, symmetric, and transitive relation.

Note: The definitions for reflexive, symmetric, transitive, antisymmetric, and equivalence relation are given in the Notation, Definitions, and Formulas pages that are provided.

Arithmetic and Geometric Sequences and Series

For this topic, you must be able to use finite and infinite arithmetic and geometric sequences and series to model simple phenomena (for example: compound interest, annuity, growth, decay) (*Mathematics: Content Knowledge (0061) Test at a Glance*, page 6).

Arithmetic and Geometric Sequences

In an arithmetic sequence, the same number (called the "common difference") is *added* (algebraically) to each term to find the next term in the sequence. Here are examples.

What is the next term in the sequence 4, 9, 14, 19, 24,...?

The number 5 is added to a term to get the term that follows it, so the next term in the sequence is $24 + 5 = 29$.

What is the next term in the sequence 10, 6, 2, –2, –6, . . .?

The number –4 is added to a term to get the term that follows it, so the next term in the sequence is $-6 + -4 = -10$.

In general, an arithmetic sequence has the form

$a_1, a_1 + d, a_1 + 2d, \ldots, a_1 + (n-1)d, \ldots$

where a_1 is the first term, d is the common difference between terms, and $a_n = a_1 + (n-1)d$ is the general term, which you can use to find the nth term of the sequence. Here is an example.

What is the 50th term in the sequence –2, 2, 6, 10, 14,. . .?

The first term a_1 is –2. The common difference is 4. The general term is $a_n = -2 + (n-1)(4)$. Thus, the 50th term is $a_{50} = -2 + (50-1)(4) = -2 + (49)(4) = -2 + 196 = 194$.

In a geometric sequence each term in the sequence is *multiplied* by the same number (called the common ratio) to find the next term in the sequence. Here are examples.

What is the next term in the sequence 4, 8, 16, 32, 64,. . .?

Each term is multiplied by 2 to get the term that follows it, so the next term in the sequence is $64 \cdot 2 = 128$.

What is the next term in the sequence 25, 5, 1, $\frac{1}{5}$, $\frac{1}{25}$,...?

Each term is multiplied by $\frac{1}{5}$ to get the term that follows it, so the next term in the sequence is $\frac{1}{25} \cdot \frac{1}{5} = \frac{1}{125}$.

In general, a geometric sequence has the form

$$a_1, a_1r, a_1r^2, \ldots, a_1r^{n-1}, \ldots$$

where a_1 is the first term, r is the common ratio between terms, and $a_n = a_1r^{n-1}$ is the general term, which you can use to find the nth term of the sequence. Here is an example.

What is the 9th term in the sequence $-1, -2, -4, -8, -16, \ldots$?

The first term a_1 is -1. The common ratio is 2. The general term is $a_n = (-1)2^{n-1}$. Thus, the 9th term is $a_9 = (-1)2^{9-1} = (-1)2^8 = (-1)(256) = -256$.

Of course, you could have worked this problem by continuing to multiply by 2 until you reached the 9th term as shown here.

$$\underset{1^{st}}{-1}, \; \underset{2^{nd}}{-2}, \; \underset{3^{rd}}{-4}, \; \underset{4^{th}}{-8}, \; \underset{5^{th}}{-16}, \; \underset{6^{th}}{-32}, \; \underset{7^{th}}{-64}, \; \underset{8^{th}}{-128}, \; \underset{9^{th}}{-256}$$

If you use this approach, count the terms to be sure you have the correct term.

Tip: Sometimes it is convenient to begin an arithmetic or geometric sequence at $n = 0$ instead of $n = 1$, so be sure to check for the starting value of n when you work problems involving sequences on the Mathematics CK.

Arithmetic and Geometric Series

Given a finite number of terms of a sequence, $a_1, a_2, a_3, a_4, \ldots, a_n$, the sum of the terms $s_n = a_1 + a_2 + a_3 + a_4 + \ldots + a_n$ is a finite series. You can write this sum using the sigma (summation) notation as $s_n = \sum_{k=1}^{n} a_k$, where k is the summing index. Some useful properties of sigma notation are the following:

$$\sum_{k=1}^{n} c = nc \qquad \sum_{k=1}^{n}(a_k \pm b_k) = \sum_{k=1}^{n} a_k \pm \sum_{k=1}^{n} b_k$$

$$\sum_{k=1}^{n} ca_k = c\sum_{k=1}^{n} a_k \qquad \sum_{k=1}^{n} a_k = \sum_{k=1}^{m} a_k + \sum_{k=m+1}^{n} a_k, \text{ where } 1 \leq m < n$$

$$\sum_{k=1}^{n} a_k = a_1 + a_2 + \sum_{k=3}^{n-1} a_k + a_n$$

Here is an example of using sigma notation.

Expand and then sum: $\sum_{k=1}^{4}(5k - 3)$.

$$\sum_{k=1}^{4}(5k - 3) = (5 \cdot 1 - 3) + (5 \cdot 2 - 3) + (5 \cdot 3 - 3) + (5 \cdot 4 - 3) = 2 + 7 + 12 + 17 = 38$$

The sum of a finite arithmetic series is given by:

$$s_n = a_1 + a_2 + \ldots + a_n = \sum_{k=1}^{n} a_k = \frac{n(a_1 + a_n)}{2}$$

The sum of a finite geometric series is given by: $s_n = a_1 + a_1r + \ldots + a_1r^{n-1} = \sum_{k=1}^{n} a_1r^{k-1} = \frac{a_1 - a_1r^n}{1-r} = \frac{a_1(1-r^n)}{1-r}$
provided $r \neq 1$. If $r = 1$, then $s_n = na_1$.

Here is an example of summing a finite series.

Find the sum of the first 60 positive odd numbers.

The odd numbers are an arithmetic sequence with general term $a_n = 2n - 1$. Therefore,

$$s_{60} = 1 + 3 + 5 + \ldots + 119 = \frac{n(a_1 + a_n)}{2} = \frac{60(1 + 119)}{2} = 3600.$$

If $|r| < 1$, then the sum of the infinite geometric series $a_1 + a_1 r + \ldots + a_1 r^{n-1} + \ldots$ is given by $S = \frac{a_1}{1-r}$.

Here is an example.

Find the sum of the infinite geometric series $4 + 2 + 1 + \frac{1}{2} + \cdots$, if possible.

The first term $a_1 = 4$ and the common ratio $r = \frac{1}{2}$. Since $|r| < 1$,

$$4 + 2 + 1 + \frac{1}{2} + \cdots = S = \frac{a_1}{1-r} = \frac{4}{1 - \frac{1}{2}} = \frac{4}{\frac{1}{2}} = 8.$$

If $|r| \geq 1$, then the infinite geometric series $a_1 + a_1 r \ldots + a_1 r^{n-1} + \ldots$ does not have a sum.

Note: See "Limits of Sequences and Series" in Chapter 7, "Calculus," for an additional discussion of sequences and series.

Discrete and Continuous Representations

For this topic, you must demonstrate an understanding of the relationship between discrete and continuous representations and how they can be used to model various phenomena (*Mathematics: Content Knowledge (0061) Test at a Glance*, page 6).

Discrete mathematics (also called "finite mathematics") is the study of processes with discrete or unconnected objects. Discrete mathematics does not require the notion of continuity. (See the section "Continuity" in Chapter 7, "Calculus" for a discussion of the term *continuity*.) Generally, processes studied in discrete mathematics have a finite (or countable) number of objects. Discrete mathematics has widespread uses in a variety of areas such as number theory, computer security, networking, robotics, social choice theory, and linear programming.

The techniques of algebra and the powerful tools of calculus are needed for dealing with continuous processes. For example, functions with graphs that have no gaps, jumps, or holes are continuous functions. Applications of continuous functions are found in many fields such as in the sciences and in business and industry.

Modeling and Solving Problems

For this topic you must be able to use difference equations, vertex-edge graphs, trees, and networks to model and solve problems (*Mathematics: Content Knowledge (0061) Test at a Glance*, page 6).

A difference equation is an equation that describes sequential, step-by-step change. A difference equation has the form $f(n + 1) - f(n) = g(n)$, where n is a positive integer.

Note: A difference equation is the discrete mathematics analog to the first derivative equation given by $f'(x) = g(x)$. (See "Derivatives" in Chapter 7, "Calculus," for a discussion of the first derivative $f'(x)$).

A difference equation for the first difference, call it Δa_n, of a sequence $\{a_n\}$ is given by $a_{n+1} - a_n = \Delta a_n$. The first difference describes the rate of growth or decline of the sequence. When Δa_n is positive, the terms of the sequence are increasing; when Δa_n is negative, the terms of the sequence are decreasing. When Δa_n is constant, the sequence is growing or declining at a constant rate and the relationship between terms is linear. The second difference of a sequence is given by $\Delta a_{n+1} - \Delta a_n$. When the second difference is constant, the relationship between terms of the sequence is quadratic.

A vertex-edge graph is a discrete structure consisting of a nonempty, finite set of vertices (also called nodes) and a set of edges (also called lines) connecting these vertices. Vertex-edge graphs are commonly used to model and solve problems involving optimal situations for networks, paths, schedules, and relationships among finitely many objects. The following figure is a vertex-edge graph with six vertices and seven edges.

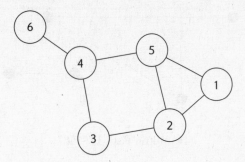

A vertex that meets an edge is an endpoint of that edge, and the edge is said to be incident with that vertex.

Two edges are adjacent if they share a common vertex. Two vertices are adjacent if they are joined by a common edge.

A loop is an edge that is incident with exactly one vertex; that is, both endpoints of the edge are the same.

A link is an edge that has two different endpoints.

A vertex's degree is the number of edges incident to that vertex (with loops being counted twice).

The Degree Sum Formula states that the sum of the degrees of the vertices of a graph is an even number equal to twice the number of edges of the graph. Consequently, there are no graphs with an odd number of vertices of odd degree.

A path in a vertex-edge graph is a sequence of vertices such that from each of its vertices there is an edge to the next vertex. A simple path is a path in which no edge is repeated.

A circuit in a vertex-edge graph is a path that begins and ends at the same vertex. A simple circuit is a circuit in which no edge is repeated.

An Euler path in a vertex-edge graph is a path that uses each edge exactly once. There is no Euler path for a graph that has more than two vertices of odd degree. Here is an example of an Euler path.

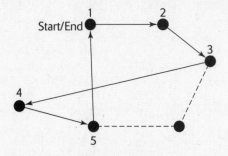

Euler Path 123451

A Hamiltonian path in a vertex-edge graph is a path that uses each vertex exactly once. Here is an example.

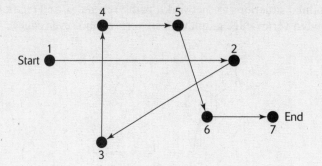

Hamilton Path 1234567

A vertex-edge graph is connected if there is a path between each pair of vertices.

A tree is a connected vertex-edge graph that contains no simple circuits. The following figure is a tree with six vertices and five edges.

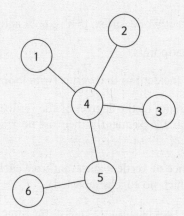

In a tree with n vertices, there are exactly $n - 1$ edges.

PART II

FULL-LENGTH PRACTICE TESTS

Scoring Your Practice Tests

Step 1. Determine your raw score. Count how many questions you answered correctly.

Step 2. Determine your percent score $= \dfrac{\text{raw score}}{50}$.

Step 3. Use the table to determine your approximate scaled score.*

Percent Score	Scaled Score
0%–40%	100
42%	102
44%	105
46%	107
48%	110
50%	112
52%	115
54%	117
56%	119
58%	121
60%	123
62%	126
64%	129
66%	132
68%	135
70%	138
72%	142
74%	146
76%	150
78%	154
80%	158
82%	162
84%	166
86%	170
88%	174
90%	178
92%	182
94%	186
96%	190
98%	194
100%	198

*The testing company does not reveal exactly how scaled scores are determined. Each edition of a test has its own conversion table that is somewhat different from the one given here. The values in this table are approximate scaled scores for this test only. (Current in 2011)

Caution: Do not let your scaled score give you a false sense of security. You should try to achieve your personal best on the official test.

Answer Sheet for Practice Test 1

(Remove This Sheet and Use It to Mark Your Answers)

CUT HERE

1 Ⓐ Ⓑ Ⓒ Ⓓ		26 Ⓐ Ⓑ Ⓒ Ⓓ
2 Ⓐ Ⓑ Ⓒ Ⓓ		27 Ⓐ Ⓑ Ⓒ Ⓓ
3 Ⓐ Ⓑ Ⓒ Ⓓ		28 Ⓐ Ⓑ Ⓒ Ⓓ
4 Ⓐ Ⓑ Ⓒ Ⓓ		29 Ⓐ Ⓑ Ⓒ Ⓓ
5 Ⓐ Ⓑ Ⓒ Ⓓ		30 Ⓐ Ⓑ Ⓒ Ⓓ
6 Ⓐ Ⓑ Ⓒ Ⓓ		31 Ⓐ Ⓑ Ⓒ Ⓓ
7 Ⓐ Ⓑ Ⓒ Ⓓ		32 Ⓐ Ⓑ Ⓒ Ⓓ
8 Ⓐ Ⓑ Ⓒ Ⓓ		33 Ⓐ Ⓑ Ⓒ Ⓓ
9 Ⓐ Ⓑ Ⓒ Ⓓ		34 Ⓐ Ⓑ Ⓒ Ⓓ
10 Ⓐ Ⓑ Ⓒ Ⓓ		35 Ⓐ Ⓑ Ⓒ Ⓓ
11 Ⓐ Ⓑ Ⓒ Ⓓ		36 Ⓐ Ⓑ Ⓒ Ⓓ
12 Ⓐ Ⓑ Ⓒ Ⓓ		37 Ⓐ Ⓑ Ⓒ Ⓓ
13 Ⓐ Ⓑ Ⓒ Ⓓ		38 Ⓐ Ⓑ Ⓒ Ⓓ
14 Ⓐ Ⓑ Ⓒ Ⓓ		39 Ⓐ Ⓑ Ⓒ Ⓓ
15 Ⓐ Ⓑ Ⓒ Ⓓ		40 Ⓐ Ⓑ Ⓒ Ⓓ
16 Ⓐ Ⓑ Ⓒ Ⓓ		41 Ⓐ Ⓑ Ⓒ Ⓓ
17 Ⓐ Ⓑ Ⓒ Ⓓ		42 Ⓐ Ⓑ Ⓒ Ⓓ
18 Ⓐ Ⓑ Ⓒ Ⓓ		43 Ⓐ Ⓑ Ⓒ Ⓓ
19 Ⓐ Ⓑ Ⓒ Ⓓ		44 Ⓐ Ⓑ Ⓒ Ⓓ
20 Ⓐ Ⓑ Ⓒ Ⓓ		45 Ⓐ Ⓑ Ⓒ Ⓓ
21 Ⓐ Ⓑ Ⓒ Ⓓ		46 Ⓐ Ⓑ Ⓒ Ⓓ
22 Ⓐ Ⓑ Ⓒ Ⓓ		47 Ⓐ Ⓑ Ⓒ Ⓓ
23 Ⓐ Ⓑ Ⓒ Ⓓ		48 Ⓐ Ⓑ Ⓒ Ⓓ
24 Ⓐ Ⓑ Ⓒ Ⓓ		49 Ⓐ Ⓑ Ⓒ Ⓓ
25 Ⓐ Ⓑ Ⓒ Ⓓ		50 Ⓐ Ⓑ Ⓒ Ⓓ

Time —120 minutes

50 Questions

Directions: Each of the questions or incomplete statements is followed by four suggested answers or completions. Select the one that is best in each case and then fill in the corresponding lettered space on the answer sheet.

1. Rose took a cab from the bus station to her home. She gave the cab driver $20, which included the fare and a tip of $2. The cab company charges $3 for the first mile and 75 cents for each additional half mile after that. How many miles is Rose's home from the bus station?

   A. 10 miles
   B. 11 miles
   C. 20 miles
   D. 21 miles

2. The whole number y is exactly three times the whole number x. The whole number z is the sum of x and y. Which of the following CANNOT be the value of z?

   A. 314
   B. 416
   C. 524
   D. 1032

Determination of Course Grade	Percent
Average (mean) of 3 major exams	50%
Average (mean) of weekly quizzes	10%
Final exam score	40%

3. A student needs an average of at least 80 to earn a grade of B in college algebra. In determining the course grade, the instructor calculates a weighted average as shown in the table above. The student has scores of 78, 81, and 75 on the 3 major exams and an average of 92 on weekly quizzes. To the nearest tenth, what is the *lowest* score the student can make on the final exam and still receive a B in the college algebra course?

   A. 81.5
   B. 81.0
   C. 80.5
   D. 79.5

4. Which of the following statements can be proven using the principle of mathematical induction?

   A. $\sin^2\theta + \cos^2\theta = 1$, where θ is a real number

   B. $\lim\limits_{x \to 0} \dfrac{\sin x}{x} = 1$, where x is a real number

   C. $\sum\limits_{k=1}^{n} k = \dfrac{n(n+1)}{2}$, where n is a natural number

   D. $\int\limits_{a}^{b} f(x)\,dx = F(b) - F(a)$, where $F'(x) = f(x)$ and a, b are real numbers

5. Which of the following expressions is equivalent to the expression $\left(m^2 + 4\right)^{-\frac{1}{2}}$?

   A. $-\dfrac{m^2 + 4}{2}$

   B. $-\sqrt{m^2 + 4}$

   C. $\dfrac{1}{\sqrt{m^2 + 4}}$

   D. $\dfrac{1}{m + 2}$

6. A solid cube of silver has edges 4 centimeters long. A metallurgist melts the cube and uses all the molten silver to make two smaller identical solid cubes. What is the length of an edge of one of the smaller cubes?

   A. 2 centimeters
   B. $2\sqrt{2}$ centimeters
   C. $2\sqrt[3]{2}$ centimeters
   D. $2\sqrt[3]{4}$ centimeters

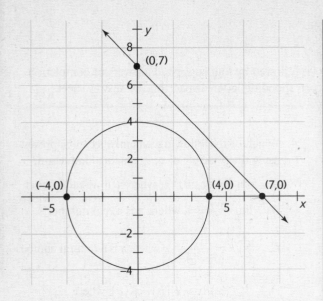

7. Which of the following statements is true about the solution set of the system of equations represented by the graphs of the circle and line shown?

   A. The system of equations has no solution because the two graphs do not intersect.

   B. The solution set is {−4, 4, 7}.

   C. An *x*-value that satisfies the system is $\frac{7}{2} + i \frac{\sqrt{41}}{2}$.

   D. An *x*-value that satisfies the system is $\frac{7}{2} - i \frac{\sqrt{17}}{2}$.

8. A line *l* passes through the point (0, 5) and is perpendicular to the line that has equation $x - 3y = 10$. Which of the following equations represents the line *l*?

   A. $x + 3y = 5$
   B. $x - 3y = 5$
   C. $3x + y = 5$
   D. $-3x + y = 5$

9. Using a digital thermometer, every morning at 8 a.m. for 5 days, a scientist measures the temperature in degrees Celsius of a lake. The temperature readings are 10.6°, 9.2°, 9.1°, 10.8°, and 10.3°. Before the temperature measurements are numerically summarized, the scientist discovers that the digital thermometer used is off by 0.7°. Which of the following is a true statement that can be made about the scientist's data?

   A. The data are unreliable.
   B. The data are imprecise.
   C. The data are inconclusive.
   D. The data are inaccurate.

10. A rectangular-shaped swimming pool is 50 feet wide and 60 feet long with an uneven bottom surface. The table that follows shows the depth of the water at 10-foot intervals.

Interval	Depth (in feet)
0 feet	3.0
10 feet	5.1
20 feet	7.5
30 feet	9.6
40 feet	10.5
50 feet	11.5
60 feet	12.0

Using the data in the table, the best approximation of the volume of the water in the pool is

   A. 22,500 ft³.
   B. 23,600 ft³.
   C. 25,850 ft³.
   D. 28,100 ft³.

11. For disaster relief in a flood-damaged area, $1.6 billion is needed. This amount of money is approximately equivalent to spending $1 per second for how many years?

   A. 10
   B. 50
   C. 100
   D. 500

12. A carpenter needs to drill a hole in a triangular piece of wood so that the center of the hole is equidistant from each side of the triangle. Which of the following constructions should the carpenter do to determine the hole's location?

   A. Find the intersection of the bisectors of the three angles.

   B. Find the intersection of the three altitudes of the triangle.

   C. Find the intersection of the perpendicular bisectors of the three sides.

   D. Find the intersection of the three medians of the triangle.

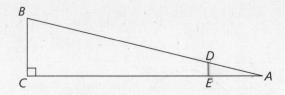

13. In triangle *ABC* shown above, segment $\overline{CE}$ has length 50 units, segment $\overline{EA}$ has length 25 units, and segment $\overline{DE}$ is perpendicular to $\overline{AC}$ and has length 10 units. What is the area of triangle *ABC*?

A. 750 square units
B. 1125 square units
C. 1500 square units
D. 2250 square units

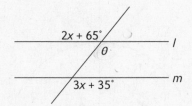

14. In the preceding figure, lines *l* and *m* are parallel. What is the measure of angle θ?

A. 125°
B. 97°
C. 30°
D. 16°

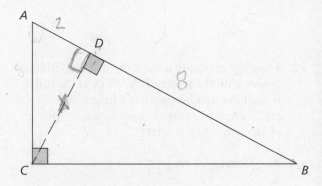

15. In the figure above, $\overline{CD}$ is an altitude of right triangle *ABC*, $\overline{AD} = 2$, and $\overline{DB} = 8$. Find the perimeter of triangle *ABC*.

A. It cannot be determined from the information given.
B. $10 + 6\sqrt{5}$
C. $10 + 2\sqrt{5}$
D. $16\sqrt{5}$

16. In the *xy*-plane, line *l* has equation $y = x$. Point *K* lies on *l* and has coordinates (–3, –3). If *l* is rotated counterclockwise 45° about the origin, what will be the coordinates of *K′*, the image of *K*, under this rotation?

A. $(0, -3)$
B. $\left(0, -3\sqrt{2}\right)$
C. $(-3, 0)$
D. $\left(-3\sqrt{2}, 0\right)$

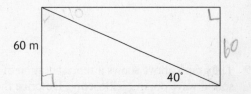

17. In the rectangle shown, what is the length of the diagonal, to the nearest tenth of a meter?

A. 71.5 m
B. 78.3 m
C. 80.5 m
D. 93.3 m

18. Which of the following is an identity for the trigonometric expression $10 \sin(4\theta)\cos(-4\theta)$?

A. $5 \sin(4\theta)$
B. $5 \sin(8\theta)$
C. $10 \sin(8\theta)$
D. $-5 \sin(4\theta)$

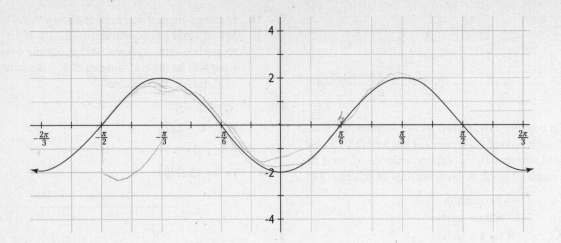

19. The graph above shows a representation of a sound wave on an oscilloscope. Describe the function that best models the curve.

A. Sine function with amplitude = 2, period = 2π, and phrase shift = $\frac{\pi}{3}$ to the right of the origin.

B. Cosine function with amplitude = 2, period = 2π, and phrase shift = $\frac{\pi}{3}$ to the right of the origin.

C. Sine function with amplitude = 2, period = $\frac{2\pi}{3}$, and phrase shift = $\frac{\pi}{6}$ to the right of the origin.

D. Cosine function with amplitude = 2, period = $\frac{2\pi}{3}$, and phrase shift = $\frac{\pi}{6}$ to the right of the origin.

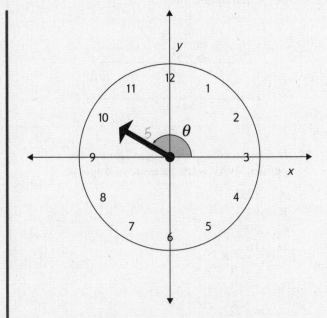

20. The diagram shows a clock on an *x-y* coordinate system with the center of the clock at the origin. If the hour hand shown has a length of 5 centimeters, what are the coordinates of the tip of the hour hand at 10:00?

A. $\left(5\cos\frac{\pi}{6}, 5\sin\frac{\pi}{6}\right)$

B. $\left(5\cos\frac{5\pi}{6}, 5\sin\frac{5\pi}{6}\right)$

C. $\left(5\sin\frac{\pi}{6}, 5\cos\frac{\pi}{6}\right)$

D. $\left(5\sin\frac{5\pi}{6}, 5\cos\frac{5\pi}{6}\right)$

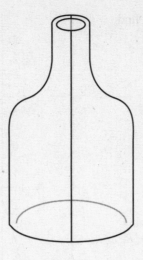

21. Water is poured at a constant rate into the container shown in the diagram. Which of the following graphs best represents the height of the water in the container as a function of time?

A.

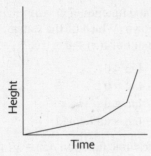

C.

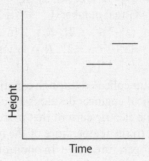

B.

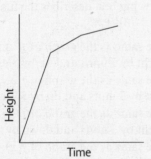

D.

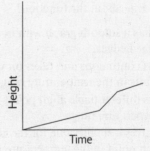

22. Given $f(x) = \dfrac{3x+4}{x+3}$ and $g(x) = x + 2$, find $f(g(a))$.

   A. $\dfrac{3a+6}{a+2}$

   B. $\dfrac{3a+4}{a+3}$

   C. $\dfrac{3a+6}{a+3}$

   D. $\dfrac{3a+10}{a+5}$

23. If $f(x) = \sqrt{x^2 - 4}$, which of the following represents the domain D_f and the range R_f of the function f?

   A. $D_f = \{x \mid x \le -2 \text{ or } x \ge 2\}$; $R_f = \{y \mid y \ge 0\}$
   B. $D_f = \{x \mid x \le -2 \text{ or } x \ge 2\}$; $R_f = \{y \mid y \in \text{real numbers}\}$
   C. $D_f = \{x \mid -2 \le x \le 2\}$; $R_f = \{y \mid y \ge 2\}$
   D. $D_f = \{x \mid -2 \le x \le 2\}$; $R_f = \{y \mid y \ge 0\}$

24. Using data collected through experimentation, an electrical engineer develops a function that relates the electric current that passes through a material to the temperature of the material in a given temperature range. In addition to being a relation, which of the following statements must be true about the function?

   A. It has a smooth graph with no cusps or jagged edges.
   B. It is continuous and takes on values at all points in the temperature range.
   C. It is differentiable at all points in the temperature range.
   D. It gives a single value for the current at each point in the temperature range.

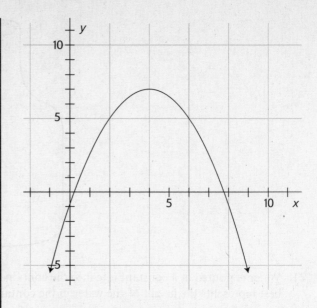

25. A quadratic function $f(x) = ax^2 + bx + c$ has the graph shown. Which of the statements about the discriminant of $f(x) = 0$ is true?

   A. $b^2 - 4ac < 0$
   B. $b^2 - 4ac = 0$
   C. $b^2 - 4ac > 0$
   D. $b^2 - 4ac$ is undefined

26. Given the cubic function $f(x) = x^3$, which of the following best describes the function $g(x) = (x - 3)^3 + 8$?

   A. the same as the graph of $f(x) = x^3$ shifted right by 3 units and up by 8 units
   B. the same as the graph of $f(x) = x^3$ shifted left by 3 units and up by 8 units
   C. the same as the graph of $f(x) = x^3$ shifted right by 3 units and down by 8 units
   D. the same as the graph of $f(x) = x^3$ shifted left by 3 units and down by 8 units

27. In the xy-plane, the graphs defined by
$f(x) = \dfrac{x^2 + x - 6}{(x+3)}$ and $g(x) = 2.5x + 2.5$ intersect
in how many distinct points?

   A. 0
   B. 1
   C. 2
   D. 4

x	$f(x)$	$g(x)$
1	3	3
2	1	4
3	4	2
4	2	1

28. Selected values of the functions f and g are given in the table shown. What is the value of $g(f(3))$?

   A. 1
   B. 2
   C. 3
   D. 4

29. A quality control engineer has determined that a machine can produce $Q(d)$ units per day after
d days in operation, where $Q(d) = \dfrac{5(6d + 14)}{d + 7}$.
Assuming the machine continues to work efficiently, approximately how many components is the machine able to produce per day after being in operation for an extended period of time?

   A. 6 units
   B. 10 units
   C. 14 units
   D. 30 units

30. The value of the first derivative on the graph of an acceleration curve $a(t)$ at numbers t_1, t_2, t_3, and t_4 are as follows:

$a'(t_1) = -0.8$
$a'(t_2) = -0.35$
$a'(t_3) = 0.5$
$a'(t_4) = 0.72$

At which number is the acceleration changing most rapidly?

   A. t_1
   B. t_2
   C. t_3
   D. t_4

31. Find the area of the region in the plane
bounded by the curve $y = \dfrac{x^2}{2}$ and the line $y = 2$.

   A. $\dfrac{8}{3}$
   B. $\dfrac{16}{3}$
   C. $\dfrac{24}{3}$
   D. $\dfrac{40}{3}$

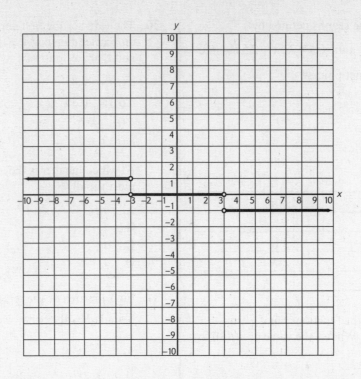

32. The figure above is a graph of $y = f'(x)$. Which of the following graphs is a possible representation of f?

A.

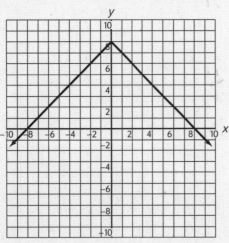

C.

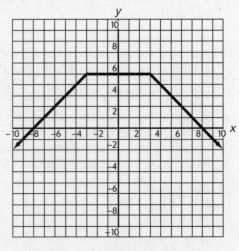

B.

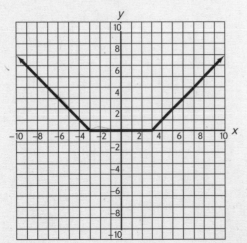

D.

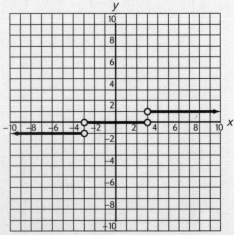

33. The velocity in feet per second of a car during the first 10 seconds of a test run is given by $v(t) = 0.9t^2$. What is the distance the car has traveled after 10 seconds?

    A. 30 feet
    B. 90 feet
    C. 300 feet
    D. 900 feet

34. A rectangular pen is to be adjacent to a brick wall and is to have fencing on three sides, the side on the brick wall requiring no fencing. If 550 yards of fencing is available, find the length parallel to the wall of the pen with largest area.

    A. 110 yards
    B. 137.5 yards
    C. 183.3 yards
    D. 275 yards

Weights in Pounds of 35 Female High School Seniors	
Stem	**Leaves**
12	3 8 8
13	1 3 4 4 5 6 8
14	0 0 2 4 5 5 7 7 7 8 9
15	0 1 3 3 5 6 7 8 9 9
16	1 2 2 9
Legend: 12|3 = 123	

35. The stem-and-leaf plot above displays the weights of 35 high school senior girls. What is the median weight of the 35 girls?

    A. 138 pounds
    B. 140 pounds
    C. 147 pounds
    D. 149 pounds

Genre	Number of Students
Biography/Historical Nonfiction	22
Historical Fiction	29
Mystery	32
Science/Nature Informational	25
Science Fiction/Fantasy	52
Total	**160**

36. The table above shows the results of a poll of young readers who were asked what genre of books they read most often. If a pie chart is constructed using the data in the table, what central angle should be used to represent the Science Fiction/Fantasy category?

    A. 49.5°
    B. 52°
    C. 117°
    D. 187.2°

Group	Mean	Standard Deviation
A	30 cm	5 cm
B	30 cm	8 cm
C	25 cm	10 cm
D	25 cm	9 cm

37. The data in the table above are based on 5 repetitions of the same experiment performed by four different groups of students: Group A, Group B, Group C, and Group D. The data of which group are most reliable?

    A. Group A
    B. Group B
    C. Group C
    D. Group D

38. The lifetime of a certain type of disposable razor is normally distributed with a mean of 16.8 shavings and a standard deviation of 2.4 shavings. What percentage of disposable razors of this type will last more than 19.2 shavings?

    A. 2.5%
    B. 16%
    C. 34%
    D. 68%

39. A researcher is analyzing data from an experiment using a simple linear regression model. Using a graphing calculator's statistical features, the researcher entered the data into the calculator and ran a least squares linear regression. In addition to providing the regression coefficients, the calculator gave a correlation coefficient of 0.03. What can the researcher infer from this coefficient?

   A. The linear model is not a good fit for the data.

   B. The dependent and independent variables have a strong positive correlation.

   C. The linear model has a 3% probability of fitting the data.

   D. The slope of the linear model is 0.03.

	Positive Diagnosis	Negative Diagnosis
Smoker	25	5
Nonsmoker	15	155

40. The data in the table above show the diagnoses of 200 smokers and nonsmokers tested for lung cancer in a certain clinic. If one of the 200 subjects tested is randomly selected, what is the probability that the subject was positively diagnosed as having lung cancer, given that the subject is a smoker?

   A. $\dfrac{1}{8}$

   B. $\dfrac{1}{6}$

   C. $\dfrac{5}{8}$

   D. $\dfrac{5}{6}$

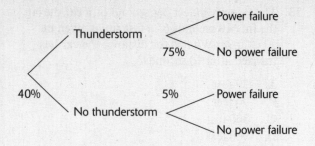

41. The probability diagram above represents the incidence of power failure during weather in which a thunderstorm might or might not develop. What is the probability that both a thunderstorm develops and a power failure occurs?

   A. 2%

   B. 15%

   C. 65%

   D. 85%

42. Only 1 of 10 remote controls in a box is defective. The remote controls are tested one at a time. If the first three remote controls tested are not defective, what is the probability that the fourth remote control tested is defective?

   A. $\dfrac{99}{100}$

   B. $\dfrac{1}{10}$

   C. $\dfrac{1}{7}$

   D. $\dfrac{7}{10}$

$$7x - 8y + 5z = 5$$
$$-4x + 5y - 3z = -3$$
$$x - y + z = 0$$

43. Solve the system of equations for y.

   A. −2

   B. −1

   C. 0

   D. 1

44. Given $\triangle ABC$ with vertices $A(0, 0)$, $B(3, 0)$, and $C(0, 4)$ in the x-y plane, which of the following matrix transformations represents a dilation of $\triangle ABC$ with center $(0, 0)$ and scale factor 3?

A. $\begin{bmatrix} 0 & 3 \\ 0 & 3 \end{bmatrix} \begin{bmatrix} 0 & 3 & 0 \\ 0 & 0 & 4 \end{bmatrix}$

B. $\begin{bmatrix} 3 & 3 \\ 0 & 0 \end{bmatrix} \begin{bmatrix} 0 & 3 & 0 \\ 0 & 0 & 4 \end{bmatrix}$

C. $\begin{bmatrix} 3 & 3 \\ 3 & 3 \end{bmatrix} \begin{bmatrix} 0 & 3 & 0 \\ 0 & 0 & 4 \end{bmatrix}$

D. $\begin{bmatrix} 3 & 0 \\ 0 & 3 \end{bmatrix} \begin{bmatrix} 0 & 3 & 0 \\ 0 & 0 & 4 \end{bmatrix}$

45. For which of the following transformations will the magnitude of a vector be unchanged?

 I. rotation of the vector by an angle θ

 II. translation of the vector by h units to the right and k units up

 III. dilation of the vector with center at the origin by a scale factor of m

A. I and II only

B. I and III only

C. II and III only

D. I, II, and III

$$\begin{bmatrix} 5 & 1.5 \\ 2 & d \end{bmatrix}$$

46. For what value of d is the 2×2 matrix shown NOT invertible?

A. -0.6

B. 0

C. 0.6

D. 3

47. Given the recursive function defined by

 $f(0) = 3$,

 $f(n) = 2f(n - 1) + 3$ for $n \geq 1$,

 what is the value of $f(3)$?

A. 9

B. 21

C. 45

D. 93

48. How many different license plate alphanumeric codes consisting of two digits followed by four uppercase letters are possible?

A. $2 \cdot 4$

B. $(_{10}C_2)(_{26}C_4)$

C. 36^6

D. $10^2 \cdot 26^4$

49. How many ways can four people sit in seven empty identical chairs that are placed in a row?

A. 24

B. 35

C. 840

D. 5040

50. The relation "is a subset of" satisfies which of the following properties?

 I. reflexive

 II. symmetric

 III. transitive

A. II only

B. III only

C. I and III only

D. II and III only

Answer Key for Practice Test 1

Question Number	Correct Answer	Content Category	Question Number	Correct Answer	Content Category
1.	B	Algebra and Number Theory	26.	A	Functions
2.	A	Algebra and Number Theory	27.	A	Functions
3.	D	Algebra and Number Theory	28.	A	Functions
4.	C	Algebra and Number Theory	29.	D	Calculus
5.	C	Algebra and Number Theory	30.	A	Calculus
6.	D	Algebra and Number Theory	31.	B	Calculus
7.	D	Algebra and Number Theory	32.	C	Calculus
8.	C	Algebra and Number Theory	33.	C	Calculus
9.	D	Measurement	34.	D	Calculus
10.	C	Measurement	35.	C	Data Analysis and Statistics
11.	B	Measurement	36.	C	Data Analysis and Statistics
12.	A	Geometry	37.	A	Data Analysis and Statistics
13.	B	Geometry	38.	B	Data Analysis and Statistics
14.	A	Geometry	39.	A	Data Analysis and Statistics
15.	B	Geometry	40.	D	Probability
16.	B	Geometry	41.	B	Probability
17.	D	Trigonometry	42.	C	Probability
18.	B	Trigonometry	43.	B	Matrix Algebra
19.	C	Trigonometry	44.	D	Matrix Algebra
20.	B	Trigonometry	45.	A	Matrix Algebra
21.	A	Functions	46.	C	Matrix Algebra
22.	D	Functions	47.	C	Discrete Mathematics
23.	A	Functions	48.	D	Discrete Mathematics
24.	D	Functions	49.	C	Discrete Mathematics
25.	C	Functions	50.	C	Discrete Mathematics

Answer Explanations for Practice Test 1

1. **B.** The fare is $3 for the first mile plus 75 cents for each additional half mile.

   Method 1: To solve the problem, break the distance into a 1-mile portion plus a portion composed of half-mile segments. Then write and solve an equation that models the situation.

   Let n = the number of half-mile segments

   Distance from the bus station to Rose's home $= 1 \text{ mile} + \frac{1}{2} \cdot n$ miles

   Fare $= \$3 + \$0.75n$

   $$\text{Fare} + \text{Tip} = \$20$$
   $$\$3 + \$0.75n + \$2 = \$20$$
   $$\$0.75n = \$15$$
   $$n = \frac{\$15}{\$0.75}$$
   $$n = 20 \text{ half-mile segments}$$

   Distance from the bus station to Rose's home $= 1 \text{ mile} + \frac{1}{2} \cdot n \text{ miles} = 1 \text{ mile} + \frac{1}{2} \cdot 20 \text{ miles} = 11 \text{ miles}$, choice B.

   Method 2. Another way to work this problem is to check the answer choices—a smart test-taking strategy for multiple-choice math tests.

   Checking choice A: If the distance to Rose's home is 10 miles, then the trip is broken into a 1-mile portion plus 9 miles $= 1 \text{ mile} + 18 \text{ half-miles}$. The fare for the trip $= \$3 \text{ (for the first mile)} + \left(\frac{\$0.75}{\text{half-mile}}\right)(18 \text{ half-miles}) = \$3 + \$13.50 = \$16.50$. When you add the $2 tip, the total is $18.50 \neq \$20$, so eliminate A.

   Checking choice B: If the distance to Rose's home is 11 miles, then the trip is broken into a 1 mile portion plus 10 miles $= 1 \text{ mile} + 20 \text{ half-miles}$. The fare for the trip $= \$3 \text{ (for the first mile)} + \left(\frac{\$0.75}{\text{half-mile}}\right)(20 \text{ half-miles}) = \$3 + \$15 = \$18$. When you add the $2 tip, the total is $20, which is correct. Choice B is the correct response.

   In a test situation, you should go on to the next question since you have found the correct answer. You would not check choices C and D; but for your information choice C gives $33.50 and choice D gives $35, both of which are too high.

   Tip: Most graphing calculators allow you to recall and edit the last expression you entered. Use this convenient calculator feature to save time with the checking process.

2. **A.** Since x and y are whole numbers and $z = x + y = x + 3x = 4x$, then z is a multiple of 4. Therefore, z represents a whole number that is divisible by 4. A number is divisible by 4 if and only if the last 2 digits form a number that is divisible by 4. Looking at the answer choices, you can see that only choice A fails the test for divisibility by 4—because the last 2 digits of 314 are 14, which is not divisible by 4.

3. D. The question asks: What is the *lowest* score the student can make on the final exam and still receive a B in the course? Examine the table to review the instructor's grading guidelines.

Determination of Course Grade	Percent
Average (mean) of 3 major exams	50%
Average (mean) of weekly quizzes	10%
Final exam score	40%

From the table, you can see that you first must calculate the mean of the student's 3 major exam scores:

$$\text{mean} = \frac{78 + 81 + 75}{3} = 78$$

Let x = the lowest score the student can make on the final and still have at least an 80 average.

Solve the following equation for x:

$$50\%(78) + 10\%(92) + 40\%(x) = 80$$
$$0.5(78) + 0.1(92) + 0.4(x) = 80$$
$$39 + 9.2 + 0.4(x) = 80$$
$$0.4(x) = 31.8$$
$$x = 79.5$$

The lowest score that will yield an average of at least 80 is 79.5, choice D.

4. C. The principle of mathematical induction states that any set of counting numbers that contains the number 1 and also contains $k + 1$, whenever it contains the counting number k, contains all the counting numbers. Eliminate A, B, and D, which are statements about the real numbers. Choice C is a statement about the sum of the first n natural numbers. The natural numbers is another name for the counting numbers, so the statement in C can be proven using the principle of mathematical induction. Choice A can be proven using trigonometric concepts and the Pythagorean theorem. Choices B and D can be proven using techniques from calculus.

5. C. The exponent for the quantity $\left(m^2 + 4\right)^{-\frac{1}{2}}$ is $-\frac{1}{2}$. Recall that negative exponents indicate reciprocals and fractional exponents indicate roots. Thus, the exponent $-\frac{1}{2}$ indicates to write the reciprocal of the square root of $m^2 + 4$, which is choice C: $\dfrac{1}{\sqrt{m^2 + 4}}$.

6. D. The volume V of a cube with edge s is given by $V = s^3$. The volume of the original cube will equal the sum of the volumes of the two smaller cubes.

The volume V_o of the original cube is $V_o = (4 \text{ cm})^3 = 64 \text{ cm}^3$.

The volume V_s of one of the smaller cubes $= \frac{1}{2}V_o = \frac{1}{2} \cdot 64 \text{ cm}^3 = 32 \text{ cm}^3$.

Let e = the length of an edge of one of the smaller cubes. Then $e^3 = 32 \text{ cm}^3$, so

$e = \sqrt[3]{32 \text{ cm}^3} = \sqrt[3]{8 \text{cm}^3 \cdot 4} = 2\sqrt[3]{4}$ centimeters, choice D.

7. D. The figure shows a circle centered at 0 with radius 4 units and a line that passes through the points (0, 7) and (7, 0).

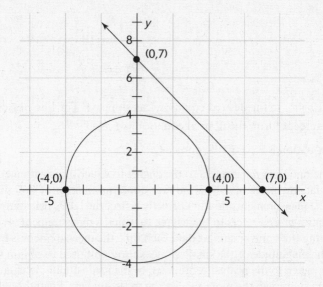

Write equations that represent each of the graphs shown, and then find the simultaneous solution of the two equations.

The equation of a circle centered at 0 with radius 4 is $x^2 + y^2 = 16$.

The slope of the line that passes through the points (0, 7) and (7, 0) is

$m = \dfrac{0-7}{7-0} = \dfrac{-7}{7} = -1$. The y-intercept b is 7. The equation of the line is $y = -x + 7$.

The system of two equations is

$x^2 + y^2 = 16$

$y = -x + 7$

Caution: When an equation or a system of equations has real solutions, you can use a graphing calculator's Trace feature to find a solution. This method will not work when the graphs do not intersect, as in this problem.

Substituting $y = -x + 7$ into the equation $x^2 + y^2 = 16$ yields

$$x^2 + (-x + 7)^2 = 16$$
$$x^2 + x^2 - 14x + 49 = 16$$
$$2x^2 - 14x + 33 = 0$$
$$a = 2, b = -14, c = 33$$

$$x = \frac{-(-14) \pm \sqrt{(-14)^2 - 4 \cdot 2 \cdot 33}}{2 \cdot 2} = \frac{14 \pm \sqrt{196 - 264}}{4} = \frac{14 \pm \sqrt{-68}}{4} = \frac{14 \pm 2i\sqrt{17}}{4} = \frac{7}{2} \pm i\frac{\sqrt{17}}{2}$$

Thus, $\dfrac{7}{2} - i\dfrac{\sqrt{17}}{2}$ is an x-value that satisfies the system, choice D.

Tip: When using your calculator to solve a quadratic equation always set the calculator in complex number mode. Complex number mode will display both real solutions and complex solutions.

8. **C.** When two lines are perpendicular, their slopes are negative reciprocals of each other.

Solve $x - 3y = 10$ for y to find its slope.

$$x - 3y = 10$$
$$-3y = -x + 10$$
$$y = \frac{1}{3}x - \frac{10}{3}$$

The slope of $x - 3y = 10$ is $\frac{1}{3}$, so the desired equation has slope -3. The line passes through $(0, 5)$, so 5 is the y-intercept. In slope-intercept form, the desired equation is $y = -3x + 5$.

In standard form the equation is $3x + y = 5$, choice C.

9. **D.** In science and mathematics *accurate* refers to the degree to which a measurement is true or correct. The scientist's temperature data are inaccurate because each contains an error of $0.7°$ due to the miscalibrated digital thermometer. The measurements do not correctly reflect the lake's true temperature on the given days. In science and mathematics *precise* refers to the degree to which a measurement is repeatable and reliable; that is, consistently getting the same or similar data each time the measurement is taken. A measurement's precision depends on the magnitude of the smallest measuring unit used to obtain the measurement (for example: to the nearest meter, to the nearest centimeter, to the nearest millimeter, and so on). In theory, the smaller the measurement unit used, the more precise the measurement. Even though the measurements are inaccurate, they are precise (eliminate B) and reliable (eliminate A) because they are consistently determined within close specified limits. The scientist's data are not *inconclusive* since the scientist can draw conclusions, although the conclusions will be inaccurate due to the faulty measuring device (eliminate C).

10. **C.** From the information given in the table, you can surmise that the swimming pool has an uneven bottom surface. Thus, none of the standard formulas for the volume of a geometric solid can be used to directly calculate the volume of the water in the pool. However, you can use the methods of successive approximation to approximate the volume of such geometric figures. With these methods, the volume of the figure is partitioned in two different ways—so that one partitioning overestimates the volume, yielding an upper bound, and the other partitioning underestimates the volume, yielding a lower bound. The average of the upper and lower bounds will yield a good approximation of the geometric figure's volume.

Find an upper bound for the volume of water in the pool using the *right* endpoint values. Do this by partitioning the water in the pool into six 10 feet (length) by 50 feet (width) rectangular prisms, whose heights, in order, are 5.1 feet, 7.5 feet, 9.6 feet, 10.5 feet, 11.5 feet, and 12.0 feet.

The sum of the volumes of these six rectangular prisms is an upper bound for the volume of the water in the pool.

Upper bound for the volume of water in the pool = 10 ft · 50 ft · 5.1 ft + 10 ft · 50 ft · 7.5 ft + 10 ft · 50 ft · 9.6 ft + 10 ft · 50 ft · 10.5 ft + 10 ft · 50 ft · 11.5 ft + 10 ft · 50 ft · 12 ft = 10 ft · 50 ft (5.1 ft + 7.5 ft + 9.6 ft + 10.5 ft + 11.5 ft + 12.0 ft) = 10 ft · 50 ft (56.2 ft) = 28,100 ft³.

Tip: Notice that you can simplify the calculation by factoring out 10 ft · 50 ft from each term.

In a similar manner, a lower bound for the volume of water in the pool using the *left* endpoint values is

Lower bound for the volume in the pool = 10 ft · 50 ft · 3.0 ft + 10 ft · 50 ft · 5.1 ft + 10 ft · 50 ft · 7.5 ft + 10 ft · 50 ft · 9.6 ft + 10 ft · 50 ft · 10.5 ft + 10 ft · 50 ft · 11.5 ft = 10 ft · 50 ft (3.0 ft + 5.1 ft + 7.5 ft + 9.6 ft + 10.5 ft + 11.5 ft) = 10 ft · 50 ft (47.2 ft) = 23,600 ft³.

Tip: Most graphing calculators allow you to recall and edit the last expression you entered. To save keystrokes (and, importantly, time), you can recall the calculation you performed in Step 1 and replace 12.0 with 3.0 to find the lower bound.

Averaging the upper and lower bounds gives

$$\frac{28,100 \text{ ft}^3 + 23,600 \text{ ft}^3}{2} = 25,850 \text{ ft}^3, \text{ choice C.}$$

Note: Of course, sequences of increasingly accurate approximations can be found by refining the precision of the partitioning (for example, measuring the depth of the water at 5-foot intervals, rather than 10-foot intervals). The upper and lower bounds get increasingly close to each other, and their average will approach the geometric figure's true volume.

11. **B.** You want to know how many years it would take to spend $1.6 billion at the rate of $1 per second.

$$\frac{\$1,600,000,000}{1} \cdot \frac{1 \text{ sec}}{\$1} \cdot \frac{1 \text{ min}}{60 \text{ sec}} \cdot \frac{1 \text{ hr}}{60 \text{ min}} \cdot \frac{1 \text{ day}}{24 \text{ hr}} \cdot \frac{1 \text{ yr}}{365 \text{ days}} = 50.73566\ldots \text{ or approximately 50 years, choice B.}$$

12. **A.** The angle bisectors of a triangle are concurrent in a point that is equidistant from the three sides, which means A is the correct response. Choice B is incorrect because the altitudes of a triangle are concurrent in a point, called the orthocenter of the triangle; but, in general, the point of concurrency is not equidistant from the three sides. Choice C is incorrect because the perpendicular bisectors of a triangle are concurrent in a point that is equidistant from the vertices of the triangle; but, in general, the point of concurrency is not equidistant from the three sides. Choice D is incorrect because the medians of a triangle are concurrent in a point, called the centroid of the triangle; but, in general, the point of concurrency is not equidistant from the three sides.

13. **B.** From the figure, you can see that triangles ABC and ADE are similar right triangles.

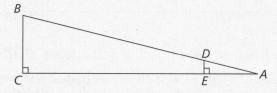

The area of triangle $ABC = \frac{1}{2}\big(\text{length of } \overline{CA}\big)\big(\text{length of } \overline{BC}\big)$

$\overline{CA} = \big(\text{length of } \overline{CE}\big) + \big(\text{length of } \overline{EA}\big) = 50 \text{ units} + 25 \text{ units} = 75 \text{ units}$

To find the length of $\overline{BC}$, call it x, set up a proportion and solve it, omitting units for convenience:

$$\frac{x}{75} = \frac{10}{25}$$
$$25x = 750$$
$$x = 30 \text{ units}$$

area of triangle $ABC = \frac{1}{2}(75 \text{ units})(30 \text{ units}) = 1125 \text{ square units, choice B.}$

14. A. From the figure, you can see that angles $2x + 65°$ and θ are vertical angles, so they are equal. Angles θ and $3x + 35°$ are corresponding angles of parallel lines, so they are equal. Thus, angles $2x + 65°$ and $3x + 35°$ are equal.

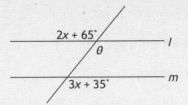

Thus, you have,

$$2x + 65° = 3x + 35°$$
$$30° = x$$

Substituting this value for x into $2x + 65°$ yields

$\theta = 2x + 65° = 2(30°) + 65° = 125°$, choice A.

15. B. Mark on the figure. Let x = length of $\overline{CD}$.

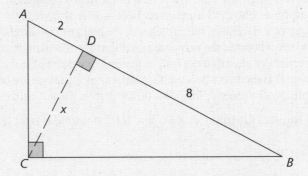

The perimeter of $\triangle ABC = \left(\text{length of } \overline{AB}\right) + \left(\text{length of } \overline{BC}\right) + \left(\text{length of } \overline{AC}\right)$

The altitude to the hypotenuse of a right triangle divides the triangle into two right triangles that are similar to each other and to the original right triangle. Furthermore, the length of that altitude is the geometric mean of the lengths of the two segments into which it separates the hypotenuse. Therefore, in the figure shown, $\triangle ABC \sim \triangle ACD \sim \triangle CBD$; and $\dfrac{\overline{AD}}{x} = \dfrac{x}{\overline{DB}}$.

Thus,

$\dfrac{2}{x} = \dfrac{x}{8}$

$x^2 = 16$

$x = 4$

Using the Pythagorean theorem, you have

$\overline{BC} = \sqrt{4^2 + 8^2} = \sqrt{80} = 4\sqrt{5}$ and

$\overline{AC} = \sqrt{4^2 + 2^2} = \sqrt{20} = 2\sqrt{5}$

From the information given, $\overline{AB} = 2 + 8 = 10$

Therefore, the perimeter of $\triangle ABC = 10 + 4\sqrt{5} + 2\sqrt{5} = 10 + 6\sqrt{5}$, choice B.

16. B. Make a rough sketch.

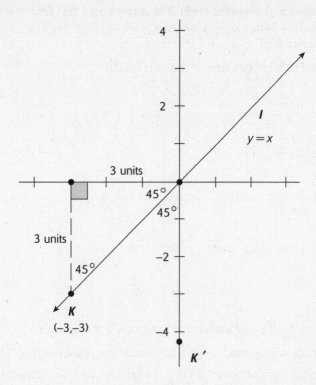

The line segment from the origin to K is the hypotenuse of a 45°-45°-90° right triangle, so it has length $3\sqrt{2}$ units. The image K' of K under a rotation of 45° counterclockwise lies $3\sqrt{2}$ units below the origin on the y-axis, so its coordinates are $\left(0, -3\sqrt{2}\right)$, choice B.

17. D. Mark on the diagram. Label the diagonal d.

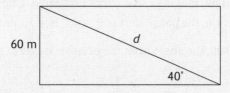

From the figure, you can see that the diagonal divides the rectangle into two right triangles. In the lower-right triangle, the side 60 m is opposite the angle 40°.

To find d, use the definition of the sine function, and then solve for d.

$$\sin 40° = \frac{\text{length of side opposite } 40° \text{ angle}}{\text{length of hypotenuse}}$$

$$\sin 40° = \frac{60 \text{ m}}{d}$$

$$d = \frac{60 \text{ m}}{\sin 40°} = 93.3 \text{ m (rounded to nearest tenth of a meter), choice D.}$$

Tip: Be sure to check that your calculator is in degree mode when the angle given is in degrees.

18. **B.** The cosine is an even function, so $10 \sin(4\theta)\cos(-4\theta) = 10 \sin(4\theta)\cos(4\theta)$.

Rewrite $10 \sin(4\theta)\cos(4\theta)$ as $5 \cdot 2 \sin(4\theta)\cos(4\theta)$. The expression $2 \sin(4\theta)\cos(4\theta)$ has the form of the double-angle formula $\sin 2x = 2 \sin(x)\cos(x)$, where $x = 4\theta$ and $2x = 8\theta$. Thus, $5 \cdot 2 \sin(4\theta)\cos(4\theta) = 5 \cdot \sin(8\theta) = 5 \sin(8\theta)$, choice B.

19. **C.** The graph's shape indicates either a sine or a cosine function.

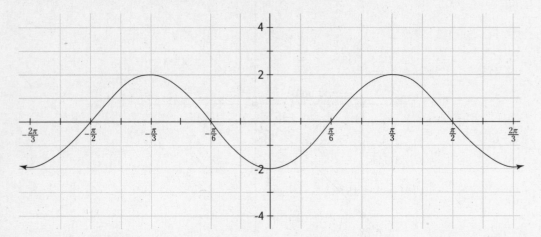

If $b > 0$, the general forms for the sine and cosine functions, $y = a \sin(bx + c) + k$ and $y = a \cos(bx + c) + k$, have graphs with amplitude $= |a|$, period $= \frac{2\pi}{b}$, a horizontal (or phase) shift of $\frac{|c|}{b}$ units (to the left of the origin if $\frac{c}{b}$ is positive; to the right of the origin if $\frac{c}{b}$ is negative), and a vertical shift of $|k|$ units (up from the origin if k is positive; down from the origin if k is negative).

Regardless whether you view the graph as a sine or a cosine function, the graph has amplitude 2, period $= \frac{2\pi}{3}$, and no vertical shift (that is, $k = 0$). Eliminate A and B because the period in these choices is 2π. Looking at the graph, you can see that if you view the graph as a sine function, the graph has a phase shift of $\frac{\pi}{6}$ units to the right of the origin, making C the correct response. Choice D is incorrect because if you view the graph as a cosine function, the phase shift is $\frac{\pi}{3}$ units, not $\frac{\pi}{6}$ units, to the right of the origin.

20. **B.** Since the hour hand is at 10:00, the angle from the positive x-axis to the hour hand is $120° = \frac{5\pi}{6}$.

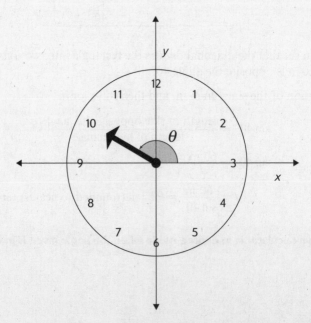

The length of the hour hand is 5 centimeters. In polar coordinates, the tip of the hour hand is located at $\left(5, \frac{5\pi}{6}\right)$. To change from polar (r, θ) to rectangular (x, y), use $x = r \cos \theta$ and $y = r \sin \theta$. (These formulas are included in the provided Notation, Definitions, and Formulas pages.) Substituting into the formulas, the coordinates of the tip of the hour hand are $\left(5 \cos \frac{5\pi}{6}, 5 \sin \frac{5\pi}{6}\right)$, choice B.

21. **A.** Analyze the figure.

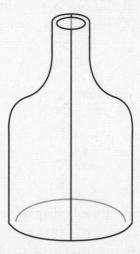

From the figure, you can see that as water is poured into the container at a constant rate, the height of the water rises at a constant rate until it reaches the point near the top where the bottle narrows. At that point, the water rises at a faster, but still constant, rate until it reaches the bottle's neck, where it rises at an even faster rate. The graph that corresponds to this analysis is given in A. Choice B is incorrect because it indicates that the rate at which the water rises slows down as the water reaches the top of the bottle. Choice C is incorrect because it indicates that the height of the water in the bottle is constant at first, then suddenly leaps to a higher level and remains constant at that level for a while and, finally, leaps to an even higher level, where it remains. Choice D is incorrect because it indicates that the rate at which the water rises initially is the same as the rate at which it rises when it reaches the bottle's neck.

22. **D.** $f\left(g\left(a\right)\right) = f\left(a + 2\right) = \frac{3\left(a+2\right)+4}{\left(a+2\right)+3} = \frac{3a+6+4}{a+2+3} = \frac{3a+10}{a+5}$, choice D.

23. **A.** The function f is defined when $x^2 - 4 \geq 0$. Solving this quadratic inequality yields $x \leq 2$ or $x \geq 2$. Therefore, $D_f = \{x | x \leq -2 \text{ or } x \geq 2\}$. Eliminate C and D because these answer choices have incorrect domains. The expression $\sqrt{x^2 - 4}$ is always nonnegative, so $R_f = \{y | y \geq 0\}$. Thus, A is the correct response.

24. **D.** Only the statement given in D will always be true about the engineer's function. By definition, each first component (temperature value) is paired with one and only one second component (current value). None of the other statements are guaranteed to be true about the engineer's function.

25. C. Examine the graph.

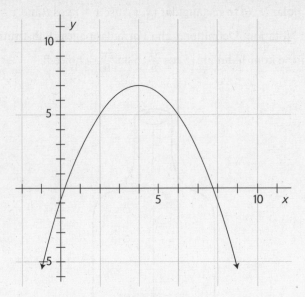

The graph intersects the real axis at two points, indicating the function has two real zeros. Therefore, $b^2 - 4ac > 0$, choice C.

26. A. Subtracting 3 from x will result in a horizontal shift of 3 units to the right. Adding 8 to $f(x)$ will result in a vertical shift of 8 units up. Thus, the graph of $g(x) = (x - 3)^3 + 8$ is the same as the graph of $f(x) = x^3$ shifted right by 3 units and up by 8 units, choice A.

Tip: If you are unsure whether the shift is to the right or left, graph the functions on your graphing calculator to check.

27. A. The rational function f defined by $f(x) = \dfrac{x^2 + x - 6}{(x+3)} = \dfrac{(x+3)(x-2)}{(x+3)}$ is undefined when $x = -3$. Simplified $f(x) = \dfrac{(x+3)(x-2)}{(x+3)} = x - 2$, so the graph of f is the line whose equation is $y = x - 2$, but with a "hole" at the point $(-3, -5)$. The graph of the linear function g defined by $g(x) = 2.5x + 2.5$ is the line $y = 2.5x + 2.5$ that intersects the line $y = x - 2$ at $(-3, -5)$; that is, $(-3, -5)$ satisfies both $y = x - 2$ and $y = 2.5x + 2.5$. However, since -3 is not in the domain of f, the graphs of f and g do not intersect, choice A.

Caution: Using your graphing calculator for problems involving holes in graphs can lead to incorrect answer choices.

28. A. Examine the table.

x	f(x)	g(x)
1	3	3
2	1	4
3	4	2
4	2	1

According to the table $f(3) = 4$ and $g(4) = 1$. Therefore, $g(f(3)) = g(4) = 1$.

29. D. The phrase "an extended period of time" is a clue that this is a calculus problem involving the limit of a function as the variable approaches infinity. To answer the question, find the limit of the function $Q(d) = \dfrac{5(6d+14)}{d+7}$ as d approaches infinity:

$$\lim_{d\to\infty} \frac{5(6d+14)}{d+7} = \lim_{d\to\infty} \frac{30d+70}{d+7} = \lim_{d\to\infty} \frac{30+\dfrac{70}{d}}{1+\dfrac{7}{d}} = \frac{30+0}{1+0} = \frac{30}{1} = 30 \text{ units, choice D.}$$

30. A. The value of the first derivative at each number t_1, t_2, t_3, and t_4 is the instantaneous rate of change of the acceleration curve at that number. The acceleration is changing most rapidly at the number t_1 because the magnitude of the change is greatest at this number, choice A.

Tip: To avoid making a careless mistake, add 0s to make the number of decimal places in each value the same before making a comparison: $a'(t_1) = -0.80$, $a'(t_2) = -0.35$, $a'(t_3) = 0.50$, $a'(t_4) = 0.72$.

31. B. Make a quick sketch of the two graphs.

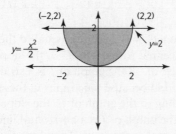

The two graphs intersect at the points $(-2, 2)$ and $(2, 2)$, and $y = 2$ lies above $y = \dfrac{x^2}{2}$ between $x = -2$ and $x = 2$. To find the area of the region bounded by the two graphs, evaluate $\displaystyle\int_{-2}^{2}\left(2 - \frac{x^2}{2}\right)dx$.

Method 1. The fastest and most efficient way to calculate this numerical integral is with your graphing calculator. Here are the steps using a TI-83 Plus calculator. Before you enter functions, you must select Func mode from the $\boxed{\text{MODE}}$ menu. Enter the function $y = 2 - \dfrac{x^2}{2}$ into the $\boxed{\text{Y} =}$ editor. As a precaution, clear any previously entered functions before you enter the function. Check the viewing $\boxed{\text{WINDOW}}$ to make sure that the interval between -2 and 2 falls between Xmin and Xmax. If not, change Xmin and/or Xmax, as needed. Go to the $\boxed{\text{CALC}}$ (calculate) menu. Select $7: \int f(x)\,dx$. Type -2 when prompted for the lower limit and then press $\boxed{\text{ENTER}}$. Type 2 when prompted for the upper limit and then press $\boxed{\text{ENTER}}$. The integral value is displayed as $\int f(x)\,dx = 5.3333333$ and the graph is shaded. (Note: The shaded region is the mirror image of what you've shaded above because you entered the difference of the two functions into the function editor.) Since the answer choices are given as fractions, select $1 :\triangleright$ Frac from the $\boxed{\text{MATH}}$ menu. The display will show Ans $:\triangleright$ Frac. Press $\boxed{\text{ENTER}}$. The display shows 16/3, choice B.

Tip: Be sure to use the negative key, not the subtraction key, when you enter negative numbers into the calculator.

Method 2. Integrate the function using methods of calculus.

$$\int_{-2}^{2}\left(2 - \frac{x^2}{2}\right)dx = \left(2x - \frac{x^3}{6}\right)\Big|_{-2}^{2} = \left(2\cdot 2 - \frac{2^3}{6}\right) - \left(2\cdot -2 - \frac{(-2)^3}{6}\right) = \left(4 - \frac{8}{6}\right) - \left(-4 - \frac{-8}{6}\right) =$$

$$4 - \frac{4}{3} + 4 - \frac{4}{3} = 8 - \frac{8}{3} = \frac{24}{3} - \frac{8}{3} = \frac{16}{3}, \text{ choice B.}$$

32. C. Analyze the graph of f'.

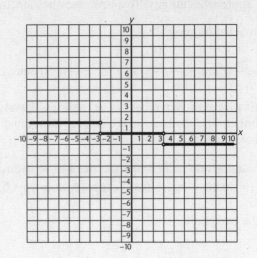

Recall that the first derivative of a function at a point is equal to the slope of the graph at that point. By inspecting the graph of f', you can see that to the left of –3, the slope of the graph of f is a constant value of positive 1, indicating that to the left of –3 the graph of f is a straight line slanting upward from left to right with slope of 1. Eliminate B and D because the graphs in these answer choices do not meet this condition. Between –3 and 3, according to the graph of f', the slope of the graph of f is a constant value of 0, indicating that between –3 and 3 the graph of f is a horizontal line. Eliminate A because the graph in this answer choice does not have a horizontal component. Therefore, C is the correct response. The graph in C is the only graph shown in the answer choices that is consistent with the behavior of f'.

33. C. Recall that the first derivative of a position function is the velocity function. To find the distance traveled after 10 seconds, find the numerical integral of the velocity function between 0 and 10 seconds.

That is, evaluate: $\int\limits_0^{10} 0.9t^2\, dt$.

Method 1. As in problem 31, the fastest and most efficient way to calculate this numerical integral is with your graphing calculator. Here are the steps using a TI-83 Plus calculator. Before you enter functions, you must select Func mode from the MODE menu. Enter the function $y = 0.9x^2$ into the $\boxed{Y=}$ editor. Notice that you must use y and x for the variables instead of v and t. As a precaution, clear any previously entered functions before you enter the function. Check the viewing $\boxed{\text{WINDOW}}$ to make sure that the interval between 0 and 10 falls between Xmin and Xmax. If not, change Xmin and/or Xmax, as needed. Go to the $\boxed{\text{CALC}}$ (calculate) menu. Select $7 : \int f(x)\,dx$. Type 0 when prompted for the lower limit and then press $\boxed{\text{ENTER}}$. Type 10 when prompted for the upper limit and then press $\boxed{\text{ENTER}}$. The integral value is displayed as 300. Therefore, the distance the car has traveled after 10 seconds is 300 feet, choice C.

Method 2. Integrate the function using methods of calculus.

$\int\limits_0^{10} 0.9t^2\, dt = \dfrac{0.9t^3}{3}\Big|_0^{10} = 0.3t^3\Big|_0^{10} = 0.3(10)^3 - 0.3(0)^3 = 0.3(1000) - 0.3(0) = 300 - 0 = 300.$

Therefore, the distance the car has traveled after 10 seconds is 300 feet, choice C.

34. D. Let the two sides of the pen that are perpendicular to the brick wall each have length of x yards. Then the side parallel to the wall has length 550 yards $-2x$, since the sum of the three sides is 550 yards. Sketch a diagram to illustrate the problem:

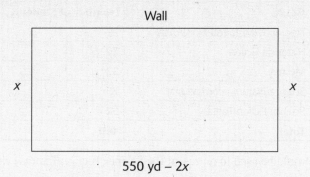

Wall

x

x

550 yd $- 2x$

The area of the field is width times length and is given by the function f, where $f(x) = x(550 - 2x) = 550x - 2x^2$.

The pen will have maximum area when $f(x)$ is the maximum value of f. To find the length of the pen with largest area, first solve $f'(x) = 0$ to find the critical numbers(s) for f.

$f(x) = 550x - 2x^2$

$f'(x) = 550 - 4x = 0$

  $x = 137.5$ is a critical number of f.

Then check $f''(137.5)$ to determine whether $f(137.5)$ is a maximum.

$$f''(x) = -4$$

Therefore, $f''(137.5) = -4 < 0$

Thus, by the second derivative test, $f(137.5)$ is the maximum area of the pen.

The length of the pen that encloses the maximum area is

550 yards $- 2(137.5$ yards$) = 275$ yards, choice D.

35. C. In an ordered set of data values, the median is the $\left(\dfrac{n+1}{2}\right)$th data value.

Weights in Pounds of 35 Female High School Seniors	
Stem	**Leaves**
12	3 8 8
13	1 3 4 4 5 6 8
14	0 0 2 4 5 5 7 7 7 8 9
15	0 1 3 3 5 6 7 8 9 9
16	1 2 2 9
Legend: 12|3 = 123	

Since there are 35 data values, the median is the $\dfrac{35+1}{2} = \dfrac{36}{2} = 18$th data value. Counting from the least weight, the 18th weight in the stem-and-leaf plot is 147 pounds, choice C.

36. C. A pie chart is made by dividing the 360 degrees of the circle that makes the pie chart into portions that correspond to the proportion for each category.

Genre	Number of Students
Biography/Historical Nonfiction	22
Historical Fiction	29
Mystery	32
Science/Nature Informational	25
Science Fiction/Fantasy	52
Total	**160**

The central angle that should be used to represent the Science Fiction/Fantasy category $= \frac{52}{160}\left(360°\right) = 117°$, choice C.

37. A. Analyze the information in the table.

Group	Mean	Standard Deviation
A	30 cm	5 cm
B	30 cm	8 cm
C	25 cm	10 cm
D	25 cm	9 cm

The standard deviation for the data obtained by Group A is less than the standard deviations of the data from the other groups. This result means the data from Group A have less variability and are, therefore, more reliable. Thus, A is the correct response.

38. B. According to the 68-95-99.7 rule, approximately 68% of the values of a random variable that is normally distributed fall within 1 standard deviation of the mean, about 95% fall within 2 standard deviations of the mean, and about 99.7% fall within 3 standard deviations of the mean. The mean number of shavings for the razors is 16.8 with a standard deviation of 2.4 shavings.

The z-score for $19.2 = \frac{\text{data value} - \text{mean}}{\text{standard deviation}} = \frac{19.2 - 16.8}{2.4} = 1$. Therefore, 19.2 is 1 standard deviation above the mean.

Find the percentage of the normal distribution that is 1 standard deviation above the mean.

By the 68-95-99.7 rule, 68% of the distribution is within 1 standard deviation of the mean. Since the normal curve is symmetric, about $\frac{1}{2}$ of 68% = 34% of the distribution is between the mean and 1 standard deviation. Make a sketch to illustrate the problem.

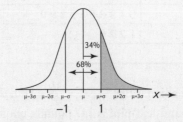

Again, due to symmetry, 50% of the distribution is above the mean. Thus, approximately 50% – 34% = 16% of the distribution is above 1 standard deviation above the mean. Thus, about 16% of the razors will last more than 19.2 shavings, choice B.

39. A. Because the correlation coefficient measures the linear relationship between the independent and dependent variables of the simple linear regression model, it can be used as an estimate of the "goodness of fit" of the regression model. Since the value 0.03 of the correlation coefficient is near 0, it fails to support a linear relationship between the variables of the linear regression, indicating that the linear model is not a good fit for the data, choice A.

40. **D.** This question asks you to find a conditional probability; that is, you are to find the probability when you already know that the subject is a smoker. Thus, when computing the probability, the number of possible subjects under consideration is no longer 200 subjects, but is reduced to the total number of smokers. To find the probability that if 1 of the 200 subjects is randomly selected, the subject was positively diagnosed with lung cancer, *given* that the subject is a smoker, find the total number of smokers, and then of these, find the probability that a smoker was diagnosed with lung cancer. Examine the table.

	Positive Diagnosis	Negative Diagnosis
Smoker	25	5
Nonsmoker	15	155

Total number of smokers = 25 + 5 = 30 smokers.

Of the 30 smokers, the probability a randomly selected smoker is diagnosed with lung cancer = P(diagnosed with lung cancer given the subject is a smoker) = $\frac{25}{30} = \frac{5}{6}$, choice D.

41. **B.** Fill in the missing probabilities.

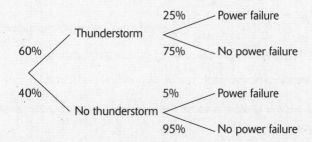

This problem requires an application of the Multiplication Rule, which states that $P(A \text{ and } B) = P(A)P(B|A)$.

P(thunderstorm and power failure)

= P(thunderstorm)•P(power failure given a thunderstorm has developed)

= $60\% \cdot 25\% = 15\%$, choice B.

42. **C.** Because there are only 7 remote controls left in the box, one of which is defective, the probability that the next remote control is defective = $\frac{1}{7}$, choice C.

43. **B.** The augmented matrix for the system is

$$\begin{bmatrix} 7 & -8 & 5 & 5 \\ -4 & 5 & -3 & -3 \\ 1 & -1 & 1 & 0 \end{bmatrix}$$

Although you can work this problem by using operations on the rows to transform the matrix so the system's solution is easily found, the process is tedious and time-consuming. Since the Mathematics CK is a timed test, you should use your graphing calculator to find the solution. Here are the steps using a TI-83 Plus calculator:

Go to $\boxed{\text{MATRX}}$ and select EDIT. Press $\boxed{\text{ENTER}}$. Define [A] to be 3 × 4: Enter 3, press $\boxed{\text{ENTER}}$; enter 4, press $\boxed{\text{ENTER}}$. Enter the elements of the augmented matrix one by one, being sure to press $\boxed{\text{ENTER}}$ after each entry. Select $\boxed{\text{QUIT}}$ ($\boxed{\text{2nd}}$ $\boxed{\text{MODE}}$). Go to $\boxed{\text{MATRX}}$ and select MATH. Select B:rref(and then press $\boxed{\text{ENTER}}$. The display will show rref(with a flashing cursor. Go to $\boxed{\text{MATRX}}$ and under NAME, select 1:[A] by pressing $\boxed{\text{ENTER}}$. Close the parentheses and press $\boxed{\text{ENTER}}$. The display will show the reduced row-echelon form of the augmented matrix:

$$\begin{bmatrix} 1 & 0 & 0 & 1 \\ 0 & 1 & 0 & -1 \\ 0 & 0 & 1 & -2 \end{bmatrix}$$. Thus, $x = 1$, $y = -1$, and $z = -2$ is the solution to the system.

Since $y = -1$, choice B is the correct response.

44. D. You can represent the triangle ABC with vertices $A(0, 0)$, $B(3, 0)$, and $C(0, 4)$ using a 2×3 matrix,

with each column $\begin{bmatrix} x \\ y \end{bmatrix}$ representing a vertex: $\begin{bmatrix} 0 & 3 & 0 \\ 0 & 0 & 4 \end{bmatrix}$. The dilation of ABC, using a scale factor of 3,

is represented by the matrix $\begin{bmatrix} 0 & 9 & 0 \\ 0 & 0 & 12 \end{bmatrix}$. Looking at the answer choices, you can see that you need to

select the 2×2 matrix that will multiply times $\begin{bmatrix} 0 & 3 & 0 \\ 0 & 0 & 4 \end{bmatrix}$ to give $\begin{bmatrix} 0 & 9 & 0 \\ 0 & 0 & 12 \end{bmatrix}$. A quick way to work this

problem is to check the answer choices.

Checking A: $\begin{bmatrix} 0 & 3 \\ 0 & 3 \end{bmatrix}\begin{bmatrix} 0 & 3 & 0 \\ 0 & 0 & 4 \end{bmatrix} = \begin{bmatrix} 0 & 0 \\ \end{bmatrix}$, eliminate A because the element in the first row second

column is not 9. There is no need to complete the multiplication.

Checking B: $\begin{bmatrix} 3 & 3 \\ 0 & 0 \end{bmatrix}\begin{bmatrix} 0 & 3 & 0 \\ 0 & 0 & 4 \end{bmatrix} = \begin{bmatrix} 0 & 9 & 12 \\ \end{bmatrix}$, eliminate B because the element in the first row third

column is not 0. There is no need to complete the multiplication.

Checking C: $\begin{bmatrix} 3 & 3 \\ 3 & 3 \end{bmatrix}\begin{bmatrix} 0 & 3 & 0 \\ 0 & 0 & 4 \end{bmatrix} = \begin{bmatrix} 0 & 9 & 12 \\ 0 & 9 & \end{bmatrix}$, eliminate C because the element in the second row

second column is not 0. There is no need to complete the multiplication.

Thus, choice D is the correct response since you've eliminated A, B, and C.

Tip: A quick way to check the answer choices is to do the multiplication with your graphing calculator. Here are the steps using a TI-83 Plus calculator:

Enter $\begin{bmatrix} 0 & 3 & 0 \\ 0 & 0 & 4 \end{bmatrix}$ as [B]. Go to $\boxed{\text{MATRX}}$ and under EDIT, select 2:[B]. Press $\boxed{\text{ENTER}}$. Define [B] to be

2×3: Enter 2, press $\boxed{\text{ENTER}}$; enter 3, press $\boxed{\text{ENTER}}$. Enter the elements of the matrix $\begin{bmatrix} 0 & 3 & 0 \\ 0 & 0 & 4 \end{bmatrix}$ one

by one, being sure to press $\boxed{\text{ENTER}}$ after each entry. Select $\boxed{\text{QUIT}}$ ($\boxed{\text{2nd}}\boxed{\text{MODE}}$). Now to check choice

A, enter $\begin{bmatrix} 0 & 3 \\ 0 & 3 \end{bmatrix}$ as [A]. Select $\boxed{\text{QUIT}}$. Next multiply [A] times [B], being sure to put [A] to the left of

[B]: Go to $\boxed{\text{MATRX}}$, select [A]; go to $\boxed{\text{MATRX}}$, select [B]; press $\boxed{\text{ENTER}}$. The display will show the

matrix $\begin{bmatrix} 0 & 0 & 12 \\ 0 & 0 & 12 \end{bmatrix}$, so eliminate A. Now edit [A], so that it has elements $\begin{bmatrix} 3 & 3 \\ 0 & 0 \end{bmatrix}$, choice B. Use the

Recall Entry feature of the calculator to do the multiplication. Repeat for C and D.

45. A. This question is an example of a multiple response set question. One approach to answering this type of question is to follow these steps:

Step 1. Read the question carefully to make sure you understand what the question is asking.

A vector has magnitude and direction. Its magnitude is the length of the vector, disregarding the direction.

Step 2. Identify choices that you know are incorrect from the Roman numeral options, and then draw a line through every answer choice that contains a Roman numeral you have eliminated.

Looking at the three transformations given in the Roman numeral options, you can immediately eliminate Roman III because dilating a vector would change its magnitude. Draw a line through B, C, and D because each of these answer choices contains Roman numeral III.

Choice A is correct because you've eliminated the other answer choices. You do not have to continue with the problem; but for your information, transformations and rotations are "rigid motions," meaning that magnitudes are preserved under these transformations.

46. **C.** The matrix $\begin{bmatrix} 5 & 1.5 \\ 2 & d \end{bmatrix}$ is not invertible if its determinant is equal to 0. Set the determinant of the matrix equal to 0 and solve for d:

$5d - (2)(1.5) = 5d - 3 = 0$

Thus, $d = \dfrac{3}{5} = 0.6$, choice C.

47. **C.** For the recursive formula given in the problem, you will need to find $f(2)$ and $f(1)$ before you can find $f(3)$. Since $f(0) = 3$ and $f(n) = 2f(n-1) + 3$ for $n \geq 1$, then

$f(1) = 2f(0) + 3 = 2(3) + 3 = 6 + 3 = 9$

$f(2) = 2f(1) + 3 = 2(9) + 3 = 18 + 3 = 21$

$f(3) = 2f(2) + 3 = 2(21) + 3 = 42 + 3 = 45$, choice C.

48. **D.** Because there are six slots to be filled, so to speak, on a license plate, you can work this problem by extending the Fundamental Counting Principle to six events. There are 10 possibilities for each of the two digits and 26 possible values for each of the four uppercase letters, which means the total number of possible license plate alphanumeric codes is $10 \cdot 10 \cdot 26 \cdot 26 \cdot 26 \cdot 26 = 10^2 \cdot 26^4$, choice D.

49. **C.** There are two tasks to be accomplished. The first task is to select 4 of the 7 chairs. Noting that different ordering of the chairs does not produce different arrangements, the number of ways to select 4 of 7 chairs is $_7C_4$. The second task is to arrange the four people in the 4 chairs. Since different orderings of the people results in different arrangements, the number of ways to seat four people in four chairs is $_4P_4$. Therefore, by the Fundamental Counting Principle, the total number of ways to seat 4 people in 7 empty identical chairs is

$_7C_4 \cdot {_4P_4} = \dfrac{7!}{4!3!} \cdot 4! = 35 \cdot 24 = 840$, choice C.

50. **C.** This question is an example of a multiple response set question. One approach to answering this type of question is to follow the following steps:

Step 1. Read the question carefully to make sure you understand what the question is asking.

Recall that a set A is a subset of set B, written $A \subseteq B$, if and only if $x \in A$ implies that $x \in B$, for every $x \in A$.

Step 2. Identify choices that you know are incorrect from the Roman numeral options and then draw a line through every answer choice that contains a Roman numeral you have eliminated.

Looking at the three properties given in the Roman numeral options, you can immediately eliminate Roman II. The relation "is a subset of" is not symmetric because, for instance, $\{1, 3\} \subseteq$ Integers, but Integers $\not\subseteq \{1, 3\}$. Draw a line through A and D because each of these answer choices contains Roman numeral II.

Step 3. Examine the remaining answer choices to determine which Roman numeral options you need to consider.

The remaining answer choices are B and C, which contain Roman numeral options I and III. Notice that both B and C contain Roman numeral III, so you know that Roman numeral III is correct and that there is no need to check it. Look at the remaining Roman numeral option I. The relation "is a subset of" is reflexive because every set is a subset of itself; that is $A \subseteq A$.

Since Roman numeral I is correct, draw a line through B. This leaves C as the correct response because it includes every Roman numeral option that is correct and no incorrect Roman numeral options.

Answer Sheet for Practice Test 2

(Remove This Sheet and Use It to Mark Your Answers)

CUT HERE

1 Ⓐ Ⓑ Ⓒ Ⓓ	26 Ⓐ Ⓑ Ⓒ Ⓓ
2 Ⓐ Ⓑ Ⓒ Ⓓ	27 Ⓐ Ⓑ Ⓒ Ⓓ
3 Ⓐ Ⓑ Ⓒ Ⓓ	28 Ⓐ Ⓑ Ⓒ Ⓓ
4 Ⓐ Ⓑ Ⓒ Ⓓ	29 Ⓐ Ⓑ Ⓒ Ⓓ
5 Ⓐ Ⓑ Ⓒ Ⓓ	30 Ⓐ Ⓑ Ⓒ Ⓓ
6 Ⓐ Ⓑ Ⓒ Ⓓ	31 Ⓐ Ⓑ Ⓒ Ⓓ
7 Ⓐ Ⓑ Ⓒ Ⓓ	32 Ⓐ Ⓑ Ⓒ Ⓓ
8 Ⓐ Ⓑ Ⓒ Ⓓ	33 Ⓐ Ⓑ Ⓒ Ⓓ
9 Ⓐ Ⓑ Ⓒ Ⓓ	34 Ⓐ Ⓑ Ⓒ Ⓓ
10 Ⓐ Ⓑ Ⓒ Ⓓ	35 Ⓐ Ⓑ Ⓒ Ⓓ
11 Ⓐ Ⓑ Ⓒ Ⓓ	36 Ⓐ Ⓑ Ⓒ Ⓓ
12 Ⓐ Ⓑ Ⓒ Ⓓ	37 Ⓐ Ⓑ Ⓒ Ⓓ
13 Ⓐ Ⓑ Ⓒ Ⓓ	38 Ⓐ Ⓑ Ⓒ Ⓓ
14 Ⓐ Ⓑ Ⓒ Ⓓ	39 Ⓐ Ⓑ Ⓒ Ⓓ
15 Ⓐ Ⓑ Ⓒ Ⓓ	40 Ⓐ Ⓑ Ⓒ Ⓓ
16 Ⓐ Ⓑ Ⓒ Ⓓ	41 Ⓐ Ⓑ Ⓒ Ⓓ
17 Ⓐ Ⓑ Ⓒ Ⓓ	42 Ⓐ Ⓑ Ⓒ Ⓓ
18 Ⓐ Ⓑ Ⓒ Ⓓ	43 Ⓐ Ⓑ Ⓒ Ⓓ
19 Ⓐ Ⓑ Ⓒ Ⓓ	44 Ⓐ Ⓑ Ⓒ Ⓓ
20 Ⓐ Ⓑ Ⓒ Ⓓ	45 Ⓐ Ⓑ Ⓒ Ⓓ
21 Ⓐ Ⓑ Ⓒ Ⓓ	46 Ⓐ Ⓑ Ⓒ Ⓓ
22 Ⓐ Ⓑ Ⓒ Ⓓ	47 Ⓐ Ⓑ Ⓒ Ⓓ
23 Ⓐ Ⓑ Ⓒ Ⓓ	48 Ⓐ Ⓑ Ⓒ Ⓓ
24 Ⓐ Ⓑ Ⓒ Ⓓ	49 Ⓐ Ⓑ Ⓒ Ⓓ
25 Ⓐ Ⓑ Ⓒ Ⓓ	50 Ⓐ Ⓑ Ⓒ Ⓓ

Time — 120 minutes

50 Questions

Directions: Each of the questions or incomplete statements is followed by four suggested answers or completions. Select the one that is best in each case, and then fill in the corresponding lettered space on the answer sheet.

1. In the xy-plane, which of the following points lies inside the circular region of radius 4 centered at $(-2, 3)$?

   A. $(-6, 3)$
   B. $(-2, -1)$
   C. $(1, 5)$
   D. $(2, 3)$

2. Which of the following sets are closed with respect to the given operation?

   I. The set of perfect squares with respect to multiplication

   II. The set of whole numbers with respect to subtraction

   III. The set of odd numbers with respect to addition

   IV. The set of integers with respect to division

   A. I only
   B. I and III only
   C. II and IV only
   D. III and IV only

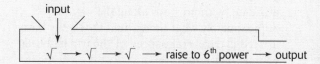

3. If a positive number x is used as the input for the function machine shown, which of the following is equivalent to the output?

   A. $x^{\frac{1}{24}}$
   B. $x^{\frac{3}{4}}$
   C. x
   D. $x^{\frac{3}{2}}$

4. For what value of k will the graph of the function defined by $y = \dfrac{k}{16x^2 + kx + 9}$ have exactly one vertical asymptote?

   A. 0
   B. 12
   C. 24
   D. 48

5. Definition: The *normal line* to the curve $y = f(x)$ at the point T is the line perpendicular to the tangent line to the curve at T. If an equation of the normal line to the graph of the function defined by $y = f(x)$ at the point $(3, 1)$ is $y = \dfrac{5}{6}x - \dfrac{3}{2}$, find the equation of the tangent line at $(3, 1)$.

   A. $5x - 6y = 9$
   B. $-6x + 5y = -13$
   C. $6x + 5y = 23$
   D. $6x + 5y = 21$

6. Given the recursive function defined by

   $f(1) = 1$,

   $f(2) = 2$, and

   $f(n) = 2f(n-1) + f(n-2)$ for $n \geq 3$,

   what is the value of $f(5)$?

   A. 5
   B. 12
   C. 29
   D. 70

7. The operation $\oplus$ is defined on the set R of real numbers by $x \oplus y = 3x + xy$ where x and y are real numbers and the operations on the right side of the equal sign denote the standard operations for the real number system. Which of the following questions tests whether the operation $\oplus$ is commutative?

   A. Does $x + y = y + x$ for all real numbers x and y?
   B. Does $3x + xy = 3x + yx$ for all real numbers x and y?
   C. Does $3x + x^2 = 3y + y^2$ for all real numbers x and y?
   D. Does $3x + xy = 3y + yx$ for all real numbers x and y?

8. The exterior of a spherical tank with radius 12 feet is to be painted with one coat of paint. The paint sells for $22.40 per gallon and can be purchased in 1-gallon cans only. If a can of paint will cover approximately 400 square feet, what is the cost of the paint needed to paint the exterior of the tank?

    A. $22.40
    B. $44.80
    C. $101.36
    D. $112.00

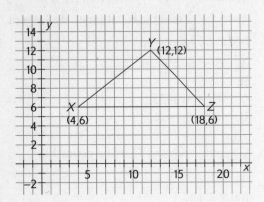

9. Which of the following properties associated with triangle XYZ shown above is an irrational quantity?

    A. perimeter of triangle XYZ
    B. area of triangle XYZ
    C. length of side $\overline{XY}$
    D. midpoint of side $\overline{XZ}$

10. To estimate the population of fish in a lake, a parks and recreation team captures and tags 500 fish and then releases the tagged fish back into the lake. One month later, the team returns and captures 100 fish from the lake, 20 of which bear tags that identify them as being among the previously captured fish. If all the tagged fish are still active in the lake when the second group of fish is captured, what is the best estimate of the fish population in the lake based on the information obtained through this capture-recapture strategy?

    A. 100 fish
    B. 1500 fish
    C. 2500 fish
    D. 3000 fish

11. Paul calls long distance to his friend J.D. in Germany. The first minute of the call costs $3.75, and each additional minute costs 55 cents. The total cost of the call is $11.45. For how many minutes did the phone call between Paul and J.D. last?

    A. 13 minutes
    B. 14 minutes
    C. 15 minutes
    D. 16 minutes

12. Given $\frac{a}{b} = 10$ and $\frac{b}{c} = 5$, with $b \cdot c \neq 0$. What is the value of $\frac{a}{b+c}$?

    A. $\frac{25}{6}$
    B. $\frac{25}{3}$
    C. $\frac{5}{3}$
    D. 12

13. $(2 \cos 10° + 2i \sin 10°)^3$ equals

    A. $4\sqrt{3} + 4i$
    B. $4 + 4\sqrt{3}i$
    C. $8 \cos 1000° + 8i \sin 1000°$
    D. $8 \sin 1000° + 8i \cos 1000°$

14. A family on vacation in an RV leaves home at 9 a.m., travels at an average speed of 50 miles per hour, and arrives at the vacation destination at 2 p.m., with no stops along the way. At approximately what time would the family have arrived if the average speed of the trip had been 65 miles per hour?

    A. 12:24 p.m.
    B. 12:50 p.m.
    C. 1:24 p.m.
    D. 1:50 p.m.

15. Triangle ABC has vertices (2, 1), (–3, 4), and (5, –3). Which of the following matrix multiplications would result in a reflection of $\triangle ABC$ over the x-axis?

A. $\begin{bmatrix} -1 & 0 \\ 0 & 1 \end{bmatrix} \begin{bmatrix} 2 & -3 & 5 \\ 1 & 4 & -3 \end{bmatrix}$

B. $\begin{bmatrix} 0 & 1 \\ -1 & 0 \end{bmatrix} \begin{bmatrix} 2 & -3 & 5 \\ 1 & 4 & -3 \end{bmatrix}$

C. $\begin{bmatrix} 0 & 1 \\ 1 & 0 \end{bmatrix} \begin{bmatrix} 2 & -3 & 5 \\ 1 & 4 & -3 \end{bmatrix}$

D. $\begin{bmatrix} 1 & 0 \\ 0 & -1 \end{bmatrix} \begin{bmatrix} 2 & -3 & 5 \\ 1 & 4 & -3 \end{bmatrix}$

16. Which of the following relations is NOT an equivalence relation?

A. "is similar to" over the set of all parallelograms
B. "is equal to" over the set of all $m \times n$ matrices
C. "is perpendicular to" over the set of all lines in the Cartesian coordinate plane
D. "is congruent to" over the set of all triangles

17. For which of the following data sets is the median clearly a preferred alternative to the mean as a measure of central tendency?

A. The data set contains some extremely high, without corresponding extremely low, data values.
B. The data set has a somewhat symmetrical distribution.
C. The data set is very large in number and has no mode.
D. The data set is very small in number and has no mode.

18. A box contains 50 one-inch square wooden tiles numbered 1 through 50. If one tile is drawn at random from the box, what is the probability that the number on the tile is a prime number?

A. $\frac{1}{50}$

B. $\frac{1}{15}$

C. $\frac{3}{10}$

D. $\frac{8}{25}$

19. To find the distance across the lake between two houses separated by the lake, a surveyor measures the angle between the houses from a distant point, X, on dry land. The surveyor then measures the straight line distance on dry land from X to each of the two houses. The distance from X to the first house is 60 feet and from X to the second house is 75 feet. If the angle measured at point X between the two houses is 60°, approximately how far apart are the two houses?

A. 39 feet
B. 69 feet
C. 96 feet
D. 4725 feet

20. The density of lead is 11.3 grams per cubic centimeter. What is the mass (to the nearest tenth of a gram) of a lead cube that measures 1.5 centimeters on a side?

A. 3.3 grams
B. 17.0 grams
C. 25.4 grams
D. 38.1 grams

21. A national health study estimates that 25% of people over age 65 in the United States will get flu shots this year. According to the study, of the people who get flu shots, an estimated 2% will have some sort of adverse reaction. If N represents the number of people over age 65 in the United States, estimate how many people over age 65 will have an adverse reaction after getting flu shots this year.

A. $0.005N$
B. $0.02N$
C. $0.25N$
D. $0.27N$

22. Given the functions $f = \{(-2, -8), (-1, 3), (0, 1), (1, 4), (2, 8)\}$ and $g = \{(-2, -7), (-1, 4), (0, -2), (1, 2), (2, 0), (3, 8)\}$. Find $g \circ f$, where $(g \circ f)(x) = g(f(x))$.

A. $\{(0, -8), (1, 8), (2, 1)\}$
B. $\{(-1, 8), (0, 2)\}$
C. $\{(-2, 56), (-1, -12), (0, -2), (1, 8), (2, 0)\}$
D. $\{(-2, -15), (-1, -1), (0, -1), (1, 6), (2, 8)\}$

23. A team of biologists introduces a herd of 2500 deer onto an uninhabited island. If the deer population doubles every 8 years, which of the following functions models the growth of the deer population on the island if t is the time in years?

   A. $(2500)^{0.125t}$
   B. $(2500)2^{0.125t}$
   C. $(2500)^{8t}$
   D. $(2500)2^{8t}$

24. For what values of x in the interval $0 \leq x \leq 2\pi$ does $\sin^2 x - 5 \sin x + 4 = 0$?

   A. $1, 4$
   B. π
   C. $\dfrac{\pi}{2}$
   D. $\dfrac{\pi}{2}, \dfrac{3\pi}{2}$

25. If $f(x) = -x^{-2}$, then $f'(2)$ is

   A. -1
   B. $-\dfrac{1}{4}$
   C. $\dfrac{1}{4}$
   D. 1

Correlation Table for Variables A, B, C, and D				
	Variable A	Variable B	Variable C	Variable D
Variable A	1			
Variable B	−0.88	1		
Variable C	0.65	0.15	1	
Variable D	−0.59	0.50	0.78	1

26. The correlation table shows the correlations between pairs of variables from among the four variables A, B, C, and D. The correlation coefficient between which of the following pairs of variables shows the strongest relationship?

   A. A and B
   B. A and C
   C. A and D
   D. C and D

27. In general, with respect to matrix multiplication on the set of $n \times n$ matrices containing elements that are real numbers only, which of the following properties do NOT hold?

   I. closure
   II. commutativity
   III. associativity
   IV. distributive property

   A. I only
   B. II only
   C. I and III only
   D. IV only

$$b2_{seven} = 134_{five}$$

28. In the equation shown, the subscript of each number identifies the base in which the number is expressed. What base-seven number does $b2_{seven}$ represent?

    A. 8_{seven}
    B. 26_{seven}
    C. 52_{seven}
    D. 62_{seven}

29. What are the units of the quantity $Y = \dfrac{Adv}{t}$, where A is measured in square centimeters (cm^2), d is expressed in grams per cm^3 $\left(\dfrac{g}{cm^3}\right)$, v is expressed in centimeters per second $\left(\dfrac{cm}{s}\right)$, and t is given in seconds (s)?

    A. g
    B. $\dfrac{g}{s^2}$
    C. $\dfrac{g - cm}{s}$
    D. $\dfrac{g - cm}{s^2}$

1 cm

30. The figure consists of a semicircle of radius 1 cm and an attached right triangle with one leg equal to the radius of the semicircle as shown. What is the figure's perimeter to the nearest tenth of a centimeter?

    A. 5.4 cm
    B. 5.9 cm
    C. 6.4 cm
    D. 9.5 cm

31. If x and y are real numbers, all of the following must be true EXCEPT

    A. $-|-x| = x$
    B. $|xy| = |x||y|$
    C. $\left|\dfrac{x}{y}\right| = \dfrac{|x|}{|y|}$, provided $y \neq 0$
    D. $|x + y| \leq |x| + |y|$

32. What is the value of $\lim\limits_{x \to 3} \dfrac{2x - 6}{x^2 - 9}$?

    A. The limit does not exist.
    B. $\dfrac{1}{6}$
    C. $\dfrac{1}{3}$
    D. 1

33. The velocity in feet per second of a car during the first 5 seconds of a test run is given by $v(t) = 1.8t^2$. What is the distance the car has traveled after 5 seconds?

    A. 15 feet
    B. 45 feet
    C. 75 feet
    D. 225 feet

34. Find a, b, c, and d if
$$\begin{bmatrix} a & 5 \\ 4b & d \end{bmatrix} - \begin{bmatrix} 3a & 2c \\ -6 & -2d \end{bmatrix} = \begin{bmatrix} -8 & 7 \\ b & 9 \end{bmatrix}$$

    A. $a = -4, b = 2, c = -1, d = 3$
    B. $a = 4, b = -2, c = -1, d = 3$
    C. $a = 4, b = -2, c = 1, d = -3$
    D. $a = -4, b = 2, c = 1, d = 3$

35. At an appliance store's grand-opening sale, 152 customers bought a washer or a dryer. Looking at the inventory, the store manager found that 94 washers and 80 dryers were sold. Of the 152 customers, how many bought only a washer?

    A. 22
    B. 58
    C. 72
    D. 130

36. The equation of the line tangent to the graph of $y = 2x^3 - x + 3$ at the point where $x = 1$ is given by

    A. $6x - y = 2$
    B. $5x - y = 1$
    C. $5x - y = 5$
    D. $5x - y = -1$

37. What is the area of the region bounded by the graph of $f(x) = 3x^2 + 1$ and the x-axis over the closed interval $[1, 3]$?

    A. 26
    B. 28
    C. 30
    D. 32

38. The heights of a certain type of indoor plant are normally distributed with a mean of 24 inches and a standard deviation of 3.5 inches. What is the approximate probability a plant of this type chosen at random will be between 20.5 inches and 27.5 inches tall?

A. 16%
B. 34%
C. 68%
D. 84%

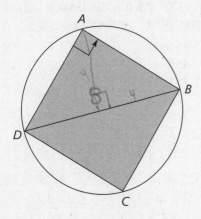

39. In the figure, the circle circumscribed about the square *ABCD* has a circumference of 8π cm. Find the area of the square *ABCD*.

A. It cannot be determined from the information given.
B. $4\sqrt{2}$ cm^2
C. 32π cm^2
D. 32 cm^2

	Exam 1	Exam 2	Exam 3	Exam 4
Student's Grade	65	87	92	70
Class Mean	55	88	86	60
Class Standard Deviation	5	2	4	10

40. The data in the table above show a student's grades on 4 exams in a college statistics class along with the means and standard deviations of the grades for all the students in the class of 50 students. On which of the exams did the student perform best relative to the performance of the student's classmates?

A. Exam 1
B. Exam 2
C. Exam 3
D. Exam 4

41. Which of the following graphs illustrates the solution to $\dfrac{2-x}{5} < 1$?

A.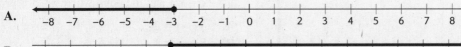

B.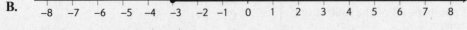

C.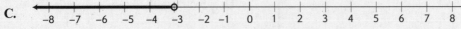

D.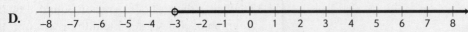

Time (minutes)	Population
0	1000
10	5000

42. The table above gives the population of a deadly bacterium at two different times. The bacteria's growth is modeled by the function defined by $Q(t) = Q_0 e^{xt}$. Based on this information, what is the value of x?

A. $\dfrac{\ln 5}{10}$

B. $\ln 5$

C. $\ln 10 - \ln 5$

D. $\ln\dfrac{1}{5}$

43. Which of the following functions is the factored form of the polynomial of lowest degree with real coefficients and leading coefficient 1 that has zeros at 0, $2 - i$, 4, and -3?

A. $P(x) = x(x - 2 + i)(x - 4)(x + 3)$

B. $P(x) = x(x + 2 - i)(x + 4)(x - 3)$

C. $P(x) = x(x - 2 - i)(x - 2 + i)(x + 4)(x - 3)$

D. $P(x) = x(x - 2 + i)(x - 2 - i)(x - 4)(x + 3)$

44. Which of the following functions have the same domain and the same range?

I. $\{(0, 0), (1, 1), (2, 4), (3, 9), (4, 16)\}$

II. $\{(x, y)|y = x^2\}$

III. $\{(0, 0), (1, 1), (2, 4), (3, 9), (4, 16), \ldots\}$

IV. $\{(x, y)|y = |x|\}$

A. I and III only

B. II and IV only

C. II, III, and IV only

D. I, II, III, and IV

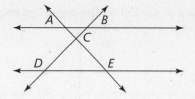

45. In the figure shown above $\overleftrightarrow{AB} \parallel \overleftrightarrow{DE}$, which of the following geometric theorems would most likely be used in proving that $\triangle ABC \sim \triangle CDE$?

I. Vertical angles of intersecting lines are congruent.

II. If two parallel lines are cut by a transversal, then any pair of alternate interior angles is congruent.

III. If two angles of one triangle are congruent to two corresponding angles of another triangle, then the triangles are similar.

A. I and II only

B. I and III only

C. II and III only

D. I, II, and III

46. In the x-y plane, triangle ABC has vertices $(0, 0)$, $(8, 0)$, and $(0, 15)$. A dilation of triangle ABC with center $(0, 0)$ and scale factor 5 is achieved by premultiplying the vertex matrix $\begin{bmatrix} x_i \\ y_i \end{bmatrix}$ by which of the following transformation matrices?

A. $\begin{bmatrix} 5 & 5 \\ 5 & 5 \end{bmatrix}$

B. $\begin{bmatrix} 5 & 0 \\ 5 & 0 \end{bmatrix}$

C. $\begin{bmatrix} 5 & 0 \\ 0 & 5 \end{bmatrix}$

D. $\begin{bmatrix} 0 & 5 \\ 0 & 5 \end{bmatrix}$

47. What is the approximate volume of a right hexagonal prism that is 30 centimeters in height and whose bases are regular hexagons that are 6 centimeters on a side?

A. 468 cm³

B. 1080 cm³

C. 2806 cm³

D. 3240 cm³

48. Which of the following vertex-edge graphs is a tree?

A.

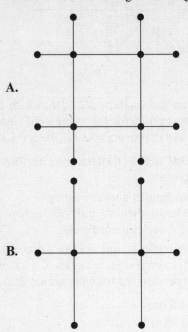

B.

C.

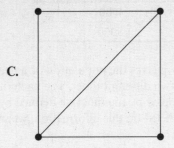

D.

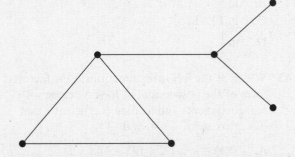

49. Find the area enclosed by the curves $y = 2x - x^2$ and $y = 2x - 4$.

A. $\dfrac{16}{3}$

B. $\dfrac{32}{3}$

C. 16

D. $\dfrac{64}{3}$

Resident Status of Second-Year Students ($n = 500$)		
	On-Campus	**Off-Campus**
Male	114	135
Female	156	95

50. The table shows the resident status, by sex, of 500 second-year students at a community college. If one of the 500 students is randomly selected, what is the probability that the student resides off-campus, given that the student selected is a female student?

A. $1 - \dfrac{156}{500}$

B. $\dfrac{95}{500}$

C. $\dfrac{251}{500} \cdot \dfrac{95}{500}$

D. $\dfrac{95}{251}$

Answer Key for Practice Test 2

Question Number	Correct Answer	Content Category	Question Number	Correct Answer	Content Category
1.	C	Geometry	26.	A	Data Analysis and Statistics
2.	A	Algebra and Number Theory	27.	B	Matrix Algebra
3.	B	Algebra and Number Theory	28.	D	Functions
4.	C	Functions	29.	B	Measurement
5.	C	Algebra and Number Theory	30.	C	Geometry
6.	C	Discrete Mathematics	31.	A	Algebra and Number Theory
7.	D	Measurement	32.	C	Calculus
8.	D	Geometry	33.	C	Calculus
9.	A	Algebra and Number Theory	34.	B	Matrix Algebra
10.	C	Data Analysis and Statistics	35.	C	Discrete Mathematics
11.	C	Algebra and Number Theory	36.	B	Calculus
12.	B	Functions	37.	B	Calculus
13.	A	Trigonometry	38.	C	Data Analysis and Statistics
14.	B	Trigonometry	39.	D	Geometry
15.	C	Matrix Algebra	40.	A	Data Analysis and Statistics
16.	C	Discrete Mathematics	41.	D	Algebra and Number Theory
17.	A	Data Analysis and Statistics	42.	A	Functions
18.	C	Probability	43.	D	Functions
19.	B	Trigonometry	44.	B	Functions
20.	D	Measurement	45.	D	Geometry
21.	A	Algebra and Number Theory	46.	C	Matrix Algebra
22.	B	Functions	47.	C	Geometry
23.	B	Functions	48.	B	Discrete Mathematics
24.	C	Trigonometry	49.	B	Calculus
25.	C	Calculus	50.	D	Probability

Answer Explanations for Practice Test 2

1. **C.** Make a sketch of the circle and plot the points given in the answer choices.

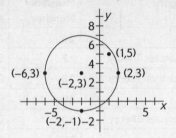

The center of the circle is at $(-2, 3)$ with radius 4, so it equation is $(x + 2)^2 + (y - 3)^2 = 16$. The points $(-6, 3)$, $(-2, -1)$, $(2, 3)$ lie on the circle. When you substitute the coordinates of these points into the equation of the circle, they satisfy the equation as shown here:

$((-6) + 2)^2 + ((3) - 3)^2 = (-4)^2 + (0)^2 = 16 + 0 = 16$

$((-2) + 2)^2 + ((-1) - 3)^2 = (0)^2 + (-4)^2 = 0 + 16 = 16$

$((2) + 2)^2 + ((3) - 3)^2 = (4)^2 + (0)^2 = 16 + 0 = 16$

Because $((1) + 2)^2 + ((5) - 3)^2 = (3)^2 + (2)^2 = 9 + 4 = 13 < 16$, only $(1, 5)$ clearly lies within the interior of the circle. Thus, C is the correct response.

2. **A.** This question is an example of a multiple response set question. One approach to answering this type of question is to do the following. First, read the question carefully to make sure you understand what the question is asking; next, identify choices you know are incorrect from the Roman numeral options, and then draw a line through every answer choice that contains a Roman numeral you have eliminated; and then examine the remaining answer choices to determine which Roman numeral options you need to consider.

A set is closed with respect to an operation if the result of performing the operation with any pair of elements in the set yields an element contained in the set. Therefore, to show a set is *not* closed, you need to find just *one* pair of elements that does not yield an element in the set when the operation is performed with that pair of elements. Eliminate answer choices that are *not* closed by selecting arbitrary pairs of values and testing them with the given operation.

Eliminate Roman II because 5 and 9 are whole numbers, but $5 - 9 = -4$, which is not a whole number. Eliminate C. Eliminate Roman III because 3 and 5 are odd numbers, but $3 + 5 = 8$, which is not an odd number. Eliminate B and D. Thus, A is the correct response. You should move on to the next problem. Notwithstanding, the following shows that the set of perfect squares is closed with respect to multiplication: Let a^2 and b^2 be any two perfect squares. Then $(a^2)(b^2) = (ab)^2$, which is also a perfect square.

3. **B.** Since the answer choices are given as exponential expressions, the best way to work this problem is to perform on x the sequence of operations indicated by the function machine, using the exponential form for the operation:

$$\left(\left(\left(\left(x\right)^{\frac{1}{2}}\right)^{\frac{1}{2}}\right)^{\frac{1}{2}}\right)^6 = x^{\frac{1}{2} \cdot \frac{1}{2} \cdot \frac{1}{2} \cdot 6} = x^{\frac{6}{8}} = x^{\frac{3}{4}}, \text{ choice B.}$$

4. C. The graph of the function defined by $y = \dfrac{k}{16x^2 + kx + 9}$ will have vertical asymptotes at values of x for which the denominator, $16x^2 + kx + 9$, equals 0. The trinomial, $16x^2 + kx + 9$, will have exactly one 0 when it is a perfect square. For $16x^2 + kx + 9$ to be a perfect square, the coefficient, k, of x needs to be $2 \cdot \sqrt{16} \cdot \sqrt{9} = 2 \cdot 4 \cdot 3 = 24$, choice C.

Tip: You can check your answer by substituting into the equation the values for k given in the answer choices and graphing the resulting functions using your graphing calculator. However, it is best that you work out the problem analytically rather than using only your graphing calculator to determine a solution because on a graphing calculator the graphs of functions that have asymptotes are sometimes misleading.

5. C. Because the normal line is perpendicular to the tangent line at (3, 1), the slope of the tangent line through the point (3, 1) is the negative reciprocal of the slope of the normal line. The slope of the normal line $y = \dfrac{5}{6}x - \dfrac{3}{2}$ is $\dfrac{5}{6}$. Therefore, the tangent line at (3, 1) has slope $-\dfrac{6}{5}$.

Use the point-slope form to determine the equation of the tangent line at (3, 1).

$y - 1 = -\dfrac{6}{5}(x - 3)$

$5y - 5 = -6x + 18$

$6x + 5y = 23$, choice C.

6. C. For the recursive function given in the problem, you will need to find $f(3)$ and $f(4)$ before you can find $f(5)$. Given $f(1) = 1$ and $f(2) = 2$ and $f(n) = 2f(n-1) + f(n-2)$ for $n \geq 3$, then

$f(3) = 2f(2) + f(1) = 2(2) + 1 = 4 + 1 = 5$

$f(4) = 2f(3) + f(2) = 2(5) + 2 = 10 + 2 = 12$

$f(5) = 2f(4) + f(3) = 2(12) + 5 = 24 + 5 = 29$, choice C.

7. D. The operation $\oplus$ is commutative on the set R of real numbers if $x \oplus y = y \oplus x$ for all real numbers x and y. By the definition of the operation, you have $x \oplus y = 3x + xy$ and $y \oplus x = 3y + yx$, so the question that tests commutativity is "Does $3x + xy = 3y + yx$ for all real numbers x and y?", choice D.

8. D. To determine the cost of the paint, first find the surface area of the sphere; next, find the number of gallons of paint needed; and then find the cost of the paint.

Find the surface area (SA) of the sphere with $r = 12$ ft.

$SA = 4\pi r^2 = 4\pi(12 \text{ ft})^2 = 576\pi \text{ ft}^2$ (Tip: Don't approximate this answer.)

Note: The formula for the surface area of a sphere is given in the Notation, Definitions, and Formulas pages provided.

Find the number of gallons needed.

$576\pi \text{ ft}^2 \div \dfrac{400 \text{ ft}^2}{1 \text{ gal}} = 576\pi \ \cancel{\text{ft}^2} \cdot \dfrac{1 \text{ gal}}{400 \ \cancel{\text{ft}^2}} = 4.5238$ gallons, so 5 gallons will need to be purchased (because the paint is sold in gallon containers only).

Find the cost of 5 gallons of paint.

$5 \ \cancel{\text{gal}} \cdot \dfrac{\$22.40}{1 \ \cancel{\text{gal}}} = \$112.00$, choice D.

9. **A.** Draw the altitude from vertex Y to side $\overline{XZ}$ and label the point of intersection P as shown here.

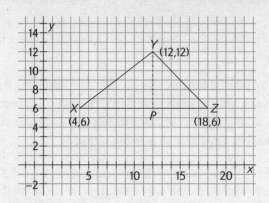

From the figure, you can determine that the length of side $\overline{XZ}$ is 14 units and that the altitude of triangle XYZ, from the vertex Y to side $\overline{XZ}$, is 6 units. The line segment $\overline{YP}$ creates two right triangles: triangles XPY and ZPY. Use the information given and the properties of right triangles to check the answer choices. Start by eliminating answer choices that are obviously rational quantities.

Eliminate B because the area of triangle XYZ is $\frac{1}{2}(\overline{XZ})(\overline{YP}) = \frac{1}{2}(14 \text{ units})(6 \text{ units})$, which is a rational quantity. Eliminate D because the length of $\overline{XZ}$ is 14 units, a rational quantity, so its midpoint is a rational quantity as well. Eliminate C because $\overline{XY}$ is the hypotenuse of a right triangle whose legs are 8 units and 6 units; thus, $\overline{XY}$ is 10 units, a rational quantity. Therefore, A is the correct response. You should move on to the next problem, but just so you know, the perimeter of triangle XYZ is irrational because it has a portion, namely $\overline{YZ}$, that is the hypotenuse of a right triangle whose legs are each 6 units; thus, the length of $\overline{YZ} = \sqrt{6^2 + 6^2} = \sqrt{72}$ units, an irrational quantity.

10. **C.** If all the tagged fish are still active in the lake when the second group of fish is captured, the proportion of tagged fish in the second group should equal to the proportion of tagged fish in the whole population, P, of fish in the lake. Set up a proportion and solve for P.

$$\frac{20}{100} = \frac{500}{P}$$

$$P = \frac{100 \cdot 500}{20} = 2500 \text{ fish, choice C.}$$

11. **C.** Let $x =$ the total number of minutes that the call lasted. Then x is the sum of the first minute and the total number of minutes talked after the first minute, which is $x - 1$. The charge for the first minute, \$3.75, plus the charge for the additional minutes, \$0.55$(x - 1)$, equals the total charge for the call, \$11.45. Write an equation and solve for x.

$$\$3.75 + \$0.55(x - 1) = \$11.45$$

$$\$3.75 + \$0.55x - \$0.55 = \$11.45$$

$$\$0.55x = \$8.25$$

$$x = 15 \text{ minutes, choice C.}$$

12. **B.** Express $\frac{a}{b+c}$ in terms of $\frac{a}{b}$ and $\frac{b}{c}$ by dividing each term in the numerator and denominator by b.

$$\frac{a}{b+c} = \frac{\dfrac{a}{b}}{\dfrac{b}{b} + \dfrac{c}{b}} = \frac{\dfrac{a}{b}}{1 + \dfrac{1}{\dfrac{b}{c}}} = \frac{10}{1 + \dfrac{1}{5}} = \frac{10}{\dfrac{6}{5}} = \frac{50}{6} = \frac{25}{3}, \text{ choice B.}$$

Note: This solution is one way you might work this problem, but not the *only* way it can be worked. For instance, you can substitute values for a, b, and c that satisfy the conditions given, and then work with your substituted numbers as shown here.

Let $a = 100$, $b = 10$, and $c = 2$. Then $\frac{a}{b} = \frac{100}{10} = 10$, $\frac{b}{c} = \frac{10}{2} = 5$, and $\frac{a}{b+c} = \frac{100}{10+2} = \frac{100}{12} = \frac{25}{3}$, choice B.

13. **A.** $(2\cos 10° + i\,2\sin 10°)^3 = 2^3(\cos 10° + i \sin 10°)^3 = 8(\cos 10° + i \sin 10°)^3$

Evaluate the second factor of this product by using DeMoivre's theorem (given in the Notation, Definitions, and Formulas pages provided), to obtain

$$8\big(\cos\,(3 \cdot 10°) + i\,\sin\,(3 \cdot 10°)\big) = 8\big(\cos 30° + i \sin 30°\big) = 8\left(\frac{\sqrt{3}}{2} + i\frac{1}{2}\right) = 4\sqrt{3} + 4i, \text{ choice A.}$$

14. **B.** At 50 miles per hour, it took the family 5 hours (9 a.m. to 2 p.m.) to reach their destination. The distance traveled $= \left(5 \text{ hr}\right) 50 \,\frac{\text{mi}}{\text{hr}} = 250$ miles. At an average speed of 65 miles per hour, the trip would have taken $\frac{250 \text{ mi}}{65 \,\frac{\text{mi}}{\text{hr}}} = 3.8$ hours $= 3$ hours 48 minutes ≈ 3 hours 50 minutes. Therefore, if the family left at 9 a.m. and traveled at an average speed of 65 miles per hours, they would have arrived at 9 a.m. plus 3 hours 50 minutes $= 12:50$ p.m. (approximately), choice B.

15. **C.** Triangle ABC with vertices $(2, 1)$, $(-3, 4)$, and $(5, -3)$ can be represented by the 2×3 (vertex) matrix $\begin{bmatrix} 2 & -3 & 5 \\ 1 & 4 & -3 \end{bmatrix}$, where the x-coordinates are in the first row and their corresponding y-coordinates are in the second row. In a reflection over the x-axis, the x-coordinates of the image will be the same as the x-coordinates of the preimage, and the y-coordinates of the image will be the negatives of the y-coordinates of the preimage. Thus, you are looking for a matrix multiplication that will yield the product matrix $\begin{bmatrix} 2 & -3 & 5 \\ -1 & -4 & 3 \end{bmatrix}$. A quick way to work this problem is to check the answer choices.

Method 1. Multiply the matrices using methods of matrix algebra.

Checking A: $\begin{bmatrix} -1 & 0 \\ 0 & 1 \end{bmatrix}\begin{bmatrix} 2 & -3 & 5 \\ 1 & 4 & -3 \end{bmatrix} = \begin{bmatrix} -2 & & \end{bmatrix}$, eliminate A because the element in the first row first column is not 2. There is no need to complete the multiplication.

Checking B: $\begin{bmatrix} 0 & 1 \\ -1 & 0 \end{bmatrix}\begin{bmatrix} 2 & -3 & 5 \\ 1 & 4 & -3 \end{bmatrix} = \begin{bmatrix} 1 & & \end{bmatrix}$, eliminate B because the element in the first row first column is not 2. There is no need to complete the multiplication.

Checking C: $\begin{bmatrix} 1 & 0 \\ 0 & -1 \end{bmatrix}\begin{bmatrix} 2 & -3 & 5 \\ 1 & 4 & -3 \end{bmatrix} = \begin{bmatrix} 2 & -3 & 5 \\ -1 & -4 & 3 \end{bmatrix}$, thus, C is the correct response. There is no need to check D. Go on to the next question.

Method 2. Multiply the matrices using your graphing calculator. Here are the steps using a TI-83 Plus calculator.

Enter $\begin{bmatrix} 2 & -3 & 5 \\ 1 & 4 & -3 \end{bmatrix}$ as [B]: Go to $\boxed{\text{MATRX}}$ and under EDIT, select 2:[B]. Press $\boxed{\text{ENTER}}$. Define [B] to be 2×3: Enter 2, press $\boxed{\text{ENTER}}$; enter 3, press $\boxed{\text{ENTER}}$. Enter the elements of the matrix $\begin{bmatrix} 2 & -3 & 5 \\ -1 & -4 & 3 \end{bmatrix}$ one by one, being sure to press $\boxed{\text{ENTER}}$ after each entry. Select $\boxed{\text{QUIT}}$ ($\boxed{\text{2nd}}\,\boxed{\text{MODE}}$). Now to check choice

A, enter $\begin{bmatrix} -1 & 0 \\ 0 & 1 \end{bmatrix}$ as [A]. Select QUIT. Next multiply [A] times [B], being sure to put [A] to the left of [B]:

Go to MATRX, select [A]; go to MATRX, select [B]; press ENTER. The display will show the matrix $\begin{bmatrix} -2 & 3 & -5 \\ 1 & 4 & -3 \end{bmatrix}$, so eliminate A. Now edit [A], so that it has elements $\begin{bmatrix} 0 & 1 \\ -1 & 0 \end{bmatrix}$, choice B. Use the Recall

Entry feature of the calculator to do the multiplication. Repeat for C and D. This method will lead to C as the correct response.

Tip: Be sure to use the negative key, not the subtraction key, when you enter negative numbers into the calculator.

16. **C.** An equivalence relation is a reflexive, symmetric, and transitive relation. Note: The definitions for reflexive, symmetric, transitive, and equivalence relation are given in the Notation, Definitions, and Formulas pages provided. The relation in C, "is perpendicular to over the set of all lines in the Cartesian coordinate plane," is not an equivalence relation because this relation is neither reflexive nor transitive. The relations in the other answer choices are equivalence relations.

17. **A.** When a data set contains some extremely high values that are not balanced by corresponding extremely low values, the mean for the data set will be misleadingly high as an indication of a "typical" or "central" value for the data set. The median, which is not influenced by extreme values, is the preferred alternative to the mean when the situation of unbalanced extremely high values occurs in a data set. Since the data set in B is somewhat symmetrical, there would be no particular reason to prefer the median over the mean as a measure of central tendency. For the data sets given in choices C and D, there is not enough information to "clearly" prefer the median over the mean.

18. **C.** The box contains 50 tiles numbered 1 through 50. The primes between 1 and 50 are 2, 3, 5, 7, 11, 13, 17, 19, 23, 29, 31, 37, 41, 43, 47, which is a total of 15 primes. (Remember, the number 1 is neither prime nor composite.)

Therefore, the probability that the number on a randomly drawn tile is prime is

$\frac{15}{50} = \frac{3}{10}$, choice C.

19. **B.** Sketch a diagram, letting d = the distance between the two houses.

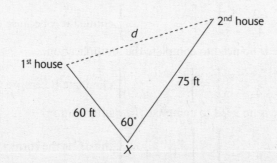

Looking at the sketch, you can see that you are given the measures of 2 sides and the included angle of an oblique triangle. To find the distance between the two houses, substitute the given information into the law of cosines and solve for d. Note: The law of cosines is given in the Notation, Definitions, and Formulas pages provided.

$c^2 = a^2 + b^2 - 2ab \cos C$

$d^2 = (60 \text{ ft})^2 + (75 \text{ ft})^2 - 2(60 \text{ ft})(75 \text{ ft})(\cos 60°)$

$d^2 = 3600 \text{ ft}^2 + 5625 \text{ ft}^2 - 4500 \text{ ft}^2 = 4725 \text{ ft}^2$

$d = 68.7386\ldots$ or approximately 69 feet, choice B.

Tip: Be sure to check that your calculator is in degree mode when the angle given is in degrees.

20. **D.** You are to find the mass, in grams, of the cube. The units for density are grams per cubic centimeter $\frac{g}{cm^3}$, so unit analysis tells you that if you want to have grams as the units of your answer then you will need to cancel cm^3 from the denominator of the density quantity. Cubic centimeters are units of volume. Therefore, find the volume of the cube, and then multiply by the density of lead.

Volume of cube = $(1.5 \text{ cm})^3 = 3.375 \text{ cm}^3$

Multiply the volume of the cube by the density of lead.

$\left(3.375 \ \cancel{cm^3}\right)\left(\frac{11.3 \ g}{\cancel{cm^3}}\right) = 38.1375 \ldots$ or approximately 38.1 grams, choice D.

21. **A.** The number of people over age 65 who get a flu shot is $25\%N = 0.25N$. Of this number, 2% will have an adverse reaction. Thus, the estimated number of people over age 65 who will have an adverse reaction after getting flu shots is $(0.02)(0.25N) = 0.005 N$), choice A.

22. **B.** The domain of $g \circ f$ is the set of elements x in the domain of f for which the image of x, $f(x)$, is in the domain of g. Only the elements -1 and 0 have images that are in the domain of g. The images of -1 and 0 under $g \circ f$ are

$(g \circ f)(-1) = g(f(-1)) = g(3) = 8$ and $(g \circ f)(0) = g(f(0)) = g(1) = 2$.

Thus, $g \circ f = \{(-1, 8), (0, 2)\}$, choice B.

23. **B.** A good way to analyze this problem is to make a chart, showing the growth of the deer population as a function of time, t.

Time in Years	$t = 0$	$t = 8$	$t = 16$	$t = 24$	...
Deer Population	2500	(2500)2	$(2500)2^2$	$(2500)2^3$	...

From the table, you can see that at 8-year intervals, you are multiplying by a power of 2. Therefore, the function that models the population growth must have an exponential factor that has base 2 in it, so you can eliminate A and C. Now you must decide whether the exponent for 2 in the expression should be $0.125t$ (choice B) or $8t$ (choice D). Again, use your table to help you decide.

Checking when $t = 0$: $(2500)2^{0.125t} = (2500)2^0 = (2500)1 = 2500$ and $(2500)2^{8t} = (2500)2^0 = (2500)1 = 2500$, which matches the table.

Checking when $t = 8$: $(2500)2^{0.125t} = (2500)2^{0.125(8)} = (2500)2$, which matches the table; but $(2500)2^{8t} = (2500)2^{8(8)} = (2500)2^{64}$, which does not match the table. Therefore, choice B is the correct response.

24. **C.** Solve the trigonometric equation $\sin^2 x - 5 \sin x + 4 = 0$.

$\sin^2 x - 5 \sin x + 4 = 0$

$(\sin x - 1)(\sin x - 4) = 0$

$\sin x = 1$ or $\sin x = 4$ (no solution)

$x = \sin^{-1}(1) = \frac{\pi}{2}$, which is the only solution in the interval $0 \le x \le 2\pi$, choice C.

25. **C.** You are to find the numerical derivative of a function.

Method 1. A fast and efficient way to calculate this numerical derivative is with your graphing calculator. Here are the steps using a TI-83 Plus calculator. Before you enter functions, you must select Func mode from the $\boxed{\text{MODE}}$ menu. Go to the $\boxed{\text{Y} =}$ editor and enter the function $y = -x \wedge (-2)$. As a precaution, clear any previously entered functions before you enter the function. Check the viewing $\boxed{\text{WINDOW}}$ to make sure that the value 2 falls between Xmin and Xmax. If not, change Xmin and/or Xmax, as needed. Go to the $\boxed{\text{CALC}}$ (calculate) menu. Select 6: dy/dx. Type 2 as the X value and then press $\boxed{\text{ENTER}}$. The derivative value is displayed as $0.25000013 \approx \frac{1}{4}$, choice C.

Method 2. Find the numerical derivative using methods of calculus.

Given $f(x) = -x^{-2}$

then $f'(x) = 2x^{-3}$ and $f'(2) = 2(2)^{-3} = 2 \cdot \dfrac{1}{8} = \dfrac{1}{4}$, choice C.

26. **A.** Examine the table.

Correlation Table for Variables *A*, *B*, *C*, and *D*				
	Variable *A*	Variable *B*	Variable *C*	Variable *D*
Variable *A*	1			
Variable *B*	−0.88	1		
Variable *C*	0.65	0.15	1	
Variable *D*	−0.59	0.50	0.78	1

Correlation values very close to either −1 or +1 indicate very *strong* correlations. The closer $|r|$ is to 1, the stronger is the relationship. Thus, the correlation coefficient between *A* and *B* (choice A) indicates the strongest relationship because $|{-0.88}|$ is greater than the absolute values of the correlation coefficients for the pairs of variables in the other answer choices.

27. **B.** On the set of $n \times n$ matrices containing elements that are real numbers only, matrix multiplication is closed (eliminate Roman I), associative (eliminate Roman III), and the distributive property holds (eliminate Roman IV); but, in general, matrix multiplication is not commutative (Roman II), choice B.

28. **D.** The number on the left of the equal sign is expressed in the base-seven system, while the number on the right is expressed in the base-five system. To find the value of b (and thus $b2_{seven}$), first expand the numbers in their respective bases to convert them to the base-ten system. Next, set the resulting base-ten expressions equal to each other, solve for b, and then put its value in the expression $b2_{seven}$.

$b2_{seven} = b \cdot 7 + 2 = (7b + 2)_{ten} = 7b + 2$

$134_{five} = 1 \cdot 25 + 3 \cdot 5 + 4 = 44_{ten} = 44$

Solve for b.

$7b + 2 = 44$

$7b = 42$

$b = 6$

Therefore, $b2_{seven} = 62_{seven}$, choice D.

29. **B.** Plug the units into the formula and simplify as you would for variable quantities.

$Y = \dfrac{Adv}{t} = \dfrac{(cm^2)\,\dfrac{g}{cm^3}\,\dfrac{cm}{s}}{s} = \dfrac{\dfrac{g}{s}}{s} = \dfrac{g}{s^2}$, choice B.

30. **C.** Examine the diagram of the figure.

1 cm

The perimeter around the figure can be broken into 3 portions: (one-half the circumference of a circle with radius 1 cm) plus (the hypotenuse of a right triangle with legs of 1 cm and 2 cm) plus (1 cm).

Find one-half the circumference of a circle with radius 1 cm.

$\frac{1}{2} \cdot 2\pi r = \frac{1}{2} \cdot 2\pi(1 \text{ cm}) = \pi \text{ cm} \times$ (Don't evaluate yet.)

Find the hypotenuse of a right triangle with legs of 1 cm and 2 cm.

$c^2 = a^2 + b^2$

$c^2 = 1^2 + 2^2 = 5$

$c = \sqrt{5}$ cm (Don't evaluate yet.)

Find the perimeter.

Perimeter = 1 cm + π cm + $\sqrt{5}$ cm = 6.3776 or approximately 6.4 cm, choice C.

31. A. You must select which statement about absolute value is not *always* true—even though it might be true for certain values of x and y. The best way to solve this problem is to substitute some values for x and y into the statements and check whether the statements hold. Only the statement in choice A is not always true. For instance, when x is 8, you have

$-|-x| = -|-(8)| = -|-8| = -8 \neq x = 8$. Choices B, C, and D are properties of absolute value that are always true.

32. C. Substituting 3 into the numerator and denominator yields the indeterminate form $\frac{0}{0}$.

Method 1. Since the $\lim\limits_{x \to 3}(2x - 6) = \lim\limits_{x \to 3}(x^2 - 9) = 0$, you can use L'Hôpital's rule to evaluate the limit by taking the derivatives of the numerator and denominator before evaluating the limit.

Thus, you have $\lim\limits_{x \to 3} \frac{2x - 6}{x^2 - 9} = \lim\limits_{x \to 3} \frac{2}{2x} = \frac{2}{6} = \frac{1}{3}$, choice C.

Method 2. $\lim\limits_{x \to 3} \frac{2x - 6}{x^2 - 9} = \lim\limits_{x \to 3} \frac{2(x - 3)}{(x - 3)(x + 3)} = \lim\limits_{x \to 3} \frac{2}{(x + 3)} = \frac{2}{6} = \frac{1}{3}$, choice C.

33. C. Recall that the first derivative of a position function is the velocity function. To find the distance traveled after 5 seconds, find the numerical integral of the velocity function between 0 and 5 seconds. That is, evaluate the following definite integral: $\int_0^5 1.8t^2 \, dt$.

Method 1. the fastest and most efficient way to calculate this numerical integral is with your graphing calculator. Here are the steps using a TI-83 Plus calculator. Before you enter functions, you must select Func mode from the MODE menu. Go to the Y = editor. Enter the function $y = 1.8x^2$. Notice that you must use y and x for the variables instead of v and t. As a precaution, clear any previously entered functions before you enter the function. Check the viewing WINDOW to make sure that the interval between 0 and 5 falls between Xmin and Xmax. If not, change Xmin and/or Xmax, as needed. Go to the CALC menu. Select 7: $\int f(x) dx$. Type 0 when prompted for the lower limit and then press ENTER. Type 5 when prompted for the upper limit and then press ENTER. The integral value is displayed as 75. Therefore, the distance the car has traveled after 5 seconds is 75 feet, choice C.

Method 2. Integrate the function using methods of calculus.

$\int_0^5 1.8t^2 \, dt = \frac{1.8t^3}{3}\Big|_0^5 = 0.6t^3\Big|_0^5 = 0.6(5)^3 - 0.6(0)^3 = 0.6(125) - 0.6(0) = 75 - 0 = 75$. Therefore, the distance the car has traveled after 5 seconds is 75 feet, choice C.

34. B. Using the rules for matrix subtraction, you can write 4 equations.

$a - 3a = -8$, $4b + 6 = b$, $5 - 2c = 7$, and $d + 2d = 9$

Solving $a - 3a = -8$ yields $a = 4$, so eliminate A and D because these answer choices have $a = -4$. Since both of the remaining answer choices have $b = -2$, go on to the next equation. You have $5 - 2c = 7$, so $c = -1$, eliminate C. Thus, B is the correct response.

35. C. Let W = the set of customers who bought washers and D = the set of customers who bought dryers. Using the notation $n(X)$ to represent the number of elements in a set, you have $n(W) = 94$ and $n(D) = 80$. Because $n(W) + n(D) = 94 + 80 = 174$, which is greater than 152, the total number of customers, you can conclude that some customers bought both a washer and a dryer. Draw a Venn diagram showing two overlapping circles representing W and D. Label the intersection, $W \cap D$.

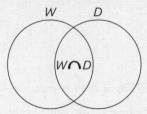

The intersection $W \cap D$ represents the set of customers who bought both a washer and a dryer. From the diagram and the information given in the problem, you have the following equation:

$152 = n(W) + n(D) - n(W \cap D)$

Thus, $152 = 94 + 80 - n(W \cap D)$

Solving for $n(W \cap D)$ yields

$n(W \cap D) = 94 + 80 - 152 = 22$

Therefore, the number of customers who bought only a washer equals

$n(W) - n(W \cap D) = 94 - 22 = 72$, choice C.

Note: The notation $n(X)$ is read "the cardinality of set X." The *cardinality* of a set is the number of elements in the set.

36. B. The y-value at the point where $x = 1$ is $f(1) = 2(1)^3 - (1) + 3 = 4$. The slope, m, of the tangent line at the point $(1, f(1))$ is given by $f'(1)$.

Given $y = f(x) = 2x^3 - x + 3$, then $f'(x) = 6x^2 - 1$. Thus, $m = f'(1) = 6(1)^2 - 1 = 5$ when $x = 1$.

Tip: You can use your graphing calculator to evaluate this numerical derivative.

Use the point-slope form to find the equation of the tangent line at the point $(1, 4)$.

$y - 4 = 5(x - 1)$

$y - 4 = 5x - 5$

$1 = 5x - y$, which is the same as B.

37. B. Make a quick sketch of the graph.

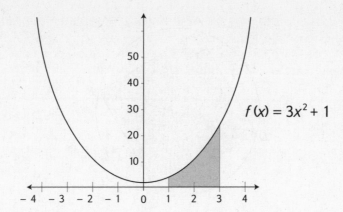

The area of the region bounded by the graph of $f(x) = 3x^2 + 1$, the x-axis, and the vertical lines $x = 1$ and $x = 3$ is given by: Area $= \int_1^3 (3x^2 + 1)dx$.

Method 1. The fastest and most efficient way to calculate this numerical integral is with your graphing calculator. Here are the steps using a TI-83 Plus calculator. Before you enter functions, you must select Func mode from the $\boxed{\text{MODE}}$ menu. Got to the $\boxed{\text{Y} =}$ editor and enter the function $y = 3x^2 + 1$. As a precaution, clear any previously entered functions before you enter the function. Check the viewing $\boxed{\text{WINDOW}}$ to make sure that the interval between 1 and 3 falls between Xmin and Xmax. If not, change Xmin and/or Xmax, as needed. Go to the $\boxed{\text{CALC}}$ (calculate) menu. Select 7: $\int f(x)dx$. Type 1 when prompted for the lower limit and then press $\boxed{\text{ENTER}}$. Type 3 when prompted for the upper limit and then press $\boxed{\text{ENTER}}$. The graph is shaded and the integral value is displayed as 28, choice B.

Method 2. Integrate the function using methods of calculus.

$\int_1^3 (3x^2 + 1)dx = (x^3 + x)\big|_1^3 = (3^3 + 3) - (1^3 + 1) = 30 - 2 = 28$, choice A.

38. **C.** According to the 68–95–99.7 rule, approximately 68% of the values of a random variable that is normally distributed fall within 1 standard deviation of the mean, about 95% fall within 2 standard deviations of the mean, and about 99.7% fall within 3 standard deviations of the mean. You want to find the approximate probability that a randomly chosen plant from a distribution with μ of 24 inches and standard deviation, σ, of 3.5 inches will be between 20.5 inches and 27.5 inches tall.

Method 1. Using the statistical features of your graphing calculator is an efficient and time-saving way to work problems involving the normal distribution. Consult your owner's manual for detailed instructions on how to find percentages and probabilities using areas under a normal curve. Here are the steps using a TI-83 Plus calculator. Go to the $\boxed{\text{DISTR}}$ (distributions) menu. Select 2:normalcdf(. The home screen will show normalcdf(with a flashing cursor after the parenthesis. Type 20.5, 27.5, 24, 3.5. Close the parentheses and press $\boxed{\text{ENTER}}$. The display will show .6826 or approximately 68%, choice C.

Method 2. To find the approximate probability that a randomly chosen plant will be between 20.5 inches and 27.5 inches tall, first determine the z-scores for 20.5 inches and 27.5 inches, and then find the percentage of the normal distribution that is between those two z-scores.

Find the z-scores for 20.5 inches and 27.5 inches.

$z\text{-score} = \dfrac{\text{data value} - \text{mean}}{\text{standard deviation}} = \dfrac{20.5 - 24}{3.5} = -1$. Therefore, 20.5 is 1 standard deviation below the mean.

$z\text{-score} = \dfrac{\text{data value} - \text{mean}}{\text{standard deviation}} = \dfrac{27.5 - 24}{3.5} = 1$. Therefore, 27.5 is 1 standard deviation above the mean.

Now find the percentage of the normal distribution that is between the z-scores –1 and 1.

According to the 68-95-99.7 rule, about 68%, choice C, of the distribution is within 1 standard deviation of the mean.

39. **D.** Let x = length of a side of the square.

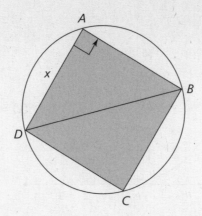

The area of square $ABCD$ is x^2. Right angle DAB is an inscribed angle. The measure of an inscribed angle is half the degree measure of its intercepted arc. Thus, the degree measure of $\overset{\frown}{DB}$ is 180°. Therefore, chord $\overline{DB}$ is a diameter of the circle that has circumference 8π cm. Also, chord $\overline{DB}$ is the diagonal of the square $ABCD$ and the hypotenuse of right triangle DAB. To find the area of square $ABCD$, first use the formula for the circumference of a circle to find the length of $\overline{DB}$. Next, use the Pythagorean Theorem to find x. Finally, use the value found for x to find the area of the square.

Let d = the length of $\overline{DB}$, then

$$C = \pi d = 8\pi \text{ cm}$$

$$d = 8 \text{ cm}$$

Applying the Pythagorean Theorem in right triangle DAB, you have

$$x^2 + x^2 = (8 \text{ cm})^2$$

$$2x^2 = 64 \text{ cm}^2$$

$$x^2 = 32 \text{ cm}^2$$

$$x = \sqrt{32} \text{ cm}$$

area of square $ABCD = \left(\sqrt{32} \text{ cm}\right)\left(\sqrt{32} \text{ cm}\right) = 32 \text{ cm}^2$, choice D.

Note: Notice that you determine x^2, the area of the square, just before you obtain x. You should skip the final step in this problem by stopping when you find x^2.

Tip: In an isosceles right-triangle, the square of the length of the hypotenuse is always twice the square of the length of a leg of the triangle.

40. **A.** A good way to compare the student's performance on the four exams relative to the performance of the student's classmates is to compute the student's z-score for each of the 4 exams.

Exam 1: z-score $= \dfrac{\text{data value} - \text{mean}}{\text{standard deviation}} = \dfrac{65 - 55}{5} = 2$. Therefore, the student scored 2 standard deviations above the mean on Exam 1.

Exam 2: z-score $= \dfrac{\text{data value} - \text{mean}}{\text{standard deviation}} = \dfrac{87 - 88}{2} = -0.5$. Therefore, the student scored 0.5 standard deviation below the mean on Exam 2.

Exam 3: $z\text{-score} = \dfrac{\text{data value} - \text{mean}}{\text{standard deviation}} = \dfrac{92-86}{4} = 1.5$. Therefore, the student scored 1.5 standard deviations above the mean on Exam 3.

Exam 4: $z\text{-score} = \dfrac{\text{data value} - \text{mean}}{\text{standard deviation}} = \dfrac{70-60}{10} = 1$. Therefore, the student scored 1 standard deviation above the mean on Exam 4.

Since the student's z-score for Exam 1 is greater than any of the z-scores for the other exams, the student's best performance was on Exam 1 (choice A) relative to that of the student's classmates.

41. D. Solve the inequality.

$$\frac{2-x}{5} < 1$$

$$2 - x < 5$$

$$-x < 3$$

$$x > -3$$

The graph for this inequality is a ray extending to the right from the point -3 with an open dot at the point -3, choice D.

Tip: Remember to reverse the inequality when you multiply both sides by a negative quantity.

42. A. You are given 2 points $(0, 1000)$ and $(10, 5000)$ that satisfy the function $Q(t) = Q_0 e^{xt}$. To find the value of x, first substitute the values for the two points into $Q(t) = Q_0 e^{xt}$, and then solve the resulting system of equations for x.

$$1000 = Q_0 e^{x(0)} = Q_0 e^0 = Q_0 \cdot 1 = Q_0$$

$$5000 = Q_0 e^{x(10)} = Q_0 e^{10x} = 1000 e^{10x} \qquad \text{(Using the results from the first equation)}$$

Solve for x:

$$5000 = 1000 e^{10x}$$

$$5 = e^{10x}$$

$$\ln 5 = \ln(e^{10x})$$

$$\ln 5 = 10x \ln e$$

$$\ln 5 = 10x$$

$$x = \frac{\ln 5}{10}, \text{ choice A.}$$

43. D. You are given that $P(x)$ has zeros 0, $2 - i$, 4, and -3. Since $P(x)$ has real coefficients, the complex conjugate, $2 + i$, of $2 - i$ is also a zero. Hence, $P(x)$ has five zeros (eliminate A and B). By the factor theorem, if r is a zero of a polynomial, $P(x)$, then $x - r$ is a factor of $P(x)$; so $P(x) = (x - 0)[x - (2 - i)][x - (2 + i)](x - 4)[x - (-3)] = x(x - 2 + i)(x - 2 - i)(x - 4)(x + 3)$, choice D.

44. B. You are to identify functions that have the same domain and the same range. The function given in Roman I is a finite function. None of the other functions are finite, so eliminate any answer choice containing Roman I. Eliminate A and D. For the functions in the other Roman numerals, compare the domains of the functions, and then compare the ranges. The domain of each of the functions given in Roman II and IV is the set of real numbers; however, the domain in Roman III is the set of whole numbers, so eliminate choice C. Thus, choice B is the correct response. You do not have to check the ranges; but, just so you know, the range of each of the functions in Roman II and IV is the nonnegative real numbers.

45. D. The question asks which theorems most likely would be used to prove $\triangle ABC$ is similar to $\triangle CDE$. Examine the figure.

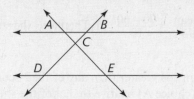

Looking at the three theorems given in the Roman numeral options, none would be eliminated from the proof. A simple way to show two triangles are similar is to show that two angles of one triangle are congruent to two corresponding angles of the other triangle (Roman III). You could proceed by showing that $\angle ACB$ is congruent to $\angle ECD$ because these angles are vertical angles of intersecting lines (Roman I), and then showing $\angle ABC$ is congruent to $\angle EDC$ because these angles form a pair of alternate-interior angles of two parallel lines cut by a transversal (Roman II). Therefore, choice D is the correct response.

46. C. From the 2×2 matrices in the answer choices, you want the one that premultiplies the vertex matrix $\begin{bmatrix} x_i \\ y_i \end{bmatrix}$ to yield $\begin{bmatrix} 5x_i \\ 5y_i \end{bmatrix}$, where $i = 1, 2, 3$. Check the answer choices.

Checking A: $\begin{bmatrix} 5 & 5 \\ 5 & 5 \end{bmatrix} \begin{bmatrix} x_i \\ y_i \end{bmatrix} = \begin{bmatrix} 5x_i + 5y_i \end{bmatrix}$, eliminate A.

Checking B: $\begin{bmatrix} 5 & 0 \\ 5 & 0 \end{bmatrix} \begin{bmatrix} x_i \\ y_i \end{bmatrix} = \begin{bmatrix} 5x_i \\ 5x_i \end{bmatrix}$, eliminate B.

Checking C: $\begin{bmatrix} 5 & 0 \\ 0 & 5 \end{bmatrix} \begin{bmatrix} x_i \\ y_i \end{bmatrix} = \begin{bmatrix} 5x_i \\ 5y_i \end{bmatrix}$; thus, C is the correct response. Go on to the next question.

47. C. The volume of a right prism is given by $V = Bh$. (Note: This formula is given in the Notation, Definitions, and Formulas pages provided.) To find the volume of the right hexagonal prism, first find the area, B, of one of the regular hexagonal bases, and then find the volume by multiplying B by the height of the prism, h.

Find the area of one of the regular hexagonal bases.

Sketch a diagram.

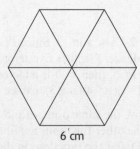

6 cm

A regular hexagon with side 6 cm can be divided into 6 equilateral triangles with each side equal to 6 cm.

The area of an equilateral triangle with side $s = 6$ cm is given by: Area $= \frac{\sqrt{3}}{4} s^2 = \frac{\sqrt{3}}{4}(6 \text{ cm})^2 = 9\sqrt{3} \text{ cm}^2$.

Tip: If you forget the formula for the area of an equilateral triangle, you can derive it by using the Pythagorean theorem or trigonometric functions to determine the height (altitude) of the triangle, and then using the formula area $= \frac{1}{2}bh$.

Thus, the area of the regular hexagonal base of the prism is given by: $B = 6(9\sqrt{3} \text{ cm}^2) = 54\sqrt{3} \text{ cm}^2$.

Volume $= (54\sqrt{3} \text{ cm}^2)(30 \text{ cm}) = 2805.9223$ or approximately 2806 cm³, choice C.

48. **B.** A tree is a connected vertex-edge graph that contains no simple circuits. Only the vertex-edge graph in choice B is a tree. The vertex-edge graphs in the other answer choices contain simple circuits, so these graphs are not trees.

49. **B.** Make a quick sketch of the two graphs.

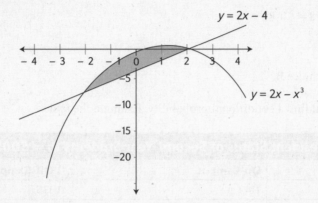

Use your graphing calculator to determine that the two graphs intersect at 2 points and the graph of $y = 2x - x^2$ lies above $y = 2x - 4$ between the points of intersection. To find the area of the region bounded by the two graphs, first find the x-values for the points of intersection of the two graphs; next, find the difference between the two functions, being sure to subtract the equation of the lower graph from the equation of the upper graph; and then evaluate the definite integral of the difference of the two graphs, between the 2 x-values of their points of intersection.

Find the x-values for the points of intersection of the two graphs.

Using substitution,

$2x - x^2 = 2x - 4$

$-x^2 = -4$

$x^2 = 4$

$x = \pm 2$

Find the difference between the 2 graphs.

Difference $= (2x - x^2) - (2x - 4) = 2x - x^2 - 2x + 4 = -x^2 + 4$

Evaluate the definite integral $\int_{-2}^{2} (-x^2 + 4)\,dx$.

Method 1. The fastest and most efficient way to calculate this numerical integral is with your graphing calculator. Here are the steps using a TI-83 Plus calculator. Before you enter functions, you must select Func mode from the $\boxed{\text{MODE}}$ menu. Go to the $\boxed{Y =}$ editor. Enter the function $y = -x^2 + 4$. As a precaution, clear any previously entered functions before you enter the function. Check the viewing $\boxed{\text{WINDOW}}$ to make sure that the interval between –2 and 2 falls between Xmin and Xmax. If not, change Xmin and/or Xmax, as needed. Go to the $\boxed{\text{CALC}}$ (calculate) menu. Select 7: $\int f(x)\,dx$. Type –2 when prompted for the lower limit and then press $\boxed{\text{ENTER}}$. Type 2 when prompted for the upper limit and then press $\boxed{\text{ENTER}}$. The integral value is displayed as 10.666667 and the graph is shaded. (Note: The graph and the shaded region will not look like what you've sketched above because you entered the difference of the two functions into the function editor.) Since the answer choices are given as fractions, select 1▸Frac from the $\boxed{\text{MATH}}$ menu. The display shows Ans▸Frac. Press $\boxed{\text{ENTER}}$. The display shows 32/3, choice B.

Method 2. Integrate the function using methods of calculus.

$$\int_{-2}^{2}\left(-x^2+4\right)dx=\left(-\frac{x^3}{3}+4x\right)\Bigg|_{-2}^{2}$$

$$=\left(-\frac{2^3}{3}+4\cdot 2\right)-\left(-\frac{(-2)^3}{3}+4\cdot(-2)\right)$$

$$=\left(-\frac{8}{3}+8\right)-\left(\frac{8}{3}-8\right)$$

$$=-\frac{8}{3}+8-\frac{8}{3}+8$$

$$=16-\frac{16}{3}$$

$$=\frac{32}{3}, \text{ choice B}$$

50. **D.** In this problem, you find a conditional probability. Examine the table.

Resident Status of Second-Year Students ($n = 500$)		
	On-Campus	**Off-Campus**
Male	114	135
Female	156	95

You want to find a probability when you already know that the student is female. Thus, when computing the probability, the number of possible students under consideration is no longer 500, but is reduced to the total number of female students. In other words, once you know that the selected person is a female student, you are dealing only with the students in the second row of the table. To find the probability, first find the total number of female students. Next, among those, determine the number who reside off-campus, and then compute the conditional probability.

Total female students = 156 + 95 = 251.

Among the 251 female students, 95 reside off-campus. Thus,

P(resides off-campus given student is female) = $\frac{95}{251}$, choice D.

Answer Sheet for Practice Test 3

(Remove This Sheet and Use It to Mark Your Answers)

CUT HERE

1 (A) (B) (C) (D)	26 (A) (B) (C) (D)
2 (A) (B) (C) (D)	27 (A) (B) (C) (D)
3 (A) (B) (C) (D)	28 (A) (B) (C) (D)
4 (A) (B) (C) (D)	29 (A) (B) (C) (D)
5 (A) (B) (C) (D)	30 (A) (B) (C) (D)
6 (A) (B) (C) (D)	31 (A) (B) (C) (D)
7 (A) (B) (C) (D)	32 (A) (B) (C) (D)
8 (A) (B) (C) (D)	33 (A) (B) (C) (D)
9 (A) (B) (C) (D)	34 (A) (B) (C) (D)
10 (A) (B) (C) (D)	35 (A) (B) (C) (D)
11 (A) (B) (C) (D)	36 (A) (B) (C) (D)
12 (A) (B) (C) (D)	37 (A) (B) (C) (D)
13 (A) (B) (C) (D)	38 (A) (B) (C) (D)
14 (A) (B) (C) (D)	39 (A) (B) (C) (D)
15 (A) (B) (C) (D)	40 (A) (B) (C) (D)
16 (A) (B) (C) (D)	41 (A) (B) (C) (D)
17 (A) (B) (C) (D)	42 (A) (B) (C) (D)
18 (A) (B) (C) (D)	43 (A) (B) (C) (D)
19 (A) (B) (C) (D)	44 (A) (B) (C) (D)
20 (A) (B) (C) (D)	45 (A) (B) (C) (D)
21 (A) (B) (C) (D)	46 (A) (B) (C) (D)
22 (A) (B) (C) (D)	47 (A) (B) (C) (D)
23 (A) (B) (C) (D)	48 (A) (B) (C) (D)
24 (A) (B) (C) (D)	49 (A) (B) (C) (D)
25 (A) (B) (C) (D)	50 (A) (B) (C) (D)

Time — 120 minutes

50 Questions

Directions: Each of the questions or incomplete statements is followed by four suggested answers or completions. Select the one that is best in each case, and then fill in the corresponding lettered space on the answer sheet.

1. To estimate the population of fish in a lake, a parks and recreation team captures and tags 300 fish, and then releases the tagged fish back into the lake. One month later, the team returns and captures 75 fish from the lake, 15 of which bear tags that identify them as being among the previously captured fish. If all the tagged fish are still active in the lake when the second group of fish is captured, what is the best estimate of the fish population in the lake based on the information gained through this capture-recapture strategy?

   A. 60 fish
   B. 1500 fish
   C. 1800 fish
   D. 2000 fish

$\otimes$	a	b
a	a	b
b	b	b

2. The table shown defines an operation $\otimes$ on the set $S = \{a, b\}$. All the following statements about S with respect to $\otimes$ are true EXCEPT

   A. S is closed.
   B. S is commutative.
   C. S contains an identity element.
   D. S contains inverses for all elements in S.

3. Sophia bought a precious stone pendant in 2004 for $500. By 2007 it had lost 10% of its value. In 2009 it was worth 10% more than in 2007. By 2012 it had lost 20% of its value from 3 years previously. What was the pendant worth in 2012?

   A. $390
   B. $396
   C. $400
   D. $404

4. If two identical machines can do a job in 10 days, how many days will take five such machines to do the same job?

   A. 4 days
   B. 5 days
   C. 8 days
   D. 25 days

5. If $y = e^{x+1}$, then $x =$

   A. $\ln(y - 1)$
   B. $\ln(y) - 1$
   C. $\dfrac{y - 1}{e}$
   D. $\dfrac{y}{e} - 1$

6. Two vehicles leave the same location at 10:45 a.m., one traveling due north at 70 miles per hour and the other due south at 60 miles per hour. If the vehicles maintain their respective speeds, at what time will they be 325 miles apart?

   A. 12:15 p.m.
   B. 1:15 p.m.
   C. 2:15 p.m.
   D. 3 p.m.

7. First prize for a television show's promotional drawing is a $24 \times 16 \times 8$ inch rectangular box filled to capacity with U. S. $20 bills. On average, U. S. $20 bills measure 6.14 inches long and 2.61 inches wide, and a stack of one hundred $20 bills is about 0.43 inch thick. What is the approximate total value of money in the first-prize box of $20 bills?

   A. $45,000
   B. $890,000
   C. $1,160,000
   D. $8,920,000

8. If the surface area of a sphere is 144π cm^2, find the sphere's volume.

   A. 36 cm^3
   B. 288 cm^3
   C. 216π cm^3
   D. 288π cm^3

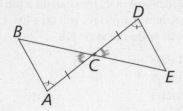

9. In the figure $\angle A \cong \angle D$ and $\overline{BE}$ bisects $\overline{AD}$. Which of the following methods should be used to show triangle ABC is congruent to triangle DEC?

   A. SSS
   B. SAS
   C. AAA
   D. ASA

10. Riqui scored at the 75th percentile on a multiple-choice history exam. The best interpretation of this information is that

   A. Riqui answered 75% of the questions on the test correctly.
   B. Only 25% of the other students did worse on the test than Riqui did.
   C. Riqui answered 75 questions correctly.
   D. Riqui did as well or better than 75% of the students who took the exam.

11. If $\sin\theta = -\dfrac{5}{13}$ and $\pi < \theta < \dfrac{3\pi}{2}$, then $\tan\theta$ is

   A. $-\dfrac{12}{5}$
   B. $-\dfrac{5}{12}$
   C. $\dfrac{12}{5}$
   D. $\dfrac{5}{12}$

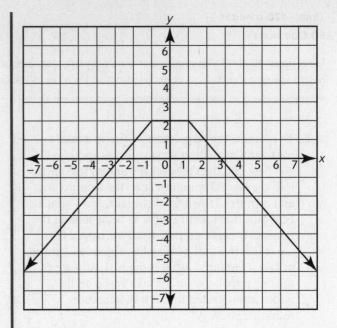

12. Which of the following sets is the range of the function shown?

   A. $\{y \mid y \text{ is a real number}\}$
   B. $\{y \mid y \text{ is a real number}, -3 \le y \le 3\}$
   C. $\{y \mid y \text{ is a real number}, -7 \le y \le 7\}$
   D. $\{y \mid y \text{ is a real number}, y \le 2\}$

13. If $y - 2.8 = 4\sin x$, what is the minimum value of y?

   A. -6.8
   B. -1.2
   C. 1.2
   D. 6.8

14. Which of the following expressions is an identity for $\dfrac{\tan\theta + \cot\theta}{\sec\theta\csc\theta}$?

   A. $\sin^2\theta + \cos^2\theta$
   B. $2\cos^2\theta$
   C. $2\sin\theta\cos\theta$
   D. $1 - 2\sin^2\theta$

15. Triangle ABC has vertices $(3, -1)$, $(-5, 7)$, and $(2, -4)$. Which of the following matrix multiplications would result in a reflection of $\triangle ABC$ over the y-axis?

    A. $\begin{bmatrix} -1 & 0 \\ 0 & 1 \end{bmatrix} \begin{bmatrix} 3 & -5 & 2 \\ -1 & 7 & -4 \end{bmatrix}$

    B. $\begin{bmatrix} 0 & 1 \\ -1 & 0 \end{bmatrix} \begin{bmatrix} 3 & -5 & 2 \\ -1 & 7 & -4 \end{bmatrix}$

    C. $\begin{bmatrix} 0 & 1 \\ 1 & 0 \end{bmatrix} \begin{bmatrix} 3 & -5 & 2 \\ -1 & 7 & -4 \end{bmatrix}$

    D. $\begin{bmatrix} 1 & 0 \\ 0 & -1 \end{bmatrix} \begin{bmatrix} 3 & -5 & 2 \\ -1 & 7 & -4 \end{bmatrix}$

16. On the set of $n \times n$ matrices, the relation "is conformable for multiplication" satisfies which of the following properties?

    I. reflexive

    II. symmetric

    III. transitive

    A. I only

    B. III only

    C. I and III only

    D. I, II, and III

Mean Score	65
Median Score	73
Modal Score	77
Range	52
Standard Deviation	15
Number of Students	50

17. The data in the table summarize the scores of 50 students on a chemistry exam. Which of the following statements best describes the distribution of the scores?

    A. The distribution is positively skewed.

    B. The distribution is negatively skewed.

    C. The distribution is symmetric.

    D. The distribution is bimodal.

18. A real estate agent selling houses located in an upscale housing development has determined the following probabilities for two neighboring houses, one of which is a model home: the probability that the model home will be sold is 0.50, the probability that the house next door will be sold is 0.40, and the probability that at least one of the two houses will be sold is 0.80. Find the probability that the house next door will be sold given that the model home has already been sold.

    A. 10%

    B. 20%

    C. 30%

    D. 40%

19. $i^{218} =$

    A. -1

    B. $-i$

    C. 1

    D. i

20. Using a graduated cylinder, a chemist measures a chemical solution's volume and uses the appropriate number of significant figures to record the volume as 40.6 milliliters (mL). Which of the following ways most accurately expresses the range of possible values of the solution's volume?

    A. 40.6 mL $\pm$ 0.005 mL

    B. 40.6 mL $\pm$ 0.05 mL

    C. 40.6 mL $\pm$ 0.5 mL

    D. 40.6 mL $\pm$ 0.1 mL

21. Which of the following expressions is equivalent to the expression $\log_{10}\left(\dfrac{x^3}{20}\right)$?

    A. $(\log_{10} x)^3 - 2$

    B. $3\log_{10} x - 2$

    C. $(\log_{10} x)^3 - \log_{10} 20$

    D. $3\log_{10} x - \log_{10} 2 - 1$

22. Which of the following matrices are nonsingular?

I. $\begin{bmatrix} -3 & 5 \\ -6 & 10 \end{bmatrix}$

II. $\begin{bmatrix} 4 & 0 \\ 0 & 4 \end{bmatrix}$

III. $\begin{bmatrix} 2 & -5 & 3 \\ 6 & 1 & -4 \\ 0 & 0 & 0 \end{bmatrix}$

IV. $\begin{bmatrix} 1 & 0 & 0 \\ 0 & 1 & 0 \\ 0 & 0 & 1 \end{bmatrix}$

A. I and II only
B. I and III only
C. II and IV only
D. III and IV only

23. A water tank can be filled in 6 hours when the input valve is open and the outlet valve is closed. When the input valve is closed and the outlet valve is open, the same tank can be emptied in 10 hours. If a tank is filled with both valves open, how long will it take to fill the tank?

A. 4 hours
B. $7\frac{1}{2}$ hours
C. 15 hours
D. 16 hours

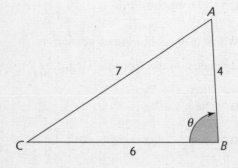

24. In triangle ABC shown, $\cos \theta =$

A. $\frac{1}{16}$

B. $\frac{29}{56}$

C. $\frac{2}{3}$

D. $\frac{6}{7}$

25. If $f(x) = -16x^{-4}$, then $f'(2)$ is

A. -2

B. $-\frac{1}{2}$

C. $\frac{1}{2}$

D. 2

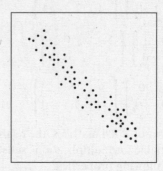

26. The graph shown is a scatterplot for a set of bivariate data, paired values of data from two variables. What does the shape of the scatterplot indicate about the relationship between the two variables?

A. There is little relationship between the two variables.
B. There is a linear, negative relationship between the two variables.
C. There is a linear, positive relationship between the two variables.
D. There is a strong exponential relationship between the two variables.

27. Given $A = \begin{bmatrix} 0 & 2 \\ 1 & 3 \end{bmatrix}$ and $B = \begin{bmatrix} -2 & 3 \\ 2 & 0 \end{bmatrix}$, then $(BA)^{-1}$ is

A. $\begin{bmatrix} 4 & 0 \\ 4 & 3 \end{bmatrix}$

B. $\begin{bmatrix} \frac{1}{3} & -\frac{5}{12} \\ 0 & \frac{1}{4} \end{bmatrix}$

C. $\begin{bmatrix} 3 & 5 \\ 0 & 4 \end{bmatrix}$

D. $\begin{bmatrix} \frac{1}{4} & 0 \\ -\frac{1}{3} & \frac{1}{3} \end{bmatrix}$

28. If $f(x) = x^2 - 4$ and $g(x) = 3x + 2$, then $(f \circ g)(x) = f(g(x)) =$

 A. $(x^2 - 4)(3x + 2)$
 B. $9x^2$
 C. $3x(3x + 4)$
 D. $3x^2 - 10$

29. On a number line, if line segment x has endpoints $6\frac{1}{4}$ and $6\frac{1}{2}$, and line segment y has endpoints $\frac{5}{\sqrt{8}}$ and $\frac{3}{\sqrt{2}}$, what is the ratio of the length of y to the length of x?

 A. $\dfrac{1}{\sqrt{2}}$

 B. $\sqrt{2}$

 C. $\dfrac{4}{\sqrt{2}}$

 D. $4\sqrt{2}$

30. Suppose that the parents of a newborn child establish a trust fund account for the child with an investment of $10,000. Assuming no withdrawals and no additional deposits are made, approximately what interest rate compounded annually is needed to double the investment in 20 years?

 A. 3.5%
 B. 5.5%
 C. 10.0%
 D. 103.5%

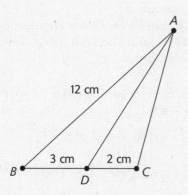

3 cm   2 cm
12 cm

31. In triangle ABC, $\angle DAB \cong \angle DAC$. What is the length of $\overline{AC}$?

 A. It cannot be determined from the information given.
 B. 6 cm
 C. 7 cm
 D. 8 cm

32. A manufacturing company purchases a robotic machine that can produce $Q(h)$ components per hour, where $Q(h) = \dfrac{10(4h + 25)}{2h + 5}$. Assuming the machine continues to work efficiently, approximately how many components is the machine able to produce per hour after being in operation for an extended period of time?

 A. 5 components
 B. 20 components
 C. 40 components
 D. 50 components

33. Water is running into a right cylindrical tank, which has a radius of 5 feet, at a constant rate of 30 cubic feet per minute $\left(\dfrac{\text{ft}^3}{\text{min}}\right)$. What is the instantaneous rate of change of the water's height after the water starts running?

 A. $0.38\dfrac{\text{ft}}{\text{min}}$

 B. $0.95\dfrac{\text{ft}}{\text{min}}$

 C. $1.05\dfrac{\text{ft}}{\text{min}}$

 D. $2.6\dfrac{\text{ft}}{\text{min}}$

$$2x + 5y - z = 5$$
$$-4x + 3y + 5z = 13$$
$$8x + 10y = -4$$

34. Solve the system of equations above for z.

 A. -3
 B. -1
 C. 0
 D. 2

35. In a certain small town all the telephone numbers have the same area code, and all the 7-digit telephone numbers listed in the town's telephone book begin with either 560, 564, or 569 (called prefixes). How many different telephone numbers are possible for that town?

 A. $3 \cdot (_{10}C_4)$
 B. $3 \cdot 10^4$
 C. 10^7
 D. 10^{12}

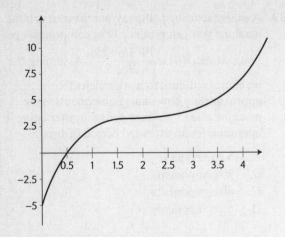

36. The graph shown is the graph of $y = x^3 - 6x^2 + 12x - 5$. Which of the following statements is true about the rate of change of y with respect to x?

- **A.** The rate of change is constant between 0 and 0.5.
- **B.** The rate of change is increasing between 0.5 and 1.5.
- **C.** The rate of change is decreasing between 2 and 3.
- **D.** The rate of change is increasing between 3 and 3.5.

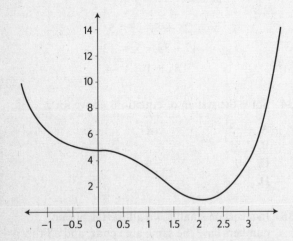

37. The graph shown is the graph of $f(x) = x^4 - 3x^3 + x^2 + 5$. What is the area of the region bounded by the graph of f and the x-axis over the closed interval $[0, 2]$?

- **A.** 1 square unit
- **B.** 5 square units
- **C.** $\frac{32}{5}$ square units
- **D.** $\frac{106}{15}$ square units

38. The gas mileage in miles per gallon (mpg) for automobiles of a certain luxury model is normally distributed with a mean of 29 mpg and a standard deviation of 4 mpg. What is the approximate probability that an automobile of this type chosen at random has gas mileage less than 25 mpg?

- **A.** 16%
- **B.** 34%
- **C.** 68%
- **D.** 84%

39. For the point $(-2, -8)$ on the graph of f defined by $f(x) = x^3$, give the coordinates of the corresponding point on the graph of g defined by $g(x) = f(2x)$.

- **A.** $(-1, -8)$
- **B.** $(-4, -8)$
- **C.** $(-2, -16)$
- **D.** $(-2, -4096)$

40. For which of the following studies would the results most likely establish a cause-effect relationship?

- **A.** An experimental study investigating the effect of a new type of fertilizer on plant growth.
- **B.** A survey of teachers' opinions about standardized testing of students.
- **C.** An observational study investigating factors related to delinquent behavior in teenagers.
- **D.** A correlational study investigating the relationship between college GPA and birth order.

41. Which of the following sets is the solution to $2x^2 - x < 1$?

- **A.** $\left\{x \in \text{reals}, x < -1 \text{ or } x > \frac{1}{2}\right\}$
- **B.** $\left\{x \in \text{reals}, x < -\frac{1}{2} \text{ or } x > 1\right\}$
- **C.** $\left\{x \in \text{reals}, -\frac{1}{2} < x < 1\right\}$
- **D.** $\left\{x \in \text{reals}, -1 < x < \frac{1}{2}\right\}$

Time (in years)	Population
0	500
5	1500

42. The table above gives the population of a deer herd at two different times in years. The population's growth is modeled by the function $P(t) = P_0 e^{xt}$. Based on this information, what is the value of x?

 A. $\dfrac{\ln 3}{5}$

 B. $\ln 3$

 C. $\ln 3 - \ln 5$

 D. $\ln\left(\dfrac{3}{5}\right)$

43. A ball is dropped from a height of 120 feet. If each rebound is $\dfrac{3}{4}$ the height of the previous bounce, which of the following functions would best model the ball's height as a function of rebound number n?

 A. quadratic
 B. polynomial
 C. linear
 D. exponential

44. The function $y = \dfrac{2x^3 + 3x - x + 1}{x^2 - 8x + 16}$ has how many asymptotes?

 A. 0
 B. 1
 C. 2
 D. 3

45. An interior decorator wants to replace a rectangular table that measures 3 feet by 4.5 feet with a circular table that has a diameter of 4 feet. Approximately how much less area does the circular table require as compared to the area of the rectangular table?

 A. 0.93 ft^2
 B. 12.57 ft^2
 C. 26.07 ft^2
 D. 36.77 ft^2

46. A sequence is defined recursively by

 $a_1 = 1$,

 $a_n = a_{n-1} + 2n + 3$ for $n \geq 2$.

 The closed-form representation of the sequence is best modeled as

 A. arithmetic
 B. geometric
 C. quadratic
 D. exponential

47. What is the approximate volume of a right triangular prism that is 25 inches in height and whose bases are equilateral triangles that are 4 inches on a side?

 A. 7 in^3
 B. 100 in^3
 C. 173 in^3
 D. 200 in^3

48. An experiment consists of flipping a coin and noting the up face 6 times. How many different outcomes are in the sample space for this experiment?

 A. $_6P_2$
 B. 2^6
 C. 6^2
 D. 6^6

49. Find the area enclosed by the curves $y = \dfrac{1}{4}x^2$ and $y = x^2 + 3x - 9$.

 A. 64 square units
 B. 118 square units
 C. 172 square units
 D. It cannot be determined from the information given.

50. A bag contains 10 blue marbles, 7 red marbles, 5 green marbles, and 3 yellow marbles. If two marbles are randomly drawn from the bag, one after the other, without replacement after the first draw, what is the probability that both marbles will be yellow?

 A. $\dfrac{3}{25} \cdot \dfrac{3}{25}$

 B. $\dfrac{3}{25} \cdot \dfrac{2}{24}$

 C. $\dfrac{3}{25}$

 D. $\dfrac{2}{24}$

Answer Key for Practice Test 3

Question Number	Correct Answer	Content Category	Question Number	Correct Answer	Content Category
1.	B	Algebra and Number Theory	26.	B	Data Analysis and Statistics
2.	D	Algebra and Number Theory	27.	B	Matrix Algebra
3.	B	Algebra and Number Theory	28.	C	Functions
4.	A	Functions	29.	B	Measurement
5.	B	Algebra and Number Theory	30.	A	Discrete Mathematics
6.	B	Algebra and Number Theory	31.	D	Geometry
7.	B	Measurement	32.	B	Calculus
8.	D	Geometry	33.	A	Calculus
9.	D	Geometry	34.	B	Matrix Algebra
10.	D	Data Analysis and Statistics	35.	B	Discrete Mathematics
11.	D	Trigonometry	36.	D	Calculus
12.	D	Functions	37.	D	Calculus
13.	B	Trigonometry	38.	A	Data Analysis and Statistics
14.	A	Trigonometry	39.	A	Functions
15.	A	Matrix Algebra	40.	A	Data Analysis and Statistics
16.	D	Discrete Mathematics	41.	C	Algebra and Number Theory
17.	B	Data Analysis and Statistics	42.	A	Functions
18.	B	Probability	43.	D	Functions
19.	A	Algebra and Number Theory	44.	C	Functions
20.	B	Measurement	45.	A	Geometry
21.	D	Algebra and Number Theory	46.	C	Discrete Mathematics
22.	C	Matrix Algebra	47.	C	Geometry
23.	C	Functions	48.	B	Probability
24.	A	Trigonometry	49.	A	Calculus
25.	D	Calculus	50.	B	Probability

Answer Explanations for Practice Test 3

1. **B.** If all the tagged fish are still active in the lake when the second group of fish is captured, the proportion of tagged fish in the second group should be equal to the proportion of tagged fish in the whole population, *P*, of fish in the lake. Set up an equation and solve for *P*.

$$\frac{15}{75} = \frac{300}{P}$$

$$P = \frac{75 \cdot 300}{15} = 1500 \text{ fish, choice B.}$$

2. **D.** Determine which of the given properties does NOT hold for *S* with respect to $\otimes$. Using the table, list the possible "products" and check for the properties given in the answer choices.

$\otimes$	*a*	*b*
a	*a*	*b*
b	*b*	*b*

From the table, you have $a \otimes a = a$, $a \otimes b = b$, $b \otimes a = b$, and $b \otimes b = b$.

Checking A: *S* is closed with respect to $\otimes$ because when $\otimes$ is performed using any 2 elements in *S*, the result is an element in *S*. Eliminate A.

Checking B: Because $a \otimes b = b$ and $b \otimes a = b$, *S* is commutative with respect to $\otimes$. Eliminate B.

Checking C: Because $a \otimes a = a$, $a \otimes b = b$, and $b \otimes a = b$, *S* contains an identity element, namely *a*, with respect to $\otimes$. Eliminate C.

Thus, D is the correct response. You should go on to the next problem. However, for your information *S* does not contain an inverse for every element in *S*. In particular, the element *b* does not have an inverse because there is no element in *S* such that $b \otimes$ (that element) = *a* (the identity element).

3. **B.** In 2004, the value is $500.

In 2007, the value is $500 − 10%($500) = 90%($500) = 0.90($500) = $450.

In 2009, the value is $450 + 10%($450) = $450 + 0.10($450) = $495.

In 2012, the value is $495 − 20%($495) = 0.80($495) = $396, choice B.

4. **A.** Determine the rate at which 1 machine works.

Let *r* rate of 1 machine, then

$$2 \cdot r \cdot 10 \text{ days} = 1 \text{ job}$$

$$20r = 1 \text{ job}$$

$$r = \frac{1}{20} \text{ job per day per machine} = \frac{1}{20} \frac{\text{job}}{\text{day}} \Big/ \text{machine}$$

let *d* = number of days it will take 5 machines to do the job

$$(5 \text{ machines}) \cdot \left(\frac{1}{20} \frac{\text{job}}{\text{day}} \Big/ \text{machine} \right) \cdot d = 1 \text{ job}$$

$$\frac{1}{4}d = 1 \text{ (omitting units for convenience)}$$

$$d = 4 \text{ days, choice A.}$$

5. **B.** $y = e^{x+1}$

$\ln y = \ln(e^{x+1})$

$\ln y = (x + 1)\ln(e)$

$\ln y = x + 1$

$\ln (y) - 1 = x$, choice B.

6. **B.** Distance traveled by vehicle traveling north = (rate)(time) = $70 \frac{\text{mi}}{\text{hr}} \cdot t$.

Distance traveled by vehicle traveling south = (rate)(time) = $60 \frac{\text{mi}}{\text{hr}} \cdot t$.

Therefore, the total distance traveled =

325 miles = $70 \frac{\text{mi}}{\text{hr}} t + 60 \frac{\text{mi}}{\text{hr}} t$, where t is the time traveled.

Solve for t (omitting the units for convenience):

$325 = 70t + 60t$

$325 = 130t$

$130t = 325$

$t = 2.5$ hours = 2 hours 30 minutes

Clock time = 10:45 a.m. + 2 hours 30 minutes = 1:15 p.m., choice B.

7. **B.** The thickness of a single U. S. $20 bill = $\frac{0.43 \text{ in}}{100} = 0.0043$ in, so the dimensions of a U. S. $20 bill are $6.14 \times 2.61 \times 0.0043$ inches. Thus, the approximate total value of money in the first-prize box of $20 bills is given by

$$\frac{(24 \text{ in})(16 \text{ in})(8 \text{ in})}{(6.14 \text{ in})(2.61 \text{ in})(0.0043 \text{ in}) \Big/ \$20} = \frac{3072 \text{ in}^3}{0.0890922 \text{ in}^3} \cdot \$20 = \$891,607.83 \approx \$890,000, \text{ choice B.}$$

8. **D.** The formula for a sphere's surface area is $S.A. = 4\pi r^2$. The formula for a sphere's volume is $\frac{4}{3}\pi r^3$. To find the sphere's volume, first, using surface area, find the sphere's radius. Next, use the radius to find the volume.

$S.A. = 4\pi r^2 = 144\pi \text{ cm}^2$

$r^2 = 36 \text{ cm}^2$

$r = 6 \text{ cm}$

Volume $V = \frac{4}{3}\pi r^3 = \frac{4}{3}\pi(6 \text{ cm})^3 = 288\pi \text{ cm}^3$, choice D.

9. **D.** Eliminate C because this approach is not a method for proving congruence. Looking at the figure,

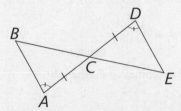

you have $\angle ACB \cong \angle DCE$ because they are vertical angles. You know that $\overline{AC} \cong \overline{DC}$ because $\overline{BE}$ bisects $\overline{AD}$. You are given that $\angle A \cong \angle D$. Thus, you have two angles and the included side of triangle ABC congruent to two angles and the included side of triangle DEC. Therefore, ASA, choice D, is the correct response.

10. **D.** The 75th percentile is a value at or below which 75% of the data fall. Therefore, the best interpretation of Riqui's score is that he did as well or better than 75% of the students who took the exam, choice D.

11. **D.** Make a sketch to illustrate the problem.

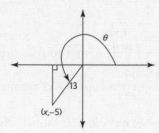

Because the Mathematics CK is a multiple-choice test, for problems of this type a clever approach is to eliminate answer choices based on the information provided. From the sketch, you can see that $\tan\theta = \dfrac{y}{x} = \dfrac{-5}{x}$ and that $x < 0$. Therefore, $\tan\theta > 0$ because it is the quotient of two negative numbers. This allows you to eliminate A and B because these answer choices contain negative values. Looking at the two remaining answer choices, you can see that only D has a 5 in the numerator for the tangent, meaning that D must be the correct response. Of course, a more conventional way to work the problem is to use the formulas, $r^2 = x^2 + y^2$ and $\tan\theta = \dfrac{y}{x}$ (which are provided in the Notation, Definitions, and Formulas pages) to determine that $x = \sqrt{13^2 - (-5)^2} = \sqrt{144} = \pm 12$. Since x is to the left of the origin, $x = -12$. Thus, $\tan\theta = \dfrac{y}{x} = \dfrac{-5}{-12} = \dfrac{5}{12}$, choice D.

12. **D.** You are to identify the range of the function shown.

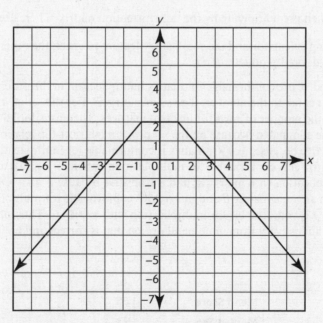

The range of a function is the set of possible second components. From the graph, you can see that the values of y are less than or equal to 2. Thus, choice D is the correct response.

13. **B.** First, rewrite $y - 2.8 = 4\sin x$ as $y = 4\sin x + 2.8$. The minimum value of the sine function is -1, so the minimum value of $4\sin x$ is -4. Thus, the minimum value of $y = 4\sin x + 2.8 = -4 + 2.8 = -1.2$, choice B.

14. **A.** **Method 1.** Since all the answer choices are given in terms of sine and cosine, rewrite $\dfrac{\tan\theta+\cot\theta}{\sec\theta\csc\theta}$ as
$$\dfrac{\dfrac{\sin\theta}{\cos\theta}+\dfrac{\cos\theta}{\sin\theta}}{\dfrac{1}{\cos\theta}\cdot\dfrac{1}{\sin\theta}}=\dfrac{\dfrac{\sin^2\theta+\cos^2\theta}{\cos\theta\sin\theta}}{\dfrac{1}{\cos\theta\sin\theta}}=\sin^2\theta+\cos^2\theta,\text{ choice A.}$$

Method 2. Rewrite $\dfrac{\tan\theta+\cot\theta}{\sec\theta\csc\theta}$ as $\dfrac{\tan\theta+\dfrac{1}{\tan\theta}}{\dfrac{1}{\cos\theta}\cdot\dfrac{1}{\sin\theta}}$, so that you can use the trigonometric function keys on your graphing calculator to evaluate the expression for a convenient value of θ, say 30°. When you

evaluate $\dfrac{\tan 30°+\dfrac{1}{\tan 30°}}{\dfrac{1}{\cos 30°}\cdot\dfrac{1}{\sin 30°}}$, you get 1 for an answer. You should recognize that $\sin^2\theta+\cos^2\theta$ (choice A) is

an identity that equals 1 for all values of θ, so A is the correct response. In a test situation, you should go on to the next question since you have found the correct answer. You would not have to check the other answer choices; but for your information, when $\theta=30°$ B, yields 1.5, C yields .8660..., and D yields 0.5.

15. **A.** In a reflection over the y-axis, the x-coordinates of the image will be the negatives of the x-coordinates of the preimage, and the y-coordinates of the image will be the same as the y-coordinates of the preimage.

Thus, you are looking for a matrix multiplication that will yield the product matrix $\begin{bmatrix}-3 & 5 & -2\\-1 & 7 & -4\end{bmatrix}$. A quick

way to determine which product given in the answer choices will result in the matrix $\begin{bmatrix}-3 & 5 & -2\\-1 & 7 & -4\end{bmatrix}$ is to

perform the matrix multiplications shown in each of the answer choices using your graphing calculator. You can expedite the process by first entering the transformation matrix given in A, entering the vertex matrix $\begin{bmatrix}3 & -5 & 2\\-1 & 7 & -4\end{bmatrix}$, and then premultiplying by the transformation matrix. Thereafter, you can use the edit

feature of your graphing calculator and the recall entry feature to check the other answer choices. Only choice A will yield the desired product matrix.

16. **D.** Two matrices, A and B, are conformable for matrix multiplication in the order AB, only if the number of columns of matrix A is equal to the number of rows of matrix B. For the set of $n\times n$ matrices, the number of columns will equal the number of rows for any two matrices. Therefore, looking at the Roman numeral options, none would be eliminated because on the set of $n\times n$ matrices the relation "is conformable for multiplication" is reflexive because an $n\times n$ matrix is conformable for multiplication with itself; is symmetric because if an $n\times n$ matrix A is conformable for multiplication with an $n\times n$ matrix B, then matrix B is conformable for multiplication with matrix A; and is transitive because if an $n\times n$ matrix A is conformable for multiplication with an $n\times n$ matrix B and matrix B is conformable for multiplication with an $n\times n$ matrix C, then matrix A is conformable for multiplication with matrix C. Thus, choice D is the correct response because it includes every Roman numeral option that is correct and no incorrect Roman numeral options.

17. **B.** Examine the table.

Mean Score	65
Median Score	73
Modal Score	77
Range	52
Standard Deviation	15
Number of Students	50

If the data were represented using a histogram, the mean would lie to the left of both the median and the mode on the horizontal axis, indicating that the data are skewed, with a tail on the left. Thus, the distribution is negatively skewed, choice B.

18. B. The problem asks: Find the probability that the house next door will be sold given that the model home has already been sold. This probability is a conditional probability. If A is the event that the model home will be sold and B is the event that the house next door will be sold, then you need to find $P(B|A) = \dfrac{P(A \text{ and } B)}{P(A)}$. Looking at the formula, you see that you are given $P(A) = 0.50$, but you are not given $P(A \text{ and } B)$, which is the probability that both houses are sold. The problem states "the probability that at least one of the two houses will be sold is 0.80." For this problem situation, the probability that at least one of the two houses will be sold is $P(A \text{ or } B)$. Recall that $P(A \text{ or } B) = P(A) + P(B) - P(A \text{ and } B)$. Thus, since you know $P(A) = 0.50$, $P(B) = 0.40$, and $P(A \text{ or } B) = 0.80$, you can determine $P(A \text{ and } B)$. To find $P(B|A)$, first determine $P(A \text{ and } B)$. Next, use the information found and information given in the problem to calculate $P(B|A)$.

$$P(A \text{ or } B) = P(A) + P(B) - P(A \text{ and } B)$$

$$0.80 = 0.50 + 0.40 - P(A \text{ and } B)$$

$$0.80 = 0.90 - P(A \text{ and } B)$$

$$P(A \text{ and } B) = 0.90 - 0.80 = 0.10$$

Thus, $P(B|A) = \dfrac{P(A \text{ and } B)}{P(A)} = \dfrac{0.10}{0.50} = 0.20 = 20\%$, choice B.

19. A. The powers of the complex number i are cyclic; that is, $i = i$, $i^2 = -1$, $i^3 = -i$, $i^4 = 1$, $i^5 = i$, $i^6 = -1$, $i^7 = -i$, $i^8 = 1$, $i^9 = i$, and so on. In general,

$i^{4k+1} = i$, $i^{4k+2} = i^2 = -1$, $i^{4k+3} = i^3 = -i$, and $i^{4k+4} = i^4 = 1$.

Therefore, to evaluate a power of i, you divide its exponent by 4 and use the remainder as the exponent for i. Thus, $i^{218} = i^{4(54)+2} = i^2 = -1$, choice A.

20. B. The maximum possible error of a measurement is half the magnitude of the smallest measurement unit used to find the measurement. The most accurate way of expressing the measurement is as an interval. Thus, a measurement of 40.6 mL should be reported as 40.6 mL $\pm$ 0.05 mL, choice B.

21. D. Method 1. Using the properties for logarithms,

$\log_{10}\left(\dfrac{x^3}{20}\right) = \log_{10} x^3 - \log_{10} 20 = 3\log_{10} x - \log_{10}(2 \cdot 10) = 3\log_{10} x - (\log_{10} 2 + \log_{10} 10) =$

$3\log_{10} x - \log_{10} 2 - \log_{10} 10 = 3\log_{10} x - \log_{10} 2 - 1$, choice D.

Method 2. Select a convenient value for x, say 5, and evaluate $\log_{10}\left(\dfrac{5^3}{20}\right)$, which is 0.79588..., and then evaluate each of the expressions given in the answer choices for x equal to 5. Choice A yields 1.65851..., choice B yields .09691..., choice C yields –.95954..., and choice D yields 0.79588.... Thus, choice D is the correct response.

22. C. A matrix that has an inverse is nonsingular. A matrix has an inverse if and only if its determinant does *not* equal 0. Therefore, to determine which of the matrices are nonsingular, compute the determinant for each. If the determinant is *not* equal to 0, the matrix is nonsingular.

You can eliminate Roman III because the matrix $\begin{bmatrix} 2 & -5 & 3 \\ 6 & 1 & -4 \\ 0 & 0 & 0 \end{bmatrix}$ has a row of 0s. If a square matrix has a

row or column consisting of only 0s, the determinant of the matrix equals 0. Therefore, $\begin{bmatrix} 2 & -5 & 3 \\ 6 & 1 & -4 \\ 0 & 0 & 0 \end{bmatrix}$ is

not a nonsingular matrix. Draw a line through B and D because these answer choices contain Roman III. The remaining answer choices, A and C, both contain Roman II, so you need to check the matrices in Roman I and Roman IV only.

Starting with the 2×2 matrix in Roman I, the determinant is computed as follows.

$$\begin{bmatrix} -3 & 5 \\ -6 & 10 \end{bmatrix} = (-3 \cdot 10) - 5(-6) = -30 - (-30) = -30 + 30 = 0, \text{ so } \begin{bmatrix} -3 & 5 \\ -6 & 10 \end{bmatrix} \text{ is } not \text{ a nonsingular matrix.}$$

Eliminate A because it contains Roman I. This leaves C as the correct response because it includes every Roman numeral option that is correct and no incorrect Roman numeral options.

23. **C.** This problem is best analyzed as a "work problem." The key idea in a work problem is that the rate at which work is done equals the amount of work accomplished divided by the amount of time worked:

$\text{rate} = \dfrac{\text{amount of work done}}{\text{time worked}}$. For the situation in this problem, the work to be done is to fill the tank.

However, only the input valve works to fill the tank. The output valve works counter to the input valve because it works to empty the tank. Let t = time it will take to fill the tank with both valves open. To find t, first determine the rate, r_{fill}, at which the tank can be filled when the input valve is open and the outlet valve is closed and the rate r_{empty}, at which the tank can be emptied when the input valve is closed and the outlet valve is open. Next, write an equation and solve for t.

The rate for filling the tank is $r_{fill} = \dfrac{1 \text{ full tank}}{6 \text{ hr}} = \dfrac{1}{6}$ tank/hr

The rate for emptying the tank is $r_{empty} = \dfrac{1 \text{ full tank}}{10 \text{ hr}} = \dfrac{1}{10}$ tank/hr

Thus, 1 full tank when both valves are open $= \left(\dfrac{1}{6} \text{ tank/hr}\right)t - \left(\dfrac{1}{10} \text{ tank/hr}\right)t$

$$1 = \frac{1}{6}t - \frac{1}{10}t \text{ (omitting the units)}$$
$$1 = \frac{5}{30}t - \frac{3}{30}t$$
$$1 = \frac{2}{30}t$$
$$1 = \frac{1}{15}t$$
$$15 = t$$

$t = 15$ hours, choice C.

24. **A.** Examine the figure.

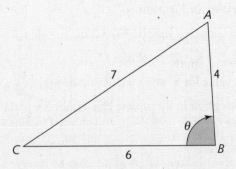

By the law of cosines,

$$7^2 = 6^2 + 4^2 - 2 \cdot 6 \cdot 4 \cos \theta$$
$$49 = 36 + 16 - 48 \cos \theta$$
$$48 \cos \theta = 36 + 16 - 49$$
$$48 \cos \theta = 3$$
$$\cos \theta = \frac{3}{48} = \frac{1}{16}, \text{ choice A.}$$

25. D. You need to find the numerical derivative of a function.

Method 1. A fast and efficient way to calculate this numerical derivative is with your graphing calculator. Here are the steps using a TI-83 Plus calculator. Before you enter functions, you must select Func mode from the $\boxed{\text{MODE}}$ menu. Go to the $\boxed{\text{Y}=}$ editor. Enter the function $y = -16x \wedge (-4)$. As a precaution, clear any previously entered functions before you enter the function. Check the viewing $\boxed{\text{WINDOW}}$ to make sure that the value 2 falls between Xmin and Xmax. If not, change Xmin and/or Xmax, as needed. Go to $\boxed{\text{CALC}}$ menu. Select 6: dy/dx. Type 2 as the X value and then press $\boxed{\text{ENTER}}$. The derivative value is displayed as 2.0000..., choice D.

Tip: Be sure to use the negative key, not the subtraction key when you enter negative numbers into the calculator.

Method 2. Find the numerical derivative using methods of calculus.

$$f(x) = -16x^{-4}$$
$$f'(x) = 64x^{-5}$$
$$f'(2) = 64(2)^{-5} = 64 \cdot \frac{1}{32} = 2,\ \text{choice D.}$$

26. B. Examine the scatterplot.

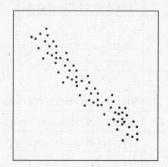

From the scatterplot; it appears that a linear relationship exists between the two variables. Since the line of best fit would slant to the left, the relationship is negative. Thus, choice B is the correct response. None of the statements in the other answer choices is an accurate interpretation of the scatterplot's shape.

27. B. Method 1. The best way to work this problem is to use your graphing calculator's matrix features. Using the $\boxed{\text{MATRX}}$ menu, enter the two matrices into the calculator. Type $\boxed{(}$. Select [B] from the $\boxed{\text{MATRX}}$ menu. Press $\boxed{\text{ENTER}}$. Select [A] from the $\boxed{\text{MATRX}}$ menu. Press $\boxed{\text{ENTER}}$. Type $\boxed{)}$. Press $\boxed{x^{-1}}$. The display shows $([B][A])^{-1}$. Press $\boxed{\text{ENTER}}$. The display shows $\begin{bmatrix} .333333333 & -... \\ 0 & ... \end{bmatrix}$. Select 1:▶Frac from the $\boxed{\text{MATH}}$ menu. The display shows Ans▶Frac. Press $\boxed{\text{ENTER}}$. The display shows $\begin{bmatrix} \frac{1}{3} & -\frac{5}{12} \\ 0 & \frac{1}{4} \end{bmatrix}$, choice B.

Method 2. Using the definition for matrix multiplication, compute the product BA, which is given by

$$\begin{bmatrix} -2 & 3 \\ 2 & 0 \end{bmatrix} \begin{bmatrix} 0 & 2 \\ 1 & 3 \end{bmatrix} = \begin{bmatrix} -2\cdot 0 + 3\cdot 1 & -2\cdot 2 + 3\cdot 3 \\ 2\cdot 0 + 0\cdot 1 & 2\cdot 2 + 0\cdot 3 \end{bmatrix} = \begin{bmatrix} 3 & 5 \\ 0 & 4 \end{bmatrix}.$$

Now determine the inverse of $\begin{bmatrix} 3 & 5 \\ 0 & 4 \end{bmatrix}$. The determinant is $3 \cdot 4 - 5 \cdot 0 = 12$. Thus, $(BA)^{-1} =$

$$\begin{bmatrix} 3 & 5 \\ 0 & 4 \end{bmatrix}^{-1} = \frac{1}{12} \begin{bmatrix} 4 & -5 \\ 0 & 3 \end{bmatrix} = \begin{bmatrix} \frac{1}{3} & -\frac{5}{12} \\ 0 & \frac{1}{4} \end{bmatrix} \text{choice B.}$$

28. C. $(f \circ g)(x) = f(g(x)) = f(3x + 2) = (3x + 2)^2 - 4 = 9x^2 + 12x + 4 - 4 = 9x^2 + 12x = 3x(3x + 4)$, choice C.

29. B. Length of $x = 6\frac{1}{2} - 6\frac{1}{4} = \frac{1}{4}$

length of $y = y = \frac{3}{\sqrt{2}} - \frac{5}{\sqrt{8}} = \frac{3}{\sqrt{2}} - \frac{5}{\sqrt{4 \cdot 2}} = \frac{3}{\sqrt{2}} - \frac{5}{2\sqrt{2}} = \frac{6}{2\sqrt{2}} - \frac{5}{2\sqrt{2}} = \frac{1}{2\sqrt{2}} = \frac{1 \cdot \sqrt{2}}{2\sqrt{2} \cdot \sqrt{2}} = \frac{\sqrt{2}}{4}$

ratio of the length of y to the length of $x = \dfrac{y}{x} = \dfrac{\frac{\sqrt{2}}{4}}{\frac{1}{4}} = \sqrt{2}$, choice B.

30. A. The compound interest formula is $P = P_0(1 + r)^t$, where r is the rate, compounded annually, and P is the value after t years of an initial investment of P_0. You need to find the rate, compounded annually, that will double an investment of \$10,000 in 20 years. In other words, you need to find the rate, compounded annually, that will yield a value of \$20,000 for P in 20 years.

Method 1. A very efficient way to work this problem is to use the finance features of your graphing calculator. For the TI-83 Plus, go to the $\boxed{\text{APPS}}$ menu. Press $\boxed{\text{ENTER}}$ to select 1:Finance…. Press $\boxed{\text{ENTER}}$ again to select 1:TVM Solver…. Use the information in the problem to fill in the values for the variables, including a zero for the unknown value of **I%** as shown in the table. Note: Because no payments are involved when you solve compound interest problems, **PMT** must be set to **0** and **P/Y** must be set to **1**.

N = 20		Number of Payments
I% = 0	unknown	
PV	= –10000	present value (entered as negative because it is an outflow of money—be sure to use the negative key, not the minus key)
PMT = 0	not applicable	
FV	= 20000	future value (entered as positive because it is an inflow of money)
P/Y	= 1	number of payments per year (must be set to 1 for this problem)
C/Y	= 1	number of compounding periods per year
PMT:END	BEGIN	

Scroll to the **I%** line, and then press $\boxed{\text{ALPHA}}$ $\boxed{\text{ENTER}}$. The **I%** line will show **I%**=3.526492384. Thus, 3.5% is the interest rate needed, choice A.

Tip: Be sure to enter PV as a negative value.

Method 2. Substitute into the formula (omitting the units) and solve for r.

$P = P_0(1 + r)^t$

$20{,}000 = 10{,}000(1 + r)^{20}$

$2 = (1 + r)^{20}$

$\ln 2 = \ln (1 + r)^{20}$

$\ln 2 = 20 \ln (1 + r)$

$\dfrac{\ln 2}{20} = \ln(1 + r)$

$1 + r = e^{\frac{\ln 2}{20}}$

$r = e^{\frac{\ln 2}{20}} - 1 = .03526$ or approximately 3.5%, choice A.

Method 3. You can work this problem by checking the answer choices.

Checking A: $10,000(1 + 0.035)^{20} = 19,897.8886$ or approximately 20,000, indicating choice A is the correct response.

In a test situation, you should go on to the next question since you have found the correct answer. You would not have to check the other answer choices; but for your information, choice B yields 29,177.5749..., choice C yields 67274.9994..., and choice D yields 1.4835...×E10.

31. **D.** Analyze the figure.

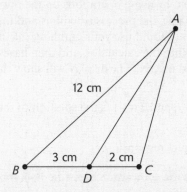

Given $\angle DAB \cong \angle DAC$, then $\overline{AD}$ bisects $\angle A$. Recall that the angle bisector of an angle of a triangle divides the opposite side in the ratio of the sides that form the angle bisected. Thus, $\dfrac{\overline{BD}}{\overline{DC}} = \dfrac{\overline{AB}}{\overline{AC}}$ and $\dfrac{\overline{DC}}{\overline{BD}} = \dfrac{\overline{AC}}{\overline{AB}}$. Set up a proportion and solve for $\overline{AC}$.

$$\frac{\overline{DC}}{\overline{BD}} = \frac{\overline{AC}}{\overline{AB}}$$

$$\frac{\overline{AC}}{\overline{AB}} = \frac{\overline{DC}}{\overline{BD}}$$

$$\frac{\overline{AC}}{12 \text{ cm}} = \frac{2 \text{ cm}}{3 \text{ cm}}$$

$$\overline{AC} = 8 \text{ cm, choice D.}$$

32. **B.** The phrase "an extended period of time" is a clue that this is a calculus problem in which you need to find the limit of a function as the variable approaches infinity. To answer the question, find the limit of the function $Q(h) = \dfrac{10(4h+25)}{2h+5}$ as h approaches infinity:

$$\lim_{h \to \infty} \frac{10(4h+25)}{2h+5} = \lim_{h \to \infty} \frac{40h+250}{2h+5} = \lim_{h \to \infty} \frac{40 + \dfrac{250}{h}}{2 + \dfrac{5}{h}} = \frac{40+0}{2+0} = \frac{40}{2} = 20 \text{ components, choice B.}$$

33. **A.** At any time t after the water starts running, let $h(t)$ be the height of the water in the tank. Using the formula for the volume of a right cylinder, which is provided in the Notation, Definitions, and Formulas pages, you have

$$V = \pi r^2 h(t) = \pi(5)^2 h(t) = 25\pi h(t)$$

The volume of water at any time t is $30\dfrac{\text{ft}^3}{\text{min}} t$. Thus, omitting the units,

$$30t = 25\pi h(t)$$

$$h(t) = \frac{30t}{25\pi}$$

The instantaneous rate of change of the height of the water at any time t is

$$h'(t) = \frac{30}{25\pi} = 0.3819... \text{ or approximately } 0.38\frac{\text{ft}}{\text{min}}, \text{ choice A.}$$

34. B. The augmented matrix for the system is

$$\begin{bmatrix} 2 & 5 & -1 & 5 \\ -4 & 3 & 5 & 13 \\ 8 & 10 & 0 & -4 \end{bmatrix}.$$

Note: You must enter a 0 for the coefficient when a variable does not appear in an equation.

Although you can work this problem by using operations on the rows to transform the matrix so that the solution to the system is easily findable, the process is tedious and time-consuming. Given that the Mathematics CK is a timed test, you should use your graphing calculator to find the solution. Enter the elements of the augmented matrix into the calculator, and then have the calculator produce the reduced row-echelon form of the augmented matrix. The display will show the following.

$$\begin{bmatrix} 1 & 0 & 0 & -3 \\ 0 & 1 & 0 & 2 \\ 0 & 0 & 1 & -1 \end{bmatrix}.$$ Thus, $x = -3$, $y = 2$, and $z = -1$ is the solution to the system.

Because $z = -1$, choice B is the correct response.

> **Tip: Be sure to use the negation key, not the subtraction key, when entering negative numbers as elements of the augmented matrix.**

35. B. You can extend the Fundamental Counting Principle to determine the number of possible telephone numbers for each prefix as follows. After the prefix, there are 4 slots, so to speak, to fill. For each slot, 10 digits are available, which means the number of possible telephone numbers for each prefix is $10 \cdot 10 \cdot 10 \cdot 10 = 10^4$. By the Addition Principle, the total number of possible telephone numbers if all 3 prefixes are used is $10^4 + 10^4 + 10^4 = 3 \cdot 10^4$ choice B.

36. D. The rate of change of a curve at a point is described by the slope of the tangent to the curve at the point. The best way to work this problem is to check each statement against the behavior of the graph of the function. Choice A is incorrect because the slope of the tangent line is decreasing between 0 and 0.5, not constant. Choice B is incorrect because the slope of the tangent line is decreasing between 0.5 and 1.5. Choice C is incorrect because the slope of the tangent line is increasing between 2 and 3. Choice D is correct because the slope of the tangent line is increasing between 3 and 3.5.

37. D. The area of the region bounded by the graph of $f(x) = x^4 - 3x^3 + x^2 + 5$, the x-axis, and the vertical lines $x = 0$ (y-axis) and $x = 2$ is given by: Area $= \int_0^2 (x^4 - 3x^3 + x^2 + 5) dx$.

Method 1. The fastest and most efficient way to calculate this numerical integral is with your graphing calculator. Here are the steps using a TI-83 Plus calculator. Before you enter functions, you must select Func mode from the $\boxed{\text{MODE}}$ menu. Go to the $\boxed{\text{Y}=}$ editor. Enter the function $y = x \wedge 4 - 3x \wedge 3 + x^2 + 5$. As a precaution, clear any previously entered functions before you enter the function. Check the viewing $\boxed{\text{WINDOW}}$ to make sure that the interval between 0 and 2 falls between Xmin and Xmax. If not, change Xmin and/or Xmax, as needed. Go to the $\boxed{\text{CALC}}$ menu. Select 7: $\int f(x) dx$. Type 0 when prompted for the lower limit and then press $\boxed{\text{ENTER}}$. Type 2 when prompted for the upper limit and then press $\boxed{\text{ENTER}}$. The graph is shaded and the integral value is displayed as 7.06666.... select 1:▶Frac from the $\boxed{\text{MATH}}$ menu. The display shows Ans▶Frac. Press $\boxed{\text{ENTER}}$. The display shows 106/15, choice D.

Method 2. Integrate the function using methods of calculus.

$$\int_0^2 (x^4 - 3x^3 + x^2 + 5) dx = \left(\frac{x^5}{5} - \frac{3x^4}{4} + \frac{x^3}{3} + 5x \right)\Big|_0^2$$

$$= \left(\frac{2^5}{5} - \frac{3 \cdot 2^4}{4} + \frac{2^3}{3} + 5 \cdot 2 \right) - \left(\frac{0^5}{5} - \frac{3 \cdot 0^4}{4} + \frac{0^3}{3} + 5 \cdot 0 \right)$$

$$= \frac{32}{5} - \frac{48}{4} + \frac{8}{3} + 10 = \frac{106}{15}, \text{ choice D.}$$

38. A. According to the 68-95-99.7 rule, approximately 68% of the values of a random variable that is normally distributed fall within 1 standard deviation of the mean, about 95% fall within 2 standard deviations of the mean, and about 99.7% fall within 3 standard deviations of the mean. The mean miles per gallon, μ, of the automobiles is 29 mpg with standard deviation, σ, of 4 mpg.

Method 1. Using your graphing calculator's statistical features is an efficient and time-saving way to work problems involving the normal distribution. Consult your owner's manual for detailed instructions on how to find percentages and probabilities using areas under a normal curve.

Using a TI-83 Plus calculator, here are the steps to find the approximate probability that a randomly selected automobile of this type will have gas mileage less than 25 mpg from a distribution with μ of 29 mpg and standard deviation of 4 mpg. Go to the $\boxed{\text{DISTR}}$ menu. Select 2:normalcdf(to paste normalcdf(to the home screen. Type –1E99, 25, 29, 4 inside the parentheses. (Note: –1E99 is used as a proxy for $-\infty$.) Close the parentheses and press $\boxed{\text{ENTER}}$. The display will show .1586. . ., or approximately 16%. Thus, the approximate probability that an automobile of this type chosen at random has gas mileage less than 25 mpg is 16%, choice A.

Method 2. To find the approximate probability that a randomly chosen automobile will have gas mileage less than 25 mpg, first determine the z-score for 25 mpg, and then find the percentage of the normal distribution that is below this z-score.

$z\text{-score} = \dfrac{\text{data value} - \text{mean}}{\text{standard deviation}} = \dfrac{25 - 29}{4} = -1$. Therefore, 25 is 1 standard deviation below the mean. Find the percentage of the normal distribution that is below a z-score of –1.

You know that about 68% of the distribution is within standard deviation of the mean. Make a sketch to illustrate the problem.

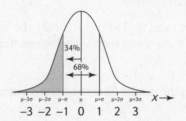

Since the normal curve is symmetric, about $34\% \left(\dfrac{1}{2} \text{ of 68 percent}\right)$ of the distribution is between the mean and a z-score of –1. Again, due to symmetry, 50% of the total distribution is to the left of the mean. Thus, approximately $50 - 34 = 16\%$ of the distribution is below a z-score of –1. Thus, the approximate probability that an automobile of this type chosen at random has gas mileage less than 25 mpg is 16%, choice A.

39. A. When $b > 1$, the graph defined by $g(x) = f(bx)$ is a horizontal compression toward the y-axis of the graph defined by $y = f(x)$. If (x, y) is on the graph defined by $y = f(x)$, then $\left(\dfrac{x}{b}, y\right)$ is on the graph defined by $g(x) = f(bx)$. Thus, if $(-2, -8)$ is on the graph of f defined by $f(x) = x^3$, then the corresponding point on the graph of g defined by $g(x) = f(2x)$ is $\left(\dfrac{-2}{2}, -8\right) = (-1, -8)$, choice A.

40. A. Establishing cause-and-effect relationships is most likely when investigators conduct well-designed experimental studies, so choice A is the correct response. Choices B and C are incorrect because cause-effect relationships are not established with the types of studies given in these answer choices. Choice D is incorrect because establishing cause-effect relationships in observational studies is problematic given that the investigators are unable to manipulate variables of interest.

41. C. Rewrite $2x^2 - x < 1$ as $2x^2 - x - 1 < 0$.

Factor the left side of the inequality to obtain $(2x + 1)(x - 1) < 0$. Now determine when the product $(2x + 1)(x - 1)$ is negative. First, find the values for x at which the factors change sign; that is, find the zero for each factor.

Set each factor equal to 0 and solve for x.

$2x + 1 = 0$ yields $x = -\frac{1}{2}$ and $x - 1 = 0$ yields $x = 1$.

The two values $-\frac{1}{2}$ and 1 divide the number line into 3 intervals: $\left(-\infty, -\frac{1}{2}\right), \left(-\frac{1}{2}, 1\right)$, and $(1, \infty)$.

Next, determine in which interval(s) the product of the two factors is negative.

Method 1. Make an organized chart to determine the sign of $(2x + 1)(x - 1)$ for each of these intervals.

Interval	Sign of $(2x + 1)$	Sign of $(x - 1)$	Sign of $(2x + 1)(x - 1)$
$\left(-\infty, -\frac{1}{2}\right)$	negative	negative	positive
$\left(-\frac{1}{2}, 1\right)$	positive	negative	negative
$(1, \infty)$	positive	positive	positive

Thus, $(2x + 1)(x - 1)$ is negative only in the interval $\left(-\frac{1}{2}, 1\right)$, choice C.

Method 2. Use your graphing calculator to graph $y = 2x^2 - x - 1$.

You know that the graph intersects the x-axis at $x = -\frac{1}{2}$ and $x = 1$. You can see that the graph is below the x-axis (and, therefore, negative) between these two points and above the x-axis otherwise. Thus, $2x^2 - x - 1$ is negative only in the interval $\left(-\frac{1}{2}, 1\right)$, choice C.

42. **A.** You are given two points $(0, 500)$ and $(5, 1500)$ that satisfy the function $P(t) = P_0 e^{xt}$. First, substitute the values for the two points into $P(t) = P_0 e^{xt}$, and then solve the resulting system of equations for x.

$500 = P_0 e^{x(0)} = P_0 e^0 = P_0 \cdot 1 = P_0$

$1500 = P_0 e^{x(5)} = P_0 e^{5x} = 500 e^{5x}$ (using the results from the first equation)

$1500 = 500 e^{5x}$

$3 = e^{5x}$

$\ln 3 = \ln (e^{5x})$

$\ln 3 = 5x \ln e$

$\ln 3 = 5x$

$x = \frac{\ln 3}{5}$, choice A.

43. **D.** Make a chart showing the height of the ball as a function of rebound number.

Height of Ball (in feet)	120	$120 \cdot \frac{3}{4}$	$120 \cdot \frac{3}{4} \cdot \frac{3}{4}$	$120 \cdot \frac{3}{4} \cdot \frac{3}{4} \cdot \frac{3}{4}$	...
Rebound Number n	0	1	2	3	...

Examination of the table leads to a general term for the nth bounce: $120 \cdot \left(\frac{3}{4}\right)^n$, where $n = 0, 1, 2, \ldots$. Thus, an exponential function (choice D) would best model the height of the ball as a function of rebound number n. None of the functions in the other answer choices works as well as an exponential model.

44. **C.** The function $y = \frac{2x^3 + 3x - x + 1}{x^2 - 8x + 16}$ will have vertical asymptotes at any value for x that makes the denominator equal 0. Set $x^2 - 8x + 16 = 0$ and solve for x.

$$x^2 - 8x + 16 = 0$$
$$(x - 4)^2 = 0$$
$$x = 4$$

Thus, y has 1 vertical asymptote at $x = 4$. Since the degree of the numerator of y exceeds the degree of the denominator of y by exactly 1, y will have 1 oblique asymptote. Thus, y has a total of 2 asymptotes, choice C.

45. **A.** Find the difference in the areas of the two tables.

Area of the rectangular table =

$A = lw = (4.5 \text{ ft})(3 \text{ ft}) = 13.5 \text{ ft}^2$

Area of the circular table =

$A = \pi r^2 = \pi(2 \text{ ft})^2 = 4\pi \text{ ft}^2$ (Note: Because the diameter is 4 ft, the radius r is 2 ft.)

Find the difference between the two areas:

$13.5 \text{ ft}^2 - 4\pi \text{ ft}^2 = 0.9336...$ or approximately 0.93 ft^2, choice A.

> **Tip:** Use your calculator's recall answer feature to find the difference without rounding until the final computation.

46. **C.** To determine the closed-form for a sequence requires looking for a pattern in the terms of the sequence or in the first and second differences between terms. Make a table that includes the terms of the sequence and the first and second differences between terms, and then look for a pattern.

n	a_n	1st Difference	2nd Difference
1	1	$8 - 1 = 7$	
2	8	$17 - 8 = 9$	$9 - 7 = 2$
3	17	$28 - 17 = 11$	$11 - 9 = 2$
4	28		$13 - 11 = 2$
5	41	$41 - 28 = 13$	$15 - 13 = 2$
6	56	$56 - 41 = 15$	

The table shows that the second differences are constant. When the second difference is constant, the relationship between terms of the sequence is quadratic, choice C.

47. **C.** The volume of a right prism is given by $V = Bh$. (Note: This formula is provided in the Notation, Definitions, and Formulas pages.) First, find the area, B, of one of the equilateral triangular bases, and then find the volume by multiplying B by the height of the prism, h.

The area of an equilateral triangle with sides of 4 in is given by: Area $= \dfrac{\sqrt{3}}{4}s^2 = \dfrac{\sqrt{3}}{4}(4 \text{ in})^2 = 4\sqrt{3} \text{ in}^2$

> **Tip:** If you forget the formula for the area of an equilateral triangle, you can derive it by using the Pythagorean theorem or trigonometric functions to determine the height (altitude) of the triangle, and then using the formula, area $= \dfrac{1}{2}bh$, to find the area of the equilateral triangle.

Volume $= \left(4\sqrt{3} \text{ in}^2\right)(25 \text{ in}) = 173.2050...$ or approximately 173 in^3, choice C.

48. **B.** Given the coin is to be flipped 6 times, you can work this problem by extending the Fundamental Counting Principle to 6 events. There are 2 possibilities for each of the 6 coin flips, which means the total number of possible outcomes in the sample space is $2 \cdot 2 \cdot 2 \cdot 2 \cdot 2 \cdot 2 = 2^6$, choice B.

Practice Test 3

49. A. Make a quick sketch of the two graphs.

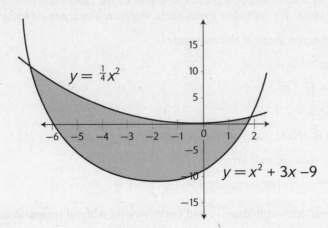

The two graphs intersect at two points and the graph of $y = \frac{1}{4}x^2$ lies above $y = x^2 + 3x - 9$ between the points of intersection. First, find the x-values for the points of intersection of the two graphs; next, find the difference between the two functions, being sure to subtract the equation of the lower graph from the equation of the upper graph; and then evaluate the definite integral of the difference of the two graphs between the two x-values of their intersection.

Step 1. Find the x-values for the points of intersection of the two graphs.

Using substitution,

$$\frac{1}{4}x^2 = x^2 + 3x - 9$$

$$0 = \frac{3}{4}x^2 + 3x - 9$$

$$0 = 3x^2 + 12x - 36$$

$$0 = x^2 + 4x - 12$$

$$0 = (x + 6)(x - 2)$$

$$x = -6 \text{ or } x = 2$$

Step 2. Find the difference between the two graphs.

Difference $= \left(\frac{1}{4}x^2\right) - \left(x^2 + 3x - 9\right) = \frac{1}{4}x^2 - x^2 - 3x + 9 = -\frac{3}{4}x^2 - 3x + 9$

Step 3. Evaluate the definite integral $\int_{-6}^{2}\left(-\frac{3}{4}x^2 - 3x + 9\right)dx$.

Method 1. The fastest and most efficient way to calculate this numerical integral is with your graphing calculator. Here are the steps using a TI-83 Plus calculator. Before you enter functions, you must select Func mode from the $\boxed{\text{MODE}}$ menu. Go to the $\boxed{Y =}$ editor. Enter the function $y = -(3/4)x^2 - 3x + 9$. As a precaution, clear any previously entered functions before you enter the function. Check the viewing $\boxed{\text{WINDOW}}$ to make sure that the interval between –6 and 2 falls between Xmin and Xmax. If not, change Xmin and/or Xmax, as needed. Go to the $\boxed{\text{CALC}}$ menu. Select 7: $\int f(x)dx$. Type –6 when prompted for the lower limit and then press $\boxed{\text{ENTER}}$. Type 2 when prompted for the upper limit and then press $\boxed{\text{ENTER}}$. The integral value is displayed as 64 (choice A) and the graph is shaded. (Note: The graph and the shaded region will not look like what you've sketched above because you entered the difference of the two functions into the function editor.)

Method 2. Integrate the function using methods of calculus.

$$\int_{-6}^{2}\left(-\frac{3}{4}x^2-3x+9\right)dx=\left(-\frac{x^3}{4}-\frac{3x^2}{2}+9x\right)\Bigg|_{-6}^{2}$$

$$=\left(-\frac{2^3}{4}-\frac{3\cdot 2^2}{2}+9\cdot 2\right)-\left(-\frac{(-6)^3}{4}-\frac{3\cdot(-6)^2}{2}+9\cdot -6\right)$$

$$=(-2-6+18)-(54-54-54)$$

$$=10+54=64\text{, choice A.}$$

50. **B.** In this problem, you are to find a conditional probability. By the Multiplication Rule, $P(A$ and $B) = P(A)P(B|A)$. That is, to find the probability that an event A occurs on the first trial and an event B occurs on the second trial, multiply the probability of event A times the probability of event B, where you have determined the probability of B by taking into account that the event A has already occurred. The probability that a yellow marble is drawn on the first draw is given by:

$$P(\text{yellow on first draw}) = \frac{\text{Number of yellow marbles in bag}}{\text{Total number of marbles}} = \frac{3}{25}$$

After this event occurs since the yellow marble drawn first is not put back in the bag, the probability that a yellow marble will be drawn on the second draw is given by:

$$P(\text{yellow on second draw given first draw is yellow}) = \frac{2}{24}$$

Thus, the probability that both marbles will be yellow when two marbles are randomly drawn from the bag without replacement is given by:

$\frac{3}{25}\cdot\frac{2}{24}$, choice B.

Appendix A

Long Division of Polynomials and Synthetic Division

Here is an example of long division of polynomials.

$$\frac{4x^3 + 8x - 6x^2 + 1}{2x - 1} =$$

$2x-1\overline{\smash{)}4x^3 - 6x^2 + 8x + 1}$	1. Arrange the terms of both the dividend and divisor in descending powers of the variable x.
$\begin{array}{r} 2x^2 \\ 2x-1\overline{\smash{)}4x^3 - 6x^2 + 8x + 1} \end{array}$	2. Divide the first term of the dividend by the first term of the divisor, and write the answer as the first term of the quotient.
$\begin{array}{r} 2x^2 \\ 2x-1\overline{\smash{)}4x^3 - 6x^2 + 8x + 1} \\ 4x^3 - 2x^2 \end{array}$	3. Multiply $2x^2$ by $2x - 1$, and enter the product under the dividend.
$\begin{array}{r} 2x^2 \\ 2x-1\overline{\smash{)}4x^3 - 6x^2 + 8x + 1} \\ \underline{4x^3 - 2x^2 } \\ -4x^2 \end{array}$	4. Subtract $4x^3 - 2x^2$ from the dividend, being sure to mentally change the signs of both terms.
$\begin{array}{r} 2x^2 - 2x \\ 2x-1\overline{\smash{)}4x^3 - 6x^2 + 8x + 1} \\ \underline{4x^3 - 2x^2 } \\ -4x^2 + 8x \\ \underline{-4x^2 + 2x} \\ 6x \end{array}$	5. Bring down $8x$, the next term of the dividend, and repeat steps 2–4.
$\begin{array}{r} 2x^2 - 2x + 3 \\ 2x-1\overline{\smash{)}4x^3 - 6x^2 + 8x + 1} \\ \underline{4x^3 - 2x^2 } \\ -4x^2 + 8x \\ \underline{-4x^2 + 2x} \\ 6x + 1 \\ \underline{6x - 3} \\ 4 \end{array}$	6. Bring down 1, the last term of the dividend, and repeat steps 2–4.
$\dfrac{4x^3 + 8x - 6x^2 + 1}{2x - 1} = 2x^2 - 2x + 3 + \dfrac{4}{2x - 1}$	7. Write the answer as quotient $+ \dfrac{\text{remainder}}{\text{divisor}}$.

Here is a completed example in which the divisor has the form $x - r$.

$$\frac{2x^3 + x^2 - 13x + 6}{x - 4} = \quad x - 4{\overline{\smash{\big)}\,2x^3 + x^2 - 13x + 6}}^{\textstyle 2x^2 + 9x + 23}$$

$$\underline{2x^3 - 8x^2}$$
$$9x^2 - 13x$$
$$\underline{9x^2 - 36x}$$
$$23x + 6$$
$$\underline{23x - 92}$$
$$\text{R } 98$$

Thus, $\dfrac{2x^3 + x^2 - 13x + 6}{x - 4} = 2x^2 + 9x + 23 + \dfrac{98}{x - 4}$

You can shorten the division process when the divisor has the form $x - r$ by using synthetic division.

Synthetic division is a shortcut method for dividing a polynomial by a binomial, $x - r$. You simplify the process by working only with r and the coefficients of the polynomial—being careful to use 0 as a coefficient for missing powers of x. Here are the synthetic division steps for the previous problem.

$$\frac{2x^3 + x^2 - 13x + 6}{x - 4} =$$

$2x^3 + x^2 - 13x + 6$	1. Write the polynomial in descending powers of *x*, using a coefficient of 0 when a power of *x* is missing, if needed.
2 1 −13 6	2. Write only the coefficients as shown here.
4 $\rfloor$ 2 1 −13 6	3. Write *r* = 4 as shown here.
4 $\rfloor$ 2 1 −13 6 2	4. Bring down the first coefficient.
4 $\rfloor$ 2 1 −13 6 8 2 9	5. Multiply the first coefficient by *r* = 4, write the product under the second coefficient, and then add.
4 $\rfloor$ 2 1 −13 6 8 36 2 9 23	6. Multiply the sum by *r* = 4, write the product under the third coefficient, and then add.
4 $\rfloor$ 2 1 −13 6 8 36 92 2 9 23 98	7. Repeat step 6 until you use up all the coefficients in the polynomial.
4 $\rfloor$ 2 1 −13 6 8 36 92 2 9 23 $\lfloor$98	8. Separate the final sum, which is the remainder, as shown here.
$\dfrac{2x^3 + x^2 - 13x + 6}{x - 4}$ is $2x^2 + 9x + 23$ R 98	9. Write the quotient and remainder using the coefficients.

Simplifying Radicals

A radical is simplified when the radicand contains no variable factor raised to a power equal to or greater than the index of the radical; the radicand contains no constant factor that can be expressed as a power equal to or greater than the index of the radical; the radicand contains no fractions; no fractions contain radicals in the denominator; and the index of the radical is reduced to its lowest value.

For example,

$$\sqrt[3]{24a^5b^6} = \left(\sqrt[3]{8a^3b^6}\right) \cdot \left(\sqrt[3]{3a^2}\right) = 2ab^2\left(\sqrt[3]{3a^2}\right) \text{ is simplified.}$$

$$\sqrt{12} = \left(\sqrt{4}\right)\left(\sqrt{3}\right) = 2\left(\sqrt{3}\right) \text{ is simplified.}$$

$$\frac{\sqrt{54}}{\sqrt{6}} = \sqrt{9} = 3 \text{ is simplified.}$$

$$\frac{1}{\sqrt{2}} = \left(\frac{1}{\sqrt{2}}\right)\frac{\sqrt{2}}{\sqrt{2}} = \frac{\sqrt{2}}{2} \text{ is simplified.}$$

$$\sqrt[4]{a^2} = \sqrt{a} \text{ is simplified.}$$

Because square roots occur so frequently, the remainder of the examples will use only square root radicals.

Radicals that have the same index and the same radicand are like radicals. To add or subtract like radicals, combine their coefficients and write the result as the coefficient of the common radical factor. Indicate the sum or difference of unlike radicals.

$$5\sqrt{3} + 2\sqrt{3} = 7\sqrt{3}$$

You may have to simplify the radical expressions before combining them.

$$5\sqrt{3} + \sqrt{12} = 5\sqrt{3} + \sqrt{4 \cdot 3} = 5\sqrt{3} + 2\sqrt{3} = 7\sqrt{3}$$

To multiply radicals that have the same index, multiply their coefficients to find the coefficient of the product. Multiply the radicands to find the radicand of the product. Simplify the results.

$$5\sqrt{3} \cdot 2\sqrt{3} = 10 \cdot 3 = 30$$

For a sum or difference, treat the factors as you would binomials, being sure to simplify radicals after you multiply.

$$\left(2\sqrt{3} + 5\sqrt{7}\right)\left(\sqrt{3} - 3\sqrt{6}\right) = 2\sqrt{9} - 6\sqrt{18} + 5\sqrt{21} - 15\sqrt{42} = 2(3) - 6\sqrt{9 \cdot 2} + 5\sqrt{21} - 15\sqrt{42} = 6 - 18\sqrt{2} + 5\sqrt{21} - 15\sqrt{42}$$

$$\left(1 - \sqrt{3}\right)\left(1 + \sqrt{3}\right) = 1 + \sqrt{3} - \sqrt{3} - 3 = 1 - 3 = -2$$

The technique of rationalizing is used to remove radicals from the denominator (or numerator) of a fraction. For square root radicals, if the denominator (numerator) contains a single term, multiply the numerator and denominator by the smallest radical that will produce a perfect square in the denominator (numerator). For example:

$$\frac{5}{\sqrt{3}} = \frac{5}{\sqrt{3}} \cdot \frac{\sqrt{3}}{\sqrt{3}} = \frac{5\sqrt{3}}{3}$$

If the denominator (numerator) contains a sum or difference involving square roots, multiply the numerator and denominator by a difference or sum that will cause the middle terms to sum to 0 when you multiply. For example:

$$\frac{5}{1 - \sqrt{3}} = \frac{5}{\left(1 - \sqrt{3}\right)} \frac{\left(1 + \sqrt{3}\right)}{\left(1 + \sqrt{3}\right)} = \frac{5\left(1 + \sqrt{3}\right)}{1 - 3} = -\frac{5 + 5\sqrt{3}}{2}$$